Fire and Desire

FIRE & DESIRE

*Mixed-Race Movies
in the Silent Era*

Jane M. Gaines

THE UNIVERSITY OF CHICAGO PRESS
CHICAGO AND LONDON

Jane M. Gaines is associate professor of Literature and English at Duke University. She is author of *Contested Culture: The Image, the Voice, and the Law* (1991), editor of *Classical Hollywood Narrative: The Paradigm of Wars* (1992), and coeditor of *Fabrications: Costume and the Female Body* (1990, with Charlotte Herzog) and of *Collecting Visible Evidence* (1999, with Michael Renov).

The University of Chicago Press, Chicago 60637
The University of Chicago Press, Ltd., London
© 2001 by The University of Chicago
All rights reserved. Published 2001
Printed in the United States of America
10 09 08 07 06 05 04 03 02 01   1 2 3 4 5

ISBN: 0-226-27874-3 (cloth)
ISBN: 0-226-27875-1 (paper)

An earlier version of chapter 1 will appear in *Hollywood Spectatorship*, ed. Melvyn Stokes and Richard Maltby (London: British Film Institute, forthcoming). Chapter 5 originally appeared in *Black American Cinema*, ed. Manthia Diawara (New York: Routledge, 1993). Copyright © 1993; reproduced by permission of Taylor & Francis, Inc./Routledge, Inc., http://www.routledge-ny.com. Portions of chapter 6 will appear as part of *"Within Our Gates:* From Race Melodrama to Opportunity Narrative" in *Oscar Micheaux and His Circle: African American Filmmaking and Race Cinema of the Silent Era,* ed. Pearl Bowser, Jane Gaines, and Charles Musser (Pordenone-Sacile, Italy: Giornate del Cinema Muto, forthcoming).

Photo credits: figures on pages 32, 101, 214, 215, 224, 240—The Museum of Modern Art/ Film Stills Archive; figures on pages 50, 151, 231—Photographs and Prints Division, Schomburg Center for Research in Black Culture, The New York Public Library, Astor, Lenox, and Tilden Foundations; figures on pages 100, 114, 115, 142—George P. Johnson Collection, Department of Special Collections, University Research Library, UCLA; figure on page 209—Bruccoli Clark Layman, Inc.

Library of Congress Cataloging-in-Publication Data

Gaines, Jane M.
    Fire and desire : mixed-race movies in the silent era / Jane M. Gaines.
        p.   cm.
    Includes bibliographical references and index.
    ISBN 0-226-27874-3 (cloth : alk. paper); ISBN 0-226-27875-1 (pbk. : alk. paper)
    1. Afro-Americans in motion pictures. 2. Micheaux, Oscar, 1884–1951—Criticism and interpretation. 3. Racially mixed people—United States. 4. Afro-Americans—Color—Social aspects. I. Title.

PN1995.9.N4 G35   2001
791.43′65203896073—dc21

                                                                                00-055952

♾ The paper used in this publication meets the minimum requirements of the American National Standard for Information Sciences—Permanence of Paper for Printed Library Materials, ANSI Z39.48-1992.

For the Johnson brothers

Contents

Illustrations

FRAME ENLARGEMENTS FROM
Within Our Gates (dir. Oscar Micheaux, 1920)

FRAME ENLARGEMENTS FROM

The Symbol of the Unconquered (dir. Oscar Micheaux, 1920)

Acknowledgments

There are, of course, different ways of conceiving of book acknowledgments. One way is just to thank the institutions and individuals who were major players and be done with it. This approach has the advantage of economy. Another approach is to attempt to reconstruct the formation of the interests that became the book, tracing the genesis of the ideas and rethinking the history of the project. I have seriously considered both options. In the end, my decision to attempt to retrace my steps was a political one. Along the way to writing this book some interesting and important educational institutions and projects came into being. Whether these venues for disseminating information about early African American film were by-products of the research or the research was a by-product of the projects, I am not entirely certain. What I do know is that within the last decade a community of Oscar Micheaux scholars and enthusiasts has come together, and that this community has changed the way it feels to be doing historical research.

First, I want to mention *The Oscar Micheaux Society Newsletter,* "dedicated to African American Film History and Preservation," founded in 1993 with the original support and encouragement of Pearl Bowser. Co-editor Charlene Regester, at Afro-American Studies, University of North Carolina, Chapel Hill, has been the most dedicated of colleagues in this endeavor, and the two of us benefited over the years from the editorial assistance of Sheila Smith McCoy and Mikki Bruner, with Lisa Poteet coordinating the production. The *Micheaux Society* is an unusual mix of scholars, collectors, fans, and community arts organizers. Although the annual meeting is held at the Society for Cinema Studies conference, the organization has grown by picking up friends at homegrown festivals like the Oscar Micheaux Film Festival, organized by Richard Papousek in Gregory, South Dakota, the location of Micheaux's homestead between 1906 and 1911.

Second, the conception of this book parallels the discovery and restoration of "lost" films, which means that the existence of the "new" Micheaux scholarship owes much to the generosity of archivists as well as the hard work of other scholars who paved the way. Even before these discoveries, Jan-Chris Horak, then head of the film archive at the International Museum of Photography, George Eastman House, in Rochester, New York, had been involved in the preservation of a 35mm print of *Body and Soul*. Then, almost ten years ago, Susan Dalton, archivist at the American Film Institute Preservation Project in Washington, D.C., and Phyllis Klotman, founder of the Black Film Center/Archive at Indiana University, Bloomington, called my attention to the Library of Congress acquisition of Micheaux's *Within Our Gates* (1920), then titled *La Negra*, a 35mm print that had been discovered in the Filmoteca Española in Madrid. At the Library of Congress Motion Picture and Sound Recording Division, Brian Taves, Patrick Loughney, David Francis, and Madeline Matz were important early supporters of a project that began to involve many more scholars. At this early stage, Kathleen Newman translated the Spanish intertitles into English, and later Scott Simmon produced the English-version videotape now used by many film teachers. A few years later, after the Museum of Modern Art Film Department received a 35mm print of *The Symbol of the Unconquered* from the Cinémathèque Royale in Belgium, Steve Higgins became involved in the production of the English-language version, joining Bill Sloan and Mary Lea Bandy, original supporters at the museum of the idea of a touring package of early films by African Americans.

So, third, and perhaps most important, this book has been conceived in the context of an exhibition plan, a plan to tour the work of Oscar Micheaux and his contemporaries, a dream that will be realized when the group of films will premiere in 2001 at the 19th Annual Silent Film Festival in Pordenone, Italy. Here is the place I want to thank Charles Musser and Pearl Bowser, the other curators as well as the coeditors with me of the catalog, *Oscar Micheaux and His Circle: African American Filmmaking and Race Cinema of the Silent Era,* and to say that their early vision of this project and their long dedication to it through its many manifestations have been remarkable. There have been many exhibition dress rehearsals for this event. The high point was undoubtedly the July 1998 premiere of the restored version of *The Symbol of the Unconquered* at the Apollo Theatre with live percussion accompaniment by jazz legend Max Roach. Turner Classic Movies funded this restoration and the premiere, tied to a month of cable television programming, and here we need to thank Turner vice presidents Katherine Evans and Tom Kirsch.

But there have been many more local exhibitions and discussions around early black cinema, and I want to remember the organizers of some of these events, such as Laura Brooker and Darrell Stover who organized the event funded by the North Carolina Humanities Council at St. Joseph's Black Cultural Center in Durham, North Carolina. Terree Caldwell-Johnson did an event at the Des Moines Art Center in Iowa, and Karmello Brooks-Coleman organized a Micheaux talk as part of the African Caribbean Film Festival in Kansas City, Missouri. As part of the Library of Congress Film Registry Tour, Tom Whiteside, Bertie Howard, Louise Stone, and Del Avent helped to organize a Micheaux day in Page Auditorium at Duke University along with Rebecca Fitzgerald and Mike Mashon from the Library of Congress. Thanks to Rick Powell, Oscar Micheaux was given another place in history as part of the "Art of the Harlem Renaissance" tour he curated, and here I benefited from the feedback of a different kind of audience at the Palace of Legion of Honor in San Francisco and the Corcoran Gallery in Washington, D.C. These are but a few examples. In a decade of rediscovery, Micheaux's work has been exhibited internationally in Japan, France, and the Netherlands, and in the United States at festivals and conferences in Seattle, Chicago, Los Angeles, New York, Atlanta, and Philadelphia as well as Columbus, Ohio, and Columbia, South Carolina. The culmination will most certainly be the "Oscar Micheaux Golden Anniversary Memorial Celebration" in Great Bend, Kansas, in March 2001, commemorating the fiftieth anniversary of the director's death.

The community interest in early "race cinema" has, not surprisingly, been equaled by academic interest, an indication of which is the range of institutions at which I have presented papers on Micheaux over the decade: Warwick University, Coventry, England; University of California, Santa Cruz; Vassar College; Princeton University; the University of Texas, Austin; New York University; Eastern Carolina University; University College, London; and universities of the Western Cape, Capetown, and Natal in South Africa. One of the Columbia University seminars on early cinema at the Museum of Modern Art in New York was devoted to this work-in-progress. Charlie Musser and Hazel Carby organized the "Oscar Micheaux and His Circle" conference at the Whitney Humanities Center at Yale University, a dry run for the essays that make up the collection that would become the catalog for the touring package.

Within these film history venues it is clear that there is much at stake for politics as well as for critical theory, but this is somewhat predictable since film studies has historically been a relatively progressive field. So my first thank-you here goes to Chuck Kleinhans for the role he played early on in my own politicization. Other film scholars made contributions in some way to the shape of this book and I should mention Todd Boyd (especially for the title), Jackie Bobo, Anne Friedberg, Clyde Taylor, Kobena Mercer, Linda Williams, Manthia Diawara, Richard Grupenhoff, Michele Wallace, Greg Waller, Gloria Gibson-Hudson, Tom Gunning, Arthur Knight, Corey Creekmur, Richard Dyer, Isaac Julien, and especially Miriam Hansen, whose example proves that history is not necessarily incompatible with theory. In a separate category because of their dedication to the cause as well as their generosity with other scholars, I would put Ron Green and Tom Cripps.

What has been most gratifying has been the growing enthusiasm in fields outside film studies for the integration of early black cinema into other disciplines, most notably literary studies and history, and it has been a dream of film scholars that some day every educational screening of *The Birth of a Nation* would be paired with either *Within Our Gates* or *The Symbol of the Unconquered*. A fellowship year at the National Humanities Center in Research Triangle Park, North Carolina, was interdisciplinary mingling at its best, and my own study was considerably enriched that year through contact with Donald Lopez, Fitz Brundage, Kevin Gaines, and Penny Von Eschen, among others. Also from outside film studies, Susan Gilman, Cedric Robinson, Helen Taylor, and Joel Williamson influenced my thinking. At Duke, Nahum Chandler, David Freeman, and Maurice Wallace were intellectually instrumental, and Susan Willis helped sync up the conclusion. And I should not forget that the first two scholars to urge me to work in this area were the eminent black historians John Hope Franklin and David Barry Gaspar.

At some point all historians of early black cinema must pay tribute to George P. Johnson, African American film pioneer and inveterate collector of black film materials. As Ann Caiger, head of the Department of Special Collections, Young Research Library, University of California, Los Angeles, will tell you, the George Johnson papers get more use than perhaps any other collection housed there. Also at UCLA, I want to thank Alva Moore Stevenson in the Oral History Program for her special help. For expert editing I want to thank Richard Audet and my sister, Sally Mosher. And, finally, I relied throughout the arduous stages of manuscript preparation on Hank Okazaki and Vince Brown, graduate students at Duke.

Note on Film Dates

Readers familiar with the literature on race movies will note that the dates given here for some of the films of Oscar Micheaux as well as The Colored Players of Philadelphia are different from those found in earlier published works and even reference books. Dating has been difficult for these particular films because on the films themselves the credits do not list a copyright year. The question for scholars of early cinema (where films themselves are not always dated) arises when one is faced with the question of whether to assign the film the date of its production or the date of its exhibition. In a case such as *Within Our Gates,* for instance, some scholars have dated it 1919 (the year of production) and others 1920 (the year of exhibition). *The Scar of Shame,* another example, was dated by scholars as 1926 for many years, but recent research would indicate that it was first exhibited in 1929. It was not unusual for these early filmmakers to release their films in an order other than that in which they were shot, with many months and even years between shooting and exhibition.

In response to the irregularity of dating, scholars working on the filmography for the forthcoming *Oscar Micheaux and His Circle* catalogue attempted to establish the date of the earliest documented public exhibition on each film included. They consulted sources in the period, most notably African American newspapers from key cities. Still, dating proved challenging, as in the case of *The House behind the Cedars* where although the film was previewed publically in 1924 it did not premiere until 1925. The authors of the new filmography thus list the date for that film as 1924/25. As much as possible, I have followed their new guidelines in an attempt to regularize the dates on these important films. I should add that this filmography is an invaluable resource, including not only cast, length, film descriptions, and selected articles from newspapers, but archival sources where films are extant. See Corey K. Creekmur, Charles Musser, Pearl Bowser, J. Ronald Green, and Charlene Regester, "An Oscar Micheaux Filmography: From Silents through His Transition to Sound, 1919–1931," in *Oscar Micheaux and His Circle: African American Filmmaking and Race Cinema of the Silent Era,* ed. Pearl Bowser, Jane Gaines, and Charles Musser (Pordenone-Sacile, Italy: Giornate de Cinema Muto, forthcoming).

Readers interested in the availability of 16mm as well as 35mm prints for rental or videotapes for purchase should consult the issues of *The Oscar Micheaux Newsletter* for frequently updated information. On the Web: http://www.duke.edu/web/film/Micheaux.

The "Race" in Race Movies

In 1929 the British journal *Close-up* devoted an entire issue to "The Negro in Film." Editor Kenneth Macpherson, in introducing the issue, captured its tone by lamenting the passing of the silent film: he concurred with others that the only consolation was that the talkies now made it possible to *hear* the Negro for the first time. One receives the impression from the special issue that the Negro was in vogue in London as never before. Amid this sudden burst on the British scene of a new flavor of cultural fare, of literature, theater, and film about black American life, the contributors to the issue begin to think along similar lines—to wonder at the possibilities and to imagine a new cinema. "The negro documentaire of the negro," writes Macpherson, "Think what might be in it. The negro as observer of himself. As his own historian. As his own agitator." This dream of a cinema, not surprisingly, is tied to technological change. For the imagination of a new world cinema is critically linked with the loss of the silent film and the arrival of the talkies: "Talking films took films from us but they have given us a glimpse of [the negro] . . . fanning something entirely and wholly new, that may expand not in the negroid alone, but throughout the world of a rationalised international cinema."[1] Another contributor echoes Macpherson: "You wonder, could there be a Negro cinema?"[2]

One would think from all of the excited speculation about this cinema that was to be produced by the "marvelously photogenic"[3] Negro that there had *never* been a cinema produced, directed, and distributed by blacks anywhere in the world in the thirty years since the invention of cinema. It is indeed strange to think that the appearance in 1929 of the Fox musical *Hearts in Dixie* and the touted promise that same year of Metro-Goldwyn-Mayer's *Hallelujah* would lead critics to wish for an all-black cinema produced by blacks themselves. In the more familiar account of these events, Hollywood's production of musicals with all-black casts killed the very possibility of black cinema. Thus *Close-up*'s eager anticipation directly contradicts the version of film history told from the other side of the Atlantic, a version in which Hollywood's "discovery" of black entertainment effectively drove the fledgling "race movie" companies out of business.[4] In this, *Close-up* seems oddly out of touch. Are these critics, writing here in the preeminent avant-garde film journal in Europe, entirely unaware of the existence of the race movie tradition that thrived in the silent era before the coming of sound? One might conclude that Europeans could not have known about this short-lived movement. But it is not just white British critics who seem oblivious of race movies; the same seems true for the prominent black Americans whose supporting letters are published in the journal—Walter White, secretary of the NAACP, who is impressed that William Fox would produce *Hearts in Dixie,* and Elmer Anderson Carter, editor of *Opportunity* magazine, who looks forward to King Vidor's *Hallelujah.* Neither White nor Carter mentions race movies but, it should be said, neither indulges in pipe dreams about blacks magically producing their own films either.

At least two *Close-up* contributors, however, do seem aware of some of the activity of the race movie pioneers who made silent films for the segregated theater circuit. Harry Alan Potamkin refers to black companies that made films on the New Jersey lots that had been vacated by white companies when they moved to California and recalls the highly acclaimed black actor Charles Gilpin's role in *Ten Nights in a Barroom* as well as Paul Robeson's involvement in black productions.[5] The fullest information, however, comes from the black American writer Geraldyn Dismond who, looking back on his early moviegoing years, vividly recalls seeing black character actor Noble Johnson play the part of a Mexican bandit.[6] It is Dismond who mentions the Micheaux Company as well as the Colored Players of Philadelphia, making reference to African American filmmaker Oscar Micheaux's *Wages of Sin* (1928) and *The Broken Violin* (1926) as well as the Colored Players' *The Children of Fate* (1926), *A Prince of His Race* (1926), and (like Potamkin) *Ten Nights in a Barroom* (1926), the all-black remake of a popular stage melodrama that, Dismond recalls, also starred Charles Gilpin.[7] Here we will be concerned to some extent with the white-owned Philadelphia company, but more than anything we will be concerned with the question, Who was Oscar Micheaux?

Oscar Micheaux, frontispiece from his novel *The Conquest* (1913)

Not Negro Modernism

It is also Geraldyn Dismond who supplies a functioning definition of the *race movie*, explaining these films as the product of Hollywood's "slow recognition of the Negro as movie material." In this vacuum and in response to Hollywood's inertia, the argument goes, there appeared "Negro film corporations, Negro and white film corporations, and white corporations, all for the production of Negro pictures. They have the same motive, namely, to present Negro films about and for Negroes, showing them not as fools and servants, but as human beings with the same emotions, desires and weaknesses as other people's; and to share in the profits of this great industry."[8] Dismond appears to know something about the ideals and aspirations of this effort, this dogged attempt to produce motion pictures against incredible odds for the enthusiastic patrons of segregated theaters. And yet he should be counted among the dubious critics of the black press who by the late 1920s were growing increasingly critical of the race movie product. Thus it is not surprising that Dismond should dismissively write that the films had all been "second rate in subject matter, direction and photography."[9]

Whether the other *Close-up* critics concurred with Dismond in his evaluation or were just unfamiliar with the race movie output is not clear, but they were asking for "all-Negro films" as though such films had never existed. We have to realize, however, that the American race movies, familiar genre films with all-black casts, wildly popular with their black audiences, were *not* the films that these elite British critics were calling for at the end of the silent era. These critics envisioned a sleek experimental aesthetic, not the rough conventionality of race movies. Macpherson himself would soon put the *Close-up* avant-gardism to the test as director of *Borderline* (1930), Paul Robeson's second film role after Micheaux's *Body and Soul* (1925), and in his introduction the editor seems to be working out a justification for his own experiments.[10] Favorably reviewed in the same issue are the European avant-garde darlings of 1929: Dziga Vertov's *The Man with a Movie Camera* and Jean Epstein's *La Chute de la Maison Usher*. Luis Buñuel's *Un Chien Andalou* takes some strong criticism, but Alfred Hitchcock's *Blackmail* is reviewed as though it were a new experiment in sound and silence. True to their politics, the *Close-up* critics imagine a by-blacks, for-blacks cinema as a political cinema, hence the recurring association with the Russian revolutionary avant-garde that this journal was so instrumental in promoting and, in addition, Macpherson's reference to the Negro as his "own agitator." To film studies scholars, *Close-up*'s anxious avant-gardism should have a familiar ring. Pinning their hopes on a political cinema, on an aesthetic vanguard based on the black experience, the *Close-up* critics stage a dress rehearsal for a moment more than fifty years later when radical film critics would give preferential attention to an avant-garde black British cinema over the popular American cinema of Spike Lee.[11] We find ourselves again caught in between, wondering why we must always choose between progressive politics and popular audiences.

In the end, however, *Close-up* is not advocating a separate cinema as anything more than a fascinating exercise, and more important to the authors than avant-garde aesthetics is the challenge to the continued dominance of white cinema. The audience, too, is on the mind of one contributor, who confesses: "For surely they are as tired of all that as of white, yellow, white—nothing but white—films; and heaven knows I am."[12] *Close-up* rehearses the Left's love affair with political modernism but still flirts with the essentialism that should be starkly antithetical to it. Several of the essays exhibit some slight fascination with the possibility that the Negro might possess a certain "something" that naturally lends itself to the screen. Let us call this fascination a tentative essentialism. On the one hand, there is a reticence to suggest that this "something" might be a "sense of rhythm" and, on the other hand, there is an eagerness to find what it is about the Negro that makes him different, a hopefulness that that "something" would reproduce on film. This same white writer for *Close-up* continues. Perhaps it is a "difference of mentality," perhaps not. At any rate, it is "[s]omething which we have not got, but which we may respond to."[13] Here *Close-up* appears to be painfully aware of the more politically compromised aspects of the Harlem Renaissance, the vicarious and envious connoisseurship referenced in the remark, "We want no van Vechtens of the films."[14] And yet it is clear that the Harlem Renaissance *is* revisited. The magazine's vision of indigenous Negro modernism is one and the same as Alain Locke's New Negro movement essentialism.[15]

During the 1920s, many attempts were made by white and black critics alike to try to locate this "something" in black art, and the search has continued into the present, a search for "blackness" extended to popular culture but with more attention on music than on popular film. Despite ever more sophisticated critiques, the most recent of which can be found in Clyde Taylor's *The Mask of Art*, the interest in the black aesthetic continues to grow with every new generation.[16] But questions about how the "black" actually got into the work still persist; though in sympathy with these questions, this book about race movies will not go down that road. Neither will this book be an attempt to attach race movies to the Harlem Renaissance, which would be an historical error since the Harlem elite virtually ignored these popular films and wrote them off as having nothing to do with art.[17]

There is another reason to resist the temptation to annex this tradition to the legacy of the Harlem Renaissance. To merge race movies with any fine art and literature tradition would be to lose the high/low distinction that we will need in order to explain the broad ballyhoo and brouhaha, the hype and the hucksterism that defined American movie culture in the teens and twenties. Race movies never were nor can they ever be *understood* as high culture, elevated though they may become over time. Ideally, we should be devising different critical tools in our attempt to draw significance from these works since we already know that the value-laden vocabulary of high culture criticism will never be able to grasp the aesthetics of necessity, the production of mass culture against incredible odds and under impossible economic conditions. These works challenge the need to automatically ascribe greatness to cultural objects that we deem worthy of study, the need to justify our interest, our awe, and our respect with the elevation of some works and the denigration of others. Thus race movies provide the opportunity to confront the vocabulary of valuation and the institutions of cultural elevation and to find ways to circumvent them. The answer here is not to find the hand of the *auteur* genius in these works but to use the works to reject the judgments that hierarchize and exclude so many cultural objects. While it can be argued that authorship as an approach has successfully secured the revaluation of so many marginalized objects, the same mechanism that values can also be used to devalue, the one move predicated on the other.

Raced Relations in the Silent Era

This is not, then, an authorship study. Neither is this approach to race movies a study of black culture alone since it attempts to trace the uncanny parallels and volatile intersections between black and white American cultures, to demonstrate what Cornel West once called the "interracial interdependence" from which we cannot escape.[18] And, in retrospect, one of the most productive connecting points for delineating this interdependence was the historical production of race movies in response to D. W. Griffith's *The Birth of a Nation* (1915), that cultural and political time bomb that set off a series of black responses that have continued through the 1990s.[19] Granted, I am reading an outright antagonism as a productive moment, but early black filmmaking is inextricably tied to the release of this film, and Griffith's offensive epic was the irritant around which a pearl formed. Further reason to return to Griffith is the current incompleteness of the historical record, as I will show in chapter 7. Revisiting this traumatic moment, we may be surprised to find that the black response to *The Birth of a Nation* is even feistier and more troublesome than all the restrained NAACP attacks reprinted over several decades have given us to believe. I will have issues as well with the NAACP strategy, which needs to be reconsidered in the light of the censorship apparatus that turned so quickly from Griffith to Oscar Micheaux. We have begun to reach a fuller understanding of the trouble surrounding *The Birth of a Nation* from recently discovered race films, and also from contemporary black newspaper critics such as the *Chicago Defender*'s Juli Jones, who satirically imagines an answer to Griffith based on the realities of white-on-black murder, rape, and incest titled "The Birth of a Mixed Race."[20] One of the reasons it has been difficult if not impossible to analyze this penetrating response to Griffith as well as the point of convergence between white and black cinema in the silent era is that the film texts in question have been considered "lost." The disappearance of these films is now understood as the consequence of their banishment from the United States and their export to Europe where some were saved but subsequently forgotten. Such is the case with two of the films I will consider. Both Micheaux's *The Symbol of the Unconquered* (1920), located recently in Belgium, and *Within Our Gates* (1920), returned to this country from Spain in the late 1990s, are eerie answers to *The Birth of a Nation*.[21]

Thus it will be important for me to return one more time to D. W. Griffith's unfortunate epic, to add more about the conditions surrounding its reception in an effort to compare the real riots accompanying its exhibition with the imagined riots that city fathers feared would break out at showings of so many of Oscar Micheaux's silent films. For it is in the reception to the release of Micheaux's *Within Our Gates*, as contrasted with the exhibition history of Griffith's *Birth of a Nation*, that one begins to see not only the political discrepancy and economic unevenness that produce cultural distinctiveness and the exclusion that produces difference, but also the antagonism that produces inextricability rather than distance. In this book D. W. Griffith and Oscar Micheaux meet as antagonists but also as parallel fathers—one, the white father of American cinema; the other, one might say, the black father—the most prolific and the most daring of the early film pioneers. To bring the two fathers closer together is to see what the two have in common: one a white Kentuckian and proud southerner, the other the descendent of former slaves born in Metropolis, Illinois, in 1884, just nine years after Griffith. Ron Green's efficient contrast reveals the commonality between the two as he compares Griffith's big capital "expensive vision of the Dream" with Micheaux's small capital (i.e., low budget) "inexpensive revision of the American Dream."[22] Here we see two outsiders striving to produce their versions of American life on an enormous scale, two undaunted egos, and two artist-entrepreneurs, both working at precisely the same historical moment.

The discovery of new films by Micheaux and the uncovering of the work of other race pioneers from the period before 1927 demand a significant revision of American film history.[23] Until recently, there has been no chapter on black film in the silent era, and the reasons for this go beyond the problem of the number of surviving prints. The *Close-up* writers, it would seem by the contents of their 1929 special issue, are not only thinking about black film but closing the chapter on the sound era. And in closing this chapter, they are waxing nostalgic about the silent film, sounding uncannily like Rudolph Arnheim, who looked back at the silent film, contrasting it with the too-easy excesses of the technically imperfect talkies, and who, looking at all culture from the high art "less is more" position, declared the silent film to be a superior art.[24] The Negro is clearly implicated in this. For all of *Close-Up*'s heralding of the talkies for their discovery of the Negro's "voice," in their association of the Negro with this noisy and new and, by many accounts, audibly intolerable form, these critics disassociated him from the perfection of the silent film. How could the Negro possibly have produced silent film? The silent film was so aesthetically pure. Or so they seemed to imply.

Another question about the contemporary reception of Micheaux grows out of the issue of the purity and potency of the silent film aesthetic, particularly if we take the question of aesthetic perfection a step further and supplement the Arnheimian insight about the limitations of silence producing the apex of the form with Peter Brooks's view of the transcendence of muteness. We wonder why Micheaux's critical reputation, based solely on his sound films, should be so dramatically reversed with the recent discovery of his silent film work. Why was Micheaux's sound work dismissed and his silent work, once discovered, immediately embraced by film scholars? Why does it promise so much? I would answer this question not with recourse to the aesthetics of perfection, the connotations of which would now seem to accrue to Micheaux, but with an acknowledgment of a fortuitous bonus of the silent aesthetic, a paradoxical situation that has been considered by at least one critic. Micheaux's silent films, gesturing in the tradition in which everything is shown and nothing is heard, gesturing into the acoustic void that is silent cinema, do appear to *say more* than his sound films. In contrast with the shallow tinniness of his sound films, the silent films seem a bottomless well of meaning.

Peter Brooks would explain this resonance of silence as an aesthetic of deprivation whereby a type of drama is stricken right at the source of its particular forte, at its time of greatest need.[25] For example, since melodrama is about expression, when it is "struck dumb," so to speak, it is at its most eloquent. Silent cinema exemplifies this principle on a different scale since, unlike theatrical melodrama, which relies on the eloquence of hushed moments, silent film is eternally mute, totally speechless with or without musical accompaniment. Neither the problematic production values of Micheaux's early talkies nor his actors' inflectionless delivery of often banal dialogue explains the reputation of his films: the question resides in the relative eloquence of silence. By this principle more than from any lack of profundity of the written dialogue in his sound films,

Micheaux's silent features are seen to throb with meaning. The mute gesture, which Brooks tells us is particulary adept at rendering the ineffable, bears the fuller burden of signifying those inexpressible dilemmas that were concerning the black community in the 1918–1931 period—the period in which Micheaux completed his silent film work.[26] But it was not only the way the aesthetics of the unutterable strained to portray the miseries of fathers addicted to gambling, children dragged down by parents, parishioners betrayed by their preachers, and brothers who drove businesses into bankruptcy. Silent melodrama also suited Micheaux's purposes because it tended toward the hyperbolic and the grandiose. It makes sense that a man who would want to homestead the vast plains of South Dakota would also want to fill the screen with the largest and most deeply felt images of black life.

Micheaux's silent oeuvre would then seem to benefit from the critical reevaluation of film melodrama, an evaluation that has allowed scholars to think through the long-standing appeal of the form without needing to dismiss its loyal audience following. But this is not the only way in which the critical moment has made a difference in the reception of race movies. Now that we are beyond the value judgments of an earlier era and even beyond the strictures of 1970s Marxist aesthetics that would dismiss these films out of hand because of their formal conventionality, it becomes possible to look at early black cinema for new reasons. Perhaps the burden of proof is now on the theory and not on the films themselves. Clearly, these new discoveries highlight the inadequacy of existing theories, and here it is not the films but film criticism that must rise to the occasion—the reverse of the situation with the old value judgment criticism that would require the work to meet pre-set standards. For it could be said that the work studied will often rise to the level of its criticism. I have also found that the questions that arise out of the study of race movies in the silent era have benefited from the recent confluence of postcolonial theory and a more seasoned feminism as well as the formulations of "race theory" in response to identity politics. In addition, recent works by film and television studies scholars have made it possible to establish the seriousness of the popular and important new work on contemporary black American film that has discovered an entire territory overlooked by traditional white criticism.[27] White criticism has had to adapt and change. So, too, the excavation of race movies, this smaller territory within black American film, has shuffled knowledges as approaches that served us well (psychoanalysis and media effects studies) no longer seem serviceable in their current form. Old concepts are rehabilitated (mimesis), and others are reformulated (utopianism).

Race Theory / Film Theory

In undertaking this study, I was surprised to discover the degree to which film theory needed to be reconceived in order to even attempt to answer key questions raised by a group of films whose audience was self-selected along racial lines. For some time it has been acknowledged that existing theories of spectatorship did not anticipate the question of raced spectatorship. Simultaneously, it seemed, the question of the dichotomy between the abstract subject of 1970s film theory and the real historical spectator was posed, and Judith Mayne, for one, expressed the hope that the issue of black as opposed to white spectatorship would help us move beyond this dichotomy.[28] The question still remains a difficult one since what is needed is a theory that accounts for variety as well as generality, a theory that considers *everyone as well as someone* in the audience. In the current political climate in which the question of identities is so pressing, we will need to imagine the spectator as both singular and plural, as the hub where many identities intersect, a position as well as a person. Mayne also raises the adjacent question of the ostensible race of the critic, a question sometimes posed in terms of the way the white as opposed to the black critic may, by virtue of experience, produce significantly different interpretations.[29] Ann duCille represents a model for all of us when she says, "Readings are never neutral." She goes on, "All criticisms are local, situational. My own interpretations are colored by my race and my gender, by my blackness and my feminism."[30]

While I think that sensitivity to these differences is important, particularly as we check the tendency of white critics to be taken as automatically expert in all areas of knowledge, I have other concerns as well. One is that we may want to imagine a future in which the attributed race and gender of the writer may no longer be an issue. Within the next decades we may also see a reaction against the contemporary interest in referring the spectator's response to a cultural text back to his or her gender, race, or class position. A future generation may criticize the way the race or gender of the critic serves as verification of the authenticity of the critical or the creative work. But in this particular period, there is an unwritten assumption that the question of the race or gender of the unseen author will be resolved at some point and will prove to be an important political factor. We assume that the authorial identity question will be resolved because of the relatively small community of readers in the field of cultural studies within which authors are known as this or that. We seldom read the work of an author without knowing key details about his or her

identity, and the fact that we want to know suggests that "race matters."[31] Significantly, one of the themes of this book is the impossibility
of knowing, the ambiguity of the concept of race as well as the difficulty
of determining who is what. So, race *does* matter, and yet there have historically been and will continue to be ways in which it does not. Race
does / doesn't matter.

The fact that white feminists have circled the question of race and
spectatorship for so long is only one more indication of how much race
now matters.[32] Several years ago, dissatisfied with the way feminist film
theory addressed questions of racial difference, I attempted to rethink
the established model of looking relations, by which I meant not just the
shot structure but the film–spectator–character connecting points.[33] At
the time, there was a strong academic emphasis on the way gender is
"built in" to cultural forms ("structured," in the terminology of the
times), and I was interested in the way "race difference" might be similarly "built in," although often built in by exclusion. The beauty of the
sexual difference model of reception in vogue at the time was its utter
predictability. Soon it became a formula as conventionalized as the shot–
countershot editing structure itself. When you "plugged in" the interpre-
tive model, feminist readings fit perfectly (male characters controlled the
gaze and female characters were objects of desire). But perhaps too perfectly since aberrations and extenuating circumstances could and did
trouble the model. This is not, however, to say that a theoretical model
should just be more accommodating.[34] Now at a juncture in which the
limitations of the sexual difference / racial difference analogy are clear,
we may be in a position to rethink what it is that we want from a theory
of film that takes race into account. More concretely, what we are asking
is how to develop theoretical language that would sensitize us to race as
identity as well as to existing racialized structures at the level of representation as well as reception.

When I set out to think about the impact that race movies would
have on existing theories of spectatorship, I didn't expect that I would
need to do more than raise questions. In the end, however, I have argued
the need for a healthy suspicion of some theories, taking to task the dominant model, here the psychoanalytic theory of identification in film, and
made an attempt to point the way toward a new formulation. My short-
term solution has been to shift the emphasis from the motion picture as
a looking machine to a device for showing the one to the other, to conceive of the entire apparatus as an "othering machine." Othering calls attention to the way identities are formed across and through others, in relation to those who are like and not like us. It emphasizes the distinction

between "I" and "not-I" as corresponding to positions on- and off-screen, in the theater auditorium and on the screen in front of the audience, and finally it allows for processes of making the other as well as being other than. But what I am suggesting is only intended as an orientation toward new theories of how people view, a transition to another approach.

Such an approach does not necessarily need to start, as feminist film theory began, with the structural analysis of classical Hollywood narrative. We could conceivably begin with the critical work of influential black intellectuals. One such productive beginning is suggested by Saidiya Hartman and Farah Griffin, who use Ralph Ellison's "The Shadow and the Act" in their analysis of Julie Dash's *Illusions* (1982).[35] "In the beginning was not the shadow, but the act, and the province of Hollywood is not action, but illusion," says Ellison, who in this statement both summarizes everything that was wrong with the NAACP campaign against *The Birth of a Nation*—its assumption that you fought racism by fighting an image of it—and a repetition of the NAACP's error—the argument that motion pictures are lies or illusions.[36] The analysis of the cinema as shadow world has been and continues to be important. But it is crucial that we now turn from that criticism forged out of the response to *The Birth of a Nation,* which for so many decades defined the conditions of the consideration of race in American cinema and even set up the terms of debates about "images of" women and minorities in popular motion pictures.[37] Hartman and Griffin in their epigraphs (a theoretically rich set of quotations) suggest starting places for theories of racialized looking in cinema. These hypothetical starting points range from Frantz Fanon to Richard Wright to Zora Neale Hurston and subtly address ways in which acts of seeing have been historically complicit in the constitution of raced subjecthood. The authors end with W. E. B. Du Bois's important theorization of double consciousness, which, from the point of view of film theory, is all about looking relations. Double consciousness, he says in the familiar quotation, is that "peculiar sensation," that "sense of always looking at one's self through the eyes of others, of measuring one's soul by the tape of a world that looks on in amused contempt and pity."[38] Suddenly one of the foundational statements in race theory appears as film theory, addressing the question of the execution of power through the trajectory of the eye.

The "seeing ourselves being seen"—shades of feminist film theory—is undeniably there in Du Bois, and for a minute we may experience a theoretical déjà vu, may find ourselves in that moment when, in the early 1970s, John Berger (echoing Simone de Beauvoir who echoes

Sartre) noted the self-surveillance of women who saw themselves always through male eyes *in* as well as outside representation.[39] But although the analogy between women and blacks points up a striking similarity (both destined always to be objects of the look of another and thus to see themselves only as objects), it fails to tell us enough about what we need to know most. We need to know about social relations. The social dimension of looking relations has been too long implied and needs now to be spelled out. This entails taking the emphasis off "looking" and putting it instead on "relations." And returning to Du Bois, this would mean stressing the concept of "through" rather than "eyes," producing his famous definition of double consciousness as an analysis of hegemony in which everything the black man knows about himself is first routed "through" the white man against whom he is always "measuring" himself, "measuring" with the rigged tape measure that is handed to him by the white world that watches, hoping that he won't succeed. Here is a strange surveillance, a mix of "contempt and pity" and, worse, "amusement." And stranger still, for blacks there is the hegemonic absurdity of looking at themselves through the same distorted lens that eyes them so contemptuously. For blacks within white society who have historically been looking through the wrong lens, race movies offered a corrected view of things, not a radically new view but certainly an improved one.

The significance of race movies would be the way in which they could be counterhegemonic without symmetrically "countering" white culture on every point; for their oppositionality, if it could be called that, was in the circumvention, in the way they produced images that didn't go *through* white culture. Seen by blacks, unseen by whites, race movies featured an all-black world, a utopian vision of "all-black everything," as I argue. And yet, at the level of the building blocks of culture, all-black had to be premised on all-white, the one effectively deciding the other by the process of inclusion and exclusion, by addition and elimination. One must also emphasize that neither cultures nor peoples are constituted by gazes alone. Even the gaze structure, if one goes back to the origins of the concept, turns out to be less about looking than about relationality, and if about seeing, about seeing likenesses, an exercise into which a comparative dimension always enters by way of the elaborate system of substitution that holds language and culture in place. And likeness is not only where realism works wonders, but also where questions of identification and imitation arise, where one understands every phenomenon as like or not-like me, where we see realism with a vengeance in the insistence on "like." But in the racial construction of the self, relationality is difficult to determine if it is a question of relative to another, the very other to whom one wants no relation at all. Frantz Fanon summarized the asymmetry of this system of racial meaning in his observation that "not only must the black man be black; he must be black in relation to the white man."[40]

This charged relativity is most pronounced, of course, in every case in which the color line is enforced, where there is daily demonstration of separate but not different, parallel but not equal. One can begin to see here where the economic gets constructed on the semiotic, where in the race movie period, in neighborhoods, in businesses, and in the motion picture theater itself, the separate entrances and divided houses testified to the epitome of the social relation of antagonism: the Jim Crow principle. Consider here also the oddity of black capitalism, its success based on a lapse in a white capitalism that would for a limited time forsake its imperative to expand in order to better serve the ideology of racial superiority. So it is these exceptional relations of production that will concern us as they test the rule, these "raced" relations of production that expand out from the economic as what was originally understood as a labor relation gets transposed into the realm of sexual relations. Certainly it is Marx whose efficient philosophical system originally gave us a theory not just of society but, as Bertell Ollman says, of "society conceived 'relationally.'" Marx probably used the German word for "relation" (*Verhältnis*) with more frequency than any other in his written works.[41] Yet as we fill in the connection between "race" and "sex," those more immediately compelling "relations of production," we are reminded that Marx did not anticipate the significance of either, leaving us with his unfinished job. But let us not forget that there is an entire chapter of human history covering several centuries in which sexual relations *were* literally economic relations, a deformation of family relations expressed as mixed parentage and experienced as a race identity complex. In how many ways have these particular strained relations organized American culture over the past centuries?

How many times have we almost said that "looking relations" are "sexual relations"? In feminist film theory, we originally meant to say that "looking relations" are "gender relations" and made the mistake of talking about them as "sexed relations," or relations of sexual difference, thinking "gender" but saying "sex."[42] We face the difficulty now when, in connection with race, we genuinely need to talk about sexual relations in cinema, a new approach to analysis in which the historical prohibitions are seen as figuring significantly in the representational system that is classical Hollywood narrative. Nick Browne has suggested that there is a semiotics of race relations that has historically regulated classical cinema, and that this system is itself linked with a system of sexuality, linked by means of a "constituting prohibition," simply stated as "no nonwhite man can have sanctioned sexual relations with a white woman." Carried over from the broader culture into American cinema, this prohibition legislates against certain narrative occurrences and enactments, replicating the familiar asymmetry of mixed-race relations: white female and nonwhite male marriage is a taboo but nonwhite female and white male sexual relations are frequent.[43] While Browne considers this scheme as determining narrative options, thus representing a strict governance of American cinema, I will consider this "constituting prohibition" somewhat differently, studying its ramifications for melodrama. For in my analysis, this characteristic American prohibition provides opportunity for melodrama, the genre that specializes in the transposition of social asymmetry and relational dysfunction into the inexpressible dilemmas that make such compelling narratives.

The "Race" in Race Movies

We should immediately acknowledge the undeniable political gains attributable to understanding the social construction of race. It is not only that this vantage helps us to see the historical opportunism in the shifting definitions of "who is and who isn't." The idea that race is a powerful fiction has an important job to do as ammunition against a subtle essentialism and a treacherous biologism. It is a counter to every assertion of the naturalness of behavior and bodily appearance in groups of people who are identified as "this or that." Certainly the self-fulfilling prophecy of the identification of the peoples of the world as automatically "this or that" is objectionable at this time in history. But there is much more to object to. The category of race, socially convenient as it is, has no scientific standing, as biologists now confirm, so it is also a matter of which peoples *verifiably* belong in what group.[44] And it has largely been this scientific untenability as well as the philosophical incoherence of the concept of race that has inspired the most radical position, Anthony Appiah's assertion that *there is no such thing as race,* a position that he has recently reaffirmed, stating that, in the final analysis, "nobody has a race."[45] And yet something has to stand for all of the things that we need race to stand for.

While the argument that "there is no such thing as race" is politically compelling as it combats biologism, other arguments on behalf of the political necessity of the concept of race are equally compelling and may not be exactly incompatible with the fictionality of race. I would single out Hortense Spillers's assertion that "[i]f we did not already have 'race' and its quite impressive powers of proliferation, we would need to invent them," since, as she suggests, something more than a figure or a metaphor is working to hierarchize difference.[46] *Something* is using difference as a means of sorting and separating us. Hazel Carby tightens this argument somewhat, basing her case for the centrality of the concept of race on the need for analyzing the particular power relations that produce the "racialization of our social order," emphasizing that it is not race per se but the "racialization" process that is determining.[47] And, finally, let us not forget the importance of racial self-construction, which makes its argument by turning race to the advantage of historical subjects who vehemently claim and celebrate "blackness" as their own. The question here, of course, is whether that "claiming" is a knowing invention or an unknowing assertion of a preexisting racial something.

The understanding of race as an invention informs the following discussion of race movies as well as racial themes in American cinema in the first two decades of the twentieth century. My hope is that in answer to concerns about the denial of race, an assertion of the fictionality of race should bring the historical specificity of race questions into sharper relief. The existence of a cinema separate from and parallel to Hollywood, founded on the premise that it was "other than white," helps us to see the unacknowledged whiteness of the majority cinema. Ideally, race movies should defamiliarize the dominant cinema, should make that cinema seem strangely white. In contrast with the "all-black cast" silent movies in the 1913–1931 period, Hollywood cinema was snowy white and totally blind to its selectivity as well as to its increasingly successful illusionism.[48] Not only did this cinema not think about its own illusionistic devices, but it did not think about the race makeup of the actors in the acting pool or the racial characterizations it disseminated, although this was a cinema that clearly *did* think about lightness and darkness.

Race movies were a significant part of the attempt in the teens and twenties to define black entertainment produced for black Americans, and in this the films themselves helped to construct "the race." Ironically, although the race film pioneers started from the assumption that they knew who they were and who the race audience would be, they were, as they produced, directed, and exhibited their product, actually *constituting* that race community. Was the "race" in race movies then meant to refer to the producers or to the subjects of these films or to the audience for them or to all of the above? We would not want to argue tautologically that race movies were called race movies because they were largely by, for, and always about the Negro race. This is too easy. The chain of historical events that produced this short-lived cinema were not self-evident or inevitable but contingent and unexpected. The race pioneers carved something significant out of nothing—race movies were an audacious invention that helped to make an audience that most white entrepreneurs did not see, that helped to imagine a separate community into existence.

One could argue that in their separateness, race movies could produce a vision of life without reference to the white community, a vision that made it seem as though there were no other communities, so seldom did a white character appear on screen. Race movies aspired to a condition of blackness from top to bottom and celebrated striving and loving and laughing in an all-black world. In their heyday, race movies took something from every existing Hollywood genre; thus it is difficult to generalize about them in terms of narrative structure, although, as I do argue, in every way imaginable they espoused uplift. And one of the unspoken ways in which they advocated uplift was in their consistent use of what could be called the "light-skinned aesthetic." It is not only that the black press noted the preference for light over dark-skinned heroes and heroines in these films, but that contemporary viewers in discussions following retrospective screenings invariably question the prevalence of light skin on the screen. The paradox of race movies is that they celebrate blackness, but blackness as performed by actors who *look almost white*. In race movies, while blackness is celebrated, the lightness that flirts with passing, that is almost a "play" on passing, suggests that the celebration is toned down. These players, although not exactly "passing," are performing blackness of a particular kind, a "high" or rarefied blackness. It could be said that they are able to enact this white–black vision on the screen because, as historian of the American mulatto Joel Williamson has argued, in North America, for all intents and purposes, "white is black" because of the one-drop rule.[49]

The distinction between *being* a light-skinned black actor or actress and representing blackness as idealized lightness in a screen performance is significant in that it helps us to understand the ontology of passing, which in turn is a way into the difficult question of the social construction of race. There is more to the ontology of passing than meets the eye: it may have been downplayed in the early years of African American studies in history and literature because the instances were undocumentable or because the number of racially indeterminate persons, potential candidates for passing, was relatively small. As a paradigm, however, passing continues to structure our way into African

American literature as a rich, as well as a deeply American, ambiguity.[50] For my purposes the inconsistency implicit in the possibility of passing is instructive as it indicates a culture that is of two minds, a culture that is in so many respects contradictory to the core. Here also is the best case to be made for the social construction of race, for its arbitrariness as a category, a case that rests on the existence of people who could conceivably fit the definition of one or more categories and live in one community or the other within the larger culture.[51] Passing, however, is admittedly an odd paradigm since it is often only about a possibility. Because it is not necessarily an ongoing practice, passing is by definition undetectable.

It is interesting in this respect to consider the impact of what is now called "White Studies" on the paradigm of passing, a paradigm that is becoming basic to the study of American literature.[52] Walter Benn Michaels, for instance, has considered the asymmetry between passing and crossing over, both examples of what might be called "race treason," the abandonment of one race for another.[53] In reference to James Weldon Johnson's "treatise" on passing, *Autobiography of an Ex-Colored Man*, Michaels argues that there is no such thing as an ex-colored man and neither can there be such a thing as an ex-white man, a controversial argument *against* the social construction of race that is still not an argument for essentialism. It is, it would seem, a question of representation, of what might be called the semiotics of race identity. Simply stated, it is a question of whether as a black person passing for white you *become white*. Or, put another way, when you pass, do you become what you are passing as? Constructivism would say that you do. Michaels would say that you don't—you can never become an "ex-colored man," by which he means you can never stop being a "colored man" even if you are passing as a white man. The visible–invisible dialectic of the racial signifier requires that in order for black blood to be known it must be *represented*. This is the dictum of the notorious one-drop rule. In passing, then, is one deliberately concealing the invisible or passively failing to signify? It is, he says, a problem of misrepresentation: "That race can be invisible . . . means that it *must* be either misrepresented or represented, since to leave it unrepresented will be to misrepresent it. In other words, if you are invisibly black, either you must find some way to represent your blackness or you must pass for white."[54] Thus the "invisibly black" are caught in a double bind—they can only represent or misrepresent. Whether light or dark, skin color, that inadvertent sign, signifies one way when *you* might want to signify another. White, wanting to cross over, or black, wanting to pass, you cannot (in these terms) represent; you can only misrepresent.

Most difficult for me to accept about Michaels's argument is the reliance on the notion of "really," reinforced by the frequent recourse to the finality of the state of being verbs "is" and "are." One wants to know if the race question is finally resolved if Michaels can (without reliance on essence or biology) say of the impossibility of representation and the inevitability of misrepresentation: "And once we recognize this, we recognize also that even if you can't pass (even if you can't help but look like what you are), you can still fail to act like *what you are*" (emphasis mine).[55] But isn't this argument one and the same as the highly ideological "you are who you are," sometimes extended to "you are who your people are"? This recourse to "really" is further problematic because it would negate the subversive possibilities of passing, the way the practice might undermine the ideology of the visible or the mistaken wisdom of "what you see is what you get." Passing, with its internal tension between two possibilities, with its ability to point up the discrepancies between looking like and acting like, can bring home the point that race is not just a matter of color. Passing is a visual trick played on a gullible white culture.

Although the semiotics of race identity as it pertains to passing has been an important informal topic within the African American community, the politics of passing has dictated a kind of silence about the practice since passing has been historically understood as community abandonment and self-annihilation. It is never politically radical to renounce who you are, but, as I have been suggesting, there is also something politically retrograde in the commonsense wisdom that you *are who you are,* which implies that your race identity is fixed. This idea of fixedness seems in particular a contemporary anomaly given that we are everywhere encouraged by consumer culture to construct and cultivate as many identities as possible. In chapter 1, I look at this race identity conundrum through James Baldwin's ruminations on his own race identity formation, a formation in which, as a boy in 1930s Harlem, his experience of motion pictures and white female stars is crucial. Astute critic of mass culture that he was, in his essays on this early period of his life Baldwin appears to be searching for the "truth" of the self, a vain search we might think from the point of view of contemporary theories of identity. But who, it could be asked, is ever searching for the "fiction" of the self? Also in this chapter, as in every other, I attempt to consider one or more central problems in contemporary film theory. Here I introduce the problem of identification in the cinema, beginning with Christian Metz's theorization, showing how this elaboration does and does not answer the challenge of the "politics of mirroring," including the charge of marginalized groups that mainstream cinema never reflects back the image of themselves that they would like to see. The challenge to established theories of identification comes as well from queer theory and Baldwin represents an opportunity to investigate the failure as well as the imaginative possibilities of identification.

As a thematic, the problem of identification is carried over into chapter 2, which takes as its starting point the 1903 Edison short, *What Happened in the Tunnel.* Here I examine the first interracial kiss in cinema. The triangular encounter on the train opens up into a consideration of the self/other relation and its philosophical foundation in Hegel's lord and bondsman, a foundation I look at as underpinning what has become known as "the gaze," a discovery that would suggest that Hegel's racialized scenario has had its way of structuring film theory. In Hegel's conceptualization of Desire and the Other, I find the central premise of the book: that identification in the cinema is about the transformation of difference into identity and, corollary to this, in the largest sense Desire has to do with overcoming differences. Concomitant questions arise here in regard to the use of elite theory in relation to minority texts and the use of feminism as a starting point for a theory of race and cinema, issues that are introduced to a readership that may have more interest in the history of race movies than in film history and theory. Conversely, the film studies scholar is introduced to aspects of African American history and developments in contemporary race theory.

It is also my intention to situate the black independent film movement in the silent period in relation to developments in early film history as well as to trends in film studies, such as the focus on spectatorship. I also explore the impact of new film discoveries on the basics of film criticism, including the consideration of cinematic realism, illusionism, and melodrama as form, crosscutting as a device, and the facial close-up as a rhetoric. Simultaneously, I use the race movie phenomenon to critique and rethink Marxist aesthetics, authorship theory, and psychoanalysis as well as to challenge reflectionism, effects studies, and concepts of stereotypage. But theorizing about race movies in the silent era also requires knowledge of the history of such struggling companies as the Lincoln Motion Picture Company and the Micheaux Book and Film Company—hence chapter 3 is a short history of these endeavors from 1913 to 1931. Here I begin with the newer findings of film historians who locate the beginnings of this industry significantly before, not in response to and only in the aftermath of, *The Birth of a Nation*. The chapter looks at the promotion and exhibition strategies of the black film pioneers in an effort to further fill out the cultural history of black moviegoing and to understand the economics of segregation that produced, ironically, the conditions for race movies. The chapter concludes with an attempt to understand the powerful and enigmatic Oscar Micheaux through the eyes of his onetime competitor, Lincoln's George P. Johnson, who chronicled Micheaux's successes and failures over the course of his mercurial career.

As regionally separate and diverse as the race movie pioneers were, they produced motion pictures for the edification of the black audiences of the segregated theaters and can thus generally be understood as within the sphere of influence of black middle class uplift. In chapter 4, I attempt to flesh out the meanings of this uplift, modifying it in relation to the Frankfurt School notion of the utopian dimension of the popular, thereby associating race movies with the highest aspirations of the black community—with the desire for freedom for all, for change, community, leisure, and plenty. In short, the desire for a middle class way of life. Addressed here is the criticism that black films were imitative of white ones, a criticism best answered by more sophisticated theories of two-way cultural transmission in which the black culture is seen in the white dominant one and the white discerned in the black minority culture. Nevertheless, from 1913 to 1931 race movies institute an elaborate parallelism, a separate cinema on a separate track that today looks like an absurd world based on an economy of "two of everything." As strange to viewers today is the skin color code in effect in these films that uses light-skinned blacks to stand for black aspirations, that appears to say that black people are "just like" white people. And thus one hesitates to read these films as automatically progressive when they superficially appear to be based on a reactionary premise that white is best.

In chapter 5, then, I begin to take up the challenge of assessing the political and aesthetic valence of race movies in a close study of Oscar Micheaux's most controversial film, *Within Our Gates*, a film plagued by community censorship beginning in 1920, the year of its release, a film caught up, as I argue, in a linkage between race riots and lynching. Discovered in Europe and not returned to the United States until over sixty years after it disappeared, the film poses a direct challenge to the white mythologies of lynching, particularly in its representation of the brutal hanging of an innocent black man and his wife, a sequence crosscut with the attempted rape of their foster daughter by the white man who discovers when he accosts her that he is her own father. Micheaux's use of crosscutting is here contrasted with Griffith's, locating his maverick stylistics in the tradition of melodrama, countering Hollywood as it borrowed heavily from it.

An intertitle in *Within Our Gates* that refers to a "legitimate marriage" between the light-skinned heroine's mother and her white father presents us with an enigma unresolved by the film. Chapter 6, titled "The Body's Story," discusses the "telling" mark on the breast of the heroine and goes on to examine narratives of the "telltale" signs of race. These narratives include mythologies of mixed parentage and Micheaux's own *The Symbol of the Unconquered,* a narrative of racial misrecognition and black betrayal of black, a study of the hooded face of the Ku Klux Klan. These narratives allow me to look at the incontrovertible evidence of the human body, the self-evidence of the seen, and to compare human body and motion picture apparatus as mimetic technologies, as two machines of reproduction. Reading a formal photographic portrait of a mixed-race family taken in the 1920s, I consider the uncanniness of family resemblance across race.

In a concluding chapter, I return to the community contention over *The Birth of a Nation,* contrasting it with the reception of *Within Our Gates,* two films associated with blood and trouble, with real and imagined racial strife. The way in which these texts were instrumentally produced by their historical moments, shredded by censors, and rewritten by the communities within which they were exhibited, gives us a unique opportunity to consider the way the historical works itself into the popular text, to address one of the most daunting challenges for scholars working in the tradition of Marxist cultural studies. I begin this investigation into the interpenetration of cultural form and real historical force with questions about the infamous incident in which an egg was thrown at the screen during the "Gus chase" scene in *The Birth of a Nation,* inquiring about the semiotic aptitude of the egg-thrower who aims at the world and hits the screen. Returning to the thematic of identification, I ask about the community's own fear of the screen, a terror that analogizes the motion picture itself with riots and betrays a fear of overidentification and imitation by a dark and seething mass audience. The greatest fear of the motion picture censor is that the picture may become more real than the real thing. Film theory has yet to adequately address this unfounded fear, and here I offer an anthropological concept as a solution to the problem posed by *too much likeness.* Following Michael Taussig, whose work has rehabilitated the concept of mimesis, I answer the charge of imitation with the more utopian notion of mimetic powers, the transformative powers I associate with race movies, the form in which the black pioneers attempted, as Taussig says, to "manipulate reality by means of its image."[56] Race movies, I conclude, were a magical inhabitation of white forms, deriving their power from that which blacks were not (whites), using that power to become better—betterment being the watchward of the black middle class in that period. Black race movie pioneers, taking some things and leaving others, brought about change by means of a complex and imaginative incorporation, not a simple assimilation.

"Green Like Me"

There is no better account of the African American child's measurement of his likeness against the luminous screen image than James Baldwin's recollection of his own childhood in *The Devil Finds Work*. In these auto-biographical essays, the child's racial identity is drafted and redrafted between the ages of seven and seventeen, a process involving formative trips to two theaters—the black motion picture house, the Lincoln, and the black dramatic house, the Lafayette. At the Lincoln, he sees MGM and Warner Brothers films from the twenties and thirties with all-white casts, and later, at the Lafayette, he sees productions of *Macbeth* and *Native Son* with all-black casts directed by Orson Welles. Early on, it is clear to the boy that he does not see himself when he looks at the white screen. And yet the cinema mirrors back images that he claims.

The Politics of Mirroring

"Chain of many mirrors," writes film theorist Christian Metz, "the cinema is at once a weak and a robust mechanism: like the human body, like a precision tool, like a social institution. Which is to say that it is really all of these at the same time."[1] Metz's "The Imaginary Signifier," the definitive text on mirrors and mirroring as metaphor for cinema spectatorship, also, perhaps more than any other essay, bears the responsibility for introducing Lacan's reworking of Freud into contemporary film theory. Epitomizing the obtuseness as well as the baroque stylistics of French film theory of the 1970s, "The Imaginary Signifier" immediately seems a text at odds with the question of African American spectatorship. The fact that Metz never considered the black spectator should be taken seriously since it alerts us to look for ways in which his theory might serve the interests of entrenched power as opposed to serving a broader knowledge of spectatorship in all of its variety. But to look elsewhere for a preexisting theory of identification, incorporation, and representation that anticipates the theory of black spectatorship that we now need is to look for the impossible—a theory that perfectly fits the text hand in glove. Rather, we need to concentrate on how to make existing theories say what we need them to say, to grapple with high theory until it finally, reluctantly, yields useful insights.[2] The question of blacks in cinema, like the nearly parallel question of women in film, is often a problem in what I will call the "politics of mirroring," a politics that asks why the bodies of blacks and women are missing from the screen, or why, if they are not missing, they are unrecognizable to the people they are supposed to represent. This is a politics that wants to see positive images and asks why screen images are unlike real people. To this crucial question that has occupied so many African American and feminist critics, Metz has one answer: although one's own body is always reflected in the mirror, the spectator's own body is *never* reflected on the screen.

Of all of the metaphors employed in an attempt to describe the new phenomenon of moving pictures, the "window" and the "mirror" have perhaps been the most overused, exhausted to such a degree that they would appear to have little left to tell us. And one of Metz's projects is to further exhaust and to simultaneously revive the problem of the mirror, telling us that the screen *is* and *is not* like the empirical mirror that he at times seems to confuse with Lacan's mirror-stage mirror (as though that symbolic process somehow involved an actual mirror).[3] The film screen *is* like a mirror, Metz says, "But it differs from the primordial mirror in one essential point: although, as in the latter, everything may come to be projected, there is one thing, and one thing only that is never reflected in it."[4] Is it because we are so accustomed to seeing ourselves in the empirical mirror that we have this expectation of the mirrorlike screen? Stressing the self-centeredness of the empirical mirror experience, Umberto Eco, in his discussion of the semiotics of mirrors, reminds us that we are adept at using mirrors in relation to our own bodies but unable to use them in relation to the bodies of others.[5] Eco's empirical observation only confirms this idea that it is the mirror that contributes to the expectation that what we should be seeing on screen is *our own* image, and Lacan's psychoanalytic account further confirms the developmental importance of symbolic mirroring, which demonstrates to the child that the image he sees is his own.[6]

What is generally taken from "The Imaginary Signifier," however, is not the idea that the body of the viewer is missing from the mirror-like screen, but the idea that because he or she has had the cultural prerequisite (the lesson of the mirror), the sight of his or her own body on screen is no longer necessary. Or, because the spectator has already had experiences with mirrors (or known the mirror phase), he or she no longer needs to use his or her own body as a reference point in order to make sense of the screen image. To summarize Metz, "what makes *possible* the spectator's absence from the screen—or rather the intelligible unfolding of the film despite that absence—is the fact that the spectator has already known the experience of the mirror (the true mirror), and is thus able to constitute a world of objects without first having to recognize himself within it."[7] The fact of cultural initiation and the phenomenon of linguistic knowledge have been foremost during the years in which film theory established its respectability primarily through such comparisons with language.

But I want to take the rich suggestions of "The Imaginary Signifier" in a different direction and ask why there are so many complaints from women and other minorities if the cinema spectator, advanced far beyond the simple mirror, no longer needs to see himself or herself mirrored back in the theater. Why the "politics of mirroring" when no spectator can ever expect to see his or her own body anyway? Although in the cinema the spectator cannot expect the phenomenal mirror image experience that he or she has had with the looking glass (even though he or she might wish it), the spectator's experience of looking at others on the screen is relatively similar to looking at others in the mirror. In neither situation does the viewer have control over the bodies of others. But finally there is an even more important lesson that the child takes from the empirical as well as from the symbolic mirror: the others imaged appear like and not like himself. In fact, it is not so much that the child cannot move on to comprehend more complex cultural phenomena without first recognizing himself but that the child cannot enter society at all without the mirroring lessons that illustrate the semiotics of "like" and "other."

In Metz's variations on Lacan, the mother from whom the child early distinguishes itself becomes the first "other" and consequently all others, in what is a near parody of the centrality of the mother in psychoanalysis. Here "the child sees itself as an other, and beside an other. This other other is its guarantee that the first is really it." And who else is in this mirror? The other other is, of course, the mother. "Thus the child's ego is formed by identification with its like," Metz goes on. But identification is with its "like" in two senses—both metonymically and metaphorically. First, the child identifies with the "other human being who is in the glass," and second it identifies with itself, "the own reflection which is and is not the body, which is like it."[8] So the child actually requires not one but two others (itself-in-the-mirror and its mother), both of whom are "likes."

The psychoanalytic understanding of identification, summed up by Anne Friedberg as "denying the difference between the self and the other," would seem to set up a maze of mirrors within which the child finds as many selves as others, even turning itself into an other.[9] And shifting the emphasis from the mother to the ingenuity of the child in the formative stages may work productively to de-emphasize the mother who in so many accounts of the mirror stage emerges as a doting mom with a much petted only son. Who, other than a white middle class mother who doesn't work outside the home, would have the time to patiently accompany her child through the confusing stages of the mirror? Responding to the privilege implied in the theory that sees the mirror stage as a prerequisite to language, Kobena Mercer asks, "What if some subjects do not have access to the initial moment of recognition?"[10] Certainly nontraditional mothering would upset the intricate process that, as so often formulated, requires *the* mother, but it is not only that too many subjects are left in the cold outside psychoanalysis.[11] It is also that the focus on one symbolic moment, no matter how definitive, means that we miss other important formative moments. In the developmental years, there are hundreds of mirroring experiences and thousands of fascinating experiences of similitude and repetition, striking experiences that dramatize for the child the patternings of the self, the other, and the self. To look closely at the childhood spent in the motion picture theater, then, is to hopefully de-emphasize the importance of the psychoanalytic mirror in film theory.

One of the most fascinating experiences of similitude and repetition would, of course, be that of viewing figures on a screen in a darkened theater. For the black child growing up in a mixed-race society, however, the patterning of like and unlike bodies on the screen teaches special lessons. In the United States, particularly during the first half of the twentieth century, the young African American child's initiation into segregation would have involved searching for and not finding his or her likeness on the screen, looking for the "one thing, and only one thing that is never reflected in it." This child must discover early that the screen is in no way like a mirror and learn quite quickly to relate his or her body to it accordingly. The screen that is not a true mirror teaches the calculus of black and white in the mixed-race society, a lesson in white-like and unlike into which his or her own body must fit. The child must supply the black half of the mixed-race society equation, the half missing from the screen. Furthermore, the child must construct an identity based on what it is that she or he sees and doesn't see.

Like and Not-Like Me

Is there a contemporary question more fraught than the question of raced identity? Popular wisdom, of course, makes it deceptively simple: "You *are* who you *are*. You are who your people are." But what if the racial group to which you think you belong, which carries the same name as the identity you think is yours, is just an abstraction—or worse, nothing more than a functional fiction? I hesitate to continue to use the term "race" without qualification for fear of committing the error of assuming it without proving it, of contributing to the move in recent history to see race identity as "belonging" to all of us but belonging to some people more than to others. One is backed into a corner, unable to address the issues surrounding the concept of race without recourse to the terminology of race distinctions. How does one signal the trouble ahead in the category of race without using the category itself, given that no other terms signify both the *identity* that is widely claimed as well as assigned throughout the world and the disputed *category*, whether cultural or natural? But stated simply, the problem as it relates to American culture, especially in the period we are considering, is one of limitation: you are allowed only one race identity per body.[12] If you are *one* you cannot be another. Historically, you have only been able to check one box. And the problem of limiting has a corollary in the idea that identity "comes from within" rather than from without, making it difficult to imagine how one identity could be produced in relation to others. "It is an immensely important gain when one recognizes that all identity is constructed across difference," Stuart Hall has remarked, and the young James Baldwin has a particular facility for this, accumulating his identity, as he does, "across" gender as well as race.[13]

Baldwin constructs his identity "across" the bodies of glamorous white movie stars. In "Congo Square," he demonstrates how he borrowed from Joan Crawford and Bette Davis, opening the essay with a description of his epiphany. The screen *moves:*

> Joan Crawford's straight, narrow, and lonely back. We are following her through the corridors of a moving train. She is looking for someone, or she is trying to escape from someone. She is eventually intercepted by, I think, Clark Gable. I am fascinated by the movement on, and of, the screen, that movement which is

something like the heaving and swelling of the sea (though I have not been to the sea): and which is also something like the light which moves on, and especially beneath, the water. I am with my mother, or my aunt. The movie is *Dance, Fools, Dance.*[14]

While I will be taking Baldwin at his word in every other way, I must correct his memory here. The film he recalls is certainly not *Dance, Fools, Dance,* a 1931 MGM drama about a rich girl who goes to work as a reporter after her father loses all in the stock market crash, finally winning the respect of the young and dashing heir to a fortune. It seems more likely that the Crawford film Baldwin describes is *Laughing Sinners,* also released in 1931 and also costarring Clark Gable.[15] Although the first scene in this film does take place on a moving train, Crawford is neither escaping nor is she alone on the train. She isn't "intercepted" by Clark Gable until much later in the film, and what he "intercepts" is her attempt to commit suicide by throwing herself off a bridge. Baldwin does not recall the redemption subplot in this film in which Gable, the ex-sinner, recruits Crawford into the Salvation Army, nor is the young Baldwin drawn to the "torchiness" of the film, adapted from the play *Torch Song* and featuring Crawford singing "What Can I Do?—I Love That Man!" The boy goes to see the 1931 MGM drama, but he doesn't see the film that everyone else sees.

Instead, the black boy (quite immune to the powerful motion picture illusion) observes what no audience member ever seems to see—he sees that not only do shapes on the screen move, but that the screen itself moves. To the boy, the screen undulates like the sea, and the illumination of the flickering projector appears as light under moving water. Not surprisingly, then, Baldwin's anti-illusionist eye also sees race categories where others would see actresses. It does not matter what the film is "about" after all (and therefore the title is even irrelevant). He continues with his own explanation:

> I don't remember the film. The child is far too self-centered to relate to any dilemma which does not, somehow, relate to him—to his own evolving dilemma. The child escapes into what he would like his situation to be, and I certainly did not wish to be a fleeing fugitive on a moving train; and also, with quite another part of my mind, I was aware that Joan Crawford was a white lady. (p. 4)

The young James Baldwin, who sees the swelling sea where others see figures on a train, sees screen movement and everything else from the point of view of his "evolving dilemma" (the dilemma of who is and who is not "black like me"), sees Joan Crawford and thinks "white." No sooner has he situated Joan Crawford in the category of "white" than he discovers the interchangeability of race categories. Next, he transforms Joan Crawford into a black woman:

> Yet, I remember being sent to the store some time later, and a colored woman, who, to me, looked exactly like Joan Crawford, was buying something. She was so incredibly beautiful—she seemed to be wearing the sunlight, rearranging it around her from time to time, with a movement of her head, and with her smile. (p. 4)

The boy starts out of the store behind her. "His Miss Crawford," as he calls her, laughs at the boy along with the others in the store who knew him but who also knew them both. Baldwin makes the point that he is in the process of learning that he is black, and, considering that he is just learning, one might read this confusion between the beautiful black woman and the white Joan Crawford as the boy's "mistake." Actually, he gets it right. It's society that has it wrong. He has perfected the screen image and learned something about the arbitrariness of race. If he can make the black lady white, he can make Joan Crawford black. And to make Joan Crawford black is also to make the screen into his mirror—a wonderful black mirror.

"It was always said among Black women that Joan Crawford was part Black," says Michelle Wallace in her retrospective consideration of white forties stars. In her understanding of cinema spectatorship as not only bisexual but multiracial, she sees these black viewers as "possessing" the films they loved, using them to enlarge their identities instead of rejecting white female stars outright. What Wallace thinks to herself as she views Rita Hayworth and Lana Turner affords us insight into the process of racial transformation: "she is so beautiful, she looks black."[16] This racial transposition (black for white) is a magical transvaluation with the power to color the world. If whatever is wonderful and beautiful is always, *must be* always black, the wonderful and beautiful white star has to be black.

Baldwin's racial transposition (black to white and white to black) is even more pronounced and successful in the Bette Davis lesson and is a transformation with even broader implications since it is not just that he has produced race change in what he calls "the cinema of my mind" (p. 10). *When he looks at Bette Davis he sees himself.* To the young Baldwin, it is clear that Bette Davis looked just like him, but it is especially her "frog eyes"—his eyes—that confirm the likeness. Very early he is aware that his father hated his "frog eyes," and that his hatred had to do with the fact that they were his mother's eyes. They also served as a reminder that he was his mother's son by a different man. "What was he doing with these enormous eyes?" he asks himself (p. 9).[17] He enjoys the contradiction:

> So, here, now, was Bette Davis, on that Saturday afternoon, in close-up, over a champagne glass, pop-eyes popping. I was astounded. I had caught my father, not in a lie, but in an infirmity. For, here, before me, after all, was a *movie star: white:* and if she was white and a movie star she was *rich:* and she was *ugly.* (p. 8)

All of the duplicity of adult society is exposed. No, it was not as they said—that it wasn't possible to be rich and a movie star if you were ugly. It *was* possible to be white, rich, *and* ugly, or, rather, white, rich, and black. Watching Bette Davis and Spencer Tracy in *20,000 Years in Sing Sing* (1933), the black boy metamorphoses Davis on the screen, this time in a more thorough and amazing way. He makes her over as a new species, a species more benign and familiar, a species to ward off the malevolent whiteness. His explanation of his motivation suggests the necessity of protection: "Out of bewilderment, out of loyalty to my mother, probably, and also because I sensed something menacing and unhealthy (for me, certainly) in the face on the screen" (p. 8). This loyalty to his mother (who looked just like he did) is also a kind of loyalty to his race, a loyalty that keeps him from entertaining white fantasies and imagining white versions of himself.

Baldwin is no easy case of cross-race identification that simply assumes a one-way process in which all blacks envy whites. Recently, Eric Lott has opened up this question for further consideration from the other end. Blacks may be thought to envy whites but what if whites envy blacks? In his study of blackface minstrelsy, Lott gives the lie to the assumption that it was only blacks who identified across race, arguing that whites put on "blackface versions of themselves" at the same time that they ridiculed blacks.[18] In reference to the closely related phenomenon of Hollywood's "nigger minstrels," Kobena Mercer asks, "What is going on when whites assimilate and introject the degraded and devalorized signifiers of racial otherness into the cultural construction of their own identity? If imitation implies identification, in the psychoanalytic sense of the word, then what is it about whiteness that makes the white subject want to be black?"[19]

Let us also ask the companion question. If whites have wanted to be black, have blacks historically wanted to be black? The best answer to this question is probably yes and no, depending on the historical mo-

Bette Davis

ment, and not in the same way, of course. Certainly Baldwin gives the lie to the assumption that in the 1930s all blacks wanted to *be* whites, and what he does with Davis's image suggests that his relationship to whiteness is unorthodox, if not ambivalent. What he does is quite extraordinary—making out of Davis something like and not like himself, something to aid identification as well as to prevent it absolutely—to ward it off. "I gave Davis's skin the dead-white greenish cast of something crawling from under a rock," he says. Think what is accomplished by producing Bette Davis as green! She inhabits the world of mixed-race society; she is alien to it. She is a frog. She is a lizard. He goes on. Even though she is "something green crawling," he is "held, just the same, by the tense intelligence of the forehead, the disaster of the lips: and when

James Baldwin

she moved, she moved just like a nigger" (p. 8). But, no, Bette Davis is not a black version of himself; she is a *green* version—neither black nor white, but in one of those "in between" color categories that is anomalous to white but not to black society. One thinks of Kermit the Frog's lament: "It's not easy being green." In the child's skin fantasy, color distinctions are imaginary, and just as you "wear" your gender, you can also imagine your own skin color beneath, putting the one on over the other.[20]

Jimmy Baldwin has no designs on whiteness. The boy constructs Bette Davis as "ugly like me" but does not make himself into a white movie star. Instead, he meets Davis in the category of "strange," which he says he knows he was because people "treated me so strangely" (p. 9). Correspondingly, though he no longer sees whiteness as transparent obviousness, he begins to view it as somewhat "strange," a revelation that allows him increasing latitude in his skin fantasies. By now it should be clear that Baldwin is not only describing the constitution of a "raced" subject via star images, but he is also describing the constitution of a flamboyant queer. In his early appreciation of Joan Crawford and Bette Davis (as early as the age of seven), there is an undeniable precocious camp sensibility at work. Undoubtedly in his production of Davis as "strange" we also see a fledgling critique of heterosexuality that unsees the normal at the same time that it claims Davis for "strangeness."

The question of Baldwin's homosexuality raises the issue of the choice of one identity over another, as though he wasn't preoccupied enough with working out his black identity. He would have been pressed, on occasion, to answer the question, When it comes down to the wire, which identity? And in one interview he is known to have said that the "most tormenting thing" for him had been the recognition of his homosexuality.[21] Further, there is always the question of retrospective claiming, of black culture with its often homophobic identity politics wanting to claim Baldwin sans homosexuality, and of gay culture wanting to claim him as queer. It is as though the great identity crises of the culture could be resolved if only James Baldwin could be found to have sorted out his own. But increasingly we are faced with the evidence of inextricability. As Kendall Thomas has argued, "sexuality is always 'racialized' and race always 'sexuated,'" and try as we might to study the one social phenomenon in isolation, it is always modified by the other.[22] Perhaps the challenge is to situate Baldwin in such a way that through him queer theory speaks to race theory.

Disidentification

It is clear that queer theory has made an end run around the "politics of mirroring," leaving complaints about negative imaging or stereotypage in the dust. As queer theory has incontrovertibly demonstrated, selves are always concocted, never simply given and received. Following queer theory, identification is not about denying the difference between the self and the other, that mirror moment that produces normalcy; it may be more about using differences, about accumulating possible selves, a process that is more accretive than anything, and a process that is a direct challenge to the one identity per body rule.

It is this historical connection between identification and normalcy, the modeling-oneself-after-another aspect, that should alert us to the conservatism in identification, a point I will return to in a later chapter. But queer theory has suggested that there is something complicated going on *within* identification, perhaps something that undermines and prohibits and thus protects the identifier. Recently, José Muñoz has reworked the concept of disidentification, giving it a political edge, understanding it as a survival strategy, making a case, in effect, for a notion of identification that is somewhat aware of the pitfalls of identity formation, a concept that has particular relevance for an understanding of the black subject who comes of age in a white society. In Kobena Mercer's famous admission of "ambivalence" toward Robert Mapplethorpe's photographs of black nudes Muñoz locates "disidentificatory pleasure," a pleasure that (as it relishes) is all the while cognizant of the political danger (for a black gay male critic) involved in loving the very images that fetishize the black male body.[23] This doubleness is found as well in African American painter Jean-Michel Basquiat's homage to a white Superman, a disidentification that Muñoz finds particularly instructive.[24]

What I think we need from this concept of disidentification is the particular mix of danger and pleasure, a pleasure that tastes like "ambivalence." But we still must know how the concept is significantly different from other critical moves that have helped us to deal with troublesome texts, moves such as reading "against the grain" or "distanciation," the critical stance that in Brechtian approaches to film was meant to break the spell of identification. Still, "disidentification" could offer more, and clearly has the edge of provocation. Crucial components of "disidentification" seem to me to be the hissing "dis" prefix, the echo of the street slang that puts people in their place, as though identification itself is "dissed," but also the "crossing" that is characteristic of queer reading. Indeed, it is certainly the important work on literary "cross-identification" from within queer theory that is foundational here.[25] In this, we would always want to retain the closeness between "queerness" and "crossing," remembering, as Eve Sedgwick has pointed out, that the word "queer" has its etymological roots in the linguistic terms for "across," and that to be queer is to be always in motion.[26]

On the danger side, Muñoz leads us back through the Althusserian Michel Pecheux whose concept of disidentification is neither an embrace nor a rejection of the dominant ideology but rather an accommodation within it, a position that is somewhat similar to the way cultural studies understands the inhabited space of popular culture.[27] As theorized by Stuart Hall, the damage of the dominant would seem to be always ameliorated by the counterswing of popular culture, a paradigm understood as the "double movement" of the popular, which is able to both conservatively contain and radically resist what it tries to contain.[28] But cultural studies may have underestimated the hegemonic damage produced by the dominant, the damage to women, blacks, queers—outsiders whose interests are never served by the culture with which they are enamored. The classic example of hegemonic damage has been perhaps Frantz Fanon's example of the young Antillian who in colonial Fort-de-France identifies with Tarzan and "against the Negroes" but who in Paris finds that the white audience "identifies him with the savages on the screen."[29] To be caught always on the wrong side of identification is one of the situations that defines the plight of the colonial subject.

The other well-known example of the young black self, hegemonically damaged, is Toni Morrison's tragic Pecola in *The Bluest Eye*, driven to insanity by her fascination with whiteness.[30] Speaking on behalf of the other black women who, like Pecola, have had to define themselves against whiteness, Ann duCille talks about her relationship to child star Shirley Temple in perhaps the most biting assessment of the hegemony of the white star image to date. "My own relationship to Shirley Temple is a vexed one. I didn't worship the child star like the ill-fated Pecola, but I didn't have the good sense to hate her either," she says. And then the erudite and self-assured persona of the essay remarks, "The truth is, much of the time I wanted to be Shirley Temple. That is, I wanted that trademark Shirley Temple."[31] Here duCille anticipates an important position that I will explore in later chapters. To want to *be* Shirley Temple is not exactly to want to be Shirley Temple instead of oneself. If we confuse black appropriations of the powers of whiteness with the negation of blackness, we may miss what these confessions of ambivalent attraction have to tell us about the enormous imagination of black aspiration. For what it may finally come down to is the potency of the imagination that can conceivably override the hegemonic danger of white star imagery.

In the traditional response to hegemonic dangers, the minority focus has been predominantly on underrepresentation and exclusion, a paradigm that is always silently informed by an assumption that if only blacks, Asians, and women could gain access to the means of media production then and only then can the problems of image, identity, and identification be addressed if not resolved. But queer theory has never really been involved in the *"our* images of ourselves vs. *your* images of us" debates. From queer theory we gain instead not only a sense of the psychic damage potential in, but, even more important, an analysis of the total failure of, identification. One only needs to think of James Baldwin's identificatory frustrations to get a sense of the challenge to the child—black and queer—who searched for selves in all the wrong places. And yet Judith Butler finds in this "failure of identification" the starting point for politicization. "What," she says, "are the possibilities of politicizing *dis*identification, this experience of *misrecognition*, this uneasy sense of standing under a sign to which one does and does not belong?"[32] Perhaps it is this "does–does not" dialectic of unbelonging that defines the delicate balance of disidentification, the characteristic situation in which the queer self "is–is not," for instance, the excessively heterosexual figure of the opera diva.

And Muñoz is right to remember the cross-identification with the opera diva.[33] Perhaps this is where the pleasures of identification are the most intense and perhaps also where they are only comprehensible through some grasp of the relationality that is camp.[34] And it is camp relationality—that discrepant connection between the self and the world as well as the link between the "is and the isn't"—that is at the theoretical core here. If there is pleasure, it is about reveling in discrepancies, in appreciating a long chain of jokes enjoyed at the expense of straight culture. There is something in the incongruous mismatch that can reveal the makeshift structure of the most serious object of culture. To the "is and isn't" of cross-identification we thus need to add the "on–off," the modality that is often said to have its origins in the experience of passing for straight in a heterosexual world.[35] Illustrative of this modality of theatricality is Richard Dyer's analysis of stars as tragic models of the too-too close relationship between self and role.[36] The point is that with the most highly theatrical sufferers such as Judy Garland, something always slips to reveal something else, suggesting the "putting on" of roles, first the one and then the other, an acting art that is certainly one of the major tributaries that have fed into the theory of "gender as dressing."[37] In queer theory, "acting," the basic camp paradigm, is also a critique that is literally "performed, " and Baldwin, fledgling literary critic as well as emerging queer, finds his own critical paradigm in his cult actresses.[38] Here that characteristic equation between drag and distance, that ironic relation between the queer and the world, is the astute sensibility that produces Bette Davis as green.

White Not

With all of his critical acumen and the extra distance afforded by his being queer, Baldwin, however, is still tormented by the question of his blackness, now inseparable from his queerness. But how does his queerness actually impinge on his blackness? And what, if anything, does queerness tell him about blackness? James Baldwin's account of his fascination with white film stars has not been a favored text in either African American studies or gay and lesbian studies in their recent growth periods. Is this because his recruitment of white female stars in the process of discovering what it means to be black would seem to be politically retrograde? Rather than seeing it as retrograde, we need to see the ingenious eclecticism of black queer identity formation as able to find itself through whiteness, to go deeply into whiteness and take out the best parts. Black disidentification with white stars is an attraction to the glamor in danger as well as the danger in glamor, and it knows just how close to get to the flame. James Baldwin is and isn't Bette Davis.

I know of only one critic who has seriously pursued this question of black people's relation to white stars. In a provocative essay, Arthur Knight denies neither the fascination nor the repulsion. Beginning with Aaron Siskind's 1940 photograph of a black janitor in a Harlem building sleeping with his back to a wall of movie star pinups, Knight suggests that notions of oppression and dominance don't go very far toward explaining this image, sometimes titled "Sleeping with White Pin-Ups." Knight finds the hint of the complexity of the black response to the movies in Gwendolyn Brooks's poem, "The Sundays of Satin-Legs Smith," in her reference to the "booing" at the kiss and the "ivory" heroine coupled with the "sinning" that defines the looking. The African American literary figures and characters who find and lose themselves at the movies (Toni Morrison's Pauline, Malcolm X's "Detroit Red," Richard Wright's Bigger Thomas, and Ralph Ellison's Invisible Man) are active critics, but not equally critical, and sometimes more ambivalent than critical, sometimes less.[39] So a black attitude or reading is by no means uniform or predictable even while the black eye may be consistently jaundiced in the most productive of ways, as Jacqueline Bobo discovered in her important contemporary study of black women viewers.[40] Again, the question is never exactly about appropriating whiteness, since this critical engagement seems not to be about borrowing at all.

Recently, as I have said, there has been less interest in black appropriations of whiteness, no matter how novel, and more interest, as evidenced in the work of Kobena Mercer and Eric Lott, in the way white culture finds itself through blackness. Whiteness as "parasitic" on blackness has been a theme as well in the recent work of Clyde Taylor, Cornel West, and Toni Morrison, a thematic that challenges us to look at race relations in reverse, to always invert the dominant version of the way things are.[41] The way in which blacks "use" white culture may be considered by some to be too prevalent to warrant serious study, but it is interesting that in all of the new and important work on black gay men and the already voluminous literature on gay men and film stars there is still no academic analysis of white women as objects of fascination or influence in relation to black queerness.[42] The young Baldwin himself eventually comes to the conclusion that there is nothing that white folks can possibly tell him about blackness. As he sees it, if white culture is "used" at all in the process of black selfdiscovery, it is used as a foil.

And yet other white people figure significantly in Baldwin's adventures with the screen-mirror, and, most notably, all of Baldwin's early moviegoing experiences (with the exception of the 1931 experience of attending with his mother or his aunt) appear to have been in the company of a white woman with a man's name. Bill Miller ("Bill" short for Orilla), his young school teacher, was also understood in terms of Joan Crawford, the prototype for both the black as well as the white women whom he admired. Bill Miller was white, he says, but she was "not white for me in the way, for example, that Joan Crawford was white." Neither, he goes on, was she white "in the way that the landlords and the storekeepers and the cops and most of my teachers were white" (p. 6). "She, too . . . was treated like a nigger, especially by the cops, and she had no love for landlords." He learns from Bill Miller that "white people did not act as they did because they were white" (p. 7). But the observation that there is no absolutely perfect correlation between whiteness and abuse of power does not lead automatically to the idea of social class. The question is difficult because, as Baldwin finds, although it appeared as though all oppressors were white, not all whites were oppressors.

Bill Miller, a young communist, is instrumental in teaching the boy about victimization and its operations irrespective of color, illustrating with her life that if one controlled for color one could still experience oppression.[43] "Thus," Baldwin recalls, "she tried to suggest to me the extent to which the world's social and economic arrangements are responsible for [and to] the world's victims" (p. 12). Eventually not one but two white women would be instrumental in this lesson in the concept of victimization. The other would be Harriet Beecher Stowe, and Baldwin's viewing of *A Tale of Two Cities* at the Lincoln Theatre in 1936 with Bill Miller is linked with reading *Uncle Tom's Cabin*, which he would later rail at for its dishonesty.[44] From Bill he learns something about revolution: "Revolution was the only hope of the American working class—the *proletariat:* and world-wide revolution was the only hope of the world." Yet it is not clear to Baldwin whether or not he understood this as a boy. If he did grasp what was meant, he says, he understood "negatively," that is, for blacks were not in the picture. "I could not see where I fit in this formulation, and I did not see where blacks fit" (p. 17).

Blacks do *not* easily fit into the Marxist formulation, and unlike his more radical contemporary Richard Wright, Baldwin the historical figure was not exactly interested in actively attempting that fit over the course of his lifetime. And yet the question arises in the context of this discussion of mass culture and the construction of identity. Class figures, but where and how? Consider the countless ways in which race has been theorized in relation to class over the past century, the explanatory burden placed on first the one and then the other. At times, the two categories vie for ascendancy, and when the one is privileged over the other, considerable explanatory strain may be produced. Stuart Hall once described this pressure on race and class, both eager to account for so much, as a situation in which "each/both feel required to produce a single and exclusive determining principle of articulation—class *or* race—even if they disagree as to which should be accorded the privileged sign."[45] Finding ways of formulating the critical relation between the two has been difficult enough for political theorists. In some models, race and class are lived hierarchically, with one on top and the other on the bottom. In others, they are lived sequentially, with one predating the other, and in still others they are lived asymmetrically with class victimization cutting one way and race oppression another.[46] The fact that class and race are never congruent means that in historical circumstances class affinities and race solidarities divide and tear, wreaking havoc within communities and groups. Within the individual, these are the historical conflicts that translate so immediately into identities, the identities that war within one small body.

Not seeing how class could fully explain himself to himself, Baldwin continues with his search, concluding that it is blackness that is determining, blackness that must do the explaining. He concludes that Bill Miller "could not instruct me as to blackness, except obliquely, feeling that she had neither the right nor the authority, and also knowing that I was certain to find out" (p. 11). Having discovered that Bette Davis is ugly *and* white, not black, Baldwin has reason to believe that the skin system is not as straightforward as adults claim it to be. But since the peculiarity of his blackness is not completely accounted for by blackness alone, he is left with the question of who is and who isn't "black like me" with little or no hope of finding the "black" or the "like me" always in the same place.

The Race Fiction

The distance between race as an identity and race as a category is both great and small. The abstract category is indifferent to the lived identity at the same time that it impinges on it daily and directly. So to leave off the discussion of the identity question for an exploration of the category as category is to guarantee an eventual return to identity. It is hard to talk about race at this time in history, difficult to talk about either race "in" or races "of" persons as well as race as the barrier of all barriers—*the* most insurmountable of differences. It is difficult, and a silence ensues. "Race," says Toni Morrison, "is still an unspeakable thing."[47] Affirmed as it is denied by "color-blind" social policies and attitudes, race is still seen everywhere although it is never supposed to be looked at, particularly in American culture.

That race has "effects," however, is difficult to deny, especially when surveying the consequences of such human differences over the last three centuries—the deep social divisions, the elevation of some people, and the degradation of others. One approach to understanding the development of the concept of race historically has regarded it as functioning ideologically, that is, as maintaining with seeming effortlessness the social equation that ensured the economic equation. The Marxism from which Frantz Fanon and Albert Memmi both drew secures the understanding of race as ideology in such a way that Fanon, for instance, was able to see issues of race as superstructural, as "an obscure ideological emanation concealing an economic reality," and to bring the question of race always back to the necessities of colonization.[48] More recently, the race as ideology approach has been interested in attempting to separate slavery from race in an effort to further establish the historical exigencies of the concept of race difference. If it is understood that in the New World, slavery of both European whites and West Africans predated the notion of race, it can be established that race was the creation of a particular economic need, all the better to argue that race is an "invention." Summarizing her work on how slavery could and did function (for at least a century) before the introduction of the notion of race, Barbara Fields says, "Race as a coherent ideology did not spring into being simultaneously with slavery, but took even longer than slavery did to become systematic."[49] Valuable as this historical work is, it has an uphill battle against the idea that slavery and race are historically coincidental, an only slightly altered contemporary version of an earlier notion that to be born black was to be born a slave, that slavery was the natural condition of the Negro. Not only has the concept of race worked to naturalize everything adjacent to it but it creates the sense that people have been *the way they are*, that is, racially and thus economically predetermined, for time eternal.

The theoretical approach that understands race as a functioning ideology is not exactly reducible to the assertion that race is a fiction. The Marxist notion of ideology always carries with it a sense of the instrumentality of the ideological, which will always be tied to a misrepresentation of economic realities. Where we might speak of the fictionality of the ideological, ideology is never synonymous with fiction. A number of approaches to theorizing race, then, can be seen to fall under the broad category of the fictionality of race, among them an understanding of the social construction of race. Clearly, the beauty of the argument that race is nothing more than a social construction is that it so cleanly and neatly removes the categorization of peoples by race from the biological, from the genetic basis that could continue to curse some and reward others. So it is not surprising that, as an antidote to the dangerous argument about the biological basis, it might be necessary to declare that *there is no such thing as race*. The classic statement of this, to which I refer in the introduction, is Anthony Appiah's: "The truth is that there are no races: there is nothing in the world that can do all we ask race to do for us."[50] In an earlier essay in which this statement first appears, Appiah contrasts the concept of race with the actual peoples of the world to which the concept is supposed to refer, peoples who are in excess of the concept. Considering whether race might be a structure of oppositions that would include not only white as opposed to black or yellow, and Jew as opposed to Gentile or Arab, he goes on to conclude that if we search the world over we will never find the people to correspond with the category. "If," he says, "we can now hope to understand the concept embodied in this system of oppositions, we are nowhere finding referents for it." What eludes us in this exercise is finally "reality," he says, and perhaps he means the reality of bodies.[51]

And yet this strategy (there is no such thing as race) that so deftly eludes biologizing (and its close companion tendency, essentializing) has been often challenged on the basis of its apparent noncomprehension of the reality of everyday life as a black person. Of what use is the idea that there is no race, argues African American critic Houston Baker, if he can't catch a cab in New York? The very features (hair, bone, skin) that Appiah argues away are the very features that, to quote Baker's famous retort, "always make a painfully significant difference—perhaps *the only* difference where life and limb are concerned."[52] Baker's response is an eerie echo of W. E. B. Du Bois's fictional "conversation with a white man":

> "But what is this group; and how do you differentiate it; and how can you call it 'black' when you admit it is not 'black'?"
> "I recognize it quite easily and with full legal sanction; the black man is a person who must ride 'Jim Crow' in Georgia."[53]

Translated into contemporary terms, this is the rule that "you are what the police think you are," a rule that flies in the face of race as a fiction.[54] While you are holding your own conviction about race as a fiction, you may be assaulted by someone somewhere on the basis of the very race that you hold does not exist (or so this argument goes). Another way of putting this would be to say that you don't construct yourself so much as you are "given" your race identity, or, even, it is forced on you.[55]

Baker's is only one of two well-known challenges to the extreme constructivist position. The other, the reverse of the idea that race is assigned, goes to the heart of the way race has been claimed historically by African Americans. As articulated by African American critic Joyce Joyce, the deconstruction of the concept of race destroys black identity.[56] Here the argument depends on seeing how race has been taken over and inhabited by the very people it would separate out for purposes of suspending liberties and denying rights. Once it has been taken over, it can't be taken back. "There is no such thing as race" is heard as "there is no black community, no black culture, and no black person." Actually, the historical occupation of the concept of race makes a better argument for the constructedness of race than it does for the existence of any natural group. One has only to think here of Stuart Hall's contemporary example of the construction of blackness as beautiful, referencing the way black Americans during the 1960s reinflected the signs of blackness, creating, for instance, the Afro hairstyle as a badge.[57] This reasserts the variability within the concept of race as racial characteristics are reclassified and reassigned to meet historical imperatives. If there is a compromise position here, it might be Henry Louis Gates's argument that race is the "ultimate trope of difference," so powerful that it explains and invokes community divisions, whether linguistic, cultural, or religious.[58] As a "trope," race has measurable functions and effects but is not put to any other tests of "realness."

One might also consider another development in response to the constructivist assertion that there is no such thing as race, a move that draws the question of the race category away from the clear-cut debate and into the realm of philosophy, complicating and deepening the discussion. Recent developments in feminist theory and philosophy have looked again at the ramifications of one of the theoretical backbones of feminism, the constructedness of gender. Important to feminists as a way around the plague on women of biology as destiny, the notion that gender is a construction has proven politically empowering. Feminist theory has been able to thoroughly investigate as well as reconstruct "woman" as a concept, a project that has basically been built on a constructivist foundation. Recently, however, Judith Butler has reconsidered, from the point of view of feminist philosophy, the coverage of the construction, that is, the degree to which absolutely everything is constructed and whether there is anything left over that is *not* produced by social discourse. And she finds quite a lot left uncovered. Reminding us of what one has to ignore in order to make a case for the social construction of gender, Butler says, "the constructivist refutes the reality of bodies, the relevance of science, the alleged facts of birth, aging, illness, and death."[59] She also provocatively asks whether, given this blanketedness, anything of "sex" remains once "gender" has "absorbed" it, whether there is any body "reality" that gets away, that remains unconstructed.[60] But does race theory have the political luxury to go this route? Perhaps feminist theory, from its somewhat more established position, can afford to speculate about that which gender might not have constructed. Whether race theory follows feminist theory in this line of questioning remains to be seen, for the dangers of conceding the biological, even to the slightest degree, might turn us back.

And is race to biology as gender is to biological sex, anyway? Yes and no. If gender "absorbs and displaces" sex, what can race do to biology?[61] It would seem that race is both always in danger of becoming biologized and almost at the point of culturalizing the biological. Race, with its chameleon-like capacity, can be nature, culture, nationality, or biology. But again what *do* we do with the "grosser physical differences of color, hair, and bone," to pose Du Bois's question? [62] These physical distinctions are, of course, natural signs, with the emphasis on "signs," natural "marks," that are mistakenly taken as the origin rather than the product of existing social relations.[63] But just as soon as they are seen as signs, they are renaturalized, reasserted in such a way that we lose sight of any arbitrariness we might have momentarily glimpsed. As we consider the power of naturalization to place phenomena beyond the reach of culture, we may be tempted to think that it is too late to argue the constructedness of race. And yet, it is the very history, the recent history of the concept of race, that tells us otherwise. If the case for the social construction of race can be made anywhere, it would be in the vicissitudes of the one-drop rule, the rule that has classified American peoples as black if they had any percentage of Negro ancestry, no matter how small.

A peculiarity of American culture, the one-drop rule is the key to comprehending how the United States has historically understood itself. All the canny self-deception along with the cavalier opportunism is there in the written and unwritten race codes. The characteristic American indecision about racial classification can be seen as early as the reversal of the 1662 Virginia law that decreed that the status of the slave followed that of the father, establishing a tradition in which slave mothers begot slave children.[64] Children, henceforth, would follow the condition of the mother. Thus it was established that blacks begot blacks and whites begot whites, even though the one-drop rule, evolved by the middle of the nineteenth century, asserted that this was not the case either. Whites *did* beget blacks if any percentage of the child's ancestry was black.[65] The one-drop rule was, of course, a stopgap solution to dangerous blood-mixing, and the long-term consequences of the dictum were the furthest thing from the minds of the white fathers who instituted it. Originally a property rule, this hard code became the social scheme that eventually solidified a rigid caste system. The paradigm that ruled out the light-skinned mulatto who had historically been "white," the one-drop rule finally eradicated the mulatto, the in-between group. But even as the one-drop rule went into effect, at least one state, South Carolina, was a holdout, ironically because the rule would prevent marriage between whites who otherwise would be unable to marry each other because of the preponderance of people with black ancestry in the state.[66] It is well known that by 1920 the mulatto had more or less disappeared, the "neither/nor proposition," as Hortense Spillers calls this "peculiar new-world invention," a casualty of intermarriage.[67]

But, as no one anticipated, the rule that was designed to criminalize intermarriage between black and white instead *fostered* intermarriage between black and white, that is, former "whites" (light-skinned blacks) married darker-skinned blacks within the black community.[68] Thus the lightening of the black population was not produced by interracial intermarriage, as some sociologists mistakenly thought, but by intraracial unions as the white blood that was not supposed to be mixed was instead spread further throughout the black population.[69] The one-drop rule would underwrite the dread practice of "passing" for white, the condition of playing on the discrepancy between appearance and "essence," that controversial core that is thought to be the final determination of race. And it is the final determination that gives us so much difficulty. It is a determination poised to go either but not both ways. As Nahum Chandler has written about the "discourse of the Negro," it is a matter of European purity, but no small matter, for "purity" has historically come down to a difficult philosophical question, a question of the one or the other. "For at its root," he says, "the implied question of this discourse, the hidden question about European American or White identity, brings into view the fact that the adjudication of the status of the Negro implies a prior determination of the grounds for deciding any 'racial' identity as one thing or another." A claim always has to be made for one or the other. As he goes on, "The only manner in which such a claim could be made was to assume, in the philosophical sense, that a distinction could be made absolute, oppositional or pure, according to Aristotle's law of non-contradiction."[70] To restate that law, which so succinctly summarizes what we are up against when we ask questions about racial identity: "For it is impossible for anyone to believe the same thing to be and not to be."[71] So what do we do with a person who *is* and *is not* black?

Both / And and Neither / Nor[72]

Ben Nightingale's life is a parable of the neither/nor. Adopted and raised in a loving family in the warmth of a black community in Philadelphia, he felt black, through and through. "I saw, I felt, I absorbed," he says, recalling the "choir marching around the church aisles, clapping and singing."[73] But although Ben merged, he never really blended with his community. He might have felt himself to be thoroughly black but he appeared to be thoroughly white. Furthermore, the unusual circumstances of his adoption led him to believe first that his father was white and later that he might have been a Negro. He was in possession of two different birth certificates—one declaring him to be white, the other declaring him to be black. An investigation into the details of his adoption brought him to an inconclusive dead end. Later in his life, Ben moved from Philadelphia to Los Angeles where he lived as a white person, reluctantly "passing," but he found that he could not rectify the two worlds and the two possible identities. Married to a white woman for thirteen years, he divorced when the lived discrepancy between his white self and his black self became unbearable. He concludes, "I had let only my white appearance speak for me. Never my black essence."[74] At this point, confused by the contradictory definitions of race in America but convinced that, white appearance or not, blackness was his essence, he turned to the dictionary definition of "essence" for help. The dictionary seemed to confirm his belief in an authentic self, explaining "essence" as "fundamental nature or quality . . . a substance distilled or extracted from another substance and having the special qualities of the original substance."[75] Finally, taking heart from what he learned from Webster's dictionary, Ben concluded that although he had not known his "original birth substance" for most of his life, he did know his "fundamental nature": "It is black. This feeling, this quality was 'distilled' in me by my childhood environment, a black neighborhood in South Philadelphia."[76]

The appeal of the belief in an essential nature is, of course, that it settles uncertainties and, in this case, for Ben Nightingale it resolves his racial identity question through recourse to the "truth" of his being. Note, however, that "essence" here is not biological, that it stands in for and even transcends the biological. It does not matter what he "really" is (in the verifiable, testable sense); *he* knows what he "really" is, following an almost tautological structure. But what is he to the others who for him are "black like me"? Is the black community essence that he "absorbed" through his pores "really" his if he is *not* really a Negro? And if he is? The one-drop rule of thumb, remnant of an earlier era, still holds. All it takes to resolve the question is a fraction, and the fraction makes him black. Yet the one-drop rule works the other way as well, reserving black identity only for those with (some) black "blood" and not extending it to black "wanna-bes." If Ben doesn't have the requisite "drop," is he an interloper, a fraud? Will his membership in the black community be suspect?

And what about the black community essence, the "distilled substance" that Ben Nightingale calls his own? To call this essence a substance is to suggest that it has concrete existence, that it is verifiable and measurable, although after years of attempts to isolate the essence of blackness, mostly in terms of a black aesthetic, it still eludes critics.[77] In the name of this essence, Black Studies programs have been formed and arts exhibitions mounted, excellent efforts in and of themselves on behalf of people of color and in honor of rich, often unexamined cultures. If we were to search for the black aesthetic in music, literature, and film, in the arts and folk culture produced by African Americans, what would we find? Would that something (for which we search) be the same in all of these forms? There is, of course, a difference between "finding" a preexisting cultural essence and making a case that brings it into being or, as Judith Butler would put it, "naming" it into existence. Ever skeptical of essentializing and equally critical of the experiential as transcendent, Anthony Appiah has argued that "to talk of the Afro-American experience treats the complex worlds of millions of men and women as homogeneous."[78] Given, then, the nonhomogeneity of black people, does African American culture function as a marvellous funnel, channeling diversity into an imaginary unity? And is it this imagined unity that inspires Ben Nightingale to draw an analogy between his experience and that of James Baldwin?

Like Baldwin, who escapes to Switzerland with Bessie Smith records, Ben Nightingale must return to his recordings of Marian

Anderson's spirituals whose messages "began to quicken that long-buried black life I had run from."[79] Nightingale quotes from *Nobody Knows My Name*, borrowing Baldwin's paradigm:

> There, in that absolutely alabaster landscape, armed with two Bessie Smith records and a typewriter, I began to try to re-create the life I had first known as a child and from which I had spent so many years in flight.[80]

Although Baldwin says that he never listened to Bessie Smith in America (as one would assume), in Europe she "helped to reconcile [him] to being a 'nigger.'"[81] There is a sense in both searches that "authentic" black culture is the starting point as well as the end point in a return journey to the "truth"of the self. But the self, says Stuart Hall, "is always, in a sense, a fiction," an "arbitrary closure" like those closures that create "communities of identification," examples of which might be "nation, ethnic group, families, or sexualities."[82] However, one always searches for the "truth" of the self, one never searches for the fiction of the self. But this is not something that one would say to such an important figure in African American literature. If Ben Nightingale has trouble with his blackness, it is not surprising that Baldwin, despite his "looking the part," also has trouble, for it is not so much the comprehension of one's identity assignment (incomprehensible to begin with) as it is the *finality* of that assignment. Again, it is the dictum—one identity per body—that enforces, a dictum that is daily underwritten by the Aristotelian logic that one thing cannot possibly be another.

Melodrama and the Unfathomable Question

Recall that the young Baldwin wants an answer from Bill Miller and Harriet Beecher Stowe to his "unfathomable question": "what, under heaven, or beneath the sea, or in the catacombs of hell, could cause any people to act as white people acted?"[83] He turns to melodrama, the form that specializes in the unfathomable and the incalculable but also in the inexplicable. Not a form that answers questions, melodrama is rather a form that assuages fears and manages fantasies, often by organizing inexplicable events in ways that appeal to the dispossessed—to blacks and women.[84] In its biblical proportions, its rhythms of confrontation and release, its intense clash of villainy with righteousness, and its miraculous righting of wrongs, melodrama enhances the point of view of the powerless. Baldwin, feeling the powerlessness of his existence, is drawn to the great tumultuous narratives of English and American literature—*A Tale of Two Cities* and *Uncle Tom's Cabin*—narratives that speak to him, although he says he did not know what either novel was about, "which was why I read them both so obsessively." He continues to read *Uncle Tom's Cabin*, "trying to find out something, sensing something in the book of some immense import for me," and his mother, terrified, hides the book above the bathtub on a high shelf (pp. 16–17). But what the white author has to tell him is limited. In another essay Baldwin rails against Stowe and her book because she left "unanswered and unnoticed the only important question: what was it, after all, that moved her people to such deeds."[85] Obsessively reading *Uncle Tom's Cabin*, he says, "was this particular child's way of circling around the question of what it meant to be a nigger" (p. 12). Still circling, still obsessively reading, not only did he not see where blacks fit (and not daring to ask Bill Miller, whom his father "distrusted and disliked"), he continued "partly because I hadn't really accepted, or understood that *I* was black" (p. 17). "That *I* was black," he concludes with emphasis.

We are given the sense that Baldwin's resolution in favor of blackness comes finally with the rewarding mirroring experience of live black theater. Bill Miller takes him to the Lafayette Theatre to see the Orson Welles production of *Macbeth*, set in Haiti with an all-black cast.[86] This, he says, was the "first time I ever really saw black actors at work: and it is important to emphasize that the people I was watching were black, like me" (p. 33). As formative was another, later, experience in which he sees the African American actor Canada Lee as Bigger Thomas in the Orson Welles production of *Native Son* (p. 40). For Baldwin, the crucial difference between his earlier moviegoing and the experience of live black theater is one of "shadows" as opposed to "living black actors on a living stage: we are *all* each other's flesh and blood" (p. 36). What is the difference for him? It is a matter of distance, he says, for the distance between audience and screen is "paradoxically absolute," paradoxical because of the illusion of closeness in the face of the actuality of distance, of separation. The motion picture, he concludes, is only "masquerading as intimacy" (p. 34).[87]

Baldwin's quarrel with the cinema is not just that it fails to return his own image to him. The motion picture creates the illusion of intimacy but holds the viewer at a distance. In his hierarchy, flesh-and-blood theater is *over* shadowy film, the "like me"of theater over the "not-like me" of film. The theater offers him a continuity of liveness and blackness, provides him a lifeline between his black body and that of the actors on stage. On the screen, the closest thing to Baldwin's own face is the frog-eyed face of Bette Davis. And part of what riles him is that in a

Lafayette Theatre, Harlem

mixed-race society to understand *that one is black* is to understand what one is not. Sometimes one is black and other times one is *not-white*. The politics of mirroring only confounds the problem since the African American child is doubly separated from the already distant screen. Not only is the "me" missing from the screen, as with all spectators, but there is no "like me" there either.

In later chapters I want to think about the experience Baldwin apparently never had in his formative years—the experience of watching an all-black-cast film on the screen. I want to extrapolate from Baldwin's theorization of his own childhood experience, seeing what it offers us toward a theory of the African American audience for silent race films, those products exhibited in black theaters between 1913 and 1931, roughly four years into what is known as the sound period in film history. In contrast with early African American literature, which was produced to be read only by white people, early African American films were produced to be viewed by black people, playing exclusively at black theaters during the historical period of American segregation. Seen by blacks and unseen by whites, race movies present us with an exception to the rule of spectatorship. But before race films there were hundreds of films that used black figures, many of them in exceedingly curious ways. The race question, as I find it in 1903, is a foundational fiction wrapped up in a silly diversion.

Desiring Others

In 1903 the Edison Manufacturing Company released a short "kiss in the tunnel" film of no longer than one minute. *What Happened in the Tunnel*, composed of two live action shots separated by one strip of black leader, is actually a "before and after" narrative joke based on the familiar format of a seduction. In the interior of the train we see a stylishly dressed young woman seated in front of a gentleman who has taken her hand and who is attempting to move aggressively toward her. Seated beside the woman is her black maid. The young woman appears as though she might respond to the man's advances, but before anything happens, the tête-à-tête is interrupted and the screen goes black, signifying the train's entrance into a tunnel. When the image returns to the screen seconds later, the dramatic scenario has been rewritten: the woman and her maid have changed seats. The gentleman is embracing the maid whom he has mistaken for the original woman. Seeing in the light that he has been deceived, he returns sheepishly to his seat while the two women turn to look at each other and laugh.

What Happened in the Tunnel

So "What Happened in the Tunnel"? Due to the use of an ingenious dramatic device—the insertion of a brief moment of darkness—the film reveals and covers up its scene in an instant; it both tells all and tells nothing. This odd phrase, this declamatory statement of the title, leads the viewer to expect that the film will show *what happened* in the dark, an impossibility, of course, because the whole problem of seeing in the dark is that one can't exactly "see" anything and therefore one doesn't try to do so, except, perhaps, in the darkened house of the cinema. For a moment, we are confronted with that interesting distinction between literary tell-

What Happened in the Tunnel (dir. Edwin S. Porter, 1903)

ing and cinematic showing: it is not just that the viewer is promised a "telling" but that he or she expects a "showing," popularly, a "show." It could be said that this is what every viewer knows—that cinema cannot help itself: it cannot "tell without showing."[1] But we are tricked. The title announces that it will tell the viewer what happened in the tunnel, but this is only a lure—the viewer must surmise what happened in the tunnel since *what happened* is never shown. The viewer is led to believe that what happened is that the two women changed places, and that one of the two was kissed. But since the would-be seducer may have been thwarted, the answer to the question "What Happened in the Tunnel?" might be "Nothing. Nothing at all happened in the tunnel." And yet the appeal of this very brief dramatic short is its assertion that *something* happened within the section of the narrative that the viewer does not get to see. The story is interrupted and a key link in the narrative chain is withheld from the viewer.

In the history of film narrative 1903 was a milestone year, a year most often connected with the development of editing, and it is noteworthy that this edited film was "photographed" by Edison Company cameraman Edwin S. Porter just at the time he was beginning to be regarded more as a director than as a cameraman. Equally significant, *What Happened in the Tunnel* was released in 1903 between Porter's *The Life of an American Fireman* and *The Great Train Robbery*, both of which are textbook examples of the problem of the evolution of crosscutting.[2] Clearly this short appears at the moment in the transition from the single shot to the multishot film when filmmakers were thinking about what happens *between* shots as well as what happens *next* when shots are connected end to end. In this example more action transpires in the time and space between shots than was previously thought possible. To the early film producers, *What Happened in the Tunnel* presents the dilemma of how to keep the narrative going when the camera cuts or when something on screen changes significantly. Here is only one of the many ways in which, as Lynne Kirby has shown us, the motion picture has an affinity with the locomotive train.[3] Given the dilemma of editing, the narrative can be likened to the movement of the cars of a train—each linked segment speedily moving in a single direction, one following another.

At this moment when the cinema is only beginning to evolve from the uninterrupted storyline to the highly interruptible (crosscut) one requisite to the more complex narrative, cinema is in its adolescent growing phase, the phase in which it is often said to have been exhibiting or "showing off" its newly discovered devices.[4] In recent years film scholars have urged a reconsideration of the amusement park and carnival sideshow aspect of early cinema, a move that has occasioned a new attentiveness to the seaminess as well as to the viscerality of early cinema, particularly in the years prior to 1906.[5] The years between the 1895 Lumière exhibition in Paris and 1906 are, of course, characterized by technological experiments but also by a naughty subject matter warmed over from vaudeville and burlesque. Like Sally Rand's fan and the ubiquitous screen behind which showgirls undressed as well as the numerous keyhole shots, the "kiss in the tunnel" films, of which there were several, were the cinematic equivalent of the kind of sexual teasing perfected earlier on the stage.[6] Newspapers were also a source of similar comic sketches. As Charles Musser tells us, a newspaper anecdote supplied the idea behind Sigmund Lubin's *Love in a Railroad Train* (1902), most notable because the woman passenger tricks the male passenger who tries to steal a kiss by substituting her baby's bottom in the dark tunnel.[7] *What Happened in the Tunnel*, appearing the next year, substitutes the maid's black cheeks for the baby's white ones, and it is the place where the "kiss in the tunnel" films meet the "racial mistake" films (films in which the black female character is accidentally kissed, thus making the lady-killer the target of the joke).[8]

Lynne Kirby makes a case for understanding the movements of the train as "underwriting" the many "romance of the rail" films, films in which, as she says, "desire . . . is an effect of the machine and its movement." The opposite effect, however, is produced in *What Happened in the Tunnel*, which Kirby says is illustrative of the "chance juxtaposition typical of train travel" with its uncertainties and instabilities that "gave rise to scenarios of confusion and inversion of identity."[9] Not a romantic space but a thrilling space was created, a space that tried to replicate as much as possible all of the sense experiences of riding the train, the viscerality of which becomes more understandable when one imagines the exhibition spaces of Hale's Tours, the popular amusement that turned actual train cars into a "theater ride" with shorts like *What Happened in the Tunnel* projected at one end and spectator-passengers at the other facing the screen.[10] In Hale's Tours the origins of cinema in amusement parks such as Coney Island are unmistakable, and it is not much of a leap from the jostling, whistling picture show to John Kasson's analysis of the rides at that great turn-of-the-century fairground as "broad parodies of urban experiences."[11] And it is the amusement park that brings to mind that parody of the tension between public and private sex, the tunnel-of-love ride. Not until Alfred Hitchcock's abstract tunnel of love in *Strangers on a Train* (1951), which connects the tunnel with murder, do we fully understand, however, the sexual charge of the image withheld by means of the tunnel device. The tunnel is especially titillating as represented on the screen because it places us in relation to a double darkness—the theater auditorium *and* the screen—referencing the thrilling frustration of the old carnival attraction in which we are thrust into darkness and whisked out again.

Placing the screen's first interracial kiss in context, that taboo kiss appears in an era of narrative experimentation and within the carnival sideshow phase of cinema history. Perhaps this transgressive kiss could only be represented as a joke since the structure of jokes is based so clearly on negativity and denial. The slip tells all.[12] Although the gentleman appears to have made a mistake and kissed the wrong woman, he is still *shown* as having kissed the black maid. But who or what is telling us that the maid has been kissed (by *showing* us that the maid has been kissed)? Following Judith Mayne, we understand the vignette as organized by a "primitive narrator," an abstract entity that she likens to a conjurer.[13] What is effected by that narrator is a magical transformation, a sleight of hand facilitated by the dark tunnel. One should add here that this is a very very primitive use of the "presto-chango" stop-motion capabilities of cinema technology, capabilities that were employed with even more invention by Georg Méliès in France around the same time.[14]

In its brief flirtation with racial inversion, this short also looks forward to the later silent, *A Florida Enchantment* (1915), a Selig Company two-reel comedy featuring gender change as well as magical race change.[15] That the possibility of racial inversion was suggested almost as soon as gender inversion in early cinema tells us that this use of cinema's "presto-chango" devices was premised on the imagination of the world upside down, a fantasy that has proved to be such a staple in the comedy genre.[16] The "primitive narrator" shows us the transgressive moment—an interracial kiss—and then cancels it. (The two women look at each other and laugh.)[17] Feminists have recently been interested in transgressive substitution in comedy, and what this work on gender and comedy has told us about gender change, for instance, is that the substitution of male for female bodies is ultimately conservative if order is restored and gender-body discrepancies are corrected. In 1903 the mistakenness of the transgressive act is admitted by a laugh, a laugh that would seem to restore the racial order of things. But the laugh doesn't completely discount the kiss. Comedy doesn't always correct *everything*. An indiscretion has been committed and the unimaginable is still imagined. It is, however, a strange kiss that we see—even a strained kiss in which there is really no reciprocity. The maid sits in for the sake of the joke, not for the sake of the kiss (to which she appears totally indifferent). And yet she *has* been kissed.

Since a number of feminist critics have been intrigued by this film it is understandable that it would come to exemplify important critical paradigms. Judith Mayne's interest in this scene, as she tells us, is the fleeting moment of resistance it offers—the opportunity taken by the "primitive narrator," who, aligned with the women, enters dangerous territory in order to play a joke on the male. In the end, however, the transgression is short-lived. As Mayne argues, the transgression is fleeting because it is constrained by two hierarchies, the hierarchy of the gendered "look" that positions the two women on screen in relation to the male and the hierarchy of "racial difference." The transgressive laugh is modified by the "firmly established structure of self and other."[18] The initial reference is to the "male look" about which volumes have been written, a concept that may have reached the point where it can no longer be used with any precision since it would seem to be absolutely everywhere on the screen.[19] My concern here, however, is not with the "look" but with the "structure of self and other" about which Mayne says very little. It is not even clear whether the maid is other to the mistress or to the masher, or is it that the two white characters are other to the black maid? This self/other dichotomy, as we will call it, has been an important construct in recent film theory although it has never been properly laid out, a situation that may be the consequence of the perception that questions of "the other" have come in through the back door of postcolonial theory rather than the front door of film criticism (where the critical concept of "the look" entered). A short overview of the uses of the concept of "the other," never far from the antithetical "self" in film theory, reveals, if nothing else, the centrality of a concept that has perhaps been too often assumed to stand for all marginality and too seldom explicated.

The Other in Film Theory

As introduced into film theory in Homi Bhabha's "The Other Question," the postcolonial concept of the other has to do with the colonizer's way of knowing the colonized, a knowing that is found in the representational figure we understand as a stereotype. In the contradictory image of the other is concentrated all of the "ambivalence," the hate and the admiration of the colonizer for whom the very "visibility" of the signs of difference in the other is decisive.[20] At this moment and in this particular article by Bhabha, postcolonial theory undergoes a cross-fertilization with feminist film theory as the image of the other emerges as yet another "object of difference," even a fetish like the figure of woman, thus close to the secret sexual fetish of Freudian theory.[21] But the mutual concern with image was short-lived, and after some initial shared starting points, feminist film theory and postcolonial theory went their separate ways, following agendas significantly different in kind and scope.[22] Feminism, it would seem, has been historically concerned with the problem of the representation of the sexualized body of woman, and postcolonial theory with the problem of the First World *knowledge of* the Third World, two distinct problems, worlds apart.[23] More recently, however, feminists have begun to adjust film theory to the requirements of a field transformed by the concerns of postcolonial theory.[24] Areas of interest and inquiry have begun to fan out from the old centers.[25]

It may be necessary, however awkward, to speak of several feminisms, the First World white one and those feminisms that black British, African American, and Asian American scholars forge in answer to the first white feminism. It is in response to this forgetful white feminism that we see a kind of economy of the use of the construct "other" in the work of black and Third World feminists who identify a doubled otherness. One thinks here of Michelle Wallace's comment that for black women the problem does not stop with the lived existence of the "woman as other" because she is more accurately the "other of the other."[26] Likewise, Trinh T. Minh-ha, from the standpoint of a Third World anthropologist living in the First World, has worked through the positions of knowing others as the same and as the not-same, as culturally once removed and as culturally synonymous.[27] Sometimes interchangeable with "woman" and sometimes not, the other has shared many of the critical attributes that feminism has ascribed to those outside the patriarchal sphere of influence. As "unspeakable," "objectified," "misrecognized," "negated," and "disempowered," it seemed to early Second Wave feminists that the concept of "the other" was theoretically and structurally close to "woman." This association through analogous subjectivization has been particularly strong in feminist film theory where the comparison between "woman" and "black" has been shored up with reference to Freud's portrayal of woman as the "dark continent."[28] If such an analogy has persisted, it is certainly out of a long habit of feminist identification with alterity. But has this identification continued even after the great strides made by First World (white) feminists? These strides, after all, have finally distanced First World feminists (black as well as white) from those who are "truly other" in the postcolonial sense.[29]

Another tradition has evolved in academic discourse, a practice of "othering" everything and anything outside, strange, or just unlike something else. In recent years, whole bodies of knowledge have been restructured in accordance with the need to center what was once marginal, a rearrangement that often seems designed to benefit from the current vogue in alterity studies. Indeed, "the other" as a term may have already exhausted its utility even before its possibilities as a concept have been thoroughly explored.[30] Still, within academic fields, it is not surprising to find epistemological territories now organized in terms of that which is established and that which is unconventional or outside and therefore designated as "other." Film theory and criticism, for example, have had recourse to the concept of "the other" in relation to the characterization of its own historical phases as well as in relation to schools of filmmaking ("other" cinemas).

Here we will be concerned with race movies, an outsider cinema, as well as with the unconventional aesthetics of motion pictures in the silent era. What is understood as the radical otherness of early cinema signals the absolute divide between the familiar scenes of classical cinema and the relatively strange aesthetics of the earliest moving pictures to which contemporary audiences are thoroughly unaccustomed. In one way, "othering" early cinema serves as a kind of caution to all who dare to watch and to all who, after watching, might find these films disappointingly incoherent or virtually unwatchable. In another way, however, constructing early film as other to classical Hollywood narrative romanticizes the study of cinema between 1895 and 1906 as a kind of imperial adventure in which the scholar is encouraged to find the strange and exotic. Further, the degree to which early cinema has been referenced as "primitive" may be the product of a kind of uncritical receptivity to concepts that have blown in on academic headwinds carrying assumptions about Western versus non-Western art, assumptions that travel from field to field and eventually take stubborn root.[31] Whether or not we want to emphasize any likeness between pre-1906 cinema and artistic "primitivism" in other fields, the understanding of early cinema as other to highly evolved classical narrative may still be useful. What needs to be emphasized, however, particularly in the following chapters on silent film, is the way early cinema is both "of" and "not of" the classical cinema it would become, and therefore that the one cannot be conceived without the other. It would seem, then, that this long-standing usage from within film history and film theory advances our understanding of the situatedness or the *relation* of interdependency between the classical and the not-classical that we want to retain.

If the use of the concept of otherness to divide one period from another, an earlier from a later, borrows loosely from postcolonial theory, the use of the other in relation to cinematic identification comes quite unmistakably from psychoanalytic theory. I want to alert the reader to the fact that although I am proceeding with my overview of the way the other is essential to standard accounts of cinematic identification, this does not mean that I am yet satisfied with this account, an account whose reconsideration, as I indicated in the last chapter, is long overdue. Looking back to the origins of the fullest version of cinematic identification in Christian Metz's "The Imaginary Signifier," introduced in chapter 1, the concept of the other proliferates and is soon filling every anonymous space, confirming our analysis of that concept as theoretically rich and provocative but somewhat unruly.[32] Emerging immediately out of Metz there are at least two places or positions that have been understood as spaces of the other in film language, both requisite to the formation of the subject. My discussion is by no means exhaustive and is not meant to suggest that there are only two ways in which the concept of the other has been significant in the development of film theory as it pertains to cinematic language. The first, what I will call the use of the other in the theory of cinematic subject constitution, starts from the premise that cinema, as a strange mirror, doesn't exactly return the image of the viewer-subject. As a familiar theorization, Lacan's mirror-stage account of identity formation enters here and is generally invoked to suggest an analogy between the viewing process and the child's initiation into the culture via the acquisition of language, as I discussed in the last chapter. An other is required in this process of language learning in order to give confirmation of its existence back to the tentative self who stands before the metaphorical mirror. The theory of cinematic identification based on Lacan enriches the basic structure that predicates identity on the distinction between the self and the other, and supplements it with an account of misrecognition and disavowal. In this account gender is secured by means of a denial of difference between self and other (designated male or female), a denial basic to the formation of the ego in psychoanalytic theory. I will return to this theory of spectatorship in somewhat more detail after the section later in this chapter, "What Psychoanalysis Can and Can't Tell Us about Race."

If this first notion of the other is basic to the theory of spectatorship, particularly as it draws on psychoanalysis, a second, complementary notion has filled out the theory of how classical film grammar works to constitute this same spectator-subject. This second other, still in a position opposite the self, is referenced in the theorization of the classical shot/reverse shot construction, which is sometimes described as an alternation between the seeing and the seen. For the shot construction to make sense to the viewer, the vantage point off-screen from which the on-screen image is seen is "authorized" by an unseen placeholder (sometimes a character, sometimes not a character). And it is this absent one who is said to be other to the visible figures on the screen as well as to the viewer whose identification is enlisted and secured via this powerful placeholder, this "not-I."[33] A note of caution should be injected here. I do not want to give the impression that this particular usage has been thought through systematically in film theory, but the notion of a mysterious faceless placeholder (an off-screen placeholder, other to the on-screen figures) has been a productive one. (It is this placeholder who we suspect has switched the woman with her maid on the train.) Without a doubt, thinking about this placeholder, even naming it, has contributed to a particular view of the peculiarity of cinematic shot construction. To characterize this cinematic structural function as a process controlled by an anonymous other gives that function an enlarged significance. Looking at it more pragmatically, othering the off-screen space is nothing more than an attempt to come to terms with the way viewers are called on to connect shots.

Although refined in classical cinema, this patterning is already pronounced in the first decades of cinema. Even before continuity editing was fully developed, one might find an alternation between what we are calling the one and the other (both off-screen and on-screen), an exchange that plays a part in the solicitation of spectator allegiance at the level of shot and therefore in relation to on-screen figures—that is, characters. Noel Burch, for instance, has discussed the "programming" of spectator identification in these terms, demonstrating how spectators are encouraged to see one set of characters as other through their alignment with another set, even when those characters are not on the screen. In other words, the other need not always be off-screen. Considering D. W. Griffith's *Gold Is Not All* (1910), for instance, Burch notes that the "rich Others" appear more often than the poor on the screen, the rich made "other" by the positioning of the poor. He explains that "it is established from the beginning of the film that 'our' gaze has become the gaze of the 'happy poor,' *even in their absence.*" And it is this positioning of the largely unseen poor vis-à-vis the highly visible "rich Others" that makes it possible for the film to argue that "the poor are happier than the rich."[34]

While these accounts of cinematic structuring may often seem hopelessly difficult to unravel, there is a constant that should be emphasized; whether off-screen or on, "the other" is distinguished from the "I," the spectator-subject for whom the viewing pleasure in the scene is organized. Further, it is crucial that the spectator-subject and the other are never in the same place at the same time. So what is certain is that the other is not us. Although one would expect that in this us-other relation the other would always be disenfranchised in some way—off-screen, faceless, and mute—this is not necessarily the case. For as Burch's example shows, the power of the off-screen position is its ability to elevate one set of characters (or views) over another, even to align the spectator-subject with the poor "others" against the "rich Others," thus effecting the textual disempowerment of the rich.

So we want to understand why, when the subject-other distinction sometimes appears to be nothing other than a question of alternation, the asymmetry obtains. We want to understand the *difference* between the "subject," here aligned with the self, and its "other" since the two concepts would at this point seem to rival one another in their ability to say everything and nothing, and we look with dismay on the current status of the discursive "subject" in critical theory, once a potent tool, now an empty shell of a concept.[35] The distinction between these two philosophical concepts is not easily simplified (indeed nothing about them can be simplified). Though their recent histories demonstrate their divergence, there is at least one way in which the two concepts would seem to echo one another. Whereas the "subject," the creature of the Enlightenment, is central, or centered, and singular (but not necessarily on top since it is "subject to" that which constitutes it), the "other" is always off-center and contingent, that is, defined always in relation to another, which is *its* "other." The history of the Enlightenment subject, so crucial to understanding the ideological functioning of classical works of art, including the cinema in our time, has helped us to hold on to a slippery concept on which we seem always to be in danger of losing our theoretical grip.[36] So, too, some history of the development of "the other," that philosophical concept whose origins can be traced to Plato, may be insurance against *its* further dilution.[37] Our concern, it should be recalled, is to trace the history of a philosophical concept in order to ask who is who to whom in the 1903 scene on the train.

Desire and the Other

It is only where the other is brought back into relation with the concept of "Desire" that the two terms begin to fill out one another in such a way as to offer a more complete theory of the production of identity, which has its implications for theories of cinematic identification. As philosophical concepts, the two make their debut together in Hegel's 1807 *Phenomenology of Spirit,* producing an account of human interrelatedness that has provided the point of departure for the major philosophical influences on contemporary critical theory: Marx, Sartre, Lacan, Foucault.[38] In Hegel, it is "the one" or the "I" that stands in opposition to the "other," and it is this entity that must go through another entity in order to finally become itself. An apparent paradox, this famous dialectical "overcoming" of the one by the other, so startling in its symmetry, would seem to have been lost in later versions of this notorious philosophical encounter. Most surprising of all in Hegel's original formulation, after the legendary struggle between the positions he names "lord" and "bondsman," it is the bondsman, now in the position of the one and not the other, who finally lands on his feet, a free man.

Desire in Hegel only bears a slim resemblance to the contemporary concept, a concept that today is almost always synonymous with sexual desire. One could say that in Hegel, Desire, always capitalized, stands for so much more, expressing as it does the effort to encompass the external world. More than anything, however, Desire in Hegel is deeply involved with the problem of identity: it is the way in which difference becomes identity in *The Phenomenology of Spirit* that has consequences for film theory, as I will show. Consider, for instance, the dilemma of the young James Baldwin who formulates his identity against and across the images of Bette Davis and Joan Crawford. For Baldwin, difference would, quite literally, become identity as he questioned his relationship to the white images on the screen and formulated himself as black and queer. But it is only after two waves of reconsideration (divided by five decades) that Hegel has begun to sound at all relevant to the contemporary moment, and here I refer to Alexander Kojève's famous lectures delivered in the 1930s and Judith Butler's more recent rereading, two distinct but equally significant returns.

Appropriately, Kojève pulls the theme of recognition out of Hegel's concept of Desire where Butler emphasizes the theme of satisfaction. Butler wants us to see the one as striving to achieve identity by means of another, a process that requires an exchange in which the subject is able to "become oneself by becoming another."[39] Satisfaction of Desire absolutely requires others, and only another can give back confirmation of one's existence. But the Hegelian model of Desire is no simple mirroring process, and as Butler explicates Hegel's famous concept of "mutual overcoming," it involves a novel form of bodily incorporation, a taking into oneself as well as a taking out of oneself. She thus summarizes Hegel's concept of Desire as "the incessant human effort to overcome external differences, a project to become a self-sufficient subject for whom all things apparently different emerge as immanent features of the subject itself."[40] Here is a variant on the more familiar concept of the social construction of the self—things that seem different eventually turn out to be part of the self, a generation of things out of themselves. This also anticipates here, it would seem, the much more fluid concept of subjecthood that expects genders (or identities) to be temporarily inhabited or "tried on," a concept central to Butler's later work in queer theory, a concept that, as I earlier suggested, has already had its impact on contemporary theories of identification.[41]

Let us not forget, however, that Hegel's encounter between lord and bondsman, master and slave, is a struggle, a concept seemingly at odds with any theory of identification. In Hegel, the one attempts to wrest his identity from the other from whom he demands recognition. This very process by which the one tries to establish who or what he is through the passive object or other is the process that produces inequality. It should be no surprise, then, that the unequal being is unable to return the desired recognition, for how can an unequal confer the recognition on the very master who has prohibited recognition in the first place? The master's refusal to grant the slave humanity (and freedom) is turned back on the master himself when he needs, expects, and desires recognition of his existence from the slave whom he is unable to recognize.[42] As this structure, Hegel's "reciprocal recognition," has been translated, almost verbatim, into postcolonial theory, the impasse between the two has been stressed as much as the mirroring, a stalemate that produces a face-to-face standoff between the lord and the bondsman. One cannot help but think of Fanon's "dual narcissism" and Sartre's "relentless reciprocity" as well as Albert Memmi's description of the colonizer's confrontation with the colonized, the two forever locked horn to horn.[43]

But Kojève insists on seeing reciprocal recognition as a condition for the satisfaction of Desire, again for him a prerequisite to the development of what Hegel terms self-consciousness, a concept within which the more contemporary understanding of "the search for one's identity" might be found. Butler summarizes Kojève as seeing "the satisfaction of desire in the successful recognition of each individual by every other," and following Kojève through to his conclusion we have a relatively benign reading of Hegel as resolving the master–slave impasse in favor of the slave and a conclusive equality between men.[44] In fact, Kojève imagines a world in which the master and the slave are finally indistinguishable: "Generally speaking, the I of Desire is an emptiness that receives a real positive content only by negating action that satisfies Desire in destroying, transforming, and 'assimilating' the desired non-I."[45]

This answers the question as to what has become of the "Other" (always capitalized by Kojève), the "non-I," the entity who always seems to disappear into the one in the mysterious Hegelian "switcheroo" in which "opposites pass over into each other" at their most extreme point. On second consideration, however, Kojève's "destruction" and "assimilation" of the other is a solution to the problem of the other who is no longer "other," a solution that seems to point outside philosophy to historical events of the past century. Assimilation as a solution seems to suggest the need to overcome otherness, hinting that otherness is a temporary and intolerable condition that must somehow be eradicated. Especially given Kojève's inflections, it is difficult not to see Hegel's philosophical scenario as a metaphor for the colonial condition as so many have indeed seen it.[46]

Hegel's scenario, however, has a different ending, an abstract conclusion that appears indifferent to history. In this foundational scene, operating almost simultaneously with the degradation of the other is this unmistakable attempt to set the two face to face, to take something from the one and to give it to the other in order to equalize the situation, and finally to *put the other over the one.* The relevant passage in Hegel is this:

> Self-consciousness is faced by another self-consciousness; it has come *out of itself.* This has a twofold significance: first, it has lost itself, for it finds itself as an *other* being; secondly, in doing so it has superseded the other, for it does not see the other as an essential being, but in the other sees its own self.[47]

Also pronounced in Hegel, at this stage in the encounter between the two, is a cruel narcissism, evidenced in the one's insistence on seeing only itself in the other (a narcissism that, with some modifications, will metamorphose into Edward Said's notion of Orientalism).[48] Here, to summarize, is the requirement of the other, the standoff, the movement of the one into the other, and finally the remarkable mirroring. But an amazing mirroring not of two philosophical positions but of two gendered and raced entities.

While critics have established that Hegel's characterization of his abstract positions as "the lord" and "the bondsman" renders his philosophy race-specific to a fault, the exclusive maleness of the famous encounter has yet to draw comment. But for feminists there is much more at stake here than the proverbial exclusion of women. Following Judith Butler back to Hegel we discover the origins of more than one foundational paradigm. For instance, feminists can find in Hegel an early use of the term "object of desire," the term that has become for them a theoretical cornerstone. Here is the old passivity and the "thingness" as well as the interchangeability of "other" and "object," and, perhaps most familiar, the idea that Desire fixates on something outside of itself that will materialize as a fetish. Further, the idea that Desire *must have* an object is given a rationale in Hegel, where it is reiterated to the point where the having of an object becomes a defining feature of Desire. But the desired object for Hegel is only a means to the goal of "self-consciousness" or the expansive annexation of what is outside oneself. Curiously, pre-Freud, Hegel's antagonists seem quite innocent of the sex drive, having only the need for food, although in their strange dance they anticipate the contemporary configuration we associate with Sartre.

It is only later in Sartre's *Being and Nothingness* that Desire undergoes the sexualization that produces the self and the other as a prototype of the heterosexual couple. In Sartre, each is an object for the other, and here the "Other," emphatically capitalized, appears to have grown in stature as well as significance, no longer aligned with servitude or work, but a fully participating partner. So Sartre's debt to Hegel is the apparent reciprocity in the self-other relation, a mutuality in which the partners produce or create each other. I say "apparent" reciprocity, however, because Sartre is critical of Hegel on the question of reciprocity and corrects him: it is in my 'being-in-the-world' that the Other determines me. Our relation is not a *frontal* opposition but rather an *oblique* interdependence."[49] The difference between self and other, instead of producing a demand for the rectification of an intolerable inequity, becomes in Sartre the basis for erotic attraction. Even given Sartre's phenomenological exhaustiveness, his gradual move from Hegel's theorization to his own, the new characterization seems at some points abrupt: "What the Hegelian Master is for the Slave, the lover wants to be for the beloved. But the analogy soon stops here, for with Hegel the Master demands the Slave's freedom only laterally and, so to speak, implicitly, while the lover wants the beloved's freedom *first and foremost*."[50] A sexual scenario also suggests itself in the emphasis on the way the one becomes an object *for* the other; Desire, as it becomes sexual desire, is born of the clash between the selves.[51]

If there is a theme in the philosophical self/other encounter from Hegel to Sartre, then, it would be antagonism, a deep-seated hostility that will branch off into postcolonial theory.[52] However, in its development from Hegel to Sartre to Lacan, antagonism becomes less and less about conflict and stalemate and eventually takes an unrecognizable form—that of utter impossibility. Thus what is tension in Hegel and Kojève, Lacan's teacher, becomes frustration in Lacan where desire, by definition, can never be fulfilled.[53] Lacanian desire, still desire for the other, cannot ever be satisfied but not because the other is an opposite, a separated being. Desire stands no chance of satisfaction because the other is a separated part of the self. In Lacan, the other, no longer capitalized, comes to have a new site. The other is the unconscious itself, and thus it is that desire also signifies the unlikelihood that the subject will ever cohere. There is a kind of irresistible logic to this in that the very opacity of the unconscious, its constant evasion of attempts to pin it down, instantiates the impossibility that characterizes desire. Thus it is that, on the model of the disjuncture between conscious and unconscious, radical otherness has been theorized as the discrepancy between language and intention. Still more emphasis on the impossibility of satisfaction is needed, however, for this is where Lacan swerves away from the Hegelian resolution of the paradox and where deconstruction reiterates the Lacanian theme song: the forever desired, the never achieved. Indeed, to explain the impossibility of ever completely deconstructing a text Gayatri Spivak invokes desire as both the means as well as the structural key: "The tool for this, indeed for any deconstruction, is our desire, itself a deconstructive and grammatological structure that forever differs from (we ony desire what is not ourselves) and defers (desire is never fulfilled) the text of our selves."[54]

Desiring Machines

Having given some idea of the sources of the currents that have delivered the concepts of "other" and "desire" (no longer capitalized) to contemporary film theory, I want to return one more time to "The Imaginary Signifier" where these concepts come together as an explanation as to how it is that we find ourselves in the cinema. I want to know if the knowledge of the philosophical legacy of these concepts affects in any way our habituated uses of them. But first I want to call attention to a contemporary development that requires the theorization of the relation between "desire" and "other" as machinelike. Metz early alerted us to the productivity of understanding the cinema as two connected machines—the "outer machine" (cinema as industry) and the "inner machine" (spectator psychology), which have both a metonymic and metaphoric relationship to one another.[55] As often within film studies, the human being is a "desiring machine," a concept introduced into critical discourse by Gilles Deleuze and Félix Guattari, who in their provocative metaphor capture the confluence of capitalism and psychoanalysis.[56] Here, changing places, desire has become efficient and the machine has become sensuous, an insight I wish to retain. For Deleuze and Guattari, the cinema is one of those desiring machines that has to do with both gadgets and fantasies. Metz concurs with his description of cinema as "a weak and a robust mechanism: like the human body, like a precision tool, like a social institution."[57] Like the human body, thus like a desiring machine, the cinema meets that other desiring machine, the spectator.[58] Now let us see what the machine does to the Lacanian understanding of desire as interminably held out, held out because of the totally impossible relation between self and other (an other, as we will recall, now relocated to the unconscious itself).

What Metz adds to the "forever desired, never achieved" paradigm in his psychoanalytic film theory is the prototype of a magical machine that produces desire in inverse relation to the possibility of achieving its object. (The more impossible the more desirable.) In Metz, that imaginary object longed for and preferred because of its absence is gone forever—is "lost":

In the end it has no object, at any rate no real object; through real objects which are all substitutes . . . it pursues an imaginary object (a "lost object") which is its truest object, an object that has always been lost and is always desired as such.[59]

This object, missing from the beginning, forever out of reach, helps us understand what Metz means by the "imaginary signifier." The cinematic image, likened to the child's mirror image, "is imaginary because the viewer takes as really present what is absent," says Elizabeth Cowie.[60] Metz's cryptic title poses the question as to how something that is "only imaginary" could so successfully signify the "real" that is not in fact there in the motion picture theater. But the use of the term "imaginary" always seems to suggest that the cinematic signifier itself is finally *not there* (not that it is signifying things not there), and for this reason I have always maintained that a better title would have been the "imaginariness of the signifier." Important for my argument here is the understanding that the cinema signifier, because it will never ever be there, produces the very condition of being unsatisfied and unfulfilled, produces the very Lacanian "forever desired, never achieved."

In Metz all of the various "mechanisms" of cinematic desire (a term coordinating the two machines, the psychic and the industrial) are attached to this structure of utter impossibility. For instance, Metz refers to "wandering framings" (which dress and undress space in a "generalized strip-tease") and various "postponements," among which would certainly be the use of editing to create suspense by withholding parts of the action, as I will discuss further in relation to crosscutting.[61] By such technical means, the means of signifying these structures of impossibility, cinema ensures the "excitation of desire." None of its techniques of desire, however, excites more than the voyeuristic mechanism about which so much has been written.[62] In Metz's discussion of voyeurism we glimpse the founding antagonism between lord and bondsman as seen in his characterization of voyeuristic desire (as well as sadism) as the desire that depends on the distance that stands for "the gap" between subject and object, a "fundamental rent."[63] Voyeuristic desire, says Metz, is particularly suited to the evocation of this gap, the "something missing" that summarizes for him the experience of cinema spectatorship, the experience defined by the eternal search for the lost or absent object and the consequent impossibility of finding satisfaction. What the cinema gives, he says, is only given "in effigy"; what it offers is imaginariness and elusive substitutes of which it is in constant pursuit.[64] Again and again, the gap between subject and object arises to frustrate.[65]

Although Metz's references to voyeurism and its object in "The Imaginary Signifier" appeared almost simultaneously with the publication of Laura Mulvey's "Visual Pleasure and Narrative Cinema," the two articles were conceived independently. Their basic conceptions, drawing as they both do on Freud and Lacan, are remarkably similar, but in the long run Mulvey's theorization has become the definitive one. There, as in Metz, voyeurism is both technique and psychic process located in relation to the camera, the screen, and the spectator. Voyeuristic scopophilia is the Freudian instinct that requires an object held at a distance; the voyeurism of the camera is its operation as a surrogate eye, the voyeurism of the spectator is the motionless seat before the drama that unfolds in front of him. Voyeurism in feminist film theory following Mulvey has become closely associated with the eyeline match, the shot / reverse shot pattern, and the point of view shot, suggesting its absolute centrality in film grammar. What is most unmistakable about Mulvey's understanding of voyeurism in "Visual Pleasure and Narrative Cinema," however, is that the process is exclusively male. As Teresa de Lauretis summed up the consequences for female desire, "sexual desire belongs to the other, originates in him."[66] With this emphasis, Mulvey's theory of cinematic desire (through voyeurism) suddenly appears as a feminist lament, a complaint that while desire is understood as male, neither the lesbian nor the straight woman has access to it. If one is an object *for* the other, the other has desire while the one cannot have desire—the other even has desire at the expense of the one who is deprived of it. Feminists take this for granted as a paradigm of the history of the imbalanced sexual practice between males and females, and for this reason, if no other, the paradigm of desire in recent feminist theory probably owes as much to the allegory of the contemporary bedroom as it does to the bedroom of Freud's primal scene.

Feminists could also complain about the way neither Metz nor Mulvey had much to say about the bodily pleasures, leaving these questions entirely to later feminists who would expand and critique Mulvey in their analysis of hard-core pornography. It is still the case, however, that we have had too little work seriously considering ways in which the machine could be seen as "producing the body," which has also meant that film theory as a whole has had relatively little to say about bodily desires although it has had much to say about desire.[67] Quite safely, desire in 1970s film theory is almost always an unrequited or unconsummated desire. Having arrived at this point in its journey, traveling from Hegel's obsession with overcoming differences (Desire) through Sartre's erotics of difference and Lacan's distances, the philosophical concept seems almost, but not quite, transformed beyond recognition. We might as well conclude that this earlier Hegelian concept of Desire has no relation whatsoever to carnal desires, and yet we recall the origin of the other that Lacan has transformed into the unconscious itself. In addition to having a structure, the unconscious also has content, and it is here that (in psychoanalytic theory) cinema finds its material, where, in the depository of taboo wishes, are found desires in the plural—desires galore.

Gaze Theory and the Other

We began by looking for a structure that we suspected was buried deep in the psychoanalytic theory of spectatorship, a theory that has been notoriously uninterested in questions of alterity. What would it mean to find that the theory that we thought was oblivious to racialized differences between peoples owed something to a philosophical scenario that reminds us of these differences, that puts them constantly before us? One cannot make a case that the forgotten ancestry of this philosophical position produces an ineradicable tainting. While we may be able to prove that philosophical antecedents were buried and forgotten, this does not mean that they are in any sense *there*. It remains for us to keep the connections alive, and this means in the critique that counteracts the forgetting. To begin with, I want to assert that "the gaze" is not now and never was about looking.

What has become known as "gaze theory" has recently become somewhat more tightly defined in Linda Williams's feminist reference to the "eye as organ" and perhaps forever literalized in a quotation from French critic Jean Clair: "the gaze is an erection of the eye."[68] Does Williams's association of the gaze with the penis finally resolve the question not just of "who owns the gaze" but of "what is the gaze"? It is actually a question of whether what is wanted is more specificity rather than less for a concept that seems at once entirely too formulaic and too incomprehensibly vague. Furthermore, the popularity of the concept has not contributed to its careful elaboration, for as the concept of "the gaze" has come into wide use, particularly outside feminist film theory in other disciplines, it would appear that this "gaze" is everywhere. It has come to seem that there are as many gazes as there are eyes in the image.[69] This is not to say that the concept has not had its productive applications, and here I would mention Bob Stam and Ella Shohat's notion of the Eurocentric gaze, which would seem also to usefully encompass an analysis of a hegemonic function.[70] In the concluding chapter I discuss what I call the censorial gaze, which I propose in hopes of annexing the connotations that accrue to a more complex theorization of the concept.

However, a wide discrepancy has arisen in the use of the term. In its critical usage "the gaze" is sometimes a theoretical concept having to do with the difficulty of signifying relations and at other times it is nothing more than a synonym for looking at or being looked at. Certainly the most compelling uses always seem to imply a tight circular structure wherein two entities (the one and the other) are interrelated although related *without touching*. Both Metz in "The Imaginary Signifier" and Mulvey in "Visual Pleasure and Narrative Cinema" appear to have looked to Lacan's intriguing but highly idiosyncratic development of the concept, although it has been Mulvey's designation of the maleness of the gaze, reinforced early by Ann Kaplan, that has become the standard usage in the field.[71] Heretofore, however, gaze theory, as used in feminism and film, has been oblivious of its debt to Hegel, a connection only discovered in a return to Lacan. And there in the French psychoanalytic discussion of the gaze we see the pronounced indebtedness to the Hegelian allegory of the one and its other, which is there in the structure of reciprocity of Lacan's "gaze and gazed at" as well as in the apparatus that both looks as well as shows.[72]

But try as hard as we can, we cannot find the formula in Lacan for gazing as equal to seeing. This may simply have to do with translation of the French *le regard* as "the gaze," which may have been a translator's way of actually discouraging the understanding of Lacan's concept as nothing more than a look.[73] Lacan is adamant that the gaze is not the eye itself, and neither, apparently, for him is "the gaze" synonymous with looking or "the look." Instead, it is the crucial *division* between vision and the gaze that defines the function of what in psychoanalytic theory is known as the scopic drive.[74] So it is again this "never together" version of the constitution of a representation through vision that seems to sum up "the gaze," which, it is now clear (if we go directly back to Lacan) is always about our difficult relation to the things we try to signify:

> In our relation to things, in so far as this relation is constituted by the way of vision, and ordered in the figures of representation, something slips, passes, is transmitted, from stage to stage, and is always to some degree eluded in it—that is what we call the gaze.[75]

This mysterious something that "slips" but is still "transmitted" (although not completely) would seem to summarize all of the problems we have with signification—the eternal absences of the things signified, the losses in translation, and the need for substitution. Joan Copjec goes further in her conclusions about the Lacanian gaze, which she associates with the " 'terrifying alterity' the representation takes on, an alterity that stands in the way of the subject straightforwardly seeing itself in that representation."[76] The very otherness of the other as well as the grappling with this otherness (this never together aspect) repeats the founding philosophical moment of coming to self-consciousness.

One would hope that this exercise would make it possible for us to see the silhouette of the master-slave relation in the Lacanian concept of "the gaze," and to read back into it a more political implication, one aware not only of the politics of signification but of the raced relations of looking. Such a reading may perhaps only be reinforced by remembering Sartre, who always seems mysteriously left out of the 1970s film theory that echoes without referencing his concept of "The Look." In Sartre, the most basic architecture of Mulvey's popular account of the male gaze, without relinquishing Hegel, is unmistakable: "If someone looks at me, I am conscious *of being* an object. But this consciousness can be produced only in and through the existence of the Other."[77] Countless phrases are reminiscent of feminist film theory, from "the Other's look fashions my body" to the reference to "being-a-look to being looked-at," which anticipates Mulvey's characterization of the "to-be-looked-at-ness" of the female body, a refusal of Sartre that remembers him.[78] While feminism papered over Sartre, totally replacing his concerns with the contingency of the existence of the other on the self with the equally valid (and politically imperative) project of critiquing the uses of the image of woman, other theoretical possibilities in Sartre languished. Kaja Silverman, in her discussion of Sartre in relation to the evolution of *le regard,* reminds us that *Being and Nothingness* predated Lacan's *Four Fundamental Concepts* by thirty years and, in stressing the importance of seeing the connection between the two works, helps significantly to enlarge our understanding of this concept.[79]

Of course, it could be said of Sartre that in his elaboration of "the look" he was not thinking so much about representation as about the constitution of selves in the social arena, even that he was as much if not more intent on exploring the class implications of looking relations than in confirming his male idea of heterosexual relations. Fredric Jameson brings this out in Sartre in his discussion of the "charged electrical tension of a coexistence" that prefigures the antagonism of class struggle. The preference for the class struggle that Marx forged out of Hegel is there in Jameson's discussion from the early 1970s of "the look" as mediating the relations between classes: "It comes to define oneself against the other, by interiorizing the other's look, and transforming what initially was experienced as shame into a sense of pride or identity (what on the level of class is known as class consciousness)."[80] Confronted again with the question of whether to read one fundamental opposition for another, we experience a theoretical déjà vu, reminded of a time when, as Marxists, it did not seem that we always had to "choose" one oppression over another. But even with the emphasis on class struggle, Sartre keeps the master–slave paradigm alive—alive enough for us to claim the paradigm as a lost ancestor for film theory.

So if the paradigm we are tracing has found its way into psychoanalytic film theory, albeit in much altered form, it reveals itself in this discovery that "the gaze" implies a structure of relationality—our relation to things and the relative positionality of terms—that makes language possible. Certainly it is there in the "standing in" function of language in which something is always missing (or has slipped), since whatever it is that is being signified is never ever there. An impossibility makes language possible. But perhaps the connection between "the gaze" and Hegel's self/other standoff becomes more clear when Stuart Hall, thinking of Saussure, asks us to take note of the analogy between identity and language: "I know who 'I' am in relation to 'the other' (e.g. my mother) whom I cannot be."[81] Undeniably, the substitutions that are the foundation of language as the system we use to make meaning work on another scale in identity formation. Now that I have taken the trouble to demonstrate the deep relevance of psychoanalytic theory to questions of identity, my reader may assume that I will next recommend this route as we consider how to refine film theory in such a way that it takes account of race. There are, however, several reasons for instead recommending caution, not the least of which is the style of psychoanalytic discourse itself. As many have noted, psychoanalytic theory replicates the problem of substitution (this sense of "never together") in its own discourse, in its own notorious circularity suggesting the impossibility of clear definition. The consequent linguistic impenetrability has political implications.

What Psychoanalysis Can and Can't Tell Us about Race

It is the very circuitousness of psychoanalytic discourse that has made its poor reputation among black scholars, a discourse that Claudia Tate has talked about as its "irritating baggage that has made it virtually an anathema to the black intellectual community."[82] Here, then, is perhaps the best place to raise again the issue of the compatibility between psychoanalytic theory and the question of racial identity, an issue that has been raised with relative frequency in recent years without, however, producing definitive answers.[83] The most compelling arguments against the use of psychoanalysis in African and African American studies are still essentially political ones since scholars have yet to mount the kind of campaign that either successfully disproves or seriously discredits this discourse. And psychoanalysis as a theory that has transcended the clinical studies upon which it was once based can neither exactly be disproven nor supplanted anyway.[84] Still, following the feminist challenges to Freud that questioned a system that infantilized and pathologized women, black scholars want to know how the system that historically excluded blacks in its schema could possibly have anything to contribute to the study of the people of the black diaspora. Reminding ourselves of Mary Ann Doane's astute observation that psychoanalysis is a written "ethnography" of the white Western psyche, the question is how this white science can possibly comprehend societies so dramatically different from the one Freudians have studied with such obsessive thoroughness.[85] So it would seem that scholars working on black culture will have different issues with Freud.

The political objections made on behalf of black diaspora studies will have to be distinctly different from those made by feminism. It is not only that psychoanalysis has had a total blind spot where it comes to people of color, but that the science was not designed for them, Freud having completely written off what he called the "lower strata of civilized races" as, in Doane's terms, totally "unpsychoanalyzable."[86] Freud's reason for dismissing them, ironically, is that the relative sexual freedom enjoyed by children reared in these societies produced adults who he thought would not be prone to neuroses, who were "protected" from it, in his words. It would seem that Freud has here liberated entire continents from the plague of psychic disorder, and it would even seem that these neurosis-free people might be elevated above others if it were not for his suggestion in the next sentence that the lack of neurosis correlates with backwardness and, by implication, that pathology produces cultural achievement. Thus it is that Freud sees backwardness where he would (in the case of the neurosis-free white middle class) see success and psychological health and, not stopping there, he wrests an explanation for cultural superiority from the very miasma of psychopathology, a familiar move in the history of white dominance that has so often abandoned science and logic as it created a world in its image. On these grounds alone, protest against psychoanalysis and refusal of its methodology would seem to be justified. The point would be that historically psychoanalysis had no cognizance of black people nor was any attempt made to understand them. Since Freud never studied the lower strata of civilization, why should his science have any application for groups who are neither white nor middle class? How many more times will psychoanalysis get it as wrong as Freud got it, Freud who reads the sexuality of the "lower orders" as both a psychological ideal and the source of cultural retardedness?

Clearly Freud's glaring mistake has implications for the black critique of psychoanalysis. Scholars of African American culture cannot argue as feminists did that psychoanalysis was useful to them because it contained the key to the construction of "woman" in the very patriarchal culture they were critiquing since psychoanalysis has historically never claimed to take black people as its object of study. Strategically, it would make sense that any challenge to psychoanalysis would have to be mounted from the outside rather than from the inside, highlighting its exclusions, featuring at the most basic level the black culture exceptions to the Oedipal rule, the most dramatic example of which is the black mother. Elizabeth Abel, drawing on Hortense Spillers, has noted in slave societies a deformation of the classic maternal function since the black woman had been assigned a purely reproductive function in which she was expected to be a breeder rather than a mother to her children.[87] It would seem that plantation society was full of exceptions. In this upside-down world the black woman was not expected to "mother" the black child but to be "mother" to the white child who then had two mothers, one white and one black, a situation that, as Lillian Smith described it, made the Oedipal seem by comparison "almost a simple adjustment."[88]

And yet the very complexity and exceptionality of that culture that would appear to elude any attempts to try to understand it in psychoanalytic terms attracts the interest of the approach that the slave culture would seem to defy. Of the slave society that Spillers says compromised the black mother she also writes: "threads of an incestuous, interracial geneaology uncover slavery in the U.S. as one of the richest displays of the psychological dimension of culture before the science of European psychology takes hold."[89] Spillers calls our attention here to the sexual dynamics of Linda Brent's slave narrative, a horrible family romance featuring an insanely jealous white wife and a philandering plantation owner in which the black heroine lives for years under threat of rape by her master.[90] To this example of the psychosexual horrors of the interracial slave geneaology could be added the case of Celia, the Missouri slave who murdered her master, the father of her children, rather than submit to him one more time.[91] A compelling argument can be made (echoing Frantz Fanon, to whom I will shortly turn) that white middle class society has historically "infected" African arrivals with New World pathologies. But before we become too interested in the psychodynamics of these cases of symbolic incest and real patricide, we should ask ourselves what exactly this kind of interpretation can do to the history of slave women, how it may or may not write their history *for* psychoanalysis. We should ask whether psychoanalysis is the only interpretative tool available, and also how it would be possible for there to be a "display of the psychological dimension" *before* the development of the European science that could retrospectively construct New World slave culture as a psychological case study.

While it is understandable that we would want to use contemporary critical tools in an effort to fill out and comprehend the past in modern terms—that is what we do as scholars—it is another thing to rewrite the past in an effort to prove the comprehensiveness of a model into which has been built a politically suspect worldview. Here is where one wants to recall Deleuze and Guattari's warning that "Oedipus is always colonization pursued by other means."[92] Certainly it can be demonstrated that studying African or North American and Caribbean slave cultures in terms of psychoanalytic categories is a way of making non-European phenomena fit into existing European knowledges, is a utilization of these peoples' lives in order to advance those knowledges. It is an invisible and apparently painless exploitation of the inner lives of colonial subjects in an effort to advance a science that will not necessarily serve them, and here I am putting an emphasis on the *utilization* of European theory in an effort to shift the emphasis away from the argument that that theory is *inherently* corrupt. It would be convenient to be able to find that there is something *inherent* in a philosophical school, system of knowledge, or theoretical position that makes that discourse predictably serve one political position above another. In past decades, brilliant feminist arguments have been made in an attempt to uncover the patriarchal structure of apparently innocent texts; deconstruction has taught us to turn discourses against themselves in such a way that they are made to reveal their own complicity in reactionary projects. However, to locate the racist message or the capitalist assumption in European knowledge systems, to argue against these messages and assumptions, is not the same as finding that these systems are essentially and finally locked into this or that ideology for all time. Besides, the very act of engagement can be a disarmament. In the process of discourse analysis, we are *shifting* ideological structures *as we study them,* and continued scrutiny has political benefits. We always find these theories *in use,* and to the degree that we engage with psychoanalytic theory, for instance, in order to put it "in check," to *that* degree we will be countering the Western tendency to colonize objects of study *for* traditional knowledges. Anthony Appiah has perhaps a better way of describing the project that takes something from the master's knowledge without losing anything to it. "European languages and disciplines," he says, "have been 'turned,' like double agents, from the projects of the metropole to the intellectual work of post colonial cultural life. But though officially in the service of new masters, these tools remain, like all double agents, perpetually under suspicion."[93]

High on our list of Third World theorists who have taken up the tools of the European masters with skepticism and suspicion would be Frantz Fanon, who should be regarded as one of those critics who makes truly imaginative use of psychoanalysis. In its unorthodox use of Freud and creative use of Lacan, *Brown Skin/White Masks* marks a shift *away* from the tradition that seems always to be attempting to better understand psychoanalytic theory, to read it in such a way as to finally produce the science of incoherence as coherent. To my mind, however, Fanon's approach is still entirely too deferential and respectful. Both Homi Bhabha and Henry Louis Gates, in their discovery of Fanon as an honorary deconstructionist in recent years, open the door to a much more irreverent engagement with psychoanalysis, but of the two, Gates is the more critical, pointing out the dilemma of the incompatability between Marx and Freud that is only exacerbated when colonial repression is conflated with psychic repression.[94] More recent readings of Fanon by Mary Ann Doane and Diana Fuss, however, take this criticism further, acknowledging Fanon's breakthrough—the "discovery" of neuroses in Algerian and Tunisian peoples that emerge coincident with their colonization—but suggesting that the West Indian psychoanalyst's own political blinders are too significant to overlook.

In his rush to make everything that is politically reprehensible to him pathological, Fanon locates Negrophobia in the fear that is really desire directed toward the black man by the white woman and the homosexual white man.[95] In his pathologization of interracial sexual relations that so symmetrically mirrors his own cultural attitudes, Fanon scarcely conceals his male West Indian bias against alliances between light-skinned women and white men. It is well known that he writes off as incurable the unfortunate Margotte Capécia who is so desirous of marrying a white man, producing a much less dire prognosis for Jean

Veneuse, the black male "neurotic" who is attracted to the white woman. But, as Mary Ann Doane has noted, Fanon reserves his most severe condemnation (and, in contrast, his most serious symptoms) for the white woman in whom hysteria is connected to fear of sexual encounters with black men.[96] In his interest in pathologizing the white woman, Fanon totally ignores the black woman about whom he says he knows nothing. Most egregious from the standpoint of feminism, Fanon transposes Freud's "A Child Is Being Beaten" into the white woman's fantasy, "A Negro is raping me," a fantasy that to Fanon can only be read as her wish to rape herself.[97] Just as psychoanalysis has led to important "shake ups" of knowledge, it has also authorized preposterous claims and bizarre inversions and done so in the name of "science."

In an essay that represents itself as a qualified defense of psychoanalysis, Hortense Spillers offers this cautionary note before exploring the conditions under which Freud and Lacan could be used productively in African American cultural studies:

> Little or nothing in the intellectual history of African Americans within the social and political context of the United States suggests the effectiveness of a psychoanalytic discourse, revised or classical, in illuminating the problematic of "race" on an intersubjective field of play, nor do we yet know how to historicize the psychoanalytic object and objective, invade its hereditary premises and insulations, and open its insights to cultural and social forms that are disjunctive to its originary imperatives.[98]

Not only is psychoanalysis hopelessly ahistorical, but it tends to myopic universalization ("It seems that Freud wrote as if his man or woman were Everybody's") and is politically obtuse ("Lacanian psychoanalytic theory is simply heavenly, insofar as it has no eyes for the grammar and politics of power").[99] Having nailed psychoanalytic theory on every political count, demonstrating that she knows all of the pitfalls of the project, Spillers makes her case primarily on the basis that in theory what is valuable (as well as in the political interests of the black community) is the chance to reconceptualize the self. It is the self as the "one," a separate entity not the "individualist" person but something more like the self as simultaneously singular and mass, that is required.[100] But Spillers is most compelling when she challenges her reader to think how "race" might expose psychoanalysis and how a new psychoanalytic study of "interior intersubjectivity" might "throw certainty and dogma . . . into doubt."[101] Not since Fanon has a black scholar taken such productive license with psychoanalysis, and this essay leads the way for what one hopes will be more unorthodox uses of Freud and Lacan as well as more methodological eclecticism in the study of interiority.

The answer to the question "what can psychoanalysis tell us about race" is that it may be able to tell us some things but not others. Psychoanalysis is, after all, a specialized approach and can't be expected to deal equally well with all phenomena; my interest in raising the question is more than anything to suggest the need for productive suspicion as well as alternative approaches. Unlike literary theory where a range of methodologies has been developed over decades, film theory has developed fewer analytical options, and for many years it seemed as though the only film theory was psychoanalytic film theory. Film theory was exclusively psychoanalytic to the detriment of the growth of the critical analysis of cinema. Adjacent philosophical traditions predating Freud have remained unexplored in relation to the new technologies of film and television, which has meant that we have not as yet achieved the necessary distance on psychoanalysis. Yes, psychoanalysis can be *made to* comprehend questions of race, but it will always see some aspects and miss others.[102] Perhaps the better question is whether we can understand sexuality in relation to film *without* recourse to psychoanalytic theory. What would a nonpsychoanalytic discussion of race, gender, and sexuality in film sound like?

The Return of the Hegelian Paradigm

If we are to scrutinize Freud in this way, however, we can't very well let Hegel off the hook. And, again, the criticism of the philosopher's infamous scenario has been well rehearsed. In his master–slave confrontation, Hegel follows the contours of nineteenth-century imperialism in which the non-European world is encountered and incorporated by Europe. But where Freud's scenario is elusively ahistorical, Hegel's is too painfully and specifically historical since it is at every turn reminiscent of the relation between the plantation master and the New World African slave, the relation that characterized the era before the 1807 publication of *The Phenomenology of Spirit* and that would continue to organize everyday life in the English-speaking colonies until later in that century. And Hegel was extremely specific, putting historical meat on the philosophical bones of the encounter between lord and bondsman in his 1822–1823 *Lectures on the Philosophy of History*, where it is clear that his own version of world history conforms to his earlier theorization of the self and its growth by means of an encounter with that which is the farthest thing from that self.

Although in these lectures Hegel decries slavery as an injustice, he still finds this condition from Rome and Greece through to European serfdom to have been a stage of progress, a "phase of advance from the merely isolated sensual existence," and even an "education" that would lead to an improved and elevated culture. Even abolition, which he says he favors, should not come too soon but should be gradual, a position that would seem to follow from his conviction that there is a lesson to be learned in the encounter between master and slave; from this it would also follow that the institution of slavery and the concomitant human misery should be prolonged while historical figures enacted the intricate philosophical process of coming to self-consciousness.[103] On the same page, we find Hegel's infamous assertion that Africa has no history as well as the familiar mantra that Africans sold each other into slavery and, not surprisingly within the same section, references to the horrors of African polygamy and cannibalism.[104] There is reason enough in the *Lectures* to reject Hegel on political grounds alone.

More recently, however, given the interest in thinking through the colonial and the postcolonial, new arguments for returning to Hegel have been advanced, not the least important his utility in the study of every conceivable form of domination.[105] While some may take Hegel more seriously after they are reminded that he was Dr. Martin Luther King's favorite philosopher, it will most likely be Paul Gilroy's return to Hegel that will be the most influential for cultural studies.[106] Gilroy approvingly refers to Habermas, who finds Hegel's master–slave relationship, as Gilroy says, "secreted inside many of the writings of contemporary theorists of modernity."[107] And it is for this reason that Gilroy argues that a return to Hegel is part of the project of rewriting modernity, a writing that restores slavery to its historical and philosophical moment. Slavery, then, has been hidden from history, and Hegel has been "secreted" inside the work of major theoretical and philosophical thinkers, from Sartre through Lacan and from there to Christian Metz and Laura Mulvey, as I have shown.

The case of Hegel thus presents us with the dilemma of the unknown underlying paradigm, the stubborn pattern that we are doomed to repeat, unaware as we are of its silent structuring presence.[108] Looking *under* Western philosophy, then, examining the bulwarks, what if we find instead of an abstract nonracial epistemology, a racialized scenario, a scenario that reminds us as we use it of the narrative of imperial conquest? What if the most familiar and basic of philosopical paradigms, the paradigm that demonstrates that the self is constituted through the relation of one to another, that meaning is produced by means of the relation of one to another, is a paradigm drawn from the historical condition of African slavery? Desire, language, identity, everything? All understood by means of theoretical tools derived from the philosophical consideration of eighteenth-century master–slave relations? Although time-tested theoretical systems of relationality, including psychoanalysis, the dialectic, and even structural linguistics, have long been understood as race-neutral, we now have to ask how they would work if no longer trusted to be race-blind. If Gilroy is right, we need not only insist on restoring to history the chapter on slavery but to insist on remembering a racialized other much like Fanon, who, we recall, asserted that "the real Other for the white man is and will continue to be the black man."[109] And, it should be noted, Fanon looks for confirmation of this analysis where we would least expect it, in the study of Lacan.[110]

Othering Machines

I have already raised some of the objections to the use of psychoanalysis as the basis for the study of the African American self. But here I want to address its specific use in film theory where, for over twenty years, psychoanalytic film theory has offered *the* theory of subject formation and *the* theory of identification in the cinema. Considering that this has become the reigning theory, it is interesting to recall that Metz opened "The Imaginary Signifier" by asking: "What contribution can . . . psychoanalysis make to the study of the cinematic signifier?"[111] Once he demonstrated that it could make a contribution, no other theory emerged with the claim that it could account for so much. Once institutionalized, psychoanalytic film theory encouraged a kind of tautological structure in which the justification for the use of psychoanalysis was the existence of the psychoanalytic. To say, for instance, that the reason for using psychoanalysis is that the cinema "engages the processes of the unconscious more than any other artistic medium" is like saying that cinema reveals the unconscious because it *is* the unconscious, forgetting also that psychoanalysis "invented" the very unconscious processes that the cinema is now meant to engage.[112] Since at this time in history it is difficult to think how to conceptualize cinematic identification without recourse to psychoanalytic vocabulary, I begin here with a proposal that we think in terms of what is most basic to identification, which, as it has emerged, is the position of one in relation to the other—hence my term "othering machine."

Clearly it is time for a revised and expanded theory of identification in cinema.[113] More than anything, Manthia Diawara's classic argument about the recurring dilemma of the black spectator dramatizes this need. Reconsidering the black spectator's experience of viewing *The Birth of a Nation* in the light of contemporary theories of reception, Diawara asserts that the racist characterizations and scenarios in the film put that spectator in an extremely uncomfortable position. The structures of the film leave this spectator no alternative mode of engagement with the image, and he or she is thus "compelled to identify" (against all inclinations) with the white woman as victim and the black man as sexual threat, a case of what I am calling hegemonic endangerment. Resisting reading aside, the complaint is that identification is thwarted. And because identification is thwarted, a source of pleasure available to white male spectators is unavailable to black spectators, male or female.[114] "There was nothing to see. She was not us"—so bell hooks quotes her black female informants as they look back on a lifetime of viewing the white female on screen.[115] This argument makes sense based on a widespread and well-documented criticism directed at *The Birth of a Nation* by the black community, suggesting that in the process of identification viewers *want something back from the image*. From the image they want a *return*, that is, they want reciprocity. They want the screen to return to them an image of their completeness. From the vantage point of this desire for reciprocity we gain new insight into the street rioting that characterized the reception of *The Birth of a Nation* in the year of its release and the protests of more recent decades, a historical moment to which I will return in a later chapter.

"There was nothing to see. She was not us." This is a powerful argument and one that is easy to follow, that is, if we all share the same understanding of the meaning of the term "identification." If identification as a concept did not have a definition in wide circulation, however, we would be at a loss to understand what ordinary viewers mean when they say they "can't identify with" this or that popular image. But probing further is difficult because the popular definition of identification tends to be tautological: to identify with is to identify with, a repetition resorted to because of the scarcity of synonyms for the word. Identification *does* overlap with imitation at some points and *can* involve empathy but not always—if even Freud after so many attempts was unhappy with his definition of identification, why would we find it any easier?[116] So what *does* it mean to "identify with," in the awkward English vernacular that lets the preposition dangle so uncertainly? "Identifying with" would seem to be an atrophied version of "identifying oneself *with another*," and the phrase suggests that it only takes *one* to actively identify, that it is a one-way process, and that therefore the object of identification is always passive. Is it?

Academic discussions of identification in the cinema suffer from some of the same problems that plague this everyday usage, and these discussions are in fact constantly slipping out of the theoretical mode and into the everyday.[117] Only one example is the use of the term "misrecognition," which has both an ordinary meaning as a mistaken identification and a psychoanalytic definition, a specificity that involves the child's formative confusion.[118] Between the everyday usage (in reference to characters or situations) and the psychoanalytic conception, however, there is no middle area and no fully developed alternative version. Neither have we seen alternatives to psychoanalysis take hold within critical circles to explain the phenomenon that we are trying to describe here. To make matters more complicated, even alternatives must draw on the psychoanalytic theory of cinematic identification, and long-standing critical habits die hard. The now-institutionalized account starts from the assumption that identification is an unconscious process and takes from Freud the ego's need for an ideal, with the "larger than life"screen figure logically assuming this function for the spectator. The classic projection is also involved in the subject's attachment to the screen figure, most often the luminous star image. But what if we want to give a different version of the lure of the screen? Must we always do this with reference to the ego and the unconscious? Readers who are familiar with Metz's theory of identification will also wonder about his formulation of two kinds of identification, primary and secondary, a paradigm that has stood for twenty-five years without challenge. Following Metz, students of film theory have understood primary identification as "with the image itself," a conceptual and perceptual prerequisite to viewing, and secondary identification as more traditionally a relation to the characters on screen.[119] This film theory fundamental, however, is due for reconsideration, especially since, as Elizabeth Cowie has recently noted, it is peculiar to Metz.[120]

But we use one theoretical paradigm in order to reach another. In feminist film theory, the moving picture machine has primarily been understood as a machine for the establishment and perpetuation of sexual difference, which should be clear from my earlier discussion of Mulvey. Here I want to take a short detour to demonstrate how an alternative theory of identification must differentiate itself from, but also construct itself out of, this influential paradigm. For instance, while the figure of voyeurism is the eye to the hole, identification suggests a face-to-face paradigm.[121] Identification in the cinema produces faces on bodies and objects where none were seen before and, as a process, is undoubtedly instrumental in what Deleuze and Guattari from outside (as well as inside) psychoanalysis have called the "faceification" of the universe.[122] And identification, as focused in the face-to-face paradigm, will be the key to understanding how it can be said that the cinema is an othering machine. So what does the one do to the other in order to produce sexual difference in the psychoanalytic account? In the most comprehensive overview of psychoanalytic identification as it has been adapted to film theory, Anne Friedberg has explained the process as involving the "displacement" of one subject by another, an alignment that privileges the one who gets to identify (male) over the other who doesn't (female), the other who is "displaced" and perhaps even "used" as a fantasy object. Although the one subject's displacement radically alters the other subject, this is not a move that differentiates—it is instead a unilateral change since, as Friedberg states, identification "demands sameness, necessitates similarity, disavows difference." Basically, she continues, identification is the "process of denying the difference between self and other."[123] But this theory of identification, drawing as it does on the feminist theorization of sexual difference, still has its quarrels with the patriarchal organization of everything in the world according to the principle of male and female. What is the problem with denying difference if that denial is *not* a rehearsal of that most notorious of denials—the "disavowal" of difference?[124] Again, when is a disavowal an ordinary renunciation and when is it a proper psychoanalytic "disavowal," that ambivalent "does-doesn't want"?[125] And what is wrong with sameness, similarity, likeness?

We have come some distance from Hegel's original standoff between the one and the other to arrive at this point where the two have become hinged: male/female, self/other. But it has never been clear in feminist theory whether the objection was to sameness, with its conservative implications of adherence to norms, or to difference, with all of its connotations of the very sexual division that has been used to exclude and to denigrate women. To disavow or to "deny difference" is not only to express fears of castration but in another way it could be to denounce the organization of the world according to the principle of sexual difference, a denial that would actually seem to be in the long-term interests of feminism. The argument *for* difference that is also an argument *against* sameness would seem to fare less well in the political scheme of things since it is vulnerable to appropriation for an argument on behalf of individuality and against conformity, an argument that plays into the hands of an outdated apolitical humanism.

This is only to give some idea of the kinds of difficulties raised by the "sexual difference theory" that emerged out of feminism.[126] And feminism is here a case in point of what Stuart Hall has called the "divided legacy" of difference, which can be positive one minute and negative the next.[127] It should by now be clear that the social distinctions generally understood as race relations would be inadequately comprehended by any "race difference" theory that followed the "sexual difference" paradigm. Neither are the shortcomings of the paradigm rectified *for* plurality and against dichotomy by simply producing difference in the plural. I have something else in mind. I have taken my inspiration from Barbara Johnson's nuanced critique of feminist theory, a deconstruction of "difference" that suggests that even with the exhaustive emphasis on difference, feminists never looked at the concept dialectically:

> Difference is a misreading of sameness, but it must be represented in order to be erased. The resistance to finding out that the Other is the same springs out of the reluctance to admit that the same is Other. . . . The difference between difference and sameness can barely be said. It is as small and as vast as the difference between "like" and "as."[128]

Deconstruction would here seem to stress the proximity between difference and sameness in an almost Hegelian move in which the one turns out to be the other at its most extreme point.

I offer this aside about sexual difference in connection with the question of how the motion picture apparatus can be said to be an othering machine. But let us go further. If cinema is a desiring machine, it is also an othering machine, producing (again with remarkable efficiency) the I as well as the not-I. But it is not enough to say that the cinema is an othering machine (provocative as that may be) without first being able to say *how* (as an institution) the machine works. Furthermore, one must be careful not to slip back into old theoretical positions that give the impression that the cinema "produces subjects" as factories produce products. If the cinema is what I want to call an othering machine, a machine that stages the face-to-face encounter between entities in search of identity, *it must offer some satisfaction of the desire to overcome differences.* It is not that the othering machine produces *either* difference or sameness in its open invitation to the spectator to identify with it, but that it relies on the fundamentals of subject reciprocity (the one becoming the other), relies certainly on this reciprocity for the organization of desire (really the relations of desire). And in Judith Butler's creative reading of Hegel, the "satisfaction of desire [is] . . . a transformation of difference into identity."[129] There is an echo of this in C. L. R. James's enthusiastic discovery of Hegel: "Identity means difference. Difference means identity," he says, and then, discovering the application of the dialectic to "labor" and "capital," he remarks: "I think myself that all this is thrilling."[130]

The process of identification in the cinema is a "transformation of difference into identity." Identification is where the other meets the one—face pressed against face—where difference and sameness glide against one another, where they sometimes change places, and thus where the difference between them "can barely be said." The identificatory "face-off" is complemented by a "body through" whereby everything the spectator-subject sees in the cinema has come to him via another, via these particular relations of desire. If, in film theory, one goes through another in order to see, one also goes through another in order to be. The cinematic relations of identification reiterate again the premise that one receives oneself from the other, that in order to become oneself one must become the other.

It would seem that there is always some redundancy in identity, there is a quality of selfsameness. Cinematic identification as a process is so close to "wanting to become identical" that it is difficult not to acknowledge the being-like aspect that is unmistakable in its allure. But how exactly *does* the othering machine that offers faces to faces encourage the one's "becoming of" the other? As I have said, the cinema stages the face-to-face encounter between entities in search of identity. Difference is transformed into identity. But how? The othering machine produces ones as others by means of an imitation that is also an incorporation, an incorporation not unlike the Hegelian merger that satisfies desire. But incorporation how? The very root of the word suggests a body, one corporeality, that makes another a part of itself. In its function as an incorporating machine, the othering machine has a social mission, a mission in which some are represented *to* others, and one assumes here an audience that is racially mixed, that is, an integrated cinema.

As I will discuss in later chapters, the premise of the race movies from the era of the segregated cinema is the representation of audience members *to* themselves. However, whether the one is represented to the other or ones are represented to themselves, the screen-mirror experience cannot escape the long-standing association with imitation—the imitation that is thought to be the lowest form of identification. This is the imitation that plays so easily into conservative hands when it arouses fears of "mindless copying," fears that fan the flames of censorship epidemics, fears that have been associated with motion pictures since the release of *The Birth of a Nation*. And it is this imitation that seems most intolerable to conservative forces when it is associated with dark others. But to emphasize this side of imitation is to miss the transcendent aspirations credited to mimesis, for mimesis captures the longing to reproduce things *with one's own body*, the desire, above all, to bring about change through incorporation. Useful for us, utopian theorist Ernst Bloch has identified in what he calls the "mimic need" an irresistible desire—the "tempting desire to transform oneself."[131]

The Kiss on the Train

I began with the representation of a kiss on a train, a figure of desire that has an awkward position vis-à-vis classical voyeurism since the trajectory of the kiss is a transgression of the very space the voyeur puts between himself and his object. This echoes Rosalind Coward, who has written about the kiss as a "transgression" of the "conventional distance between the self and others." As an act of "mutual penetration," she goes on, the kiss offers something more to women: "the chance to actively penetrate."[132] The kiss is not easily imitated by the camera or in any way accommodated to looking relations within the spatial rules of classical cinema where the camera is known to penetrate space in the tracking long shot but not in the close-up where there is no room to travel. And this is significant because the kiss, for all intents and purposes, *is* the representation of the face-to-face incorporation of the one into the other, the attempt to act on as well as to act out the desire to become oneself by becoming the other, an efficient corporealization of identification. Kissing raises philosophical as well as proxemic issues: is it possible to become without touching or, conversely, to touch without becoming, a question reminiscent of the myth of coming without touching.[133]

The yearning for touching and becoming is only met halfway by the cinema. The spectator and the screen inhabit separate worlds, one of which, as Metz says, is *not there*. And yet, beginning with the 1896 *Irwin–Rice Kiss*, there was an expectation that the cinema, the new medium for showing all, would raise the curtain on the romantic kiss.[134] Unmistakable about that first scandalous kiss is the uncomfortable close-up solution to the problem of the representation of the intimate embrace. Where *do* you put the camera? With the triumph of illusionism in later decades, the cinematic representation of the erotic kiss would involve the exploration of variations on the over-the-shoulder reverse-angle shot as well as the tight close-up of quivering lips nearly meeting the camera lens, and would finally arrive at the 360-degree tracking shot as a convention for representing the engulfment of the kiss. In contrast, early film kisses are depthless—two-dimensional cardboard (like the stiff train interior set with a hole punched in it to show the rear-screen projected footage of moving countryside). The solution in the early *Irwin–Rice Kiss* is an awkward two-shot, two faces pressed quickly together, both facing out toward the camera. *What Happened in the Tunnel* finally opts for showing the figures "coming out of" the kiss, corresponding with the train's "coming out of" the tunnel. The kiss, it would seem, represents both the solution to and the immediate problem of the spatial representation of interpenetration—the solution to the problem in that, as everyone knows, kissing *stands in for* sexual intercourse. Both a preface to and a pale substitute for intercourse, the kiss bears the burden of representing the act that cannot be represented, of eternally standing in for the "real thing." A peculiar custom, kissing uses the lips to cover the mouth—but not always politely. Two covered mouths, hole to hole, are like two tunnels connected, really two caves pressed together into which two tongues stretch furiously, sometimes like locomotives.

It is a leap from a comic interracial kiss in early cinema, really a racist joke, to the seamy history of interracial sex in the United States. Only in recent years have scholars begun to research this history in an attempt to find out who was actually doing what to whom. More problematically, with all of the significant new work on race theory, the question of interracial sexual relations remains virtually untouched. One exception is bell hooks's remarks on the contemporary phenomenon she observed in New Haven while teaching at Yale. She analyzes the way a particular group of white male Ivy Leaguers she observed challenged each other to a kind of game of interracial conquest—to see how many racially diverse sexual experiences they could collect before graduation, with black women in the category of trophy. As hooks sees the phenomenon, the challenge went beyond the usual callous young male exploitation of young women, having as it did an unusual element of the desire for transformation, of the expectation that they would be radically altered by these encounters. "The point is to be changed by this convergence of pleasure and otherness," she explains.

Here is a changing premised on a thrust into extreme difference— into a dark unknown. To the sexual explorer, the body of the racial other represents uncharted territory, and, not surprisingly, the myth of the "primitive" is in operation as it promises pleasure in proportion to the darkness of the body. But hooks takes this question further, far beyond conventional moralism as well as beyond theoretical platitudes about others as objects. She says that there could be, at least in the one example she considers, a nostalgic desire on the part of the progeny of the conquerers to resurrect the history that brought them together with the black girls they pursue. "Imperialist nostalgia" that it is, it remembers selectively, but this is not to discount either the intensity of the longing or the political drawbacks of the inclination. "Most importantly it establishes a contemporary narrative where the suffering imposed by structures of domination on those designated Other is deflected by an emphasis on seduction and longing where the desire is not to make the Other over in one's image but to become the Other," she says. hooks puts the emphasis on displacement in this essay, where "becoming the Other" is about envy, about the radical chic that lays claim to myths of the superiority of the "primitive."[135] Desire even goes a step further; in this essay whose title is "Eating the Other," hooks indicates that the desire for the whole of the other takes on a devouring quality. And yet, one on one and one by one, mutual interpenetrations and becomings have historically transformed adjacent but racially distinct cultures, sometimes by absorption, sometimes by the inadvertent procreation that bell hooks doesn't mention here.

What I want to take from this essay more than anything else, however, is its idea that the historical asserts itself in every interracial sexual encounter. Every act is a reenactment. It is there in the tryst on the train that would seem to be a remarkable rearrangement of a historical paradigm: the white lady looks on *approvingly* as the white gentleman kisses her black maid, a historical turnabout that would seem to stand in front of the familiar paradigm in which the white lady strenuously *disapproves* of such a relation. A historical approach further suggests the aspect of sexual surrogacy in the brief moment, the "standing in," I have noted, that also recalls the plantation practice in which the black woman performed the white woman's sexual duties. The 1903 comedy, performed *over* these historical connotations, gives us that paradigm backward and upside down as comedy is wont to do: the white lady approves and the white gentleman is thwarted in his advance by the alliance of the woman and her maid. The maid gets the last word, however, rebuffing the scoundrel, and, although she laughs with the mistress, she firmly declines the role of surrogate. Or perhaps she just knows how to keep her job since she seems to be all smiles and starched white apron. If this early film fragment is finally incoherent on the subject of interracial sexuality, this merely signals the calculated oblivion of white society. If the brief comedy is coy and contradictory, it is no more so than its original audience. This is, of course, the predominantly white audience for whom interracial sexual relations simply did not exist. This is the audience that, all the while it plunks down its money to *see What Happened in the Tunnel*, still, in the end, would not want to *know* what happened on the train.

Paradigms of identification abound in *What Happened in the Tunnel*, and it could also be said that more than one cross-race "invitation" has been extended. In addition to the kisser–kissed paradigm, there is, of course, the one who gets kissed and the other who doesn't. And perhaps this is the most illustrative paradigm—the one that contains the mistress and the maid—for it is here that the audience would opt for the position of "I am being kissed" or "I am not being kissed," stronger, I would surmise, than the "I am kissing" position aligned with the hapless seducer. (I should add that I think that there is room here to consider the acceptance or rejection of the heterosexual kiss as a position equal in importance to race or gender. Wanting to be or not wanting to be kissed may override everything else.) The mistress–maid paradigm contains a host of positions, the richest possibilities of wantings-to-be, from interracial attraction to interracial envy. Importantly, bell hooks reminds us of the "white female envy of black women and their desire to 'be' imitation black women," and I should add that this is an envy that has its historical mirror image, the imitation white woman.[136] But the face-to-face encounter between the woman and her maid is no mirror encounter, and it complicates any attempt to devise a theory of cross-race identification based on the Hegelian self–other structure in which "opposites pass over into each other." Hegel, predating Marx's theory of class conflict and revolutionary change (which, as we know, was based on Hegel to begin with), gives us false hope; Kojève, writing with Marx behind him, is perhaps too sanguine when he imagines the one taking from the other in order to equalize the master–slave equation. The "switcheroo" on the train calls Hegel out and puts Kojève in check. The fantasy of the indistinguishability between master and slave is just that—a fantasy. This is neither to dispute the theory nor to dismiss the fantasy. It is just to note the similarity between our theory and the fantasy of that other other, the primitive narrator.

Race Movies: All-Black Everything

I have arrived at a place in my account where I need to leave the road of theoretical discourse in order to provide some kind of historical background. Faced with the problem of how to present this background, I confront nothing more nor less than the dilemma of how to represent real historical events with nothing more than linguistic signs lined up in rows—words on pages. Further, I face the difficulty of how to "tell" these events since my telling will by definition be a fictionalization of what is so often thought to be fact, a narrativization of not imaginary but real events. Although one could observe that most traditional historians do not conceive of what they do as having anything to do with the production of fictional narratives, at least one critical theorist has challenged historical writing on these grounds. In relation to the inescapable use of narrative in the representation of the historical real, Hayden White has asked, "How else can any past, which by definition comprises events, processes, structure, and so forth, considered to be no longer perceivable, be represented in either consciousness or discourse except in an 'imaginary' way?"[1] So I will be asking my reader to imagine and I will be imagining for my reader, but also, following the conventions of historical writing, I will need to create the perfect illusion that these past events are *not* being fictionalized but rather that they are revealing themselves, following the logic of "this happened then." This logic would seem to dictate the organization of any discourse that represents itself as historical.

African American history presents a special problem for the narrativization of the past in that its monumental project of restoration and reclamation must first claim that earlier narratives excluded significant portions of a rich and dense past and that this exclusion, this selection process, has been an ideological one. In contrast to older, highly ideological fictionalizations, then, any new account of African American history must be seen as *no longer a fiction* and—specifically—no longer a white fiction. This disparagement of older fictions is accompanied in this case by a deep longing for the irretrievable moments in the infinite past of the historical real, a wish for what cannot now and never will be again. The very attraction to the discourse of history might then be understood as a "desire for the real." Or, as Hayden White has delimited the particular appeal of this discourse, it proceeds to "make the real desirable," to "make it into an object of desire."[2] Desiring the African American past is also a way of wanting restitution as well as restoration, a desire that places a particular burden on the retelling of that past. Every retelling must be an amelioration. And note how the discourse of African American history, the narrative of inhumane treatment and brutal exclusionary practices, qualifies White's theorization. What is there to desire about such a historical past? But the real, no matter how gruesome or infuriating, still holds its attraction, even its fascination, if only because it is thought to be "the real" with an emphasis on the "the."[3]

In the history of African American film not only is the elusive real an "object of desire," but the many "lost" and consequently mourned films are coveted "objects of desire." Especially valued because they have vanished so dramatically (as in the case of Micheaux's *Within Our Gates*), these films are cherished as realizations of the real.[4] Such a discovery places a special burden on the historian. But once lost and now found, the events of the African American film past as well as the treasured objects of black culture ask to be interpreted and given form. And given the conventions of historical discourse, the historian is expected to "find" that form within the events themselves, that is, the historian cannot be seen to have "put" form and order into or onto the events. This, says Hayden White, is the "embarrassment of plot," that narrative device that must produce the order that cannot exactly be "found" in the chaos of events.[5] So it is that the writing of history, like the construction of classical Hollywood film, is the production of continuity as opposed to discontinuity, is an ironing out of the disorderly past in such a way as to give a smooth and seamless account of things.[6]

The imperatives of narrative form are no more apparent than in the rule of chronology, which dictates that the order of appearance of events in the narrative must follow the order of events in the original occurrence.[7] This happened and then this and then that. The structure demands firsts, and thus in the attempt to give form (and meaning) to the frenetic early days of black entrepreneurship in the American entertainment industry, we are obliged to locate beginning points as well as caesuras and ends, or rather to "choose" these points and, in choosing, *appear* to "locate" the preexistent. Our narrative must produce the *discovery* of blacks independently financing, shooting, and exhibiting motion pictures, and produce these events in chronological order, the order of "when" and "then." The issue of "when" is immediately before us if we consider the question of common knowledge about American film history. In the United States white and black cultural knowledge of motion picture history, then and now, has a distinct convergence at one point—the exhibition of D. W. Griffith's *The Birth of a Nation.* A serious study might reveal that whereas a few in either group would know that Griffith's film, the "masterpiece" that stirred black communities then and continues to anger so many blacks, was released as early as 1915, fewer would know anything about the blacks who themselves produced and directed motion pictures at about the same time. And fewer still would know that blacks produced and directed their own films *before* the release of *The Birth of a Nation.*[8] So dominant is *The Birth of a Nation* in the historical memory of this period that the idea of black-produced motion pictures *before* Griffith's cinematic provocation is almost unimaginable by whites and, although probably imaginable by blacks, may be completely unfamiliar to them.[9] And so to supplant this earlier narrative of beginnings, we will need to start our narrative before 1915.

This particular need to rewrite the historical record should come as no surprise to African Americans who have learned to expect that there will always be yet another case of a black artist or entrepreneur unburied and brought to light. Excavation, however, is only the first stage of reclamation; in the case of the black motion picture pioneers, although two major studies were published in the mid-1970s, the names and the discussions of the work of these trailblazers have been slow to enter popular knowledge and are only now being integrated into the scholarly overviews of the industry.[10] Common sense would suggest that if we begin the history of early African American cinema after *The Birth of a Nation,* we can account for the appearance of new black-owned companies beginning in 1916 by looking to the overwhelming African American critical response to Griffith's film, a response that could range from denunciations in the African American press to organized protest across the country. One assumes that early creative production is part of that protest, an "answer" in other terms, in another, more elaborate, rhetoric.

But there is a danger in going too far with the question of the strategy against the virulent racism of a single film. While there is every indication that the desire to produce films in order to disprove Griffith and coproducer Thomas Dixon, author of *The Clansman,* motivated the undaunted efforts of most of the early pioneers, we are still left with the question of how to account for pre-1915 production. How do we best answer this question? What motivated black motion picture producers *before The Birth of a Nation?* To focus exclusively on either Griffith's or Dixon's racism is to overlook an entire decade of offensive imagery, as we will see. To start with the black response to Griffith's film is to stress only the exceptionality of black motion picture production at the expense of seeing commonalities between white and black pioneers. Seeing the similarities means acknowledging that black directors and actors wanted to make movies for some of the same reasons that whites went into the business, and many of the same economic conditions that encouraged white successes made such black enterprises almost possible.

All such historical questions ask to be addressed straightforwardly and in the prose style of historical narrative—a style that is not allowed to comment on its own methods—and here I am reminded of Bill Nichols's description of documentary film as able to "talk about anything in the historical world except itself."[11] Historical narrative, like classical film style, requires the creation of the perfect illusion of a world without cuts or comments on itself. As I shift from one prose style into another, I am painfully aware of the prohibitions against critical interruption, the intervention of a discourse about the discourse that is doing the telling. Questions and critical points, while allowable, must be carefully blended in such a way as to respect the economy of chronology that drives historical discourse. Theoretical questions must serve the historical narrative and not threaten to become a rival discourse that attracts the attention of the reader. My reader may by now have surmised that I want to signal the difficulties of writing history that is also theoretical as well as to signal the difference between history that is theoretically informed and history that is intertwined with theoretical discourse. Here I am faced with the problem of the very conventions of writing, the structures of the writing style that would seem to require that the theory be folded into the historical narrative in such a way that it disappears—informing but not visibly altering that narrative. The alternative would be to respect the distinct style of historical writing, an acknowledgment that would produce the complete segregation of history and theory, and here I see no better way to highlight this problem than by an abrupt change in style as well as by the cautious separation of my short history from the discourse of theory.

A Short History of Race Movies

In many ways William Foster, who may have produced, written, and directed the first African American film in 1913, is typical of both black and white pioneer actors and directors in that he arrived at motion pictures through the theater, working as a business manager for Chicago's Pekin Theater. His first film, *The Railroad Porter*, a two-reel comedy in the slapstick style of Mack Sennett's Keystone Cops, was perhaps an early training ground for his later career producing black sound comedies for Pathé in Los Angeles.[12] Opening in Chicago at the States as well as the Grand theaters, the film did well, and later was exhibited with the first black newsreel featuring images of a YMCA parade. Like the later black pioneers (and most significantly Oscar Micheaux), Foster entered the field with great expectations, even traveling to Jacksonville, Florida, in 1914 to consider sites for building a studio and to investigate distribution possibilities for his films with Kalem, Lubin, and Pathé, white companies located there at that time. In his ties with the *Chicago Defender*, Foster illustrates as well what was distinctive about the early African American film industry—it diverged from the white mainstream in the strength of its connections with widely circulating black newspapers. Writing for these papers under the name of Juli Jones and later working as a marketer for the *Defender*, Foster was at the center of early attempts to establish mass communication vehicles in growing black urban centers.[13]

From this position Foster summarizes the aspirations of blacks in the first years of a new American industry in a long article in the *Indianapolis Freeman* published in 1913. The themes he touches on here encapsulate the dreams as well as the pitfalls ahead as enterprising blacks entered the untested motion picture business. In addition, Foster sketches out the public discourse on the representation of blacks in white-produced films, a discourse that would define the terms of the debate for the rest of the century. In 1913 the train was leaving the station. "What," he asks, "is the colored man doing to establish a place for himself in the motion picture world?" Already, Foster notes, the motion picture has done more than any other medium to awaken "race consciousness." However (and here is the starting place), this awakening, he says, has come as a negative reaction against the "traditional portrayal" of the Negro. As an example of this awakening, Foster refers to a number of cases in which black patrons protested caricatures, thus forcing exhibitors to take films off the screen. Two years before *The Birth of a Nation*, we have a building resentment against white portrayals of the Negro, exemplified by public protest, and we have as well the beginnings of a discourse that takes as its starting point the problem of representations that are not, as Foster says, "true to life."

Then, as now, the popular antidote to misrepresentation is the replacement of "false" with "true" representations. If protest is one side of the awakening race consciousness, the need for blacks to represent themselves is the other, for, as Foster explains: "It has made him hungry to see himself as he has come to be." The white man, Foster goes on, will not see and therefore will not show the black man's exceptionality: "Our brother white is born blind and unwilling to see the finer aspects and qualities of American Negro life."[14] And here the significant move for blacks is to take up the challenge to represent themselves as they see themselves in order to further their own cause. As important as the nascent critique of the image of the black in white film is Foster's estimation of the chances for the Negro in the motion picture business. Based on the first enthusiastic responses to *The Railroad Porter*, released five months earlier, Foster forsees that for Negroes the motion picture business could become "a great and profitable industry." In fact, more than any other industry, he asserts, motion pictures will produce "the biggest returns to Negroes for several investments."

At the same time that he predicts profits Foster also precisely pinpoints the single factor standing in the way of black success in the motion picture industry—white competition for the same profits. Uncannily describing the demise of the very enterprise that he is advocating, Foster confirms the attractiveness of the black motion picture market to the hypothetical white show business profiteer: "After awhile, however, when profit begins to loom into sight in little more than reasonable figures, then he suddenly realizes that the black will not rub off and he nestles close to the skin of the source of the profit." Despite what would appear to be "limited experience, the lack of technical knowledge, the deficiencies in business training," Foster argues that individuals or groups need to invest what they have, to boldly undertake business ventures, for if they do not, whites will inevitably "step in and grab off another rich commercial plum from what should be one of our own particular trees of desirable profit."[15] Foster would prove prophetic, and certainly by the time of the release of King Vidor's all-black-cast musical *Hallelujah* (1929), whites had discovered black culture as mainstream entertainment.[16] As numerous scholars have pointed out, there was a direct, irrefutable correspondence between the disappearance of race movies and Hollywood's discovery of the African American motion picture market, a development that produced a crisis for race movie pioneers at the end of the 1930s.[17]

Not surprisingly, for enterprising blacks like Foster, *The Birth of a Nation* only confirmed these two assumptions—the certainty that the black community would protest the images of Negros on the white screen and that there were profits to be made in the film business, as evidenced by the reports of the millions of dollars the film was taking in at the box office. At least two companies immediately took on Griffith's film in their announced promotions, and significantly these companies were backed by black professionals who bought shares of stock. In Jersey City, New Jersey, the Frederick Douglass Film Company in 1917 produced *The Colored American Winning His Suit,* stating in the pressbook: "The picture aims to offset the evil effects of certain photoplays that have libeled the Negro and criticized his friends."[18] Perhaps the most publically visible effort organized to "offset" the effects of *The Birth of a Nation,* however, was the production of *The Birth of a Race* by the Photoplay Corporation, a massive effort, organized in 1917, that solicited white as well as black investment and boasted 7,000 stockholders.[19] But this acclaimed effort was a colossal flop.

The story of the fiasco of the mixed-race *Birth of a Race* production begins with the efforts of Booker T. Washington's secretary Emmett J. Scott to negotiate the rights to *Up from Slavery,* which was originally to have been the basis of the film.[20] But over a two-year period the script took abrupt turns, with people from both the Tuskegee Institute and the NAACP involved with the white screenwriter at different times. Although W. E. B. Du Bois eventually dropped out of the project, he was for a time interested in launching a film, so interested that he and other NAACP members had discussions with Universal's Carl Laemmle.[21] As editor of the NAACP's *The Crisis,* Du Bois not only helped to formulate the terms of the protest against *The Birth of a Nation* in his editorials but also advocated the creation of a black motion picture tradition.[22] One is tempted to speculate about the contribution that Du Bois might have made to the history of African American cinema, but in retrospect it is clear that it was not intellect alone that was needed. What was needed was capital. The underfinanced *Birth of a Race* company and others were short-lived. After the fanfare of the premiere at Chicago's Blackstone Theatre in 1919, *The Birth of a Race* saw no widespread distribution. After *The Colored American Winning His Suit,* the Frederick Douglass Company went on to produce two more films, *The Scapegoat* in 1917, and a documentary in 1919, *Heroic Negro Soldiers of the World War,* a film that earned the company praise from the *New York Age:* "The company is owned and controlled by Negroes, whose aim is to present the better side of Negro life, and to use the screen as a means of bringing about better feeling between races."[23]

Despite this praise for the Frederick Douglass Company, it is the *Birth of a Race* company, more than any of the other minor companies, that has received the historical attention, perhaps because of the way it illustrates the incompatibility between Hollywood and the black community but also perhaps because of the availability of archival material—promotional materials as well as the film itself.[24] But the difference between the companies, beyond the issue of documentation, raises the question of what counts as a black film company in the silent era, finally an issue of how many produced films can be counted. Looking at the record, it would appear that the *Birth of a Race* company produced one film to the Frederick Douglass Company's three. Many other black companies produced one film that might or might not have actually been released, for it was standard practice among white as well as black independents to advertise moving pictures that might never get financing and that consequently were never shot. However, scholars are only now beginning to ask hard questions about the existence of prints. It would seem only judicious, then, given the state of research into these minor companies, to count as many as possible, which means that to our historical overview we should add the companies of Hunter C. Haynes and Peter P. Jones as well as the Unique Film Company and Virgil Williams's The Royal Gardens (Chicago); The Leigh Whipper Film Company, Colored Feature Photoplay, Inc., and The Downing Film Company (New York); Sidney P. Dones's The Booker T. Film Company and Rosebud Film Corporation (Los Angeles); Charles West's Peacock Photoplay Company (Danville, Virginia); J. William Clifford's Monumental Pictures Corporation (Washington, D.C.); and the Maurice Film Company (Detroit).[25]

Perhaps the best example of the rise and fall of early race cinema, the promise and the decline, is the Lincoln Motion Picture Company, legendary for its national distribution network as well as for its black star, Noble Johnson, whose success in Hollywood finally contributed directly first to the triumph and then to the demise of the young company. Starting in Los Angeles with an original capitalization of $75,000 and a small board of directors (Noble Johnson, company president; Clarence Brooks and his brother Dudley, actors; Dr. J. Thomas Smith, a wealthy druggist; and Harry A. Gant, the only white member, a cameraman), Lincoln completed *The Realization of a Negro's Ambition,* starring Noble Johnson, in

1916. The Lincoln Motion Picture Company had a fortuitous beginning, when an accident sidelined an actor in a Lubin Company film directed by Romaine Fielding that was shooting in Colorado in 1914.[26] An expert with horses, Noble Johnson was hired to drive a runaway stagecoach, a job that led immediately to a part as an Indian in *The Eagle's Nest* and to more employment with the Philadelphia-based company where he worked closely with Fielding, about whom he wrote to his brother, remarking that the director "did not know what race prejudice is." If he stayed with Fielding, Johnson expected that he would "push me up to the top in this business."

Quickly, the multitalented Johnson, who devised his own ingenious makeup, found his niche as a character actor, appearing in thirty-four films between 1915 and 1918. However, of all of the ethnic roles he played in his early career, from Mexicans to Native Americans, in only a few instances, such as a 1915 role in Universal's *The Lion's Ward* and later as Uncle Tom in *Topsy and Eva* (1927), did Johnson play Negro characters. Among Johnson's many minor roles in silent cinema was the part of a chariot driver in the Babylonian section of Griffith's *Intolerance* (1916); the fact that he had cast a black actor in that film apparently eluded the director.[27]

In the first years of the Lincoln Motion Picture Company the new entrepreneurs rode on the notoriety of Johnson, who starred after *The Realization of a Negro's Ambition* in both *The Trooper of Troop K* (1916) and *The Law of Nature* (1917), films in which he worked with cameraman Harry Gant, the company's only white officer. The popularity of these three films had much to do with Johnson, a box-office draw in the black community, but whereas black audiences considered that he was one of them and would go to see his Lubin or his Universal films, these companies neither promoted nor acknowledged Johnson's racial identity. The fledgling black company could not have foreseen how this very popularity would produce a competition between their films and those of the white studios.

In 1918 Universal Pictures made it a condition of Johnson's contract that although Lincoln could use his name and likeness as already employed in "existing publicity matter" for the three Lincoln pictures in which Johnson was featured, Lincoln could neither produce new advertising nor utilize existing advertising in new ways, including "any part of the negative or positive films, slides, stills, plates, cuts, heralds, or lithographs." Consistent with the legal practice at the time, the studio exerted control over the reproduction of the image of its employee under contract, but as Jesse Rhines has argued, the action against Lincoln seems

Noble Johnson, character actor, Universal Films

cutthroat, especially coming from Universal whose head, Carl Laemmle, had a reputation in the business for his generosity.[28] Effectively the arrangement speaks to the competition between two commodities—Noble Johnson as the star of Lincoln films and Noble Johnson as the costar of the currently running Universal serial *The Bull's Eye*. Although the contract made a special exception for the promotion that had already been produced for the three Lincoln films, effectively allowing the company to continue distribution of those films, implicit in the new contract was Universal's assertion of exclusive rights. Noble Johnson resigned from Lincoln, and the company's last two dramatic films, *A Man's Duty* (1919) and *By Right of Birth* (1921), starred instead Clarence Brooks.[29]

Noble Johnson as Uncle Tom
Topsy and Eva (dir. Del Lord, 1927)

While Noble Johnson's fame and popularity explained the draw of the Lincoln films, without the distribution network set up by Noble's younger brother George in Omaha, Nebraska, the Lincoln Company would never have become a national phenomenon, paving the way for others, most notably Oscar Micheaux. Starting with *The Realization of a Negro's Ambition*, which he first exhibited in two white-owned theaters in small black neighborhoods in Omaha, George Johnson established contacts with Tony Langston, editor of the *Chicago Defender*, and Romeo Daughterty, editor of New York's *Amsterdam News*, both of whom began to work as agents setting up exchanges in those major cities.[30] George had moved to Omaha from the all-black and thriving Muskogee, Oklahoma, where he ran the Johnson Real Estate Company, "The Hustling Real Estate Firm," selling lots by mail. In Omaha he divided his day between his two jobs, distributing motion pictures with the aid of a secretary out of an office in his home in the morning, and working a 3:30 P.M. to midnight shift as a postal clerk.[31]

The growth of Lincoln's distribution arm coincided with the appearance of black-owned and managed theaters around the country, a phenomenon paralleling the development of black-owned banks and hotels. Known in the South as the "Movie King," Durham, North Carolina's Frederick K. Watkins built theaters in Durham, High Point, and southern Virginia and was organizer and president of the National Negro Exhibitors of America.[32] This early rise of black capital would be understood as one of the ambiguous fruits of segregation.[33] Although some enterprising members of the black middle class would profit from the creation of white and black parallel institutions, and white society would be indecisive about whether profit was more important than racial segregation, in the end white capital cut deeply into the Negro market built by race movie producers.[34] In the short-lived heyday of race movies, which reached peak production in 1921, however, black producing companies and black exhibitors worked together to effect an arrangement somewhat like the vertical integration system of the Hollywood majors where motion picture product had an automatic exhibition guarantee in a theater owned by the producing studio.[35]

Circulated just before Noble Johnson left the company, a marketing survey conducted by Lincoln gives some indication of how this system worked and confirms the commitment of owners and managers (many of whom identified themselves as "colored" on the survey form) to screening all-black-cast films when they could find them.[36] Although the white-owned and managed Savoy in Birmingham, Alabama, as well as the black-owned and managed Washington Theatre in Okmulgee, Oklahoma, showed Noble Johnson's Universal Films to their black audiences, they reported that they could not get the Lincoln films. Several of the theaters that did show the Lincoln films reported that of the three Lincoln pictures, *The Trooper of Troop K* was the best, although the white-owned and managed Alamo in Washington, D.C., listed *The Law of Nature* as the "biggest drawing card." The black-owned and managed 700-seat Booker Washington in St. Louis and the 625-seat Palace in Louisville, Kentucky, were impressed with *Troop K*, but the Palace manager later wrote to George Johnson that *The Law of Nature* "took on like wild fire."[37]

These reports of the reception of the Lincoln films, progressively more popular with their black audiences and probably improved in production quality with each new release, suggest that the Lincoln Company was well positioned to profit just at the point when Noble Johnson resigned. However, the economics of early distribution were such that success was always elusive. The daily rental average was generally $25 and the company split the house proceeds sixty–forty with the theater, but Lincoln was always limited by the number of release prints it had in distribution, apparently never having more than five. Then there is the question of the number of theaters catering to black audiences that would need to book the films in order for Lincoln to make back the negative cost on each. Finally, although the creation of a distribution network certainly depended on advertising and reviews in an enthusiastic black press, it also relied heavily on the "wildcat" work of advance men who carried films from city to city to screen for exhibitors, who would then book them for later dates.[38]

The need for expanded markets, new capital, and more product kept George Johnson hustling, and after his brother left Lincoln in 1918, he continued to aggressively promote the company and to look for new angles. In 1919 the company produced *Lincoln News*, a composite of twenty-five scenes including footage of Kelly Miller, dean of Howard University, as well as of Madame Walker's hair preparations business at its original site in Denver. Three years later, Harry Gant shot footage of the U.S. Tenth Cavalry Unit in Fort Huachuca, Arizona; Johnson purchased newsreel footage of black troops in World War I from the French government. With the help of Robert L. Vann, publisher of The *Pittsburgh Courier* and a friend of the Lincoln Company, Johnson published a novelization of the fourth Lincoln dramatic feature, *A Man's Duty*, in his magazine, *The Competitor*. Finally, George Johnson wrote the screenplay for *By Right of Birth*, the last film to be produced by Lincoln. By that time, Johnson had moved to Los Angeles where he helped to secure the backing for the film from a wealthy dentist and supervised the premiere there—separate screenings, one for blacks and a second for whites at a theater in Riverside.[39] A sixth Lincoln drama, *The Heart of a Negro*, was planned for 1923 but was never produced.[40] Contributing to the company's difficulties were the flu epidemic and increased competition from white producers. A sign of the times: after the demise of the Lincoln Motion Picture Company, George Johnson started the National News Service out of his garage, again working his two jobs—the motion picture business by day and the U.S. post office by night. Until the end of his life he made a business and eventually a hobby of collecting and disseminating information about the status and progress of African Americans in the entertainment industry.[41]

During the same period that the Lincoln Motion Picture Company was experiencing the success that capitalized on the enthusiasm of a growing black urban audience, white producers also entered the race movies market, stepping in to meet demand. Richard J. Norman started the Norman Film Manufacturing Company in Florida in 1921, producing *The Crimson Skull,* shot in Boley, Oklahoma, another all-black town.[42] His *The Flying Ace* (1926), an action film featuring a black aviator hero, exemplifies the way traditional genres were often taken over or, one might say, "reinhabited" by an all-black cast in such a way as to rewrite the genre.[43] Another white company, New York–based Reol Productions, headed by Robert Levy, was linked to the Lafayette Players' all-black stock company, the source of talent for productions such as *The Burden of Race* (1921) and *The Call of His People* (1922), both serious dramas that dealt with the issues of interracial love and passing.[44] The films produced by the white companies have not survived any more than those of the black producing companies with the exception, perhaps, of those of the Colored Players of Philadelphia, where two of the four films completed between 1926 and 1929 are extant—*Ten Nights in a Barroom* (1926) and *The Scar of Shame* (1929).[45]

The Colored Players films represent a typical division of labor between black and white artists producing race pictures in this period. Produced specifically for black motion picture audiences, the films were directed and photographed by white professionals and improvised by black actors from a story written by the white producer, David Starkman. Although the Philadelphia production group was really run by Starkman, the idea for the Colored Players originally came from black vaudeville comedian Sherman H. Dudley, Jr., who is listed in the credits as producer of *The Scar of Shame* and who served as company president.[46] Starkman, who owned a black theater in Philadelphia, was no more successful financially than the Lincoln Company, and he went into debt after producing *The Scar of Shame.*[47]

By all accounts the race movie business was a rocky one—a new venture in an industry that in the silent era was already wild and unruly. Even after a company raised the funds to go into production through stock sales or any other creative means and finally managed to pay for a print to distribute, there was always the challenge of making back the investment through distribution in a exhibition environment that was intensely competitive and slightly shady. Richard J. Norman complained not only about the difficulty he had receiving his share of the box-office receipts from theaters but also the trouble he had on one occasion getting his money from his own employee who took the Norman films on the road.[48] Evidence of the competitiveness that marked the race movie business in the early years was George P. Johnson's effort to plant his brother-in-law as a spy within the Micheaux organization in Chicago.[49] In retrospect, it is miraculous that so many companies raised the capital to start up and that race movies were distributed and seen at all by black audiences, particularly given the relative size of the industry in the beginning. In 1921, understood as the peak year, Richard Norman estimated that there were just 121 theaters he considered outlets for his race movies as compared to the 22,000 white theaters across the country.[50] The evidence of the vitality of the race movie business based on the black press and company records is contradictory and needs to be supplemented with interviews with spectators who recall their own moviegoing experiences. Other clues may help us assess the meaning of these films for segregated audiences: some of the films themselves survive, and there is one remnant of this "lost" industry that is readily available—the plot synopsis.[51]

Uplift Narratives

All that remains of the five dramatic films produced by the Lincoln Company is one reel of *By Right of Birth*, a situation that would lead us to think of these pictures as phantom films, irretrievably lost.[52] But while the moving images may have long since been destroyed, the remains of the narratives still exist, encrypted in plot summaries. Never a respectable form, the plot summary is designed to give us substantially less than the narrative from which it has been extracted, laid out end to end. The summary is thus always thought to be a reduction and diminution of the work itself, hence its relative low esteem and the total literary indifference toward this form. And yet the plot summary has crucial elements in common with the narrative from which it is culled. It is, in fact, a minor narrative in and of itself, with its intense concentration on "what happens," its observation of the rules of narrative causality (this happened and then this), and its identification of causal agents as well as the order of events. The plot summary is also a short lesson in what it is that literary narrative tries so hard to do without the aid of iconic signs and without the appeal to "vision." Addressing this question of what it is that the literary narrative attempts to achieve, Roland Barthes argues that, contrary to popular assumptions, it neither *shows* nor *imitates*. It wants to do much more. "The function of narrative," he says, "is not to '*represent*,' it is to *constitute* a spectacle."[53] Here the literary narrative (whether novel or historical treatise) tries to "constitute" a world with nothing more than words, tries with such a poverty of signs to produce so much. In contrast, the highly iconic moving picture dramatization easily constitutes a spectacle because, so effortlessly as I have been urging, it is a "telling that is also a showing."[54] The existing plot summaries, if nothing else, tell us that race movie pioneers envisioned scenarios of success, magnified in detail as well as significance on the big screen.

For the early African American film pioneers, the chance to tell their stories on film, in public, to each other, but also to white audiences wherever possible, was a chance to tell themselves into existence as a group, to constitute themselves as a visible group in the way that they wanted to be seen. At this moment and for these people there is a double move— on the one hand a rejection of the white version of the American Negro, on the other hand a consolidation and a constitution of race identity. This double, two-pronged move from the minority position is the strategy that has been so productive in the history of African American culture. To conceive of the assertion of African American culture as a double strategy is to insist on the productiveness of the negation, which we would not want to underestimate. "We only become what we are by the radical and deep-seated refusal of that which others have made of us," Jean-Paul Sartre once wrote.[55] Following this thesis of the productiveness of the refusal, race movies were about becoming a "race" purely and simply because they were so consciously counterposed to what the Negro was not.

This understanding of the productivity of negation suggests a more nuanced approach to one of the recurring themes of the protest against *The Birth of a Nation*—the charge that the white man *did not know* the black man. If the white man did not and could not know, he had to be told: the impetus to narrate is an impetus to fill in what is missing. In the black answers to *The Birth of a Nation*, narration not only supplies knowledge; it tries to correct and even to rectify things. As Ed Branigan has written about knowledge imbalance in relation to film, "Narration comes into being when knowledge is unevenly distributed."[56] In this historical example, new tellings and retellings of old stories significantly redistribute knowledge as "what was known to be true" challenged what was "thought to be" about black American life. These race movie narratives, above all, set out to constitute a world that was the antithesis of what white America thought black America to be. But consider for a moment what it was that was totally beyond the cognizance of white Americans. What was it that the race pioneers wanted to say that would redress the situation? The world constituted by race movies was a thoroughly middle class world. The knowledge supplied by race movies was the knowledge that blacks were as educated, as rich, and as respectable as whites, a point to which I will return to in the following chapter.

Finally, it did not matter exactly how many blacks "were or weren't" middle class achievers because what was important was the challenge to white assumptions that blacks could not possibly be this or that.

Like much of the black literary production of the day, then, race movies were thoroughly imbued with the spirit and the letter of uplift, the mode in which race consciousness was publically articulated in the early part of the twentieth century. Uplift, a conflation of social and moral elevation, sent the message that moral advance meant social advance, as though the one were the effect of the other. The Lincoln narratives, in the best spirit of uplift, were moral tales of self-reliance, resourcefulness, and exceptionality in which the hero's ambitions are achieved in the same way that race prejudice is thought to be overcome—by demonstrations of the way in which he is *just as* accomplished as or *just like* a white hero. In *The Realization of a Negro's Ambition* (1916), the hero is a civil engineering graduate of Tuskegee Institute who is denied a job on a California oil field because of his race and so must prove himself worthy of the job by rescuing the white daughter of the oil company owner. The owner's gratitude wins him the job, which offers the hero a chance to drill for oil on his own father's farm. Opportunity thus leads him directly back to his "own people," a recurring narrative device in race movies, which restrict action to an all-black world within which everything is won or lost—a circumscribed miniature of the white world. In *Realization*, the hero must thus also win his way with wealthy blacks who scheme against him as well as against the light-skinned heroine whom he finally marries after he becomes wealthy as a consequence of striking oil on the family farm.

The Lincoln narratives feature middle class enigmas: Can the hero get a job commensurate with his education? Will he successfully engineer the discovery of oil on land owned by his family? Will the girl agree to marry him after he becomes rich? But *to whom* are these questions addressed? Consistent with these kinds of dilemmas, the ideology of uplift, although middle class specific, would resonate across class lines. However, these dilemmas only resonated because of the split message of uplift. With its contradictory connotations, uplift's message was really two messages, each of which could be seen as addressing a different social segment. As Kevin Gaines identifies these two connotations, the one had to do with the high-minded and generous social aspiration held over from emancipation and the other with a considerably less generous and genuinely exclusive aspiration that limited success to the few. The contradictory program imagined by these few might well have been articulated, says Gaines, as nothing more nor less than "Negro improvement through class stratification as race progress."[57] Unfortunately, one race progress strategy would cancel out the other.

While "race progress" was upholding, indeed nurturing, a black elite, enforcing a class system within the black community, "race progress" could not at the same time be the advancement of *all* of the members of the race. And it was precisely where the black elite stepped onto the lower classes on the way up that the issues arose, issues that in turn produced the feelings and fears that race movies managed. In disguised form, race movies dealt with embarrassment—the embarrassment that the upward moving group felt toward the lower classes, the group that the middle class despaired over but that they also "needed," that they "required" in an ideological sense. For uplift ideology colluded in the racism of what was called "the Negro problem," a problem concretized for all to see in the much-maligned Negro "stereotype." Thus Gaines explains stereotypage as a consequence of the double function of uplift: "While the ideology of a 'better class' of blacks challenged dehumanizing stereotypes, it also exploited them, and could never fully escape them—this elite version of uplift ideology assented to the racist formulation of 'the Negro problem' by projecting onto other blacks dominant images of racialized pathology."[58] "Betterment" was, of course, one of the more seductive versions of uplift, difficult to criticize because of the way it appeared to imagine a universal improvement. Difficult to see is the way that middle class blacks were perhaps trapped by the desire for betterment, a desire that automatically (by the alignment with white aspirations) meant distancing themselves from the lower class against whom they were measured. For our purposes it will be important to always recognize this social-class double bind, particularly as it is found behind the pejorative stereotype.[59] Without dismissing the aspirations, then, we need to look at the way uplift came down, and in the teens and twenties uplift in practice set one class against another.

In the race movie betterment narrative, the model of how to be "better" was the middle class character who might reach out to and even marry one of the downtrodden class. But note the way the elevation of the elite *one* is always predictably paid for by the problem class *other*, and since the measurement of success is always based on the distance between the one and the other, the race hierarchy is invariably affirmed. At least one character, the hapless example, must be left at the bottom, uplift's casualty. T. S. Stribling's *Birthright*, popular in the black community, illustrates this principle of the class distance that elevates the hero, here a Harvard graduate who returns to the backwardness of his southern hometown where he is only able to rescue one woman from the ignorance and lawlessness of the black community that is sunken low in the mud of white corruption.[60] He must marry the woman who is pregnant by another man and take her back to Boston with him, an act of admission that he cannot finally save the town through education. On the theory of "one by one," if he cannot save the town, he can at least lift up his new family because he has a Harvard degree. One Harvard degree is thus set against the education of the children of an entire town. An archetypal race pride narrative, *Birthright* so appealed to filmmaker Micheaux that he adapted it twice for film, producing a silent version in 1924 and a sound version in 1938.

Another example of the betterment narrative, Lincoln's highly popular *Trooper of Troop K* (1916) contrasts Noble Johnson's "Shiftless Joe" with two middle class characters, the refined Clara and her suitor. Representing two approaches to "the Negro problem"—rejection or charity—the film discredits the suitor who rejects Joe in contrast with Clara who has faith in him. Clara is in fact credited with Joe's eventual success, a feat of bravery—the rescue of his captain—for which he is decorated and promoted. Given the backdrop of the historic victory of the all-black Tenth Cavalry unit against Mexican troops at Carrizal, however, one could assume that Joe's reformation is achieved by military discipline rather than Clara's belief in him. But the issue in this film is what the middle class can do to help solve the problem of every "Shiftless Joe." The lesson is brought home by Clara's choice. Turning away the suitor who failed to see Joe's potential, she chooses Joe who is the "better" of the two because he has allowed himself to be "improved."

In many ways The Colored Players of Philadelphia's *The Scar of Shame* (1929) shares the same difficulties in dealing with "the Negro problem" as Lincoln's *Trooper of Troop K*. The "problem Negro" must be seen as redeemable, that is, worthy of redemption by a respectable Negro, a character who is unusual in his or her capacity to see the value in another. The "problem" is thus framed as a difficulty that can be met by a caring and concerned individual who single-handedly rescues the lower class Negro. However, in *The Scar of Shame*, where the attempt to uplift is also staged as a gripping rescue scene, the upper class comes into direct conflict with the lower, a conflict that is unresolved, as we will see, for ideological reasons. What are these reasons?

The central victim of the story, Louise Howard (played by Lucia Lynn Moses), is molested by her shiftless father Spike and rescued by Alvin Hillyard, an aspiring composer and pianist (Harry Henderson). Hillyard marries Louise to protect her from the father who continues to assault her, thus lifting her out of the lower class. But Alvin's upper class mother is not told of the union, and Louise feels the sting of her disapproval. Soon after their marriage, the father's gambler friend Eddie Black conspires with him to kidnap Louise and to put her to work as a "lure" in a speakeasy. Caught in a pistol crossfire between Eddie and Alvin, who tries to prevent the abduction, Louise is wounded in the neck, "her beauty marred for life," according to a newspaper headline in the film. Alvin, although innocent, goes to jail for the crime, and Louise takes up a life of prostitution and gambling. When Alvin escapes from jail and the two meet again, he has become engaged to the daughter of the powerful black lawyer Hathaway (Lawrence Chenault), who frequents Eddie's speakeasy and becomes Louise's lover. Louise tries to win Alvin back, and when at the end of the film she fails, she takes poison, expiring alone in her candlelit apartment adjacent to the speakeasy. Louise's suicide note, in which she confesses that she had been scarred by Eddie's gun and not Alvin's, symbolically frees Alvin to marry Alice Hathaway, who although not necessarily lighter than the exceedingly light-skinned Louise, is, however, his social equal.[61]

Which class is then responsible for Louise's tragic death? In the preferred version of social conflict in *The Scar of Shame*, the highest and lowest classes in black society, as I am arguing, are responsible for the reputation of the lower orders and especially for the degradation and mistreatment of black women. The dual responsibility interpretation also encourages the discovery of a second victim—Alvin (who his landlady, Mrs. Lucretia Green, expects will become "the leading composer of our race"). Alvin is imprisoned as the direct consequence of the downward pull of the more disreputable Negro element—Eddie, Spike, and even Louise (since she works in league with them). Louise's confession reveals not only that it was the shot from Eddie's gun that injured her, but that Eddie and Spike prevented her from telling the truth at the time of Alvin's trial.

The structure of *The Scar of Shame* further supports the case for the culpability of the upper as well as the lower classes. Plotting to separate Alvin and Louise by sending a fake telegram to Alvin that states that his mother is seriously ill, Eddie and Spike drag Louise back to the gutter. If the lower classes force her into prostitution, the aristocratic class contributes to the degradation of the black woman in yet another way. The arrival of the fake telegram occasions Alvin's confession to Louise that his mother does not know that they have married. (Title: "Caste is one of the things that mother is very determined about. You don't belong to our set.") The Negro aristocracy and the lower orders appear to act in league with one another. This characterization of the two classes at the extreme ends of the social spectrum corresponds with the kind of scapegoating seen in the black community during this period. While the lower classes were viewed as dragging others down, the higher were seen as erecting impossible hurdles for other blacks while clambering upward on their backs.[62] One could assume from this view of the upper and lower classes that the film was positioning its audience in the one group not implicated—the middle class.[63]

The upper or aristocratic class held to an elaborate rationale for maintaining their distinctness from the lower levels, engendering certain hostility. In justifying their separateness, those who considered themselves superior held that they would inspire the lower orders to improve themselves by example. The author of *Sketches of Higher Class of Colored Society in Philadelphia* writes: "If the virtuous and exemplary members of society should not keep aloof from the vicious and worthless, they would furnish no example to the latter to strive to make themselves reputable, and of like consideration. By associating with such persons we not only thereby give countenance to their doings, but we degrade ourselves to their level, and are adjudged accordingly."[64] Thus the upper class strategy was that full acceptance depended on proving that blacks could be equal to whites in their cultured tastes and their achievements, hence the tight circle dedicated so fiercely to pursing "finer things."

Although sensitive themselves about being mistaken for the serving class, some elite families saw nothing inconsistent in employing other blacks as servants, a phenomenon represented in *The Scar of Shame* by the scene in which the butler stands in for Alvin's snobbish mother, announcing to her son that she is not at home. This butler also represents a Philadelphia phenomenon—black servants employed by elites, or "elights" as they were sometimes called in reference to the skin color that historically underwrote their status. In his turn-of-the-century study of Philadelphia, W. E. B. Du Bois found that in the 277 upper class families he studied, 52 kept servants. Although it was Du Bois's conviction that the upper classes should help the lower to rise, he found this group too economically unstable and strategically self-protective to do so. As he explains it, "the class which should lead refused to head any race movement on the plea that thus they draw the very color line against which they protest."[65] Or to take a position against racial discrimination would be to distinguish themselves even further from whites and thus cut themselves off from the small, possibly imagined, advantage they enjoyed. And this slim imaginary advantage was the very edge that hypothetically would raise the whole.

Du Bois helps us to make a distinction between the elite blacks as portrayed in *The Scar of Shame* and the class of self-educated blacks who produced race movies, with the former hesitant to "draw the color line" at all and the latter pronouncing that line by the very production of race movies. The dilemma of the race movie producers was that while they tried fruitlessly to get their films booked into white theaters and to convince white distributors to handle their films, the very commodity they were producing "drew the line" between black and white. The all-black cast was itself an allegory for the rule that lined people up—all one race on one side and all the other on the opposite side. Curiously, as we will see, race movies were simultaneously about separation and assimilation, and the "race men" who made them, those most dedicated to advancement, were often of two minds about their goals.

The class hierarchy within the black community is relevant here, not only because it was the subtext of a number of the films produced for black audiences in the silent era. This separate class system could be understood as a system below the color line within a larger system encompassing the color line. Perhaps Adrienne Rich's explanation of the relationship between race and class helps us to understand the functioning of the double system when she says that "[c]lass breaks down over color, then is reconstituted within color lines."[66] Given this double system, black elites were placed in a dual position amounting to two class positions at once, the one stacked on top of the other. The class privilege elites enjoyed in the black community was automatically revoked when they entered the white one, a situation never acknowledged by an oblivious white society. Thus, as Kevin Gaines describes the elites, they were in the contradictory position of being at once an "aspiring social class" and a "racially subordinated caste."[67]

Within the black community in the 1920s, the class system was in the process of further reconstitution and realignment as the late nineteenth-century model concentrating a few at the top and 80 to 90 percent at the bottom was giving way to a configuration that placed more in the middle.[68] Race movies, avowedly about, by, and for the black middle class that did not yet exist, would make their contribution to this reconfiguration by depicting such a class. One could also say that as enterprising blacks raised the capital to produce their first feature films, they were shoring up their own position in the middle class. Yet social class in and of itself is not constitutive of a sociology of early black filmmaking, since region may also be a significant factor, particularly as it relates to opportunity. Although the East Coast seems to have produced some important activity, most notably the Frederick Douglass Company in New Jersey started by black professionals, one finds that it is the Midwest and the

West that "cradled" the significant black film pioneers. Chicago, for instance, can claim many more black film start-ups before 1927 than any other American city. From William A. Foster in 1913 to Oscar Micheaux, whose first production office was located there around 1918, Chicago was the urban center that offered the right conditions—a strong black press, black capital, and a growing black audience for mass entertainment.[69] To highlight Chicago, however, is not to overlook the connection between the Midwest and the West, a connection made by Micheaux himself as he left the city to homestead in South Dakota where he wrote the early novels on which his first film, *The Homesteader* (1919), was based. Micheaux was then a dramatic exception to Houston Baker's assertion that the "tales of pioneers enduring the hardships of the West for the promise of immense wealth are not the tales of black America."[70]

From the vantage of the West as Micheaux characterized it in his novels, one saw nothing but the open space of opportunity—land "free" to the black homesteader, and few, if any, white people within miles. Discrimination was diluted by the space between the homesteaders, and anything looked possible after the seasons of victory against the elements.[71] Both Noble and George Johnson, born in Colorado and raised by a father who made his living training horses, could similarly be understood in relation to the stance of the black westerner about whom we need to know more from historians.[72] There would be something audacious about starting a motion picture company as the Johnson brothers did in 1916, about taking a risk against great odds, about imagining a community of blacks stretched across the nation, a network connected by train, telegram, and postal delivery. One had to think on a very large scale of thousands of other black people willing to pay to see black-produced entertainment on the screen. From within the entertainment industry, the leap was only a little less amazing. From the vaudeville successes of Bert Williams and the traveling road shows that predated motion pictures to the black theatrical groups like the legendary Lafayette Players and to the Pekin Theatre in Chicago, the move into motion pictures was within reach.[73] To shoot a motion picture required a script, some actors, and enough capital to rent a Kodak package that included camera, lights, and operator. A studio was never absolutely necessary. Although Oscar Micheaux would later use the old Selig studio in Chicago, in these years filmmakers borrowed houses or shot outdoors on location. But the leap from outside the theatrical world into motion pictures was a much further one. What was significantly new about Oscar Micheaux and George P. Johnson was that they came from outside the theatrical world to think beyond the conception of the picture itself to

Jean Baptiste (Charles D. Lucas) and Agnes Stewart (Iris Hall)
The Homesteader (dir. Oscar Micheaux, 1919)

the promotion, distribution, and exhibition of black mass entertainment. What they envisioned was a nationally distributed cinema that would not only foster race consciousness for the good of American Negroes but a cinema that would be wildly popular with their intended audiences.

Here, at the mention of promotion and reception, is where comparisons between race movies and the Harlem Renaissance literary movement of the same period break down. In contrast with New York's cultured black elite, the race movie pioneers were by and large alien to the new middle class, and we would misunderstand them if we were to try too hard to disassociate them from the world of hucksterism and ballyhoo. We especially run the risk of mischaracterizing the paradoxical Micheaux, who George Johnson himself described as a "big unscrupulous grafter" at the same time that he praised him as "a man who produced more good Negro films than anyone."[74] Johnson watched Micheaux's fortunes as closely as he could from Omaha, Nebraska, and later from Los Angeles, critically commenting on his films and noting his mercurial

Orlean (Evelyn Preer)
The Homesteader

rise and fall, counting his rapid-fire releases (twenty between 1918 and 1927), tabulating his finances, and recording his trouble staying afloat. But aggressive as he was in promoting Lincoln Motion Pictures and expanding its markets, George Johnson never had the nerve to join the fast-talking Micheaux when the producer asked him to work as his distribution manager, apparently preferring the security of his job with the U.S. postal service.[75]

From Johnson's papers we get a sense of the way the black pioneers scrambled and conned and competed fiercely with one another. But it was not only their business practices that would set them apart from the black aristocracy as well as from many others in the black middle class— it was the fact that they produced the popular entertainment so disdained by the churches. Understandably, the very entertainment that the clean-livers would have condemned was approached by the race pioneers with a kind of missionary zeal, with the conviction that black-produced films could do a great moral service by their example. For Micheaux, it was not only the example of the characters in his films who advanced themselves but the example of his own life that he directed at an audience of those race members who lagged behind. In *The Conquest*, another one of his autobiographical characters announces: "One of the greatest tasks of my life has been to convince a certain class of my racial acquaintances that a colored man can be anything."[76]

The "Big Unscrupulous Grafter"

From Johnson's papers we also glean something of Micheaux the man, although the version presented must be understood in light of the very competition to which I have just referred, and thus through the filter of George Johnson's unabashed desire to write himself into a history from which he feared he would be excluded. It is somewhat ironic that Johnson would write at least five short accounts of Micheaux's life, insisting in these "bios" that the filmmaker's story was worthy of publication as a book, and yet, to date, no definitive biography of Micheaux has been attempted. And it is not as though these biographies bring us any closer to that biography either, especially since the five versions of Micheaux's life and career tell us perhaps as much about George Johnson, the postal worker who wanted so much to be involved in the business transactions of an emerging black middle class and ended up not one of the captains of the race movie industry but the archivist of it. For Johnson's biographies of Micheaux tell us that he is remembering selectively and reworking his version of history over time, perhaps in his retirement. Although the biographies are not dated, at least one refers to the last known Micheaux production in 1948; over the years, though the emphases change, some of the phraseology remains the same, suggesting that Johnson fixed some aspects of the Micheaux story in his mind, but also that he was returning to the same dog-eared typescripts. Clearly Johnson is also rereading correspondence between himself and Micheaux as well as telegrams that he kept, since he quotes from this material, but because the correspondence also contradicts Johnson's account, it would seem that he is relying on a memory that is overflowing with other versions of events.

Johnson at times appears to be rehearsing the story he longs to tell a reporter, a listener, someone who would write the life history of the man about whom he equivocates, calling him "one of the most colorful characters in the history of the Negro in motion pictures," but "whose record while none too ivory is at least too interesting and valuable to be overlooked."[77] While in one sketch Johnson calls Micheaux the "world's greatest producer of all Negro Film Productions," in another he is merely a "very good author and the largest producer of Negro Films," and in still another he "produced more good Negro films than anyone and many of them from books he wrote and had published."[78] Consistently the accounts state that Micheaux was born in 1884 in Metropolis, Illinois, and that at twenty-five he purchased a relinquishment on farmland in South Dakota, and one states that the large homestead amounted to 800 acres of land on the Rosebud Reservation.[79] Although Johnson does not explain why Micheaux left farming, he does place him in Sioux City, Iowa, in 1915, and repeats the legend that the writer walked through the states of South Dakota, Iowa, and Nebraska, selling his book to white farmers. For Johnson, there always seems to be only one book, although in these early years Micheaux would have been selling his first two novels, *The Conquest,* published in 1913, and *The Forged Note,* published two years later.[80]

The one book for Johnson is the 1917 *The Homesteader,* the semi-autobiographical novel that it is now clear is a rewrite of *The Conquest.*[81] While Micheaux was to write the story of his life on the prairie and publish it at least three times, the final time in *The Wind from Nowhere,* George Johnson would also try to write and rewrite Micheaux's story, but apparently without much assistance from the novels, relying instead on his correspondence files and his clouding memory.[82] He asserts at least twice that in *The Homesteader* Micheaux could be understood as substituting Negro characters for white persons he had known, a revealing observation that suggests that Johnson was recalling this from his viewing of the all-black-cast film rather than from his reading of the novel, in which there are many white characters and in which the black characters, with the exception of the light-skinned heroine, are largely the hero's family members.

Where George Johnson's memory is the most revealing, however, is in the spelling of Oscar Micheaux's surname. In the correspondence from the 1918 period in which he was in close contact with the filmmaker, Johnson often spelled the name incorrectly, at least once ending it with a "z" instead of an "x," and at other times rendering it as "Mitcheaux." In later years Johnson not only adds a "t," but he sometimes drops the "a," an Anglicization of the French name to "Mitcheux," another indication that the retired postal worker was losing touch with some of the original details. Adding to the story some details and dropping others (like the addition of a "t" and the subtraction of an "a") smoothed out the rough places in Johnson's memory, which was periodically returning to these events and establishing the short-lived Lincoln Company in relation to Micheaux's larger enterprise.[83] That Johnson was not only having difficulty remembering but that he was struggling with the relative success of the Micheaux Company is perhaps best indicated by the trouble he has settling on the number of films produced by his rival, an estimation that ranges widely from "25 or more" or "about 30," and in one of the same sketches both "over 40" and "30 or more." It should be noted that George Johnson was an inveterate chronicler, list maker, and collector who typed up lists of the film appearances of his brother Noble and other black actors, and at one point typed a list of the Micheaux films along with their release dates, a list that confirms that he had continued to follow the Micheaux career into the sound era. Johnson is closer to estimations of contemporary scholars in his "over 40," but the number of Micheaux films is still an open question.[84]

Looking back over Micheaux's fascinating life as well as his own as the postal worker who had a brief encounter with importance, George Johnson finally discovers the moment that belongs to him, that places him at the launching of Micheaux's career and that allows him to claim, "And I am responsible for it."[85] And this is the moment that he appears to have worked over more than the other moments, worked over so often, perhaps, that it becomes increasingly unclear to Johnson exactly what happened, how it was that Micheaux came to negotiate with the Lincoln Company over the production of his third book, and how it was that the novel *The Homesteader* first came to his attention in Omaha.[86]

Accounts of the negotiations between Micheaux and the Lincoln Company have become legendary, and all seem to focus on Micheaux's insistence that he direct *The Homesteader* himself.[87] However, neither the correspondence nor George Johnson's various Micheaux "memoirs" support this version, since the correspondence indicates that a cordial meeting took place between the two in Omaha in late May 1918. Although in one letter after the Omaha trip Micheaux suggests that he could be of assistance in the production of the film and even play the part of N. Justine McCarthy, the villain, most of this letter is concerned with his plan for adapting the novel.[88] Even the letter that appears to contain Micheaux's "offer" to the Lincoln Company is almost exclusively concerned with the details of book royalties, which would make sense given Micheaux's experience in book publishing and the fact that he was at this point a total novice when it came to the motion picture industry.[89] In the Micheaux "memoir" that contains the fullest account of the negotiations, George Johnson is vague about the arrangements, and it is not even clear whether it was Lincoln or Micheaux who backed out: "As he knew nothing of film production, had no Los Angeles connections or any money either, we could not come to any agreement. We offered to let him come to Los Angeles and help as an advisor."[90] It may be that George Johnson came the closest to understanding what transpired when in retrospect he began to think of the negotiations as more important for the ideas they gave Micheaux than for anything else. He concludes, "But all this had put the film bug in Mitcheaux's ear and he decided that he didn't need Lincoln."[91]

Oscar Micheaux and George Johnson would have other dealings soon after Micheaux went ahead with the production of *The Homesteader*. Most notably, around 1920, Micheaux, by then into the production of his third and fourth features, *The Brute* and *The Symbol of the Unconquered*, offered the other a position as distribution manager at $1,800 per year, an offer that Johnson finally turned down, as I earlier mentioned, even though he would still advocate a merger between the Lincoln and Micheaux companies, convinced that the latter company needed Lincoln's expertise.[92] Thomas Cripps comes to the conclusion regarding these discussions between Micheaux, Lincoln, and *Pittsburgh Courier* publisher Robert L. Vann that Vann did not trust George Johnson and most of all wanted Micheaux in on the deal.[93] Whatever the reasons, the second attempt at a Lincoln–Micheaux collaboration never materialized.[94]

Given the importance of these negotiations and the evidence that George Johnson was saving documentation and even writing this episode ("A Million Dollar Negro Film Deal Fell Through") as a separate chapter in his history of black independent cinema, it is curious why it is not included in his biographical sketch. Instead, in his history Johnson stresses the financial vicissitudes of the Micheaux operation. He relates the story of how, when it became clear that there was no arrangement with the Lincoln Company to film his book, Micheaux decided to raise the capital to produce it himself, returning to the white farmers who had bought his books to sell them stock in his production company at $100 per share. Later Johnson recorded his own attempts to locate these stockholders, who he determines never realized any dividends, but whose investment made it possible for Micheaux to raise enough of his $15,000 budget to begin shooting.[95]

Remarkably, in less than a year after his first discussions with Johnson, Micheaux had produced and directed his own version of *The Homesteader*, and Johnson, knowing the difficulties of the business, appears somewhat incredulous at the beginner's good fortune. What also impressed Johnson was the rapidity of the growth of the Micheaux organization, which, after its incarnation as the Western Book Supply Company in Sioux City, Iowa, moved to Chicago where Swan Micheaux joined his brother as manager of the new company, now the Micheaux Film Corporation, in 1920. And Johnson gleefully chronicles the demise of that company. Four of Johnson's five versions of Micheaux's career contain a reference to the February 1928 declaration of bankruptcy, and three report that at the time the company had liabilities of $7,837 and assets of $1,400.

But in sticking so closely to his interpretation of Micheaux ("quite a talker," a "big unscrupulous grafter," and a "clever manipulator"), Johnson may have missed the complexity, and he certainly only took account of a fraction of the earliest portion of a career that lasted for three decades, an especially impressive record in contrast with the five short years in which the Lincoln Company was able to produce and distribute films. Others would contradict Johnson, most notably Lorenzo Tucker, who found Micheaux generous and fair-minded, particularly with his actors.[96] Micheaux's own version of the 1928 bankruptcy became the *Wages of Sin*, in which he told the story of a brother's corruption and betrayal, generally understood to be his own view of his partnership with Swan Micheaux in the early Chicago years. It is revealing that Johnson never turns to Micheaux's version of himself available in the persona of the heroes of four of his seven novels.[97]

There is yet another angle on the "big unscrupulous grafter" characterization that George Johnson does not take. That is the one that allows us to understand Micheaux as a showman, for it must be said that the newcomer was entering a preexisting tradition and learning the motion picture business as adroitly as he must have learned farming. That the tradition into which he stepped was one in which fast talk and exaggeration were rewarded and canny manipulation a requisite for success is undeniable, and placing Micheaux in this tradition helps us to appreciate not only the particularity of his legacy but the historical specificity of it. For Micheaux in his role as motion picture exhibitor and press agent stepped into the venerable tradition of the American showman descended from the circus sideshow promoter P. T. Barnum.[98] His talents for overstatement, for public show, and for the creation of colorful popular discourse are evident as early as the publicity for *The Homesteader*, which George Johnson notes was billed as "a powerful drama of the great American Northwest into which has been deftly interwoven the most subtle American problem—the race question."[99]

Micheaux's own printed promotion, a vehicle of the new Micheaux Book and Film Company, features his credentials as a publicist, as is evident in the flyer addressed to potential stockholders where he details his experience selling his novels to bookstores, libraries, and individuals. Even his "pitch" to these largely white investors is designed to capture and hold, a persuasion that encourages them to imagine his project as bigger than ever and to which end he uses the expansive rhetoric of "never before":

> Another feature to the advantage of THE HOMESTEADER is that aside from the general public, who themselves, having never seen a picture in which the Negro race and a Negro hero is so portrayed, and can therefore, be expected to appreciate the photoplay as a diversion and a new interest, is the fact that twelve million Negro people will have their first opportunity to see their race in stellar role. Their patronage, which can be expected in immense numbers, will mean in its self [sic] alone a fortune.[100]

One of Micheaux's gifts was that not only could he talk his way but he could write his way into anything, proving, as he said, that "a Negro can be anything." And in the fund-raising flyer for *The Homesteader* he exudes confidence about the undertaking, envisioning a release pattern on the model of Hollywood and in the manner of *Quo Vadis* and *The Birth of a Nation* in the "largest theatres" in the "largest cities" and in addition "under the personal direction of Mr. Micheaux."[101] After *The Homesteader* had opened at the Vendome in Chicago to large and enthusiastic crowds, he composed a form letter for exhibitors utilizing a quote attributed to O. C. Hammond, owner of the theater, describing the long lines, the 5,700 paid admissions, the ten-cent price increase, the five-day holdover, and the return engagement at Hammond's Pickford Theatre. Urging exhibitors to book the "massive 8200-foot special," Micheaux describes the interest in the film as "of such intensity that it holds one in that peculiar thralldom from which there is no escape until the word 'finis.'" Outlining his intent to book all of the important towns in each territory and to advertise "conspicuously" in the local papers, he even volunteers to mail heralds to community residents, provided he receives a copy of the town telephone directory.[102]

The effectiveness of the *Homesteader* circular mailed to exhibitors in March 1919 was chronicled by George Johnson, who at that time would have been monitoring Micheaux as his competition since the Lincoln Company was to be in business for another year or so at least. What other reason would there be for Johnson to record *The Homesteader*'s "booking route"? The earliest date Johnson lists is May 12, 1919, at the Ruby Theatre in Louisville, Kentucky, where admission was thirty cents, including the war tax, and where "extra music" was added. In June 1919

Micheaux added the Pike in Mobile, Alabama, and the Pekin in Montgomery, and in Louisiana, theaters in Alexandria, Mobile, Shreveport, and Baton Rouge, as well as the Temple Theatre in New Orleans and a lone booking in Pensacola, Florida. *The Homesteader* played two days at the Globe Theatre in Cleveland in September, with window cards and screen slides but neither posters nor stills as the advance advertising, Johnson notes. He also records the information that the rental was at that point $50 per day and admission fifteen cents for the matinee and twenty cents for the evening show. Admission was twenty-five cents plus the war tax at the Foraker in Washington, D.C., where it also played at the Hiawatha Theatre in the fall of 1919, returning March 1, 1920, for a night at the Howard Theatre. By March 14, booked for one engagement by theater manager and film critic Lester Walton at the Lafayette Theatre in New York, the print was already showing wear, according to Johnson's marginal notes, information he may have gleaned from one of his spies. In May through July 1920 *The Homesteader* did another southern tour, playing in Tennessee at the Bijou in Nashville, the Metropolis in Memphis, and the Grand in Chattanooga, and in Alabama at the Star in Florence, the Fields in Sheffield, the Sykes in Decatur, and return engagements at the Pike in Mobile and the Pekin in Montgomery.[103]

By all accounts, Oscar Micheaux's first film venture was a solid success, due, in part, to an entrepreneurial genius that was evident earlier in his strategy for promoting his novels, a brilliant way of making productive use of his failure to succeed at homesteading, especially since his books were made dramatic by the very struggle with the environmental odds that finally led to the author's loss of his farm. But, as I discuss in a later chapter, other forces also intervened to affect the socially sensitive motion picture box office, as Micheaux found when he tried to exhibit his second feature, the controversial *Within Our Gates,* which he began to prepare to release late in 1919 on the heels of the triumph of *The Homesteader.* If the emphasis here is more on Micheaux's skills as a showman and motion picture producer rather than as a director, this is because such a large portion of his talent was invested in those aspects of the industry that we understand as the work of the producer. While film history has awarded the function of the auteur to those directors who could claim responsibility for many aspects of the completed motion picture, here analogous to a work of fine art, it is well established that there are problems with the analogy between the film director and the artist or author in the traditional sense, not the least of which is the fact that the motion picture is industrially produced, not individually created. Since there is always a question about agency in relation to those directors working with other creative personnel within the studio system, the designation of unqualified auteur has historically gone to those few directors such as D. W. Griffith, Charles Chaplin, and Buster Keaton, who, working in the early years of cinema, were responsible for more of the aspects of production, including producing, writing, acting, and editing as well as directing. The auteur, like the fine artist or literary author, has also been understood in terms of thematic consistency within his or her body of work as well as stylistic signs or visible signatures. Based on this general understanding of what counts as an auteur, there is no doubt that Oscar Micheaux qualifies, and it is probable that future studies will indeed nominate him as a great auteur and proceed to find the requisite stylistic and thematic patterns in his work.

But auteur criticism has been found to be politically bankrupt on some counts, and one of the most important challenges to it has come from theories of audience response, which take the production of meaning away from the authoritarian notion of authorship and give it to audience members who meet the popular text halfway through its devices and on their terms.[104] To some degree, then, the focus on the audience has been an attempt to democratize meaning by unseating the author.[105] The challenge to authorship, whether it comes via the assertion of genre or through an interest in ideology, is generally a return of the text to its audience. This will be exceedingly important for us in our discussion of race movies, a cycle of films if not a genre, films largely defined by the audience for which they were produced and to which they were exclusively distributed. The case of Oscar Micheaux represents an opportunity to challenge not only the elitism of authorship theory by shifting attention to the race movie audience but a chance to redefine the motion picture producer as an instigator and an actualizer, someone who not only designs the work but who orchestrates its reception. And in this mode of intervention in popular culture, Micheaux has as much in common with P. T. Barnum as he does with D. W. Griffith, and hence my emphasis on him as a showman.[106]

It is indisputable that Micheaux went beyond Griffith in the areas of distribution and exploitation. While Griffith certainly made public appearances with his films, there is no evidence that he hand-carried the prints from theater to theater as Micheaux did with his first features, literally walking his booking route and shoring up the famous network of race movie distribution to segregated houses in the East, the South, and the Midwest. While Griffith wrote articles designed for the press and may have been responsible for certain aspects of the advertising campaigns for his films as early as the Biograph years, the division of labor in Hollywood was such that the publicist was increasingly separated from the production. By all indications, Micheaux was his own publicist, in his campaign for *The Homesteader* using the word "exploitation" knowledgeably in his first promotion to potential stockholders, and especially with his first films writing the kind of "screaming" copy that creates excitement around a new release.[107]

Advertisements for *The Brute* appearing in the black press, for instance, hawked it as "The Greatest Achievement by Race People in Pictures!" This was "THE STORY OF A BEAUTIFUL AND TENDER GIRL IN THE TOILS OF A SHREWD GAMBLER AND BOSS OF THE UNDERWORLD, BULL M'GEE, WHOSE CREED IS: 'TO MAKE A WOMAN LOVE YOU, KNOCK HER DOWN.'" And in the boldface all-caps that has the ring of the circus spiel, the ad calls out: **"SEE THE GREAT SEVENTEEN-ROUND CHAMPIONSHIP FIGHT BETWEEN TWO OF THE WORLD'S BEST HEAVYWEIGHTS."** As though that hype were insufficient, the next line screams: **"Suspense, Intrigue, Romance, Excitement,"** followed by "8,000 FEET OF GRIPPING, HOLDING INTEREST, FEATURING **EVELYN PREER, SAM LANGFORD, A. B. DECOMATHIERRE & AN ALL-STAR CAST."** Micheaux's rhetoric locates him in the tradition of ballyhoo, a strong American style of communication that grew up with the emergence of the mass audience and thrived on the possibility of drawing spectators in in an attempt to make an enormous profit, the enormity of the profit synonymous with the enormity of the crowd.

Dismissed as even more obvious and crass than the popular forms it promotes, this rhetoric historically drops away in the consideration of popular theater, literature, and film. Exploitation, in particular, is often considered as just advertising, an approach that fails to understand it historically or to see its larger aspirations and wider arena, for exploitation was not exactly limited to print forms of promotion but encompassed stunts, appearances, and tie-ups as well as handbills and posters. As I have elsewhere defined it, exploitation "surpasses the one-way message of advertising and publicity in the way it produces its own inflated reception simultaneously with its transmission."[108] Etymologically, exploitation can be understood as having two poles that correspond with the crowning achievement that always seems to be canceled out by the exhaustion of resources and the carelessness of opportunism. In sum, this is the doubleness of Micheaux, the garrulous and crafty promoter whose gigantic imagination of what he *could be* proved to be an achievement for the entire race. It is in contrast to the somewhat literal-minded cautiousness of George Johnson that Micheaux's flamboyant and hyperbolic style may situate him on the side of the untrustworthy. Like the melodramatic mode within which he so often worked, Micheaux's hyperbole was both full and hollow, deep and flat, characteristics I have identified in visual rhetoric as well as linguistic "hype."[109] This is the mode of the big lie and the tall tale, the mode that finds its ideal expression in risk and overreaching.

The evaluation of Oscar Micheaux and his work resembles nothing more than a critical roller-coaster ride. At the high point, his contemporary Richard J. Norman calls him a "genius" in a letter while chastising him that his "genius has been led astray."[110] In recent years he has had a champion in popular reviewer James Hoberman, who in the phase of rediscovery between 1975 and 1994 has written intelligently about the problem of situating Micheaux in relation to Hollywood.[111] Most recently, after the discovery of Micheaux's *The Veiled Aristocrats* (1932), a remake of the silent *The House behind the Cedars* (1924/25), Hoberman commented (echoing the saying that "Once you've had a black you never go back") that "it's safe to say that once you've seen a Micheaux movie, Hollywood 'perfection' will never seem the same."[112] But the contemporary critical discussion has been haunted by the sharp criticism of an earlier black press where Theophilus Lewis thus condemned Micheaux's *A Daughter of the Congo* (1930), one of his last silent films: "As a matter of fact, the picture is thoroughly bad from every point of analysis, from the continuity which is unintelligible, to the caption writing, which is a crime."[113]

It would seem for a while that the first wave of reevaluation, with the exception of Hoberman, deferred to the black press, which may explain the reticence about Micheaux's talent that Ron Green finds in Thomas Cripps.[114] As an even better example of this phenomenon, Daniel Leab, writing before the rediscovery of two of the three extant Micheaux films from the silent period, concludes that the director's "silent motion picture works cannot be considered outstanding."[115] It would be difficult to ignore, in addition, the Baltimore *Afro-American*'s 1933 "Open Letter to Oscar Micheaux" which, although appreciative of his achievements, was hard on his "jumbly-fumbly manner of directing" and advised him to "forget for a while that colored gentlemen go West, or North . . . and become millionaires . . . and come back to Chicago and Harlem to spend their cash and kick up hell."[116] Charlene Regester, however, has cautioned us to consider the reception of Micheaux in the African American press in relation to two phases, 1918–1929 and 1930–1948, roughly corresponding to the period of his silent and his sound work.[117] This would mean that, among other things, the economics of sound recording would need to be factored into the evaluation of Micheaux's aesthetic, since his low-budget use of the expensive new technology undermined his message in the sound years.

But perhaps the most important angle to take on the critical reception of Micheaux, contemporary with his work, is the political one. An increasingly politicized black audience might find his films problematic for the way that they imaged back selves that they could no longer tolerate. The apex of discontent with Micheaux was the 1938 Young Communist League boycott of *God's Stepchildren,* which involved picketing the RKO Theatre at the Harlem premiere. Although it is important to note that the boycott was organized as part of the party's effort to recruit black membership, the boycott may also have struck another chord when spokesperson Beatrice Goodjoe repeated the black press criticism in declaring that the film "creates a false splitting of Negroes into light and dark groups." For the Communists, this splitting repeated the discriminatory labor tactic they identified in those white employers who were undermining the Harlem job campaign by dividing workers against each other on the basis of skin color.[118] The Communist party boycott, originally an attempt to use Micheaux's film to advance a political position in a labor struggle, has become a significant part of the Micheaux legend, surfacing in every reassessment and coloring the director's reputation in some parts of the black community, at times making it extremely difficult to mount an assessment of race movies that is anything but a lament about the portrayal of the race. The ways of circumventing this criticism are several, and while one critic has argued that Micheaux's portrayals are actually critiques, another has asserted that he was reacting against a "Black Victorianism" that required positive images as "propaganda" for the race.[119] I would add to the latter the observation that Micheaux would not have wanted to have had his hands tied by any race-positive party line. But, finally, it is time for us to read the race movie movement from its beginning since it has been too long clouded by events from the end of Micheaux's career. Twenty years before the Communist party boycott, the race movie pioneers were reacting to the insults of early blackface film comedy, for sure, but they were also part of a larger cultural attempt to give a new "face to the race," and in this their aspirations were politically motivated in surprisingly different ways.

World-Improving Desires

Frederick Douglass, in his public lectures and speeches, says Henry Louis Gates, always spoke in an effort to "recreate the face of the race, its public face."[1] Thus invoking Douglass, Gates goes on to locate the literary project of the inventors of the "New Negro" in this crusade to represent themselves publically, a project that was (to reclaim the historical term) a massive "reconstruction." This project, he goes on, was not new but a continuation of a long struggle: since the time they arrived as Africans, Negroes had continually been forced to "reconstruct" their own image in answer to what it was that whites made of them. In the last quarter of the nineteenth century, this representation as reconstruction was more specifically a dialogue between the positive new and the pejorative old images of blacks, images that have been understood as stereotypes. In this contentious dialogue, as the "New Negro" was reconstructed, "Sambo Art" was negated.[2]

In this overview Gates opens up a long-ignored connection between the Harlem Renaissance literary figures and popular forms, a connection not made by the elite writers themselves most likely because, for them, the very act of creation was a disassociation from the low. Retracing this connection from the point of view of popular culture, we need to be cautious not to make the same mistake in reverse—not to make a *direct* link between the literary elites and race movie pioneers when the relationship is an *indirect* one, as I have already asserted. Both literary productions and race movies were, however, reactions against the same despised stereotypes.

"Sambo Art" had its equivalent in the chicken thievery and watermelon antics of early blackface film comedy, the offensive imagery that, as we saw in the last chapter, spurred the first of the black film pioneers into action.[3] While both literary productions and race movies were dedicated to the same bidirectional project of reconstruction—the production of the image of the race *for* the race itself and then *to* whites—the audiences they addressed were not exactly congruent. Access to the works of the New Negro was limited to the literate public, white as well as black, and whites were the exception not the rule in the race movie audience. But more relevant here, where Alain Locke's Harlem Renaissance writers used the black *voice* to constitute the "face of the race," these writers paradoxically disappeared from the sight line. This literal disappearance was not *the* significant effacement, however. As Gates puts it, these writers "not only sought to *rewrite* the black term, they sought to *rewrite* the (white) text of themselves, and in so doing, they erased their racial selves, imitating those they least resembled in demonstrating the full intellectual potential of the black mind."[4] I will return momentarily to the charge of effacement through imitation, but first I want to stress my point: there *was* no literary "face of the race." This is to assert, once again, that however effectively the literary text evokes faces, it does not and cannot make them visible.

The Face of the Race

I would argue that since the Harlem Renaissance literary figures never exactly "showed" either their racial selves or the raced selves of others, if any group actually reconstructed the "face of the race" in the 1920s it was not the celebrated black writers but rather the race movie producers. In contrast with a screen peopled with black figures and faces, the printed page gives us *nothing to see* really; race movies were the "face of the race" because, as the antithesis of racial erasure, they celebrated visibility, relishing the faces and bodies of actors representing the black community. But was it enough to produce the "face of the race" if that face was seen exclusively by lower class urban blacks in the North and rural blacks in some parts of the South, only a few whites, and perhaps a handful of the elite blacks in the Harlem Renaissance circle, a group who never took these films seriously enough to write about them?

Let me return to Gates's implication that the erasure of the racial self is effected by imitation of the white forms that the New Negro authors sought to emulate. Although his point is that, in imitating a white culture to which black culture bore no resemblance, black writers reproduced white culture instead of articulating their own distinctive culture, I would take issue with this if for no other reason than that the charge of imitation is a critical dead end. Yes, the Harlem Renaissance writers effaced themselves as they took up white literary forms, if by racial effacement we mean they were no longer discernable as whatever they had been seen as before. But what is it that has been effaced? For the record, I also have to challenge, once again, the old myth of a separate culture. It would seem that Gates's use of the term "imitation" betrays an assumption that there was an untouched literary tradition that was not itself an imitation of yet another tradition.[5]

Like early black literary forms, race movies have been subject to the criticism that they were no more than imitations of white forms—a criticism that immediately closes down investigation of the mutuality of the imitation and the imitated.[6] To resort to the critical judgment that an aesthetic work is no more than an imitation is to fail to give credence to processes of cultural interpenetration and, more important, to fail to imagine the possibility of the mimetic. Gates himself has elsewhere been instrumental in rehabilitating the imitative as a critical category, certainly in his conceptualization of "signifying" as the imitation that is simultaneously a reversal of white culture.[7] But the imitativeness of race movies in the pre-sound era is not necessarily a reversal of white forms to the advantage of the black signifier; there is no textual trick. Race movies, I will argue, can be understood less as imitating white forms than as inhabiting white genres. And as they inhabited, they incorporated, which is not to say that white forms did not also absorb some blackness in this process.

Yet again we encounter a variant of the "relentless reciprocity" of the Hegelian impasse—the inextricability of the mainstream and the margin that manifests itself so intractably in echoes and resemblances. We begin to see the one in the other everywhere we look. The early race movies *were* elaborate mirrorings of aspects of white middle class family life. In some cases such as the Lincoln Company's *A Man's Duty* (1919), the middle class dilemma in the narrative—dealing with two rich playboys and the consequences of a trick one plays on the other in setting up a false charge of paternity—might have been a white parlor drama in every other sense; black characters are substituted for white. And yet this substitution also makes a point about the sociology of the black middle class whose successes were seen as accruing to the entire black community. The black performance of white dramas enabled the argument that the black middle class person was "just as" good as the white person in every way because his world was "just the same." As Donald Bogle characterizes what he considers a fantasy world, this was a world "just as affluent, just as educated, just as 'cultured,' just as well-mannered—in short—just as white—as white Americans."[8]

But the idea that this was only a fantasy world misses the way in which an all-black-cast performance of a white dramatic vehicle also radically alters the meaning of the original. Perhaps one of the best examples of this alteration is the popular stage melodrama *Ten Nights in a Barroom* (1926), "reconstructed" by the performances of the Colored Players of Philadelphia.[9] In this significant reconception, the main character, played by the famous black actor Charles Gilpin, becomes increasingly dissolute after he is betrayed by his villainous former partner. The rewriting produces a villain more vile, a victim more pathetic, and a hero more proud because of the elevated stakes. These stakes of black life produce lows that are lower and highs that are significantly higher than the dramaturgy of the original temperance melodrama. The original play structure is refurbished by the performance of the all-black cast and what emerges is a new story about a black community torn apart and tragically damaged by corruption.

The Racial Commutation Test

The phenomenon of the all-black-cast film remake allows us to ponder the semiotics of substitution. For what we are looking at in any remake is an elaborate game of substitution, a semiotic commutation test on a large scale in which every character is commuted as black, producing a world in which villainy as well as heroism is entirely "black on black" and all conflict is intraracial because all of the roles go to black actors. However, the commutation test that has intrigued film scholars, as applied to cinema by John O. Thompson, would require some adaptation if we were to think through the substitutions of race cinema in these terms. Though in our contrast between white mainstream cinema and its black cinema counterpart, elements are altered, these alterations do not present us with the kind of grammatical change that has fascinated semioticians. In the original commutation test from European structural linguistics, scholars studied how some differences in linguistic signs produced semantic differences and others didn't, with the test involving the measurement of the effect on overall meaning of this or that sound change.[10] Using this denaturalizing approach, Thompson applies the principle to the question of how the theoretical exchange of one actor for another in a significant role could change the meaning of the entire film, with the caveat that John Wayne is "more complex than a phoneme."[11] But the question of how *The Wizard of Oz* (1939) would mean differently if Shirley Temple instead of Judy Garland had played Dorothy is not necessarily the same as the question of how *The Wizard of Oz* would mean if performed by an all-black cast, something we can almost imagine if we consider the musical's transformation into *The Wiz* (1978). To strictly follow the spirit and letter of Thompson's screen acting commutation test, we might imagine the semiotic consequences of actually switching Lorenzo Tucker, the black Valentino, for Rudolph Valentino in *Blood and Sand* (1922) or Ethel Moses, the black Jean Harlow, for Harlow herself in *Bombshell* (1933), except that we would also have to imagine political consequences far beyond the semiotic.

Our question, however, has to do with the way black casting transformed Hollywood formula films, producing more than an exchange of this or that element. The result is an ensemble effect in which every character alters the meaning not only of the narrative but produces a slight shift in the system of meaning itself so that race movies are always the same but different, and different because they are white-not. It might even be useful to think of race movies as written in another key, perhaps a minor key inasmuch as the effect of the minor is always produced by its oblique relation to the major key, a key the minor knows and tells us it knows, and diverges from only to return. So black casting was not a grammatical change in the individual film text, and neither was it a complete translation into another language as from English to French. And yet it was a semiotic modification that never left the text the same, as exemplified in *Ten Nights in a Barroom* in which the Colored Players version has permanently altered what once was only a temperance play. But in general, and especially when the "race movie" is not an adaptation, we want to know how the fact of the all-black cast, against the backdrop of a historical period within which popular fare was all-white, contributed to the meaning.

It should be understood here that the resonance of the all-black cast depended on the race composition of the audience, which can also be considered, following the model of the commutation test, as substitutable, the black one for the white one. We are already beginning to think about the deep significance of the all-black-cast film for the members of the black audience in terms of the image validation and reciprocity, the return of their own image to them, a return that gives a whole new meaning to the idea of the mirror cinema. For the white viewer of race movies, however, there might be a different experience of the mirror cinema that bears consideration, an underside perhaps, particularly in the pre–civil rights era. The problem of the white perception of the all-black screen comes to mind in James Baldwin's reference to the discomfort T. E. Lawrence admits when he first discovers that the black man is also a man. Baldwin is struck by a passage from Lawrence's *Seven Pillars of Wisdom* in which, contemplating the native population, he reflects that "it hurt," and what hurt was "that they [the negroes] should possess exact counter-parts of all our bodies."[12] We, like Baldwin, are struck with the myopia of Lawrence's perception of things. We are reminded that it could as easily be said that in any number of historical encounters, blacks were astonished to find that the bodies of whites were the "exact counterparts" of their own. So for the myopic racist would the screen image of the American black in the race movie produce an anguish similar to Lawrence's? Would it produce an anxiety of resemblance? In this perfect mirror cinema, the exact counterparts of the white body and the white society are up there on the screen, enlarged and unmistakable. For much of white society, this could be a deeply troubling substitution.

Thompson's commutation test, the substitution of one for another in a role within the film, dramatizes another test, ultimately a political test. What happens when white characters are assigned particular roles within an all-black-cast film? This question, in and of itself, branches off into another story, the story of the degree to which white villainy was prohibited by censors even when the white villain was played by a black actor, as in Lorenzo Tucker's account of how, as the white man who tries to seduce the light-skinned heroine in Micheaux's *The Exile* (1931), the scene and thus his entire role were cut from the film.[13] One can deduce from the paucity of white roles that race cinema was always set up as antithetical (if not antagonistic) to the white cinema from which "blacks as blacks" were excluded, and in these films the antagonistic relationship to white culture was banned from the screen, producing an entirely segregated screen world. One could watch hours of race movies without seeing a white face.[14]

For black audiences, the screen emptied of whites was a revelation. Capturing this feeling, Joseph Beam describes the absolute ecstasy for black people of reading Zora Neal Hurston's *Their Eyes Were Watching God*, which was produced for him by the "absence of white people" in the text. It is as though, he says, "we have our own country."[15] In these powerful black fictions, blackness is top to bottom, and whiteness is either villainized or banished. Even better, as in the case of Tucker, when white characters appeared on the screen they were often played by black actors, a point to which I will later return. To the degree that these already light-skinned actors were further lightened and powdered, they represent what might be called "white face," sometimes a pointed satirization of "whitey" and at other times an attempt at realistic representation. Without a doubt, "white face" was no mere imitation but, again, an ingenious occupation of a white form—in this case a white role. To reiterate my point about cultural intermixture, it was not as though white and black had never before coexisted in the same body.

The Assimilation Machine

Inextricable yet antagonistic, deferentially imitative yet transforming, segregated yet incorporated, race movies could not be seen as simple copies of white genre films. Nor was their relationship to the mainstream one of striving for exact reproduction. Some of the difficulty we encounter as we look for the critical starting point for a theoretical understanding of American race movies has to do with this problem of imagined purity in the face of impurity and intermixture. (The more contemporary argument that Euro-American culture "rips off" African American culture is no different in this regard from the earlier argument that Negro literature and race movies "imitate" white forms.) Popular culture, as we know, is so much of a sponger that it will pick up anything regardless of the source. In its unabashed eclecticism, the popular tells us something more about the historical process by which black has mixed with white in the United States, a process of intermingling and weaving that W. E. B. Du Bois has described thus:

> Actively we have woven ourselves with the warp and woof of the nation—we fought their battles, shared their sorrow, mingled our blood with theirs, and generation after generation have pleaded with headstrong careless people to despise not Justice, Mercy, and Truth, lest the nation be smitten with a curse. Our song, our toil, our cheer, and warning have been given to the nation in blood-brotherhood. . . . Would America be America without her Negro people?[16]

Du Bois would remind us that the amalgam that is American culture has been produced in millions of ways every day over several centuries, and reminds us of what is at stake in denying the Negro contribution to the whole. Knowing how this commingling of blood and culture works, understanding the attraction of cultural signs to one another, how can we dismiss as merely imitative any product that has been part of this process of cultural intermixture?

Yet to speak about intermixture, even theoretically, in relation to the early decades of the twentieth century, is to raise the question of assimilationism, especially since, as an ideal, it would have been quietly assumed and openly espoused in the black middle class community. There are, says Cornel West, different "ways of being black," and of these ways assimilationism may be best defined as the way that starts with the assumption that "black people are really like white people." Homogenization, equally problematic, he continues, begins with the premise that "all black people are alike."[17] One could argue that popular race cinema, by depicting blacks living the lives of the white middle class, was saying that "black people are really like white people."[18] Is such an argument consonant with understanding early cinema as an assimilation machine, the machine that is credited with inducting foreign-born immigrants into the American middle class by teaching them manners and customs?[19] Race movies would hardly work as an assimilation machine in this sense if the idea is to show *not* how black people *could be* but how they are "like" white people. Thus it would seem that while early race movies taught by illustration how to be middle class as well as how *not* to be a lowlife card shark, thief, and chisler, they simultaneously made the visual argument that black people didn't need these lessons because they *already were* "just like" white people. To recall Donald Bogle, the race movie logic of "just as" leads to the representation of blacks as "just as white—as white Americans."[20] At every turn, however, the logic of assimilationism runs into trouble, especially as it must first homogenize the black community in order to make its basic point: black people are just like white people.

In the logic of "just as" taken to its obvious conclusion, assimilation produces a race–culture mixture in which blacks are so well blended that they are indistinguishable from whites. With what Donald Bogle describes as their "shameless promotion of the world of hair-straighteners and skin-lighteners," race movies seemed encouraging and approving of white-likeness and in their light-skinned casting seemed to constitute one big advertisement for race effacement.[21] Like the interracial sexual unions that have "automatically" assimilated peoples over time, race movies produced the "light brights" or light-skinned ideal, a vision of both what the entire culture would look like *if* it were to become racially mixed through breeding and what it could look like if assimilation were taken at its word. Thus it is that the paradox of assimilation is dramatized in passing: the message to blacks was that you should become white-like in every way but not *so* white that you disappeared as a black. Race movies, assimilationist though they seemed, were nonetheless not about disappearing into white culture, not at all about incorporation and absorption. On the thematic level alone, from Reol's *The Call of His People* (1922) to Micheaux's *God's Stepchildren* (1938), race movies disapproved of passing. As we will see, the narrative condemnation of passing was one of several ways that these films could be seen as giving face to the race. In the final analysis, by making race visible, these films made race-as-community palpably real, producing an answer to the racist "self-evidence of the seen" that would single out and separate. In yet another way, race movies exemplify that ingenious solution to the racist exclusions of white society—they claimed and celebrated exactly what it was that defined their visible difference—and the race movie pioneers did this merely by turning the camera on themselves.

Two of Everything

But the assimilation machine that, taken at face value, would seem to encourage the cultural loss and self-denunciation of race effacement and the full absorption and disappearance of passing (alternatives seen as unacceptable to both white and black) is much more. The machine that would seem to be an efficient mechanism for overcoming otherness turns out to be an institution that works to further the race. Race movies were a vehicle by which blacks became the other in order to become themselves. As I am arguing, race movies did take over white genres, exploring them and exploiting them to their own advantage. Consider, for instance, how the all-black cast of the Norman Company's *The Flying Ace* (1924) moved into the adventure–crime genre and replaced the exploits of the white aviator hero with a black pilot hero who performs airborne stunts and solves the crime with ingenuity and skill. Such a substitution had its appeal to black audiences for whom the sight of a genuine black hero would be a source of tremendous pride. The advantage of seeing race movies as genre inhabitation rather than as white genre imitation, then, is the way this allows us to see them as a vehicle for race advancement.

Now let us see if we can connect the phenomenon of watching race movies to the theories of identification discussed in chapters 1 and 2. How have we returned to the question of becoming the other in order to become oneself? Of cinema as an othering machine as opposed to what I am calling an assimilation machine? Recall black women's nonrecognition of the white object of desire on screen: "There was nothing to see. She was not us."[22] In contrast, bell hooks describes blacks recalling the "pleasure" of race movies, a pleasure so often "interrupted" by Hollywood.[23] Instead of the unpleasure of "nothing to see," race movies rewarded black viewers with "something to see" because "they are us." Rather than settling for the simple mirroring theory of identification, however, we should push this further in order to understand how viewers might receive the desired "return" from the image, to think how the circuit of reciprocity works to give viewers something back, something they might experience as pleasure. Again, the subject as desiring machine meets the motion picture as desiring machine in this understanding of identification as going through the other to get to the self.

Here, in the case of race movies, we see how the notion of identification as "demanding sameness" and denying the difference between self and other is unable to fully comprehend the situation in which black viewers were seeing white-like black actors, actors who were so often located in white situations within white worlds. Thus the complicated play between the black audience, the white movie world backdrop, and the black actor could produce the more dialectical alternation between sameness and difference that, as I have been arguing, fills out the theory of identification more substantially. For what we need is a theory broad enough to accommodate the double pleasure of seeing "same race, different world"—the world of the middle class parlor, nightclub, and bedroom. And in this special case of the motion picture as Metz's fish tank in which the audience is always "outside looking in," because of the reversal that puts the all-black cast on the screen, the all-black audience could be powerfully inside as well as outside the screen world.[24]

For identification *is* about becoming identical, and the aspirations of *uplift* (illustrated in lush detail in early race movies) were aspirations in which a black elite stood for the whole, replacing whites in a world that *looked just like* the well-appointed and comfortable one of the white screen. But rather than stopping at any understanding of this representation of black aspirations as imitation or mirroring, a more comprehensive approach would be to understand an elaborate paralleling—a paralleling in all aspects of life. For what was produced by the early years of segregation were two economies side by side, the black economy ironically helped to thrive, as I have pointed out, by the very enforced separation that middle class assimilationism opposed. What I want to stress in my emphasis on parallelism is both a certain surreality in the idea of double worlds, side by side, but also the waste, and it is again Du Bois who noticed this bizarre economy of twos. Du Bois's "two of everything," as Robert Steptoe has explained it, is a "dialectics of race ritual between a black and white world."[25] To me, this metaphor suggests a strange courtship in which the partners know the same steps but never dance together. But for Du Bois there is also something verging on the hallucinatory in double consciousness, which might be understood as "seeing double": "double life, with double thoughts, double duties and double social classes."[26] Thus it is that he describes and explains the conflictedness and the deep ambivalence of the lived experience of the impossible situation of being a black American.

Now that we have established the historical unfairness of this totally ridiculous and wasteful situation in which "two of everything" was the rule, let us do an about-face. Let us see if we can discern the reverse of enforced separation in the "two of everything" world, that is, *the democratic aspirations of the all-black community*. Our glimpses of this better world, totally black, are in the descriptions of communities such as the Central Avenue section of Los Angeles and, even more relevant to the history of race movies, the forgotten town of Muskogee, Oklahoma, where George P. Johnson sold real estate around 1916. As Johnson describes Muskogee, it was a town that thrived before Oklahoma's 1907 statehood largely because of the miracle of the grant that gave 160 acres of land located in what had been Creek Indian territory to the descendants of Negro freedmen. The black population of Oklahoma had increased 537 percent between 1890 and 1910, and these newcomers were concentrated in thirty black towns and communities, including Muskogee.[27]

A brochure describes a complete vision, a black-owned town from top to bottom:

> Muskogee has more modern and various Negro business enterprises than any city in the world with equal Negro population. The following enterprises are to be found in Muskogee: One bank, 1 dry goods store, 2 furniture stores, 1 hardware store, 2 jewelry stores, 6 drug stores, 3 printing offices, 3 weekly papers, 2 undertakers, 3 photographers, 1 automobile livery, 2 cab lines, 1 dairy, 2 pop factories, 1 ice cream factory, 1 laundry, 1 wholesale grocery, 16 retail groceries, 15 restaurants, 1 hospital, 10 pool halls, 3 hotels, 8 rooming houses, 7 shoe repair shops, 1 harness shop, 1 upholstery shop, 1 plumbing shop, 11 blacksmith shops, 2 theaters, 1 stationery store, 1 news stand, 2 clothing stores, 1 livery stable, 3 meat markets, 14 lawyers, 15 physicians, 2 dentists, 3 veterinaries, 2 investment companies, 10 churches, 2 brick graded schools, 1 brick high school, 1 manual training school, and many other enterprises of less importance.[28]

The Muskogee pamphlet goes on to boast that laborers do not have to worry about finding work of all kinds, citing the wage range for carpenters, brick and stone masons, hod carriers, and plasterers as well as common laborers. The Colored Schools of Muskogee, it proudly declares, enroll 1,700 students and are "second to none in the Southwest." Profiled are some of the businesses owned by the more wealthy and prosperous in this town of 30,000, each enterprise a small success story in and of itself.[29]

This vision of Muskogee is the vision of race movies. For the Negroes who bought the lots George Johnson sold by mail and for all of the others who moved to the area sight unseen, Muskogee represented a world in which there was plenty of work, the opportunity to own, and in which no white people were in charge. It would be a mistake to see this vision as nothing more than middle class aspiration for Muskogee and what it represented when it was founded in the latter part of the nineteenth century were more exceptional and miraculous than one might think.[30] As a prototype of an ideal black society modeled on the white one, Muskogee represents a utopian vision of a community within reach. But if the world of the all-black model town hints at this better existence for the race, race movies go further as they utilize the mimetic mode. As they engage the mimetic mode, race movies offer visions of even more than the "more" represented by the all-black town. Never "mere imitation," mimesis, from the point of view of utopian theory, is about total transformation.

Uplift and Utopia

As theorized by German philosopher Ernst Bloch, utopian consciousness is consciousness that anticipates, looks hard at the world and expects more, that hopes beyond hope for the better life. Having nothing in common with the familiar work descending from Sir Thomas More, Bloch's approach conceptualizes the political dimension of utopian thinking, that forward-looking aspect of the revolutionary process without which people would not be able to imagine themselves out of their circumstances, let alone act to change those circumstances.[31] Mimesis in Bloch is linked to a yearning for change, even what he calls a "mimic need" manifested, we recall, in a "tempting desire to transform oneself," and it is not far from here to motion pictures as the mimetic machine that brings about such transformations and metamorphoses.[32] Again, as I see it, the capacity to become oneself by becoming the other, this mimetic "faculty" Michael Taussig describes as "slipping into otherness, trying it on for size," is an undeniably utopian reaching toward that which is better.[33] Although we wouldn't want to argue that every film is automatically utopian, as a technology the moving picture, producing the desires of desiring subjects in such a way that these wishes appear to have their origin in the subject, is always a dreaming machine. And it is in the daydream that Bloch finds the utopian consciousness.

Careful to delineate his understanding of the forward-looking utopian dimensions of the daydream from the backward-looking regression of the psychoanalytic night dream, Bloch, who argued that there was nothing new in the unconscious, borrowed from Freud but only selectively.[34] He diverges from Freudians most significantly where he attaches the waking dream directly to the project of political change, where the dream is only important to him insofar as it is an indicator of potentially revolutionary ideas in nascent wish form. Neither is the utopian dream ever a working inward through the individual psychology; always it is a reverie outward, as in Bloch's basic concept, the "world-improving dream." The world-improving dream is generous and broad, expansive and comprehensive, the antithesis of the personal wish: "World-improving dreams in general seek the outwardness of their inwardness, they emerge like the extrovert rainbow, like a vault across the sky."[35] Furthermore, this dream rises out of a knowledge of the worst of conditions: "Above all revolutionary interest, with knowledge of how bad the world is, with acknowledgement of how good it could be if it were otherwise, needs the waking dream of world-improvement."[36]

Yet the importation of Frankfurt school theory into this discussion is an imperfect solution, and Bloch's theorization of utopia leaves something to be desired as we bring it to bear on the question of the ebullience of race cinema. I suspect that what is needed is more study of the particularity of the utopian dimension of black spirituality. As Paul Gilroy has begun to analyze jubilee, it is never a particularly rational pursuit of the utopian, but might be seen as surpassing all other ordinary utopias in its apocalyptic reach. As Gilroy suggests, the "moment of jubilee has the upper hand over the pursuit of utopia by rational means."[37] So we want to turn up the volume on this notion of the utopian dimension of race cinema. But just as we have turned up the volume, it needs to be turned down again to accommodate the modifying influence of the black middle class. This is perhaps to suggest that there would be some vacillation between celebration and moderation in the tempered utopianism that characterized uplift.

While uplift had its side that wished for nothing more than the maintenance of the black status quo, its other side, still in touch with the project of emancipation, wanted nothing less than freedom for all.[38] "Improvement" in the uplift vocabulary was similarly articulated in two distinct voices—the one that worried over the lowlife Negro who needed to be "improved up," and the other that believed that anything was possible for the race through education and application. And it is the latter, expressed in Micheaux's conviction that "a colored man can be anything," carrying with it a sense of limitless possibility, that verges on the "world-improving dream." The fierce drive for betterment might also be seen as utopian in Bloch's terms, Bloch the lone Marxist who has attempted to theorize comfort. The "day-fantasy," "fabulously inventive" and looking forward, is focused on "wanting to have better, often simply wanting to know better."[39] Characterized by cheerfulness and an undaunted optimism, the world-improving utopian desire would seem to thrive and grow under prerevolutionary social conditions where wanting more is not rooted in having something but in having next to nothing. Under such circumstances, as Fredric Jameson interprets Bloch's theory of utopia, that doctrine is "reduced to a kind of philosophy of as-if, a kind of lie which helps us to live."[40] Contrary to any idea of Bloch as "reduced," however, we should see in utopian theory the commonalities with uplift melodrama, the compensatory mode of "what if" and "as if."

The racial uplift melodrama that appeared in the first decades of the twentieth century was oriented toward race improvement, as I have argued elsewhere, as the narrative of sentimentality gave way to the story of the achievement of respectability.[41] Race movies, as we have been discussing them, featured narratives of personal improvement (*The Trooper of Troop K*) but also moral improvement, as in Lincoln's *The Law of Nature* in which a young mother leaves her wealthy rancher husband and child for the excitement of an eastern city. Instead of a black version of the classic maternal melodrama *East Lynne,* the film has the mother realize that she must adhere to "Nature's Law" and return to her husband and child.[42] By and large, race movies feature the dream of a life in which the *only* imperatives are moral imperatives, the imperatives of hunger and poverty having been vanquished.

But it is finally the dream of inherited wealth in *By Right of Birth* (1921) that tells us the most about the longings of the black community during this period. As a fantasy based on the historical miracle of the discovery of oil on Oklahoma land deeded to the children of freedmen, George P. Johnson's script incorporates the inheritance into a crime drama in which crooks scheme to defraud the rightful heir, the light-skinned heroine, who nearly loses her fortune. A co-ed at a California university, Juanita's foster parents assume that she is an Indian. When she finally comes into her fortune, aided by the young Negro lawyer with whom she attended college, she discovers lost family members and is embraced by the race that she happily claims as part of her inheritance. The dream in which slavery is reversed and negated by a legacy of wealth that allows the succeeding generation to live in upper middle class ease reveals the degree to which the uplift story may be hegemonic, a point to which I will return shortly.

Generally, it could be said that the better sensibilities of uplift lean toward the largesse of the world-improving dream, but my case for understanding the utopian dimension of race movies does not rest on the uplift narrative alone. Of perhaps greater significance is the middle class mise-en-scène of the early race movies, which produced objects and properties in deep space and offered layer upon layer of consumer goods, illustrating the lifestyles of the characters portrayed by the all-black cast. As I have argued before, the motion picture screen is a distant relation of the department store window, the new commodity landscape that appeared at the turn of the century.[43] Significantly, Bloch places a good deal of emphasis on what he calls the "wishful landscape" and sometimes the "hope-landscape," concepts that seem to take account of the way the "pictorial" appeals to utopian desires and even instills longing in its representation of the beautiful life: "And the examination of anticipatory consciousness must fundamentally serve to make comprehensible the actual reflections which now follow, in fact depictions of the wished-for, the anticipated better life, in psychological and material terms."[44] Bloch's description of what happens in the motion picture theater suggests that it is the extra-dimensionality created by the film illusion that fosters the utopian daydream: "Every background turns towards the foreground here, and the wishful action or wishful landscape so essential to the film climbs, although only photographed, into the stalls."[45]

Bloch's theorization of the wishful landscape that renders a panorama extending off the screen and into the theater suggests that he is thinking about Technicolor and the widescreen cinema, which would have been familiar to him in the 1950s. But it is now a truism in the history of film that each decade's technological advances produced awe and excitement in viewers, so that one might expect that in the 1910s and 1920s even the silent black-and-white screen could inspire larger-than-life aspirations. A still from the lost Oscar Micheaux film *The Brute* (1920) evinces a race movie set, perhaps atypical in its extreme sumptuousness but nevertheless a suggestion of the inventory of richly appointed brocade furniture and valuable objets d'art that constituted an attraction in and of themselves. In Bloch's terms, it is a short leap from such a luxuriant mise-en-scène to utopian wishes, and it is here that film studies first

"Bull" Magee (A. B. Comathiere) and Mildred Carrison (Evelyn Preer)
The Brute (dir. Oscar Micheaux, 1920)

discovered the utility of Bloch. To date, the most productive use of the notion of utopia in film studies and popular culture has been Richard Dyer's reading of Hollywood musicals as addressing the utopian imagination. For Dyer, that imagination is manifest not only in the way the collective effort of putting the show on the road addresses the need for community but in the way the opulent mise-en-scène speaks to the desire for plenty to go around.[46] It may be significant here that so many of Oscar Micheaux's sound-era films featured musical song and dance numbers, cheerful utopian islands in the middle of what by today's dramatic standards are one cardboard encounter after another.[47]

It is reasonable to think of the audiences for race movies as dreaming along with the films and wishing for the freedom from want that the luxury sets stood for. This dreaming should be contrasted with the fears expressed by early critics of motion pictures that, for less fortunate viewers, Hollywood glitter produced dissatisfaction with their lives. But the problem with such suspicions about the production of dissatisfaction is that the entirety of the narrative may not be considered, and opulence would generally have a context. The early black film companies consistently produced this vision of plenty in the mise-en-scène of the middle class living room, in many cases a vision added as a kind of epilogue in a scene that restored the beleaguered family to wholeness. In several of these films, however, the wish landscape of middle class space is at odds with narrative logic, since developments in the film lead anywhere but to the comfort of home.

Most disjunctive is the final scene of Oscar Micheaux's *Body and Soul* (1925), which comes after the main character Martha Jane has awakened from the dream-flashback that constitutes the entire film, a bad dream in which the minister she idolizes (Paul Robeson) rapes her adored daughter, who consequently dies of starvation after she has run away to Atlanta.[48] The final scene portrays Martha Jane surrounded by grandchildren in her married daughter's cozily affluent living room. The daughter is now married to the man who figures as the minister's good brother in her mother's nightmare, a man who, when he enters the room in his business suit, does so as a respectable provider who has sold the patent to his invention.[49] This scene is eerily echoed in Micheaux's much later sound film, *God's Stepchildren* (1938). A tragedy of color caste, boycotted, as noted in the previous chapter, by the Young Communist League, in this film the light-skinned Naomi, a "bad seed," causes trouble for her foster family as a child and leaves home to pass for white, eventually running away from her marriage and her dark-skinned husband. In the final happy family tableau, the film cuts to the face of Naomi in the window, outside the house looking in at her own mother playing with the children she has abandoned, children who are safely cradled in the mise-en-scène of middle class prosperity.

In both of these Micheaux films, the epilogue contributes an abrupt change in tone and style of shooting. The tableau or set piece seems an acknowledgment that despite the social realities the director feels compelled to dramatize, he is still making uplift films and is equally obligated to redirect the attention of the audience in the final frames toward the aspiration for better things. A similar mood shift occurs in the epilogue at the end of *Ten Nights in a Barroom* where the Charles Gilpin character, a self-destructive drunk for ninety minutes in the film, is restored not only to sobriety by the tragic loss of his young daughter but to a prosperity that is only justified by indications of the passage of years. The patriarch, now a leading citizen, stands by the fireplace in his elegant home, flanked by family and friends.

In these films in which the last word is the image of improvement, and in others such as *Within Our Gates* (1920) and *The Scar of Shame* (1929) that end with an image of a united couple, "family" is the face put on the race. In the uplift strategy of race progress everything is riding on the family.[50] Marriage and family, the refuge of blacks since Reconstruction, the solution for all social ills, was the face that masked the social disintegration produced by economic hardship. There was then, as I have said, an inconsistency between the face of the race shown in the epilogue and the social pathology obliquely addressed in so many of these films. And, again, the paradigm for this can be found in the basic contradiction of uplift ideology in which the wide vision of democratic progress coexists with the narrower class solution that invests everything in the leading members of the race who stand as examples and who are to be explicitly entrusted with the administration of advancement.[51] There is something familiar that we should recognize about uplift ideology, about the trust in the educated elite as well as the "bootstraps" self-help rhetoric. Isn't uplift ideology nothing more than the white point of view issuing from a different source?

While it may be true that members of the black middle class and the white middle class were speaking the same language of race, each would, of course, have *experienced* race differently.[52] This phenomenon whereby a subordinate group voices the language of the dominant, a language that cannot ultimately serve its interests, we understand according to the Gramscian notion of hegemony, a concept widely used in cultural studies but until recently not utilized as productively as it might have been to explain the historical position of the black middle class. As a classic example of the function of hegemony, this class can be understood as embracing the dominant culture as its own, enthusiastically taking up some of the same versions of the Negro that worked against black efforts to advance themselves while at the same time conscientiously protesting white offenses. Ideological hegemony *is* so successful because it works *through* the very people it cannot and will not serve, replacing their own dreams with its dreams for them. Or, as in Bloch, this is a lesson in "how the ruling class wishes the wishes of the weak to be."[53] These wishes *for* that become the wishes *of* are the wishes cherished by women and minority peoples, wishes that Julia Lesage, among others, has emphasized as "hegemonic fantasies."[54]

The Wishes of the Weak

By now the importance of distinguishing between utopian aspirations and hegemonic fantasies must be clear, particularly since these forces are often found in opposition within the same works of culture. Certainly, one of the foundational principles of cultural studies is an understanding of this very tension in the popular, theorized by Stuart Hall as the "double movement" of popular culture that can be seen as a vacillation between containment and resistance.[55] And yet cultural studies would appear to have lost connection with Ernst Bloch and the original moment of this conception of the sparkling aspect of the oppositional: although "doubleness" does give us the sense that popular culture is divided against itself (as well as the sense that the popular is not thoroughly degraded), doubleness no longer seems able to convey the sense of the spark that could ignite a revolution. In fact, in cultural studies the notion of the utopian may have become so blunted from overuse (from application to any and every upbeat moment in popular culture), that it has lost all theoretical precision.[56]

For cultural studies, one of the most important sources of the concept of the utopian is Fredric Jameson's essay on *Jaws* in which he makes reference to the requisite "genuine shred" of something without which mass culture could not manipulate because it would not appeal. Jameson's use of the concept of utopia here is atypical, particularly since of all of the attempts to work through the possibility of the transcendent aspects of the popular it is the only one that has retained any sense of Bloch's complex theorization of how mass culture must release the fantasies and dreams of the masses if it must at the same time serve the ruling order.[57] In an often-cited passage Jameson makes reference to "hope," the term that is seldom, if ever, used in relation to utopia within contemporary cultural studies, although "hope" is Bloch's own term and basic to his understanding of anticipatory consciousness. "Hope," as Bloch defines it, is not the vague and even futile emotion we have from common usage but "an exact emotion," an emotion that is "capable of sharpening," even finally a "militant emotion."[58] Further, it is hope that works on cultural material that is not as yet utopian, material that it finally "forges" into utopia.[59] And it is hope as the expectant aspect of utopia (particularly at its juncture with liberation theology) that would seem to explain the wildly enthusiastic reception of race movies in the black community. To begin with, the very fact of their production was a cause for hope, some sense of which is suggested by the consensus among scholars that in the first years of race movies it hardly made any difference what was shown—any race movie was an exhilarating experience.[60]

If, however, we argue that any and all race movies gave expression to the utopian aspirations of their black audiences, is this the same thing as arguing that these films were all equally progressive? By introducing the question of the progressive valence of the text, we are returning to one of the more fraught areas of film theory, and this for several reasons not the least of which is the problem of measurement. Although, beginning in the 1970s, significant effort was made to think through the problem of how to gauge the political dimension of the popular film text, over the ensuing decades arguments for seeing one text as more progressive than another have become less and less convincing, particularly given the critical tendency to see an increasing number of popular texts as having progressive attributes.[61] One could begin to wonder whether there is any such thing as a thoroughly reactionary popular text, to state the extreme. It is worth returning to Bloch in an attempt to clear up this question, particularly since he early anticipated this crucial aspect of the cultural studies methodology. In the history of ideological criticism, Bloch should be a more important figure than he has been to date, particularly because of his theorization of the excess in great works of literature and culture that would seem to elude the ideological project, the "surplus over and above their mere ideology," as he phrases it.[62] Utopia, in Bloch, would "fetch what is its own from the ideologies and explain the progressive element which continues to be historically effective in the great works of ideology itself," confirmation that the utopian can be extracted from traditional texts.[63] But even more important for our purposes is Bloch's role in advocating a similar approach to understanding the "surplus" within the most apparently reactionary popular forms, particularly those forms denigrated by the members of the Frankfurt School from whom he was estranged.

As Jack Zipes tells us about Bloch, he was particularly interested in listening to the wants and needs of the people through the study of fairy tales, the circus, and cartoons, and stressed the historical importance of *colportage,* the wares of the traveling booksellers, the cookbooks and romances sold to the lower classes in Europe from the seventeenth to the nineteenth centuries.[64] What Bloch was listening for, of course, were the slight, almost imperceptible indications of, but not quite manifestations of, what *could become* revolutionary consciousness. This was the revolutionary consciousness in embryo that he continued to feel was not being addressed by socialism.[65] Although not tapped by socialism in the West, these needs would be released by a great movement within several decades of the advent of race movies, a movement that produced social upheaval if not revolutionary change, and here I am speaking of the U.S. civil rights movement.

Scholars have only just begun, following the lead of Paul Gilroy and others, to look at the role of popular culture in relation to the civil rights movement.[66] But here we are faced with the question of how to deal with the coexistence of the progressive and the hegemonic in race movies of the late teens and early twenties, and the problems facing us do not only have to do with the doubleness of race movies but also with the recurring dilemma of how to gauge what is and isn't progressive given the distance from anything resembling revolutionary consciousness. While I think that the case can be made for the progressive aspect of black casting where black actors are placed in traditional white middle class roles and situations, we would go too far if we were to argue that race movies were somehow always and automatically progressive. They are only flickers of what could, but not necessarily would, become revolutionary consciousness. Certainly the sight of other blacks living it up, climbing to the top, and holding their own in difficult circumstances played to the most expectant of emotions. Without a doubt, race movies spoke to the yearnings of black folk for more and better. But after elaborately laying out an approach to theorizing the politics of these films, we confront a development that Bloch did not anticipate. Pulling against the theoretical apparatus I am outlining is a strong current, a tendency to see these films as progressive if for no other reason than they are black. Does the very blackness of these films guarantee their politics? Stuart Hall perhaps does a better job of foregrounding this problem when he says in reference to contemporary black culture that blackness is no "guarantee" that the politics will be progressive.[67]

Color Coding

I raise this question of mere blackness here in relation to a sensitive issue, an issue particular to race movies as to no other high or mass culture phenomenon at any other time in history, and that is the question of skin color coding, a question I will return to in chapter 6 from the controversial angle of the body's role. Although retrospectively, historians such as Donald Bogle have criticized race movies for their replication of the color hierarchy, citing, as I have noted, their "shameless promotion of the world of hair-straighteners and skin-lighteners."[68] Bogle is echoing an earlier criticism, that important criticism contemporary with the release of these films, a criticism that issued from the black press, as I discussed in the last chapter. By the second decade of race movies the black press was expressing hostility to what it saw as a reinforcement of the worst tendencies in color consciousness. Theophilus Lewis in the *Amsterdam*

News, in addition to attacking Micheaux's presentation style, criticized *A Daughter of the Congo* (1926) on the basis of its "persistent intraracial color fetishism." "All the noble characters are high yellows; all the ignoble ones are black," he noted, a situation that he saw as creating an "artificial association of nobility with lightness and villainy with blackness."[69] The Young Communist League was able to put a political interpretation on *God's Stepchildren* (1938) by noting that a light-skinned character rejects a dark-skinned suitor and elects to pass.[70]

Concern about Micheaux's use of skin color shades as well as his use of pejorative types would eventually produce a negative critical consensus on the filmmaker in the black press. In the process of seriously reconsidering Micheaux, however, many more interpretations of his color system have been advanced. Most recently, for instance, Ron Green has asked whether Micheaux was just reproducing an existing system that privileged lightness or inventing his own.[71] To the charge of color consciousness, Richard Grupenhoff has replied that Micheaux himself was dark-skinned (although both of the women he married were light-skinned). Why, Grupenhoff asks, would Micheaux (with the exception of Paul Robeson) prefer the light-skinned hero when he himself was dark-skinned? Ron Green, however, has recently suggested that the prevailing wisdom that Micheaux was dark may be wrong.[72] Complicating the question still further, Lorenzo Tucker, the light-skinned actor who starred in so many sound-era Micheaux films, has claimed that the director *did* cast *against* color type, employing "all the shades of the black race," and often going against stereotypes.[73]

Perhaps cinematic color coding is best explained as an adherence to the realist aesthetic, that aesthetic that claims merely to record or register all the while it actually constructs its own "reality," a reality that gives support and solidity to particular ideologies of race. This notorious ideology of realism, what I am calling *racial realism,* can also be counted on to go against sense evidence at the same time that it relies on it. And clearly, as I have argued, there is an apparent similarity in the ideology of race to which the black as well as the white middle class subscribed during this period. But when it came to the casting of the cinematic representation of blackness, the two cinemas, white and black, were at complete odds. While actors playing Negro characters in race movies had to be light-skinned, actors playing Negro characters in mainstream white cinema had to be dark-skinned. The same actor could not then play Negro roles in both cinemas, although in a few cases light-skinned actors were darkened for parts in white cinema. Evelyn Preer, the talented member of the Lafayette Players, who starred in so many of Micheaux's silent films, was literally banned from acting in white films because she was so light-skinned.[74]

What do we make of a culture that dictates that the *light* should be *darkened* under some circumstances (the cinema) and that the *dark* should be *lightened* under others (in social circumstances)? Which way does white culture want black people to be? Clearly the ideology of assimilation that leads to whitening was in conflict with what might be called the ideology of race marking, and not only during the height of race movies but, as we will see in later chapters, throughout U.S. history. In relation to this history, the paradigm of color coding in motion pictures tells us everything about the contradictoriness that characterized attitudes in the larger society, a society that in 1920 had reached the point at which so large a percentage of blacks had become racially mixed that they were impossible to classify according to existing codes. After the 1920 census, any attempt to count mulattoes was abandoned.[75] The category of "mulatto" virtually disappeared as it grew and former mulattoes were simultaneously absorbed into the more encompassing and welcoming category—"black." The "one-drop rule," the very rule that had defended slavery in the middle of the nineteenth century, was turned around to serve the interests of community and solidarity. The basis for exclusion turned into the basis for inclusion as racially mixed people descending from slaves came to claim after the Civil War the very portion of their heritage that white culture assumed they would not want.

So in this uncertain period from Reconstruction on into the 1920s it is not surprising that there would be such vacillation between whitening and blackening as solutions as well as strategies. And if there is a principle that unifies these apparently opposite poles of the color spectrum, it would be the law of eradication of ambiguity. In perhaps the most critically sophisticated work on color coding in black cinema, James Snead discusses the device of marking (and overmarking) black skin as a means of resolving this threatening ambiguity: "As if the blackness of black skin itself were not enough, we seem to find the color black repeatedly overdetermined, marked redundantly, almost as if to force the viewer to register the image's difference from white images. Marking makes it visually clear that black skin is a 'natural' condition turned into a 'man-made sign.'" And if there is a "reality" outside the ideology of realism, it is that the connection between race and skin color is indeterminate. Concludes Snead: "Marking is necessary because the *reality* of blackness or of being 'colored' cannot always, either in films or in real life, be determined."[76]

Chapter Four

Black Beauty Culture

Where the white motion picture industry "blackened" race stars, the beauty culture industry was said to "whiten" ordinary black people. Cosmetics companies, owned by whites as well as blacks, responded to the challenges for black people of living within white society by producing the very instruments that were said to make these people "other" than themselves. Consumers of hair straighteners and skin lighteners were charged with attempting to emulate whites. The harsh criticism of such black beauty practices from within as well as from outside the black community was based not only on what was perceived to be white imitation but also on a betrayal of "the natural," a denial of a "real" cultural identity and a genuine self. Black beauty culture would seem to be an embarrassing chapter in the world history of bodily transformation and ritual beautification. The sensitivity of the subject, however, is all the more reason for Anglo-American as well as African American culture critics to study these practices, which implicate white people as well as black. We are called on to find new ways of studying a suspect pleasure.

Since at this time in history we have a well-founded suspicion of any invocation of "naturalness," however, particularly any appeal that goes hand in hand with the essentialism of the "real self," we need to find some other approach to this important phenomenon. Although there is a logic to seeing these practices more complexly as part of the hegemonic fantasy of being white, we may miss something if we put black beauty culture completely on the side of white hegemony. Following Bloch, we should not entirely rule out any sign, any clue that black beauty practices might give us of the imagination of a different world. Taking this theoretical route, we know that we are looking for that wish that indicates unmet needs in the most dangerous and degraded practice or despised popular form. Not only are the habits of hair straightening and skin lightening among the most despised of Western female rituals, but they appear to be profound acts of resignation to "things as they are" in a racially stratified society.

There is another reason for not ignoring what has been construed as a politically retrograde area of culture. These questionable black beauty products, the consumers who used them, and the black entrepreneurs who produced and sold them also offer us another way into the race movie phenomenon. Popular motion pictures and cosmetology: two industries that produced race pride as they made their appeals for self-improvement directly to ordinary black people. Coincident in time and benefiting from the same historical moment, both industries were deeply

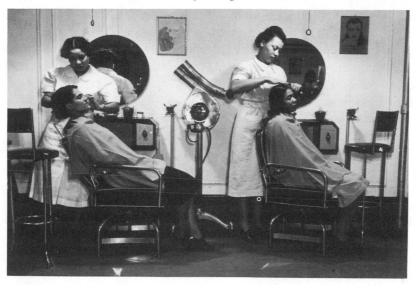

"Patrons having their hair styled"
(photographer: H. A. Brown, n.d.)

indebted to uplift and advancement—the one selling beautification-as-progress and the other marketing improved images as opportunity. Situated between everyday black existence and the white world, these products mediated a difficult relation, functioning as salves for the skin and the soul.

Comparisons between the black beauty entrepreneurs and race movie pioneers themselves are also productive as we begin to learn more about the class of industrious blacks who discovered mass culture as a means of personal profit as well as group salvation. And in the long run it is probably more reliable to draw analogies between William Foster, George and Noble Johnson, and Oscar Micheaux and the great names in black beauty culture than it is to group the race movie pioneers with the Harlem Renaissance literary figures. Here the significant common denominator is the mass-marketed commodity. Both race movie makers and beauty culturists had dreams based on a mass scale, and both mingled commerce with improvement ideals. The beauty culture pioneers—Annie Turnbo Malone (Poro Company, St. Louis, 1900), Madame C. J. Walker (Denver, 1905; Pittsburgh, 1908; Indianapolis, 1910), and Sarah Spencer Washington (Apex Company, Atlantic City, 1920)—all conceived of their businesses as advancement institutions. Beginning with personal health and hygiene and expanding out into the community, they created jobs for black women and established the beauty salon as a familial space. While their vision of all-black-owned everything was analogous to that of the movie pioneer who imagined black audiences, black theater owners, and black managers in the ideal marketplace, these industrious women came much closer to realizing their dreams for the black community and, unlike the race movie makers, they profited from their ventures. The myth about Madame Walker as a "black millionaire," while it may have been somewhat of an exaggeration, still symbolized the fact of the significant personal fortune that her beauty culture empire produced.[77]

It was the Madame C. J. Walker Company that, more than any other company targeting the black consumer, was able to successfully link the most mundane need to the larger purpose of historical advance, devising an advertising campaign that framed beauty culture in the context of Emancipation. "In 64 short years our people have cast aside the shackles of slavery—have risen to the heights of social and commercial supremacy," claimed one ad, which credited "PRIDE OF RACE, APPLIED INDUSTRY and BETTERED APPEARANCE" with this astounding progress.[78] Commenting on the enormity of this claim in relation to the ordinariness of the product, Kathy Peiss observes, "Caught up in its story of uplift and hope, a reader might be forgiven if she overlooked that this was, after all, a sales pitch for hair grower, bleach cream, and face powder."[79]

Still, the obsession with beautification appeared to be at odds with the ideals of the new racial solidarity movements so significant in the first two decades of the century, as Peiss also notes.[80] To many, skin lightening and hair straightening epitomized race betrayal and self-hatred. Stressing the contradictoriness of these practices, Peiss cites a sociologist who from the vantage of 1924 finds "conflicting forces" in operation in the black American community, which the sociologist describes as "an attempt to efface racial characteristics" matched by "an unmistakably powerful force, race pride, which is everywhere evident in Negro life"[81]—again, our theme of the confounding doubleness of black life, of the incommensurability of aspirations. Black beauty practices, like race movies, embodied the triumph over as well as the capitulation to white values. How, then, do we answer the charge of white emulation? How do we understand this particular "mimic need," that need that Bloch called the "tempting desire to transform oneself"?[82] How does the "mimic need" appear in a new light given the strong prohibitions against the self-immolation and race renunciation that always seemed to accompany the use of black beauty products?

Kathy Peiss's analysis suggests two ways of getting around the automatic denunciation of these controversial practices. First, there is the caveat that applies to the interpretation of motion pictures as well as the

use of beauty products: *we cannot assume uniform use.* A comparison between the varied uses of skin bleach and readings of narrative fictions is
not so far-fetched since such a comparison can establish, if nothing else,
that consumers have wildly differing needs and desires. But where all of
the empirical research in the world will never fully explain to us how
people engage the fantasy material they crave, sociological research can
tell us, for instance, how women use cosmetics. Thus we can know, as
Peiss suggests, that women's application of skin bleach differed enor-
mously, and for every woman who used the bleach to peal off the dark
surface of her face, another might sparingly dot it on blemishes.[83] Second, and most important, black beauty aids facilitated adaptation to difficult if not impossible situations by means of pragmatic facial and
bodily modifications. As Peiss observes about the women who worked
as maids, cooks, and housekeepers, "most adapted their beauty practices to immediate social realities, an adaptation that straighteners
and bleaches might facilitate."[84] Consider, for example, Madame C. J.
Walker's Tan-Off, sales of which rose dramatically in the 1920s, a product purporting to improve as well as to lighten the skin. In chemical composition, these products were similar to the home treatments for dark
skin that consisted usually of lemon juice, peroxide, and witch hazel, or
peroxide and ammonia. Yes, the bleaching cream that burned the face
and the straightening comb that scorched the neck and ears were instrumental in maintaining white hegemony. But health hazards aside, many
black people saw these beauty practices as nothing more than a way of
easing things for blacks in their interface with white society. As Noliwe
Rooks's grandmother told her, straightening her hair would give her a
slight advantage since it was "one less battle that would have to be
fought."[85] But while these products did actually lighten the skin, they
did not perform the miracle that at one time in history so many black
Americans wished for—the miracle of suddenly, instantaneously becoming white. And yet wanting to be white is like wishing for social access and enlarged community, for plenty to go around, for self-esteem
and respectability.

Narratives of Reversed Racial Identity

If skin lighteners addressed the hegemonic fantasy that one could suddenly, miraculously, become white, race movies would introduce the reverse: a character who is thought to be white is miraculously found to be
black, a discovery that resolves the black hero's romantic dilemma. He
may now marry the woman he loved all along because she is a woman

of his own race. The couple, separated for a time, are reunited when he discovers the "truth" of her racial identity that was before hidden to her as well as to him. "But Agnes didn't know that she was not white," writes the reviewer in the *Chicago Defender*.[86] The empirical "truth" of the light-skinned heroine's racial identity becomes the guiding light of race progress, a sign that the hero's long-suffering pioneer endurance and sacrifice have not been in vain.

Oscar Micheaux first introduced this reversal pattern as a narrative structure in his third novel, *The Homesteader*, and would return to a similar race reversal in the later *The Wind from Nowhere*.[87] A modified version of the race discovery story is utilized as well in *The Symbol of the Unconquered* (1920), although there the heroine's race is inexplicably unknown to the hero while it is known to the other characters. Not stopping there, the reversal story appears again in *The Exile* (1931), the sound film adaptation of *The Homesteader*, and from all indications it was part of his first film adaptation of the novel in 1919, a film that is now lost. And, finally, Micheaux closed his film production career with the same story he began it with, adapting, for his final effort, *The Wind from Nowhere* as *The Betrayal* (1948). A film now lost, we have only the description of the three-hour epic to tell us that Micheaux returned to his original concerns with a vengeance.

In *The Betrayal*, the South Dakota farmer hero finally marries the white woman after much soul-searching, and the marital unhappiness that immediately follows can be interpreted as a judgment against interracial marriage. Upon the discovery that the wife has Negro blood, their fortunes change and their marital harmony is ensured. The New York *Amsterdam News*, in a review that may well have been drawn from the publicity materials for the film, emphasizes a variant on the drama of passing, the question of the prevalence of black blood in white Americans:

> Posing such questions as how many whites have Negro blood and
> would be classified as colored if their neighbors knew the truth
> and how do colored women feel about Negro men marrying
> white women, the film tells the story of a colored man who settles
> out west in a community where he is the only Negro.[88]

In other words, Micheaux has upped the race relations ante, asking questions that still cause white as well as black Americans incredible discomfort. The question about black women's attitude toward sexual alliances between black men and white women is so fraught that feminism (for all of its historic courageousness in respect to difficult social issues) has remained silent.[89] Micheaux's other equally unnerving question would have all white Americans consider the possibility that, like Agnes Stewart, they, too, could discover that they had a black ancestor.

A lone voice on the subject of American race mixing, philosopher Adrian Piper has foregrounded this issue in her critical writing and contemporary performance work. Forty years after Micheaux's box-office failure broached the topic of the black blood in all of us, Piper's video installation *Cornered* (1988) faced off with the general public. Confrontational and interactive, Piper's video monitors present white viewers with facts about racial mixing in American history. Viewers who enter the exhibit room encounter monitors on which faces representing the peoples of the world instruct white people about the possibility that they are probably black. In an interview Piper explains, "The fact is that there are no genetically distinguishable white people in this country anymore, which is about what you'd expect after four hundred years of intermarrying. And the longer a person's family has been in this country, the higher the likely proportion of African ancestry—bad news for the Daughters of the American Revolution."[90] While Piper's calculated response to the incredulous seems to be to force a return to the historical, she is also subtly anticipating the first reaction of those who have been denied the historical evidence of interracial intermixture, buried so deep for so long. Immediately, white as well as black people *want to know what happened*.

In this regard, the most frequent approach to understanding Micheaux's fascination with the race reversal thematic involves recourse to autobiographical facts since, beginning with his first and third novels, *The Conquest* and *The Homesteader*, the filmmaker returned so consistently to familiar scenes and based his characters on family members, as I have noted.[91] Many scholars have remarked on the way most of Micheaux's novels and many of his films appear to have begun with the facts of the filmmaker's life, most persistently returning to the events of the years when he homesteaded in South Dakota, the years covered by *The Conquest, The Homesteader, The Wind from Nowhere*, and the films based on these novels. Often, then, scholars ask the inevitable question about the possible existence of the woman who may have inspired the character of Agnes Stewart in *The Homesteader*, the daughter of the Scot, Jack Stewart, a neighboring farmer whose wife, now dead, turns out to have had Negro blood.[92]

But the question of the existence of this woman (the prototype for Agnes Stewart) in Micheaux's life is like the question of the existence of Negro blood: it is a "test of truth" that doesn't necessarily need to be passed in order for the story to make its allegorical point. Neither question can be resolved either empirically or philosophically. For the allegory is testimony to the contradictory evidence of blood that is both visible and invisible, not there one minute and there the next. In this mysterious process of racial identification, the visible is no guarantee of anything, and ontologically there is a deep discrepancy between what is and what appears to be. Race pride resolves apparent discrepancies and overrules objections.

This paradox of race pride to which Micheaux returns so predictably asserts that if you steadfastly observe the custom of the culture that decrees that you must marry within your own race, you will be rewarded. The one you love but cannot marry (whom you believe to be of another race) will in the end be discovered to be of the *same* race. The blood that is invisible is thus made visible, forced into visibility by the act of identification. And fortuitously, in the race pride reversal, the one who is re-racialized immediately accepts and embraces his or her newfound identity. A swift narrative inversion is required by the allegory, a development that has no time for either psychological adjustment or identity crisis.[93] In its swift certainty, the race pride allegory produces a political benefit—it reverses the local logic of passing. "Since black blood is not detectable, light-skinned blacks can therefore live as whites" becomes "Since black blood is not detectable, those who discover their heritage will want to live as blacks," as in Micheaux's story. Duplicitous and malevolent passing is sharply renounced, and the problem of the invisibility of blood is overridden by a race ideology to which white and black both subscribe: although black blood may not be detectable, in the end it is *determining.*

All passing is not equal and all passing is not necessarily masquerade. It would seem that Oscar Micheaux is making a distinction between the *inadvertent* passing of Agnes Stewart, sweetly innocent of her heritage, and the malfeasance of *intentional* passing, exemplifed by the villain Driscoll in *The Symbol of the Unconquered.* The race pride allegory has its antithesis in a variant on the intentional passing story in which the light-skinned heroine is surreptitiously "passed off" as white against her will—a story of *coerced* passing. This is exemplified by Charles Chesnutt's *The House behind the Cedars,* a novel Micheaux adapted twice for the screen (first in 1924/25 and later as *The Veiled Aristocrats* in 1932). In Chesnutt's narrative the mother and brother conspire to marry the exquisite light-skinned daughter to a wealthy white man. The white man rejects her when he learns that he has been deceived, a cruelty that brings about her death.[94]

Reflecting on this thematic, Corey Creekmur has suggested that Micheaux's fascination with racial duplicity grew out of his involvement with Chesnutt's work, and therefore that passing was more Chesnutt's obsession than Micheaux's. This preoccupation Creekmur sees as the result of Chesnutt's own options as a light-skinned mulatto who could have passed but who had always resisted the temptation.[95] Micheaux, in contrast, since he was relatively dark-skinned, Creekmur argues, would have been attracted to the literary possibilities of passing as trope.[96] But far more than the literary potential that he never really mined in his novels, Micheaux was interested in the sensational aspect of the passing narrative, an angle that he could capitalize on in a motion picture campaign, and thus it was that he latched on to the amazing similarities between *The House behind the Cedars* and the scandalous Rhinelander trial. His advertisement in the Baltimore *Afro-American* hawked the passing story: "The House Behind the Cedars is a remarkable parallel to the famous Rhinelander Case. . . . It tells the story of a beautiful mulatto girl who poses as white, and is wooed and won by a young white millionaire. Although worried, she does not betray her secret. Then comes the discovery as in the Rhinelander case."[97]

To be sure, the treatment of the light-skinned heroine in Micheaux's film did pick up the themes of the contemporary Rhinelander case, but the one significant difference between the two passing narratives reveals Micheaux's viewpoint. In the Rhinelander case, the wealthy young husband and heir, under pressure from his family, tried to divorce his new wife, arguing that he had been deceived about her Negro ancestry.[98] It is not so much that the woman had passed herself off as white but that the husband, under pressure from his family, is forced to renounce her. His wife's black blood offers him a convenient exit from the marriage. It is not then the young woman who is dramatically unveiled in the Rhinelander story (as she is in Chesnutt's story); it is the motivations of the white family who seek to have the marriage annulled. What would draw Micheaux to both of these stories is this ceremonious unveiling, not of the light-skinned woman but of white duplicity. The racial mistake (the one mistaken for the other) exposes white perceptions and assumptions and proclaims that the difference between difference and sameness is negligible. In the hands of Micheaux, passing is a device for pointing up the stubborn misconceptions of white folks as well as the cruel deceptions of black ones. Neither group is left blameless. Political through it may be in motive, the passing story in Micheaux's hands is also a vehicle for inveighing against hypocrisy in general.

But there is something far more important to stress about the passing story, something beyond the possibility of Chesnutt's personal obsession and Micheaux's opportunism. The black community has historically housed a vast store of social mythology about both intentional and inadvertent passing, about blood hidden and revealed, a mythology that has only recently begun to attract the interest of white academics in the abstract. In her introduction to a recent collection of essays on boundary crossings, on the confusion of racial and sexual identities, Elaine Ginsberg suggests the density of the paradigm: "For the possibility of passing challenges a number of problematic and even antithetical assumptions about identities, the first of which is that some identity categories are inherent and unalterable essences: presumably one cannot pass for something one *is not* unless there is some other, pre-passing identity that one *is*."[99] Clearly the philosophical implications are intriguing, and my own purely academic interest in the theoretical conundrum in which one is at the same time what one is not, on the move from *is* to *is not*, and back again, should be obvious.

But in stark contrast to this theoretical puzzle are the lives of so many African Americans touched in some way by family members who "passed on" into the white community (with the implication that they might as well be deceased a functioning part of the mythology). One could surmise that passing stories have remained submerged in popular American culture because telling these stories endangered those who had passed, and Adrian Piper, again breaking the silence, speaks of the prohibition in black families against "outing" those who have gone over into white culture.[100] To further Piper's provocative assertion that all American families, white and black, have been touched by racial intermixing means that we should consider as well that every family hides incidents of passing. The more dramatic stories are there in the oral histories of African Americans, the recollections of families dispersed and siblings estranged, and typical would be George P. Johnson's own story of his older brother Virgel who, with his wife Mabel, passed as white in Little Rock, Arkansas, where he became a prosperous highway contractor, living in what his brother described as a "white colonial mansion." To shield his brother, George never put his return address on the letters he sent from Los Angeles and because of the degree of risk, entertained his brother in his home there on only two or three occasions.[101]

While I wish to argue that passing is finally subversive in the way it silently and stoically refutes white misconceptions about black characteristics and capabilities and the way it undermines white attempts to create racially pure cultural spaces, I want to defer as well to the African American argument against passing. Adrian Piper, thinking this through, concedes that blacks who have historically passed as white have wanted the advantages that accrue to them as whites, from greater rights and privileges to social status and opportunity. Weighing on the other side is all that they lose and, by her calculation, they relinquish much more than they gain. "What is harder for me to grasp is how they could want these things enough to sacrifice the history, wisdom, connectedness, and moral solidarity with their family and community in order to get them. It seems to require so much severing and forgetting, so much disowning and distancing, not simply from one's shared past, but from one's former self—as though one had cauterized one's long-term memory at the moment of entry into the white community."[102] Micheaux's argument against passing is never reasoned in this way but seems to come instead from deep conviction and black community affiliation. Broadly, in contrast with the intentional passing story where discovery leads to rejection and death, in Micheaux's race pride version of passing, based on *inadvertent* deception, discovery brings acceptance and happiness.

Micheaux was finally as much of a moralist as he was a showman, and his passing dilemmas are clearly within the tradition of African American fictions that use the narrative device to pass judgment on the practice, from Nella Larsen's novels *Quicksand* and *Passing* to the two film adaptations of Fannie Hurst's *Imitation of Life*.[103] The current popularity of these texts, certainly evidence of the increasing importance of African American studies, also attests to the magnetic attraction of the passing predicament and the pathos of this particularly American quandary: two competing identities, one person. For much of the twentieth century, however, critical practice paralleled social condemnation, and passing was virtually ignored as a trope in literary history. Only recently has it become possible to understand the multidimensionality of passing as a formal principle. In literary criticism Hazel Carby led the way, opening up the question of the mulatto as a device for contrasting black and white cultures, helping to make the study of passing as a trope legitimate and facilitating the fuller treatment it requires, a treatment that allows us even to see how passing ironically assumes the one-drop rule.[104]

Still, the actual practice haunts the study of the narrative device while it remains elusive to the historian. This characteristic elusiveness, however, seems understandable since for all the fear of passing in the white community, passing, not unlike lynching, was historically linked to entirely fabricated events. More to the point, the cases of successful passing are like the cases of black male violation of white women in one way but not another. Examples of successful passing are almost impossible to verify (and have therefore angered whites) but are more likely to be underestimated as opposed to statistically inflated. The "logic of successful passing," says Naomi Zack, "has always precluded accurate statistics."[105] So the challenge is to analyze a practice that is not supposed to exist, yet an unmistakable phenomenon, one of enormous significance that has all the same been met by vehement denial of its existence. Passing is not only "symbolically central" in American culture; it has been more prevalent than we may think.[106]

It is finally the prevalence of these two controversial practices, passing and skin lightening, that requires us to find the utopian component, the genuine lure (if there is such a thing) that would counterbalance the sacrifice of self and social solidity that Adrian Piper describes. So if we are to consider the reverse side of black beauty products, we must look to the wish to move through the white world with more ease. From this standpoint, passing is the wish for more that leads one to act on that wish. But more what—merely more money and leisure or, legitimately, more justice? Let us not dismiss passing too soon, for we need to look as well at the critical component in the possibilities of race change because in the last analysis passing is a profound statement of the total arbitrariness of the correlation between skin color and race category. On the continuum between those two politically charged practices, skin lightening and passing, it is passing that in theory appeals to the utopian imagination as it finally pragmatically proclaims that *there is no difference.*

Oscar Micheaux's dramatization of race reversal and reunion in *The Homesteader* met with great enthusiasm in black communities where it was exhibited, as I discussed in chapter 3, and this must have given him the impetus to go further in his second film—to dare to return to the origins of the race reversal scenario, to lay the blame for the great American racial mix-up where it belonged, representing the escalation of white misconceptions to their most hysterical heights. That his second film, *Within Our Gates* (1920), was originally titled *Circumstantial Evidence* suggests that the extralegal justice that sets the historical scene of the film colored his early conception of the project. In less than a year, Micheaux had leaped from a story of pioneer struggle to the epitome of racial injustice—the lynching of an innocent family. How could he have known that his tumultuous film would one day stand alone as the only African American representation of lynching in the history of silent cinema?

Fire and Desire

If *The Birth of a Nation* was history "written with lightning," *Within Our Gates* was history written in smoke.[1] When Oscar Micheaux's second feature was first exhibited in major American cities, black as well as white communities treated it like a time bomb. The very black communities that had welcomed Micheaux's first film, *The Homesteader* (1919), and applauded the success of the Micheaux Book and Film Company, protested against *Within Our Gates.* In Chicago members of the Methodist Episcopal Minister's Alliance Committee, comprised of representatives of both races, took their case against exhibiting the film to the mayor and the chief of police.[2] The request for a permit to show the film had been denied after the first screening, but a more liberal group arguing for the social value of the film's subject matter prevailed after a second screening. The film opened at the Vendome Theatre in Chicago on January 12, 1920. But the protest against it continued up until the hour before the film opened.[3] Why? What kinds of scenes could represent such a danger to public safety in 1920? And what issue could unify white and black churches in this way?

In January 1920 *Within Our Gates* was caught up in a riot-lynching linkage that characterized American race relations in the 1920s. Because of this linkage (both real and imagined), the film's release offers another case study of the way the symbolism of events (inflected as socially dangerous) can become inextricably mixed up with the events themselves, especially during racially sensitive moments in history. Micheaux's film included a sequence depicting the hanging and burning of two innocent African Americans—a man and his wife. The sequence may have been no more than a short scene in a flashback filling in the history of the mulatta heroine Sylvia Landry (played by Evelyn Preer) and may have only had minor relevance to the central narrative. But the relation of a controversial segment to the narrative whole often becomes irrelevant when such a moving image is singled out by public discourse in this way. Released in the United States the year after the "Red summer" of 1919, the film encountered especially active resistance in Chicago where in July 1919 police indifference to a white gang's drowning of a black teenager set off a chain of South Side riots, an incident to which I will return in chapter 7.[4] In Shreveport, Louisiana, the Star Theatre refused to book the film because of its "nasty story."[5] Even in Omaha, Nebraska, Lincoln Motion Pictures head George P. Johnson explained the poor attendance at an August return engagement of the film as due to the film's reminding people of the events of the year before.[6] In New Orleans an internal police memo reported that "nine negroes" were lynched in the film.[7]

In several cities Micheaux was required by officials to edit out parts of the film, a situation I will later discuss, but even this continual recutting doesn't explain the wild discrepancies in viewers' reports.[8] The groups that wanted an outright ban on exhibiting Micheaux's film saw little results from their direct appeals to city officials whose peacemaking solution was to require these cuts. But the case of *Within Our Gates* brings home one of the many lessons of the NAACP campaign against *The Birth of a Nation,* a campaign discussed extensively in a later chapter. Whereas *protest* against a film in this period did not mean that it would be banned (and might even ensure that it would draw crowds), the threat of a race riot meant that exhibitors and city officials would cooperate to keep a film off the screen.[9]

What suggests comparison between *Within Our Gates* and *The Birth of a Nation* is the caldron of protest around racial imagery into which both films were flung. However, in almost every other way Micheaux's film is the antithesis of *The Birth of a Nation,* especially in its middle class, thoroughly black-centered view of American society. Also, in contrast to the NAACP protest around *The Birth of a Nation* (centered on the notion of falsehood in representation), the *Within Our Gates* controversy implicitly focused not on the fear of too little but on the fear of "too much truth," terrifying because the status quo discourse on "truth" made no reference to the political realities of southern lynch mob justice. Such mob justice, it should be remembered, had actually contributed to the instability of northern cities, crowded in 1919 with blacks who had left southern towns in the aftermath of lynchings. The move to ban screenings of Micheaux's film, then, was both an attempt to silence the protest against lynching and a law and order move to suppress protest against worsening housing and employment conditions in the North. *Within Our Gates* was thus linked to fear of cataclysmic social change, a linkage obfuscated by the smoke screen of "race riot." And here is where the difference between the fate of this film and that of *The Birth of a Nation* is so revealing. While Griffith's "masterpiece" was enshrined, Micheaux's answer to it was "run out of town," so to speak. While the white supremacist version of the Civil War survived, Micheaux's African American history lesson disappeared and was classified by film scholars as "lost." Seventy years later, a 35mm print version of *Within Our Gates,* now titled *La Negra,* was finally returned from the Spanish National Archive in Madrid to the Library of Congress.

La Negra: Our Estranged Culture Returned

What follows is an analysis of the film that was once titled *La Negra,* the only existing version of *Within Our Gates.* To foreground the strange history of this film, which we assume was exhibited in Spain, I have retained some of the Spanish language names in my discussion in this chapter. This is a work that has had two cultural lives: the first, during the troubled year of its U.S. exhibition and the second, in Spain where audiences would have seen it as "a strange tale of the American South," in the words of the opening intertitle. Somewhat like the trade in abolitionist literature that fled an inhospitable climate of race terror in favor of publication in Britain, this film is part of that traffic of banned discourse that has historically crossed the Atlantic along with African American intellectuals, themselves often fleeing discrimination. In 1990 the film was returned to the United States with Spanish language intertitles, a return of our estranged culture as an even stranger text.

Our cultural heritage is returned to us in a language other than the original English, producing a text that is literally unreadable for monolingual American speakers of English—African American and Euro-American English speakers alike. Ironically, only the Spanish-speaking minority in this country can properly "read" this film text. The English language speaker is hopelessly "illiterate" in the face of this silent film whose intertitles are crucial narrative markers, within a film that alternates with regularity between linguistic and iconic signification. The nondiegetic (otherworldly) narrator of the realm of the intertitles signs to the monolingual English reader to no avail. But the Euro-American English speaker may be handicapped beyond his or her inability to read the Spanish titles by what may very well be a stubborn ignorance of African American history and culture, the knowledge of which is basic to understanding the moving picture story told to the viewer through the articulation of black bodies in dramatic space.

And finally there is the difficulty of analyzing a version of this film that may be only a skeleton of the original, an original shredded by censors' cuts in the year of its notorious U.S. exhibition. But my analysis is neither a lament for an original text nor for an originary moment of reception; rather it treats *La Negra* as Micheaux's surviving text, assuming that it is structurally similar to the motion picture that disturbed so many in 1920. One could assume that *La Negra* is significantly changed, but one could also argue that since no two of the "original" prints exhibited in Chicago, New Orleans, and Omaha were identical to this one extant print, it is as much a *Within Our Gates* text as any other. Given this textual fluctuation, it also stands to reason that *La Negra* might be a pale shadow of the print of *Within Our Gates* shown to Chicago censors in 1919, but then again the earlier film could also have been more tame than the surviving one. Our only clues to the image content in the earlier text are to be found in the controversy it sparked. Here also the controversy around the film becomes my justification for focusing on the lynching story, and my exaggeration of the relative importance of this sequence in the narrative should be understood as a reprise of that earlier exaggeration.

My analysis will then to some degree disconnect this sequence from the larger narrative. This is not, however, to say that the lynching story is not integral to that narrative. As told by Sylvia's cousin Alma to her suitor Dr. Vivian (Charles D. Lucas), the lynching story is offered as an explanation for Sylvia's reluctance to marry the successful black doctor. Rather than serving any direct narrative purpose, the story functions as a kind of exorcism of the past, tagged on as it is to the end of the film. Once Sylvia's history is told, the film cuts to final shots of the heroine with Dr. Vivian who reconciles her to a more optimistic point of view, arguing that black participation in World War I has changed the meaning of American patriotism for blacks. The optimistic nationalism that ends the film thus depends on seeing the scenes of racial injustice as relegated to the past, not conceivable in either the present of the film's contemporary story or in the present of the film's year of release.

We are supposing, as I have said, that *La Negra* is structurally similar to the film that was shown in the United States in 1920. However, this assumption presents us with some mysteries. Why, despite the controversy, was the film promoted in terms of the minor lynching story in city after city? Why do none of the existing publicity materials mention the "uplift" narrative about Sylvia Landry's efforts to raise money for a school in the South? Instead of featuring this respectable narrative, the advertising "cuts" for the film hawk "Who Killed Phillip Girdlestone?" and promise, in addition to the solution of the mystery, a "Spectacular Screen Version of the Most Sensational Story on the Race Question Since Uncle Tom's Cabin."[10] This then must be the key—lynching as spectacular attraction, yet another sign of Micheaux's instincts as a showman, as discussed in chapter 3.

As in the tradition of Uncle Tom's Cabin, however, spectacle and emotion do go hand in hand.[11] The film-within-the-film is also a small sentimental melodrama—so complete, it is as though one were viewing an entire D. W. Griffith short dropped down within a silent feature. Not surprisingly, the lynching narrative owes its basic formal structure to Griffith, even while its rhetorical structure produces the antithesis of The Birth of a Nation—the history of Reconstruction from the black point of view. Felipe Gridlestone/Phillip Girdlestone (Ralph Johnson) is unwilling to settle accounts with black sharecropper Gaspar/Jasper Landry (William Starks), who has earned the $685 needed to repay his debt to the wealthy planter. A fight ensues when Landry urges the white villain to treat him fairly. But we see that Landry isn't alone in his feeling of animosity toward the cruel landowner. A poor white cracker, seeing his opportunity to get rid of the hated Girdlestone, shoots the aristocrat through the window. The blame falls on Landry. Girdlestone's meddlesome black butler Efrain/"Eph"/Ephrain (E. G. Tatum) has been watching the interview with the sharecropper, but hasn't seen the shooting and thus sounds the alarm that it is Landry who has murdered old Girdlestone. Landry, his wife, his young son Emilio/Emil, and his grown daughter Sylvia flee to the woods with the lynch mob on their trail. Here I want to interrupt my own account not only for purposes of explication and background but also to call attention to interruption as a device that is so productively employed in this narrative.

Lynching as Peculiarly American

Seldom have African American and Euro-American versions of social reality been more at odds than in the historical case of lynching. In white American popular mythology, a lynching is a hanging, punishment meted out to Negro men who had sexual relations with white women. Technically, however, lynching refers to an enforcement of justice outside the law that could involve any number of brutal punishments from burning to tarring and feathering. Even despite the attempts to educate whites about the full implications of lynching, first by black journalist Ida B. Wells in the 1880s and later by white reformers like southerner

Within Our Gates (dir. Oscar Micheaux, 1920)

Old Girdlestone (Ralph Johnson) is unwilling to settle accounts with sharecropper Jasper Landry (William Starks)

A poor white cracker shoots the aristocrat through the window

"Eph" the tattletale butler (E. G. Tatum) sees Landry and sounds the alarm that he has murdered Girdlestone

Jessie Daniel Ames, the post–Civil War rape and lynching mythology has persisted for whites even into the present. For black Americans, however, the situation is significantly different, since from the 1880s there has been a strong literary and journalistic effort to write lynching sagas as a form of protest against the practice. A comparison of Micheaux's banned version of southern injustice with the white mythology, then, needs to locate the terms of this dialogue, this ideological battle in the realm of representation.

Broader accounts of lynching tell us that it is a uniquely American phenomenon, evolving out of a tradition of vigilantism going back to the Revolutionary War. Because of the long association with racial issues, it is not well known that the first victims of "lynch law," that is, mob justice, were white. The practice that reached its height in 1877 was thus adapted from a preexisting tradition but with a significant difference: the sadistic punishments inflicted on blacks during the period of Reconstruction raised the ante for brutal acts as never before. And, as Jacqueline Dowd Hall tells us, there seemed to be a direct relationship between an increase in economic tensions and the sadism of the acts against Negroes, which included burning alive and torture as well as emasculation.[12]

The act of lynching, then, is a classic displacement, that highly charged adjustment in which something of peripheral importance comes to occupy a central position. Here, the central economic concern is shifted onto the sexual, or the threat to real property gets transposed as a threat to marginal symbolic property—white womanhood. But, to follow the Freudian dream metaphor further, it is not the taboo sexual thought that is repressed; it is the economic motive. In the period we are considering, sex (even when there was none) was historically asserted and "money" was denied. But to figure the economic basis of lynching too abstractly risks overlooking the unusual mix of multiple causes of the phenomenon. For lynching can be productively seen in both the Freudian and the Marxian senses as thoroughly overdetermined.[13]

Ritualized lynching, like Freud's dream element, is the product of a whole cluster of historical causes, so tangled, inverted, and disguised that one can never hope to trace the phenomenon back to a single source. Like Althusser's overdetermined superstructural phenomenon, the links between lynching and the economic base are so varied and multilayered as to seem hopelessly indeterminate.[14] However, in the 1920s the scattershot determinations of a lynching climate do cluster around four main social developments: the extension of voting rights to black men and the question of votes for women; returning World War I veterans seeking jobs; black competition for jobs and black economic successes; and consensual interracial sexual relations. I also say scattershot "causes" to emphasize the way mob justice came down, to emphasize the utter arbitrariness of the trumped-up justifications for lynching—the nonsense of the charges against southern Negroes. It seemed, says Hall in her study of the antilynching crusade, that the "transgression of a whole range of nebulous taboos" could result in brutal beating or even hanging for the incredulous black. And this "justice" was also indiscriminate since, given the "brushfire" effect of mob justice, it often didn't matter if the black person accused of the crime could not be found. If the crowd had worked up an appetite for black flesh, any convenient Negro might be executed. Micheaux gives us this informed view of the lynch mob in his portrait of the victimization of Girdlestone's servant Eph, who, having encouraged the mob to look for Landry, is himself grabbed as a substitute when they fail to find the accused. One contemporary film reviewer, apparently attempting to deny or explain away the scene wrote, "The lynching attempt leads to the boy who dreams he is lynched. You see him hung up in the vanishing illusion."[15] Either unconscious racism or clear inability to follow the film may explain the reference to Ephrain as a "boy," but one also wonders about the construal of the superimposition as a "dream," particularly when the intertitle newspaper account in the surviving print later confirms Ephrain's fate. Discounting the intertitle, one could imagine this shot as having a complex temporality as both a premonition and a representation of a hanging. Yet note how this particular image allows Micheaux to be somewhat evasive about Ephrain's fate. Viewers are encouraged to ask: Was he or wasn't he strung up?

Perhaps Micheaux's portrait of the lynch mob is his signal achievement in this film, for he chooses to show what blacks knew and northern whites would refuse to believe—the total barbarism of the white mob. The more astounding reports collected by Ida B. Wells in *On Lynchings* confirm that lynch mobs decapitated bodies and took the parts as trophies, invented obscene tortures, and burned victims after hanging them. Women and children were not sheltered from these obscenities but participated in the horrid revelry.[16] And here is where Micheaux is at his boldest—the mob he gives us is not the usual cadre of town bullies. White men, women, and children wield sticks and torches in some of the most unsettlingly beautiful scenes in silent cinema of the late teens. His day-for-night shooting renders a grotesque black silhouette against a light sky—a kind of multilimbed spiked monster spirals from background to foreground, attacking and receding in a dynamic use of screen depth. It is all the better that these scenes are also shot in such crisp focus, for what they portray is nothing more nor less than white people as primitives. The accusation of "savagery" is turned back onto white southern culture.

Yes, this is lynching as sensational spectacle. But we should consider how it is significantly different from the white-staged lynching as public spectacle, as social control and warning to blacks. Micheaux's screen representation of the horrors of southern lynching was intended to work in the exact opposite way on black audiences. For Micheaux, to reveal these horrors was *not* to contain and control through terror, but to urge blacks to take the higher ground. As his publicity asserted, this "Preachment of Race Prejudice and the Glaring Injustices Practiced Upon Our People" was to "Hold You Spellbound" and offer you details that would make you "Grit Your Teeth in Silent Indignation."[17] In the same spirit as *Uncle Tom's Cabin*, then, Micheaux's film was meant less to inspire action or race solidarity than to work as a kind of moral self-affirmation. Much of the appeal of "race movies," as I will argue, had to do with their melodramatic structure, that is, with the fictional scheme of things in which the power structure is inverted. Here I am in complete agreement with Linda Williams, who in her recent formulation of the power of American racial melodrama refers to that dynamic as compelling us "to feel for the raced and gendered sufferings of some and to hate the raced and gendered villainy of others."[18] Melodrama elevates the weak above the powerful by putting them on a higher moral plane. Micheaux's spectacle of lynching was rhetorically organized to encourage the feeling of righteous indignation in the black spectator who it was assumed would "grit his teeth" instead of taking action.

The Politics of Crosscutting

To these ends, Micheaux makes exceedingly haunting uses of crosscutting, alternating the lynching scene with the attempted rape of Sylvia, and it is this pattern that I want to discuss in detail since it tells us so much about the way African American artists have historically used melodramatic devices. As I have noted, Micheaux characterizes the white mob as crazed and barbarically cruel, so much so that even innocents, women and children, are its victims. Landry's wife is dragged forward and beaten by the mob, the noose placed around her neck and the neck of her young son, although the boy Emil wriggles out of it and narrowly escapes on a horse. That the man and wife are to be hung together is signaled by one of the most unsettling images in the history of African American cinema: a low-angle close-up of a wooden bar frames two dangling ropes against a cloudy sky that in the Spanish Archive print appear upside down. This abstraction, as it stands in for the horrible tragedy, is then used by Micheaux as a kind of gruesome punctuation in the crosscut sequence that culminates the lynching scenario.

The fate of the family is thus established as one line of action, a line that splits into two when the film cuts from the lynchers starting a fire to Sylvia Landry returning to the family's house for provisions, unaware of the plight of her family. We see shots of Sylvia quickly gathering supplies, but she is not alone in the frame for long. She is followed and discovered by Phillip Girdlestone's elderly brother Armand / Arnold (Grant Froman) who has joined the search for his brother's killer, and Micheaux cuts away from this scene in order to intensify it. From the shot establishing Sylvia's danger, the film cuts back to the shot of the ghostly post, this time seen with one noose cut and the other still dangling. Between the shot of the one rope cut and the next shot of both ropes cut is an intertitle: "Still not satisfied with the poor victims burned in the bonfire, Girdlestone goes looking for Sylvia." That is, although the victims have not been represented on screen as hung and burned, the title tells us that Girdlestone has *already* examined their charred bodies. I wish to return to the apparent "error" of this title momentarily since it is interesting for the way in which it contradicts the temporal assumption of the crosscutting pattern that follows. For this assumption, of course, is that Sylvia is being molested *at the same moment* that her foster parents are being executed for a crime that they did not commit.

Although Arnold Girdlestone's taunting of Sylvia is alternated with shots of the hanging, the systematic crosscutting pattern begins with the conflict between the characters. Here, the struggle is interrupted five times with images of the mob burning the bodies in a raging bonfire. I say "interrupted," but there are any number of other ways in which the relationship between the two or more lines of action in a parallel editing pattern can be described. We might say, for instance, that they are "interwoven," which could indicate that the lines of action are measured out more or less equally. But here I want to emphasize how the simultaneity of the actions must work as a contrast between the two events, which still puts primary emphasis on the outcome of Sylvia's ordeal rather than that of her foster parents since we are led to believe that the mob has *already completed* its terrible work in the hanging segment.

It is the incremental *interruption* of the attack on Sylvia that builds the suspense. In the struggle, Sylvia and her attacker circle the table, her clothes are ripped from her shoulder, she throws a vase at him, and finally she faints. (See the illustration in chapter 6 at page 186.) The scene

Within Our Gates (dir. Oscar Micheaux, 1920)

"Eph": "You see him hung up in the vanishing illusion."

The gruesome punctuation in the crosscut sequence

Images of the mob burning bodies— part of the complex crosscutting

is symbolically charged—a reenactment of the white patriarch's ravishment of black womanhood, reminding viewers of all of the clandestine forced sexual acts that produced the mulatto population of the American South. The intertitle, as I have said, suggests that one script for the film may have placed the "rape" of Sylvia *after* the hanging and burning sequence, assuming that Arnold would have looked for her when he found she had not been killed along with her family. The question of the crosscut sequence in the surviving version of *Within Our Gates* thus presents us with a case somewhat similar to that of the two versions of Edwin S. Porter's *The Life of an American Fireman* (1903), versions whose discrepancies have caused scholars to consider that one of the two was later recut according to the principles of parallel editing.[19] But the similarity stops at the question of recutting. As is the case of so many African American film prints from the silent era, where it is rare for more than one version to survive, the opportunity to compare cutting patterns seldom if ever arises.

The issue of how the lynching sequence might or might not have been cut, however, gives us an opportunity to ask some additional questions about crosscutting as melodramatic form. What does the cutting contribute to the effect? How does this device manage melodramatic material? Crosscutting as a form, it could be argued, may have special meaning for the disenfranchised because of the particular way that the device inscribes power relationships. Although it is often noted, as I have said, that melodrama empowers the socially inferior by awarding them moral superiority, there are ways in which, contrary to this, crosscutting puts the viewer in a helpless position. Which is it in this case? As Tom Gunning discusses the technique of crosscutting, it is clearly marked by the intervention of a storyteller who is in the position to manipulate the narrative and especially to play on audience sensibilities by "withholding" parts of the story.[20]

Let us consider this question of power in, through, and by the text in relation to the race movie spectator. This situation in which pieces of narrative information are withheld doesn't exactly put black spectators in a controlling position. Why would they willingly submit to this? But the theatrical viewing experience by definition requires submission to the narrative. Micheaux's appeal is also to familiarity—Sylvia's fate (in which viewers cannot intervene) allows a replay of the futility of the African American historical condition. Once more, blacks look on while the white patriarch exerts his sexual prerogative.

But the scene may still afford pleasure for black spectators because although the white master appears to be prevailing, Sylvia effectively resists and eludes him again and again. The pleasure this resistance affords may be like the satisfaction offered by Harriet A. Jacobs's *Incidents in the Life of a Slave Girl* where Linda Brent (the author's fictionalized self) manages to thwart the sexual advances of her master over the course of the entire book.[21] In this important slave narrative, the odds of escaping from her master's vindictive grip and finding safety in the North for herself and her children are piled up against Linda, exponentially increased. Characteristic of much African American and abolitionist literature of the late nineteenth and early twentieth centuries is this narrative "piling on" of the overwhelming odds against freedom and safety (which is not to suggest that this isn't an accurate portrayal of the condition of enslaved peoples whose lives were daily defined by surviving humanly impossible tests).

One of the features that abolitionist fiction borrows most effectively from the melodrama form that predates it is this almost mathematical measurement of outcomes. Life's agonies are played back as the embattled forces of virtue versus the vile antagonists of virtue, *timed* to the second and rhythmically orchestrated. No device better exemplifies this mathematical feature of melodrama than narrative coincidence, and crosscutting at its most effective is really an exercise in coincidence. To return to coincidence, however, and by so doing to take it seriously, is to return to the very device that has been so often cited as proof of the "lowness" of melodrama form. Was the form maligned because audiences (readers as well as viewers) were insulted by what they thought was the affront to realism that narrative coincidence represents? Does the use of coincidence for some imply a naive reader? In spite of the critical dismissal of such narrative maneuvers, theater critic Eric Bentley, in a relatively early defense of theater melodrama, has claimed that "outrageous coincidence" is the "essence of melodrama."[22] It is, he says, like farce because of the way in which it "revels in absurdity." While I approve of Bentley's championing of "outrageous coincidence," I am not sure that "absurdity" best describes the amazing coincidences in Griffith's last-minute rescues or the many astoundingly lucky moments in both the novels and films of Oscar Micheaux. For I suspect that the swift turn of events that equalizes the unequal and the symmetrical plot development that evens scores may only be absurd and nonsensical to those in power.

In his list of melodramatic devices that may be seen by some film theorists as exceeding the constraints of classical narrative economy, Rick Altman mentions a reliance on coincidence along with spectacle and episodic presentation.[23] If he argues that "coincidence" is in excess of classical text construction, does he mean that it is illogical, overblown, or just indulgent? In terms of narrative theory, coincidence may not be an overindulgence but might instead serve as a highly economical solution for the storyteller. Thematic designs and narrative lines can be neatly unified through an accident unforeseen—for that is what coincidence is—the apparently accidental intersection of events, events coinciding to bring about swift change. And here "swift" needs as much emphasis as "change," for coincidence brings about that astonishing narrative quickening that Tzvetan Todorov says is produced most effectively by supernatural forces.[24]

Coincidence may be "excess," then, but not because it exceeds narrative economy. It must be "excess" for some other reason. Consider that coincidence is perceived as "low" and "outrageous" (sometimes illogical) when it is surprising and miraculous, as well as when it is sudden and unmotivated (that is, without justification or preparation). And to continue my argument about the appeal to the powerless, consider also how coincidence is really a secular version of divine intervention, the only invervention that can rescue the powerless in the injust world of social realist fiction. To illustrate this from *La Negra*, I might point to the series of coincidences by which Sylvia comes to receive the much-needed money to keep open Piney Woods School for Negroes in the South. While Sylvia is on a fund-raising trip to Boston, a tramp steals her purse and is quickly seen and apprehended by Dr. Vivian, the man with whom she becomes romantically involved. Next, Sylvia is hit by a car after she has saved a child who has run into the street. Coincidentally, the woman to whom the car belongs is an extremely wealthy suffragette who is sympathetic to Sylvia's cause. Although a visiting southern matron tries to dissuade her friend, the Boston suffragette decides to give the school not just the needed $5,000 but $50,000.

The miracle of coincidence is indifferent to marketplace measures of merit and worth. Instead, melodramatic coincidence dispenses rewards and punishments according to the motives of the heart, a standard directly at odds with work-world values. And so it may be the redistribution of rewards according to this alternative scheme that drags melodrama down in cultural regard. Could it be that this is one of those places where what we have come to call the "contradictions of capitalism" may be manifest? Could it be that the deep asymmetry of a culture that espouses two systems of reward (corresponding with the old public sphere/private sphere division) shows up when the reward systems are seen to be at odds with one another? The point is that African Americans have historically stood a better chance of triumphing in this fictional world. In this world, Sylvia, the tragic mulatta, survives unscathed and

Within Our Gates (dir. Oscar Micheaux, 1920)

Dr. Vivian (Charles D. Lucas) is romantically attached
to Sylvia Landry (Evelyn Preer)

A wealthy suffragette is sympathetic to Sylvia's cause

is rewarded with a $50,000 gift from heaven. The coincidence that delivers this largesse is in excess of the established system of rewards and outcomes.

This alternative moral scheme of the home and hearth that depends so thoughly on the pattern of "little" miracles also depends on comparisons. The concurrent events balanced through crosscutting are not only interwoven and matched but contrasted, as best seen in Griffith's contrast dramas where the point is not temporal simultaneity but rather relationality. Here the emphasis is not on developing action but on social inequality. I'm thinking, for example, of the scenes in Griffith's *The Usurer* (1910) and *The Corner in Wheat* (1909) where the helpless are shown suffering (waiting in breadlines and being evicted) in shots alternated with those of corpulent capitalists toasting their own successes. At least one film historian has argued that such contrasts imply a cause-and-effect relation.[25] Seen in this way, in one move (the "rescue" of the homeless or the "last gasp" of the Wheat King drowning in his own grain bin) syntagmatic causality may be complemented by paradigmatic causality. The linear chain of events as well as the contrast implied in alternating shots bears out the assertion that the Usurer and the Wheat King *caused* the suffering and death of innocent people.

Melodrama Form and African American Fiction

There is still some question as to whether Griffith's parallelism is equal to the job that the form will need to accomplish for a socially conscious African American cinema. With these issues in mind, let us return to Sylvia, cornered by the white patriarch. Micheaux's scene uses the classic double play of silent film melodrama, that is, a parallel concurrence of events (the "rape" and the lynching) as well as a coincidence that unifies the two lines of action. And this is a coincidence that asks viewers to accept an improbability that is so far-fetched that it could *only* be seen to happen if it were, indeed, "the truth," which the adage tells us is "always stranger than fiction." So it is that in the act of ripping Sylvia's dress, Girdlestone discovers a telling birthmark on her breast: *the mark is proof that he is sexually assaulting his own daughter.* (See the illustrations in chapter 6 at pages 186 and 187.) A following title explains: "A scar on her chest saved her because, once it was revealed, Girdlestone knew that Sylvia was his daughter—his legitimate daughter from marriage to a woman of her race—who was later adopted by the Landrys." Sylvia is then saved from incestual rape?

Conventions of interpretation dictate that we *not* take intertitles at their word, especially since in this period titles are so often at odds with the dramatic thrust of the silent scenes within which they are inserted. But interpreting Micheaux's scene as "rape" has a certain political significance since it can be understood as a reaction to that other controversial scene—the "Gus chase scene" from *The Birth of a Nation*. Since Flora Cameron's flight from the free black man Gus and her leap to her death from the edge of a cliff have historically been called the "rape scene" (although she would jump rather than submit), it seems only fair that we should not hesitate to call Micheaux's point of view a representation of rape, although in the following chapter I will consider other interpretations. There may be political reasons for considering this a rape scene.[26] High on that list of reasons might be the advantage of seeing the scene as the long-muffled African American retort to what Ida B. Wells condemned in 1892 as the "old threadbare lie that negro men rape white women."[27] And even more pertinently, the parallelism of the rape and the lynching scenes asserts the historical connection between the rape of the black woman and the lynching of the black man, the double reaction of the Reconstruction period to whites' nightmare vision of blacks voting and owning property.

But in representing Sylvia's deflowering as incest, *La Negra* goes deeper than the specific historical moment of lynching, attacking as it does the connecting roots of race, gender, and sexuality. For Girdlestone's attack on Sylvia stands in as protest against all of the master's sexual encounters with his own slave women, representing these encounters as acts of symbolic incest, since the paternalism of the plantation master encircled slaves in a concept of "my family, white and black."[28] Note, also, that Micheaux gives us a rescue sequence with no rescue, no Griffith-style race to protect family honor and female purity.[29] In place of the Griffith-like rescue, Micheaux's film gives us a title telling us that Girdlestone had paid for Sylvia's education, but that even after his attack on her he did not reveal that he was her father. The abrupt cut from this title to the end of Alma's conversation with Dr. Vivian in the present suggests that the doctor is offered as savior, that is, the new professional class (with education provided by philanthropic whites) would "rescue" the black race. This means that although the white patriarch cannot ride to the rescue since he himself is the real threat to the sanctity of the family, paradoxically (in the strategy of the black middle class) he can still "save the day." By this I mean that the white values that I am discussing as "uplift" are ultimately the salvation of this family. Sylvia has been educated, and she and Dr. Vivian will be properly married.

Am I making an argument for the radical nature of *La Negra* that I am gradually taking back? I have argued that Micheaux's film counters the white supremacist ideology of *The Birth of a Nation* in its images of the white lynch mob and the white patriarch's sexual assault on black women. We have in addition the historical evidence of the attempts to ban the film that suggest that the hanging of innocent Negroes was incendiary imagery for blacks as well as whites, although in different ways. Clearly the film troubled ideological waters in black as well as white communities. Now I want to consider whether there might be a kind of formal tempering of this material that is the work of the devices of melodrama in the hands of the black middle class.

Melodrama has been widely understood as politically constrained to begin with, this constraint often attributed to its status as a bourgeois form at this time in history. But we have only begun to ask questions about the political uses of melodrama in African American culture. The harshest criticism of the use of the tradition of *Uncle Tom's Cabin* (in which the earliest African American novelists all worked) has been that its sentimentality is dishonest and that its catalog of brutal acts is without justification, a criticism identified with James Baldwin whose fury at Harriet Beecher Stowe had to do with the way, he said, she left "unanswered and unnoticed the only important question: what was it, after all, that moved her people to such deeds."[30] However, without subtracting anything from the significance of Baldwin's question, we still need to ask if sentimental fiction is structurally equipped to answer this kind of question at all.

This question of the political valence of melodramatic form is not new. Eisenstein, of course, wondered if Griffith's parallel editing technique, with its contrasts of rich and poor, was capable of anything more than "liberal, slightly sentimental humanism." For Eisenstein, scenes paralleled through crosscutting stood for a dualistic understanding of social class inequality that imagined poor and rich as moving toward "reconciliation." But this visualized reconciliation was as inaccessibly distant as the point of "infinity" where the parallel lines crossed, or so Eisenstein argued.[31] What Eisenstein had in mind, of course, was a formal equivalent of Marxist dialectics—graphic clashes (mismatches) within and between his shot units—that could convey a "unity of opposites," the perfect symmetry of contradiction. To give an example closer to African American history, the cinema that could go beyond Griffith's humanism might represent something more like Homi Bhabha's three "incongruent knowledges": body, race, ancestors.[32] Such contradiction (which defines race and class relations in U.S. history), however, cannot be represented by means of Griffith's "mechanical parallelism" with its false reconciliation of the irreconcilable.[33]

Eisenstein's early attempt here to define bourgeois cinema is important as a nascent formulation of Marxist film aesthetics, and in this theorization we can see the germ of the contemporary aesthetics that began to define bourgeois form in terms of the illusionism of Hollywood-style continuity editing in the 1970s. Where what Eisenstein called bourgeois form was parallel montage (seen as a microcosm of the U.S. class structure), what later Marxist theorists saw as bourgeois was the denial of cinematic formal devices. Following the logic of Jean-Luc Godard and others, if illusionistic cinema was bourgeois, radical cinema had to be anti-illusionistic—that is, it had to foreground its devices and, ideally, it also had to evidence the material conditions of its production. But for Eisenstein, the issue was more straightforward—Griffith's early cinema was bourgeois because (although it represented class) it could not represent class struggle. This cinema for Eisenstein was also patriarchal but not in any of the ways patriarchal form has been identified by early feminist film theory, for Griffith's patriarchal provincialism was inherited from nineteenth-century melodrama and from Dickens in particular. For Eisenstein, the patriarchal and the bourgeois were epitomized in the parallel montage sequence where traditional sentiment was harnessed to the mechanics of shot alternation.[34]

This position has always seemed to imply that borrowing the corrupted form means reproducing the politics it embodies, and I would not want to dispute this, especially since so much productive work in the last ten years of film theory has been premised on the form equals politics equation. But the orthodoxy of the 1970s countercinema's antidote to Hollywood has been challenged recently, and no more emphatically than by new black British filmmakers.[35] And add to this the increasing theoretical importance of a developing Third Cinema whose early manifesto writers embraced a range of forms including the unfinished and "imperfect," the transitional, and the "incomplete."[36] This move within the field represents such a total shuffling that it is almost as though we are left with no parameters. Hopefully, this state of things will invite attempts to develop new classification schemes as we start over again to ask the same question about politics and aesthetics.[37] That the overdue consideration of Micheaux's filmmaking practice comes at this moment is fortunate since these challenges to the countercinema model may stave off attempts to pigeonhole him in preexisting categories that could preempt exploration into the ways in which his own aesthetic might shape new paradigms. Fortunately, recent considerations of Micheaux suggest that his maverick style confounds complacent assumptions about the connection between race, class, and aesthetic form, and I want to turn next to the task of situating that existing work on Micheaux's film oeuvre.

African American Culture and Bourgeois Cinema

The new Micheaux criticism suggests inventive ways to move beyond his reputation for creating unflattering characterizations of blacks, as well as his reputation for technical amateurism and aesthetic poverty.[38] In a bold move, Jim Hoberman, early to rediscover this director, has located Micheaux in an avant-garde tradition, claiming that the results of his low-budget shooting produced "surreal" effects and comparing his indifference to actors to Warhol's famous nondirection. Hoberman would like to place Micheaux outside the Hollywood tradition since he is seemingly "oblivious to the laws of cinematic continuity."[39] But here I would differ with Hoberman, arguing as I have that Micheaux should be situated in the classical Hollywood tradition that, after all, he so carefully studied and emulated. But it is not so much that he broke with Hollywood conventions, as Hoberman argues, or even that he fell short of mastering them, but that he played "fast and loose" with classical style. As master of the unmotivated cut, it is almost as though Micheaux is saying that if by 1919 audiences have learned to see discontinuous shots as fictional continuous space (always an approximation), then why can't they make sense of shots in a *really* rough approximation of that space?

Clearly, Micheaux's editing style was an ambitious improvisation with the few takes that he had, given that he shot at such a low ratio, and this meant taking temporal license with the material, even pushing the limits of conventional temporalities. Here, *Body and Soul* (1925), one of the three surviving examples of Micheaux's silent work, is exemplary for the way in which the director gives us not only the entire film as a dream-flashback but two consecutive flashbacks within that dream. Thus we are doubly deceived by the beautiful mulatta Isabelle's flashback "confessions" to her mother that the Reverend Isaiah Jenkins (played by Paul Robeson) raped her and stole the mother's money. The "confessions" within the dream are two steps removed from the overprotective mother's real fears for her daughter.[40] In addition, within this structure the temporal transitions are relatively unmarked, making it difficult for the viewer to be certain where scenes are located in time.

There is something about Micheaux's unmarked transitions and his temporal ambiguities as well as his unmotivated cuts that suggests that he is working in another mode. But does this mean that he is responding to the "call" of an indigenous African American culture? I think not, and here I am as leary of linking Micheaux's unconventional style with any hint of an essential black culture as I am with calling it prescient modernism. Perhaps to elude any attempt to essentialize it, we should treat this style as an ingenious solution to the impossible demands of the conventions of classical Hollywood style, shortcuts produced by the exigencies of economics, certainly, but also modifications produced by an independent who had nothing at stake in strictly adhering to Hollywood grammar. And I do mean grammar, for if any comparison with African American culture is useful, it may be with black usage of standard English, which linguists have argued is a shortcut that often produces refinements of an awkward and illogical standard usage. Think, in this instance, of the black usage modification of the state of being verb "is" to "bes" or "it be" to give us a perfection of the standard tense, which produces "is" as a continuous state, an improvement of that tense that still follows its logic.[41] What I want to argue with this comparison is not the miracle of one marginalized group's cultural production so much as an off-centered attitude toward using conventional forms, whether standard Hollywood or standard English. To elaborate on my comparison, in both cases, it would seem, the dominant culture has seen nonstandard, aberrant usage as failure to achieve mastery, as "mistakes" needing correction, as a "low production value" aesthetic that offends the dominant eye, or an unfamiliar grammar that offends the intolerant ear. But also in both cases, marginalized persons with less of an investment in rigid conventions simplify these rules to their own ends.

An example of Micheaux's freewheeling cinematic grammar that is both spatial error and improvement on Hollywood logic might be his use of the same close-up of one character in two different spaces. In *The Exile* (1931), for instance, Micheaux cuts to a close-up of the exquisite mulatta Agnes (who is unaware of her Ethiopian heritage and strangely attracted to the black hero John Baptiste). The close-up of Agnes, seen in an unidentified space, shows her reacting with pleasure to the presence of Baptiste who is speaking with her father in the dining room. *After* the spatially ambiguous close-up, she enters the dining room, and within that scene Micheaux cuts to the same close-up seen before to show Agnes's continued interest in Baptiste. The result is somewhat disorienting for the viewer who may be confused when Micheaux breaks continuity rules by using shots from one space in two distinctly different scenes. However, although the director may have broken a continuous space rule, he has at the same time followed the logic of inserts, which *can* be shot in the context of one recreated space and cut into another, still successfully creating the illusion of continuous space within a scene.

In his discussion of Micheaux's style, Ron Green has argued that it can be seen as having the same relation to Hollywood classicism as African American music has historically had to the classical musical style that it revitalized.[42] This seems a productive approach to the problem of form that offers the chance to theorize film in terms of music, but in such a comparison we should also be wary of the tendency to idealize an African American cinema that might have seen a Golden Age analogous to the Golden Age of jazz in the 1920s. Unfortunately, analogies between film and other forms (especially linguistic signs) have a built-in tendency to gloss over economic realities despite attempts by Marxist theory to see aesthetic forms as indelibly marked by the material conditions of their production. In contrast with the bare-bones economics of African American musical production, which allowed a community of rhythmic interchange, capital-intensive motion picture production has historically precluded the use of these forms for all but a handful of black entrepreneurs. This historical reality produces a predicament for Marxist theories of the relation between form and revolution, as exemplified by discussions of Third Cinema, for as these discussions admit, motion picture economics has historically thrust filmmakers (no matter what their class origins) into the bourgeois class.[43]

It has already been well established that Micheaux epitomized the black bourgeois class and that both his novels and his films are thematic tributes to individualism as well as testimonies to the possibility of transcending race and class handicaps.[44] He simply does not fit the current definition of radical filmmaker. The comparison between Micheaux as novelist and as filmmaker further points up the oddity of film critics' wishful tendency to consider early African American cinema in relation to avant-garde practice, a tendency that is apparent as early as the 1920s in the pages of the journal *Close-up*, as I discussed in my introductory chapter. The comparison with literary history is revealing, for to my knowledge no equivalent demand to be formally transgressive has ever been made on the earliest African American fiction writers, who as a whole worked within the conventions of narrative realism. Instead, recent approaches to this literature stress the way existing formulas were left intact at the same time that they were transformed, as in Hazel Carby's discussion of the way Francis E. W. Harper and other writers reconstructed the heroine of white sentimental fiction in their portrayals of the mulatta character.[45] Thus my sense is that the key to Micheaux's cinematic formal style as well as his thematics is to be found in the way he transformed the existing without changing it. And to some degree this aesthetic dilemma encapsulates the fate of the black bourgeois class that has historically strived for a new order but an order that is not substantially different from the one already in place.

But there is even more to be gained by an approach to Micheaux that insists on qualifying his African American heritage with his class position. Understanding Micheaux's class position gives us a way around the prevalent charges of his own race hatred, the kind of charges that led to the Young Communist League's picketing and boycott of *God's Stepchildren* (1938), to which I have referred.[46] In the work of contemporary African American theorists, such contempt is the product of internal conflict set in motion by the dual motors of dominant and subordinated cultures. And the African American intellectual, says Cornel West, has been historically prone to this "double-consciousness," a reference to W. E. B. Du Bois's "peculiar sensation," that "sense of always looking at one's self through the eyes of others, of measuring one's soul by the tape of a world that looks on in amused contempt and pity."[47] It is not, then, that this consciousness is one's own or that the voice heard speaks for one's own culture—rather, it speaks for the *other* culture, which, in the case of the black bourgeois, is also his own to the degree that he has been assimilated. It is really no wonder that the cultural products of an aspiring black intellectual in this period gave us black men as scoundrels, religious hypocrites, gamblers, and sluggards, and black women as madams, seductresses, and cheats. For Micheaux was seeing this black culture through the eyes of the white culture for which this vision of an irredeemable black underclass was flattering and entirely functional.

While the operation of "double consciousness" seems a fairly obvious way to explain Micheaux's offenses, it may be less obvious that the critique needs to be applied two ways. That is, we need to consider that the early black culture critics were part of this same divided consciousness that produced the arguments that blacks were really just like whites and that Micheaux was at fault for showing negative images. What has become known as "images of" criticism, criticism that had its most publicly visible moment in the protest around *The Birth of a Nation*, has been voided by recent work on the problem of the positive / negative formulation.[48] But this approach has remained the bulwark of popular criticism of minorities in the media, a situation I will return to in chapters 6 and 7.

One would have thought that the popularization of Gramsci's concept of hegemony, introduced in the last chapter, would have swept away this earlier formulation, would have rendered it out of date. For as a theory of hegemony explains how the oppressor's point of view is embraced by the oppressed (all the while it does not serve them), the theory could be said to lift all blame for negative self-imaging (as well as the blame for negative projection) from colonized subjects themselves. Discussing the value of Gramsci for ethnic studies, Stuart Hall emphasizes that the utility of the concept is in the way hegemony explains the " 'subjection' of the victims of racism to the mystification of the very racist ideologies which imprison and define them."[49] Thus it seems to me that there is sufficient theoretical justification for going beyond the early dismissal of Micheaux on the basis of race hatred.[50] The jury is still out on Oscar Micheaux.

What I have suggested here is an approach to this important early African American filmmaker and novelist that allows us to redeem him as well as critique him. But in some ways to try to explain Micheaux in terms of melodramatic form is entirely too tidy. As I have shown, the doubleness of black bourgeois consciousness finds its perfect expression in melodrama, the conflicted mode, the only mode within which (according to recent feminist theories) we can have classical realism and "progressive" subversion simultaneously.[51] Still, Micheaux introduces a new set of problems for melodrama as the mode of the disenfranchised, not the least of which is the question of what it meant historically for middle class white women and middle class blacks (who often held themselves above others) to profit from fictions marketed to the less fortunate.

The Body's Story

I have already discussed the cutting pattern in the scene that alternates between Arnold Girdlestone's attempt to corner Sylvia Landry and the hanging of her foster parents. As she gathers supplies for her family, she is discovered and accosted. In the act of ripping Sylvia's dress, Girdlestone discovers a telling mark seared on her breast. The close-up shot of the healed wound and the reverse-angle shot of Girdlestone's shocked reaction to seeing it tells us that this scar has deep significance for him: the mark is proof that he is assaulting his own daughter. In the English language translation of the Spanish language text of the next intertitle (itself a translation of an earlier English original), the awkward phraseology emphasizes the question of Sylvia's parentage: "A scar on her chest saved her because, once it was revealed, Gridlestone [sic] knew that Sylvia was his daughter—his legitimate daughter from marriage to a woman of her race—who was later adopted by the Landrys."[1]

"Legitimate Marriage to a Woman of Her Race"

The assault scene, crosscut as it is with the lynching scene, calls up associations with the whole tumultuous history of sexual relations between blacks and whites in the American South—from the imagined crimes of black men against white women of the Reconstruction era to the real and originary sexual attacks of the plantation masters on slave women. In this chapter I want to look at some of the racial ramifications of photographic realism, specifically at reproductive technologies and the recognition of one's own. It is, of course, the body that knows but the society that decides who is what. Large issues, issues impossible for the culture to face, grow out of this small scene. I have already argued that the scene cries out against the master's sexual encounters with his own slave

Within Our Gates (dir. Oscar Micheaux, 1920)

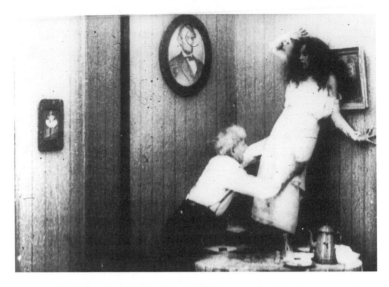

As Sylvia Landry (Evelyn Preer) gathers supplies, she is discovered
and accosted by Arnold Girdlestone (Grant Froman)

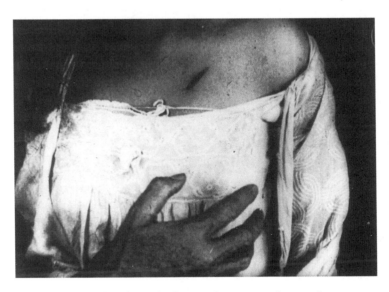

Ripping her dress, Girdlestone discovers a telling mark

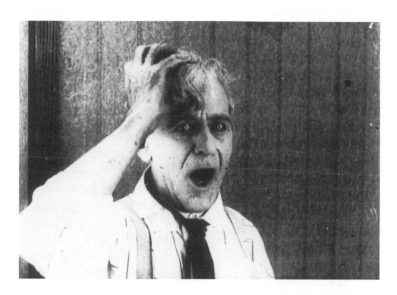

Girdlestone's shocked reaction tells us that the scar
has significance for him

A scar on her chest saved her because, once it
was revealed, Gridlestone knew that Sylvia
was his daughter—his legitimate daughter
from marriage to a woman of her race—
who was later adopted by the Landrys.

Within Our Gates intertitle translated from Spanish

women, even representing the incestuousness of every one of those acts. It is as though Micheaux were recapitulating this history in the scene, but also foregrounding the sexual secrets left out in *The Birth of a Nation*. For never once does that film intimate that the very mulatto class that it wants to discredit is the product of the indiscretion of the men of the planter class.

I have also argued elsewhere that Micheaux has it both ways in this scene, since interracial rape is "enacted as well as averted."[2] The close-up that shows Girdlestone's hand on Sylvia's breast, emphasized as it is by the technical function of the shot as an insert, stands out as a shocking testimony of guilt. The frame, discovered in the film and reemphasized here as a frame enlargement, presents irrefutable evidence that Sylvia is attacked. As a pair, the shots suggest the temporal sequence of events: we see his hand on her breast in one shot and, in the next, going to his head in a gesture of amazement, a shot order that tells us that Girdlestone is horrified to find that the woman whom he *had already* molested is actually his daughter. But there is also evidence here that the father stops short—the scene cuts back to the film's present just after Girdlestone rips Sylvia's bodice, and we are returned to Alma telling Sylvia's story to Dr. Vivian. This reading of the scene that suggests that rape is averted has the advantage of emphasizing Sylvia's purity. Politically, it would be as important to represent Sylvia as *having been raped* as it would be to represent her as innocent and *not having been raped;* this is especially so in light of new black feminist arguments that, because African American women were historically characterized as sexually willing, it was difficult to argue that they had ever been raped or sexually violated.[3] Conveniently, then, it was impossible to "rape" a black woman. As a strategic counter to the myth of black female availability, this new black feminist work thus urges us to consider black women's respectability, a consideration that inevitably leads us to the question of Sylvia's mother and the nature of the interracial relationship between her mother and father.

Another narrative of Sylvia's origins is offered in the evidence of contemporary reviews. The *Chicago Defender,* reviewing *Within Our Gates* just after the January 1920 premiere, describes a film dramatically different from the one that has survived. The reviewer relates: "You see the white man who claims the black child laid at his doorstep by the mother, because it is his own and he later gives the mother some money."[4] Contradicting the "legitimate marriage" story of the intertitles, this version confirms the "concubinage" to which Micheaux refers in his promotion for the film and in addition produces Sylvia not as legitimate but as illegitimate. It is tempting to look to this review as providing the "real" story, especially since the story of a white male taking sexual advantage of a poor black woman is confirmed a thousand times over in the historical record. But there is no "real" story, no final version, particularly with Micheaux, who was so adept at writing the same narrative a multitude of ways, beginning with the story of his own life, as Jayna Brown tells us in her study of his autobiographical novels.[5]

The existing film insists that we *interpret* what we see on the screen, and contemporary viewers consistently try to make sense of these images in relation to the curious intertitle: "A scar on her chest saved her because, once it was revealed, Girdlestone knew that Sylvia was his daughter—his legitimate daughter from marriage to a woman of her race—who was later adopted by the Landrys." Compared with the narrative fragment provided by the reviewer for the *Defender*, the existing film raises an even more interesting question of interpretation since we are faced with the evidence of the image on screen as opposed to the evidence of the intertitles. Let us consider, then, quite strictly, only the film before us. In that film, the one set of signs (the iconic) tells us that there are a wealth of interconnected relationships, and the other (the linguistic) tells us more narrowly that there is a father and a daughter and that there was at one time a "legitimate marriage." The relatively dense semiosis of the image of the white-skinned, white-haired man chasing the light-brown-skinned, black-haired young woman is portrayed in extreme contrast to the thin meaning of the linguistic signs of the intertitle; these tell a story of a respectable father who married the mother of his child, a story that would seem to completely contradict and negate the image of irresponsible lust that we see on the screen. Would the man who would so brutally ravish one helpless black woman take the trouble to marry another? It is the image, not the intertitle, that finally calls up the historical legacies and reenacts so many scenarios simultaneously, and it is the image that *can* and *does* carry the weight, the extra freight of signification.

In contrast with the full-bodied images, the linguistic signs, ghostly white letters stenciled through blackness, seem fragile, almost skeletal. Although they have relatively less semiotic density, intertitles nevertheless assert themselves with an irrefutable finality. Half book page and half theatrical title card, they give themselves to the viewer as print to be read—they ask to be attended to as literary fragments. Perhaps most important here, as the intertitles are read they place limits on the apparently unlimited semiosis of the accompanying image. Thus a Barthesian limitation of meaning is performed by the linguistic sign in proximity to the iconic.[6] As a consequence of the need to restrict the surplus meaning of the image, the motion picture intertitle produces a distinct narrative effect, interrupting the action and creating stoppage at timed intervals. More than punctuation, the intertitle exerts itself as a narrative control.

The intertitle is unsettlingly familiar. We are dimly aware that it is a hearkening back to the magic light-show origins of the motion picture, a momentary lapse into its prehistory figured by the projection lamp that shines through the lettering and the absolute stillness of the title cards. Some critics over the years, as I noted in the introduction, have argued that the speechlessness of the silent film should not be seen as a deficit.[7] At times this argument sounds like an elitist nostalgia for aesthetic purity, at other times a cranky suspicion of a newly arrived technology (in this case sound-on-film). But perhaps the most important development to come out of these arguments is the conviction that silent film should not be seen as missing something. Rather than seeing silence as a deficit, this point of view understands the ingenious compensations of the silent film. Consider, for instance, the question of sound supplementation. If the audio is not on the track, where is it? Film theorists find it in a range of different places. All of the important work on musical scoring for the silent film locates the sound in the orchestra pit or finds it coming from the honky-tonk piano. In addition, however, the silent film image itself is full of sound substitutes. Giving credence to sound substitution, Mary Ann Doane, for instance, has theorized the way missing speech is "spread over the entire body," thus assigning to the gestural continuum the burden of the conveyance of meaning.[8] The eloquence missing in the spoken word is thus given to the body in silent cinema. Perhaps, then, in the shimmering quality of silent cinema, we are seeing the image that exudes speech—all of which is to say once again that the silent image was never truly silent and that it never seems exactly mute.

For all of the eloquence of the silent image, however, we are still perplexed with its titles, which not only come from a mysterious non-diegetic netherspace (*not* belonging to the fiction within which we are immersed) but also carry an authority that has the power to overrule the image, to take its apparent meaning in another direction. Flat and impassive, the intertitle interjects its lines of prose right at the point of ambiguity. We wait for the intertitle like we wait for a stop sign. We wait, just an instant, before agreeing to its meaning in the seconds between image frames, and then we go ahead to the next frame. It is, then, a kind of tyranny of the intertitle that makes spectators into reader-viewers who are concerned about taking the insistent title "at its word." And it is this tyranny that makes it necessary to deal with the phrase "legitimate marriage with a woman of her race." Less interesting are the considerations that lead us to speculation about the way the Spanish titles might have been rewritten from the English or even about the way Micheaux wrote the titles to get around white censorship boards. More compelling is the approach that sees the mention of "legitimate marriage" as a reference to African American history and a convention in nineteenth-century African American fiction.

It is well known that part of the motivation for writing these novels in the tradition of sentimental women's fiction was to make the case that slave laws did not recognize marriage, the sacred foundation of Christian society. Perhaps it is significant that the first African American novel, *Clotel: Or, the President's Daughter,* takes the impossibility of marriage between the exquisite mulatta and the sons of the white master class as its central problematic. Its structure examines every facet of and variation on the consequences of the predicaments produced by a culture that espoused one thing and practiced another, showing up the contradictions between wife and slave and the absurdity of legally owning one's wife. The 1853 novel begins with the premise that the refined mulatta is white in every way but in the view of the law, the basis of the appeal made to white readers in the African American fiction that followed the lead of *Clotel.* In this heart-wrenching fiction, the inability of the society to condone the sacred union between the mulatta and the master has its consequences in a string of tragedies. Thus the sentimental appeal of these stories of doomed love suggests that such unions were imagined and remembered by readers. But the more interesting question is how the memory of these unions were kept alive in the African American community.

Another approach would be to look for the exceptions to the absurd law and the prevailing code in historical actuality, an approach that promises to yield examples as dramatic as those found in the fiction. Reading Catterall's *Judicial Cases* from these years, one is struck by those cases that offer up historical counters to the rule that masters generally disowned their slave mistresses as well as the children they fathered.[9] The case law record provides examples that echo the narrative of *Iola Leroy* where it is the family of Iola's planter father who sells her along with her mother and brother when the planter dies.[10] Consider the analogous case of Elijah Willis. When Willis died and left property to his slaves, his will was contested by his family, just as the villainous relatives challenged the arrangements left by Iola's father at the time of his death. Yet another man willed money to his slave or "adopted wife," and records indicate that still another slave owner, a Louisianian, took his female slave as well as their children first to Ohio and afterward to Texas, and that they lived as man and wife.[11] Inevitably, more examples will emerge as historians such as Martha Hodes begin to research the incidence and the variety of interracial coupling in U.S. history.[12] History records many even more sensational enactments of opposition to the taboo against interracial unions, such as the story of the white daughter of a North Carolina slave owner who ran away with her father's black coachman. When apprehended and tried, she reportedly drank her lover's blood so that she could claim that she was of "mixed blood."[13]

Any combination of history, literature, and legend could and did supply these counterexamples to the African American community, perhaps even through the Reconstruction period when the sociological data show interracial unions on the decline, a point I will continue to emphasize throughout my discussion.[14] So Micheaux's fiction (contained in a single title card), a fiction about the marriage of a plantation owner's son to a woman of African descent, a union that ostensibly took place around the turn of the century or before, just after Reconstruction, is important in the way it offers an alternative story. And as an alternative, it achieves some important political ground. First, the story of a perhaps secret marriage is the antithesis of the prevailing mythology about illicit interracial sexuality, and as an added bonus, the marriage makes Sylvia legitimate. Second, if the marriage story is a way around censorship boards intent on legislating morality, the assertion that Sylvia's parents were married contains an interesting irony in that as morality is upheld, interracial marriage is sanctioned.

Following the Condition of the Mother

Ingeniously, Micheaux flags all of these possibilities with the reference to "concubinage" in his promotion for *Within Our Gates*, since concubinage, with its long history dating back to the fourteenth century, has historically referred to a situation in which the man either is or is not married to the woman or women he keeps. If there is a lawful marriage, as concubinage can imply, the wife may be so inferior to the man with whom she is living that the legality of the arrangement scarcely matters. Micheaux has cannily signified the respectability of the concept of marriage at the same time that he has signaled the salaciousness of concubinage and called up all of its associations with the exotic sexuality of the Oriental harem in an effort to draw a crowd.

It is one of the ironies of culture that the logical outcome, the offspring of the illicit interracial union, always points directly back to that union. Such "abominable mixture and spurious issue" (as the North Carolina General Assembly referred to these children in 1741) always, invariably, *stood for* an act that preceded them, an act that had both everything and nothing to do with them.[15] When we reflect on this—that one's position should be both fluke of birth and absolute determination—it is extremely odd at the same time that it is predictably familiar. And yet it is strange that in this colonial custom the original act of conception should be referenced so persistently over the history and life of the offspring. This referencing is the body's own story, a story that is expected to confirm but as often contradicts official stories of paternity and procreation. And it is when the body contradicts, when it tells its own truth that counters the official story, that melodrama finds its moment, as when in Micheaux's drama, the scar on Sylvia's breast tells Girdlestone that the woman he is assaulting is his own daughter from a union with a "woman of *her* race."

The assumption that this daughter is of the same race as the mother rather than the same race as the father is an outgrowth of one of the most highly ideological assertions in recent historical memory. This assertion is a version of things that only makes sense as a desperate measure in the face of the need to maintain very peculiar social relations. We get an inkling of the exceptionality of these relations in the record of the relevant legal reversal, the 1662 Virginia law to which I have already referred. The law altered the rule that the child follows the condition of the father to one where the child follows "the condition of the mother"—a reversal that reveals the economic motive only too nakedly.[16] The audacious assumption that the interracial intercourse that produced the children in question would only and always be between black women and white men, never white women and black men, spells out that motive that was to use black women to enlarge the slave population. Here, capital and patriarchy find themselves at crosspurposes. Patriarchy, uncharacteristically, steps back, opting to claim the offspring in question as owner rather than as father. And this very atypicality poses a threat to the rule. The history of the convention whereby the child is black if the mother is black calls perhaps too much attention to the arbitrariness of racial designation, representing a danger to this assignment, possibly even as much danger to it as the child himself or herself. We have already suggested the myriad ways in which the child who is light enough to "pass" for white confounds classification. For it is important to also recall the historical time when "passing" for white might have been a subversive inversion of the "child follows the condition of the mother" rule, a time before disappearance into the white community was understood as race betrayal. And all of these glaring inconsistencies—the child who looks white but is classified black, the mother who is a producer of slave labor, the father who is but is not a father—are indicative of the trouble the social imperative encounters in its attempt to manage the incontrovertible evidence of the human body.

We speak of racial features as "telling" in those instances in which the body is read for racial clues. On this question of the one race or the other, however, the body tells its own story, a story often different from the one society tells. The body tells all about its origins, wears the signs that indicate the society's deepest secrets. But the body is mute when it comes to the details. Considering the case of the mulatto/a who signifies a secret he or she cannot divulge, Hortense Spillers writes, "In his/her face, the deceits of a culture are mirrored; the deeds of a secret and unnamed fatherhood made known."[17] The body tells but never names. And the body is stubborn in yet another sense—the reproductive body *does not know racial difference.* The biological body understands human reproduction, not racial distinction, which is why we should not be surprised that white bodies do not always automatically produce white bodies. Biologically, white bodies can produce black bodies just as easily as black bodies can produce white ones. And it is nothing more than this indiscriminate functioning of the biological reproductive system that undermines the best-laid plans of human stratification systems. Hundreds of domestic melodramas have been based on the dilemmas arising out of this foregone principle of the indiscriminateness of the reproductive system. In these narratives the inherent secrecy of the body is yet another opportunity for melodrama, the genre whose narratives relish the discovery of pregnancies concealed and identities unveiled, whose stories savor the anguish of keeping or not knowing the body's secrets.[18] This is the genre that is doomed to eternally ask, "Whose child is this?"[19]

It is the reproductive body's mechanical indifference to social outcomes that produces the melodramatic situation in Kate Chopin's late nineteenth-century short story, "Désirée's Baby," for its time a bold consideration of the scourge of black blood.[20] It is the darkness of the child born to the orphan Désirée that is telling, a blackness that reflects back on her, the child's mother, putting her whiteness in question and resurrecting the myth of the black blood that can surface after generations of whiteness. But it is Désirée's aristocratic husband Armand who is finally revealed as the parent with the black blood, although this is not disavowed until after his young wife has already walked, zombie-like, into the swamp carrying the baby in her arms. The body, the carrier of genetic mysteries, signifies its "truth," signifies a secret that, once referenced, must be revealed, although the answer to its enigma must appear to be irretrievable. In the last moments of the narrative, however, the question of racial paternity may be settled by the device of the discovery of a lost letter, as it is in Chopin's story. There, the question is answered by a letter from Armand's mother to his father, a letter in which she says she is grateful that her son will never know that she is black. Although the letter clears up the mystery of Armand's blood, we realize that although we could assume that Désirée is white, we can never be certain whether she is one way or the other because her parentage is unknown.[21] The melodrama effect again works because of the discrepancy between the body's knowledge and the characters' knowledge, intelligence that may be withheld until the last possible moment. Alternatively, genetic secrets are carried to the grave with narrative finality. Narrative, like the genetically secretive body, is indifferent to the content of outcomes—it only wants a device that works unpredictably, and once it has that device, it wants its own set of improbable options passed off as a probable situation.

So the technology of human reproduction itself gives melodrama some of its best scenarios: the simple yet complicated situation in which maternity is unambiguous and paternity in contrast is indeterminate.[22] To the indeterminacy of paternity let us add the historic fear that the child born will bear the signs of some past transgression, where the baby is incontrovertibly the effect of an earlier cause, a terrible cause. Worse, even, than the situation in which the presumed father is not the actual father is the situation in which one or the other of the two parents carries something that mysteriously passes through them to the child, that is passed by means of the blood, whether the blood carries racial information or a hereditary predisposition of some kind. The strange child delivered becomes the evidence that gives the lie to the assumption of health or normalcy or whiteness. The biological scenario recipe for this is deceptively simple: a male parent and a female parent produce a third person. The child takes the *gender* of one parent but not the other, and the *race* of only one parent if they are of different races or of both if they are of the same race.[23]

Race and Reproductive Technologies

What I have been intimating in my reference to the reproductive technology of the body is that the body is a machine not unlike that other technology of reproduction, the motion picture machine. Michel Foucault is suggestive here in his reference to the body as a machine "imbued with the mechanics of life," and others have been struck by the resemblance between the machine and the reproductive body.[24] While one would think that the possible analogy between human reproduction and the mass production of images and goods would have intrigued feminists, it was, however, Raymond Williams who was struck early on by the comparison and would seem to have used the term "reproductive institutions" rather knowingly. Quite simply, as we understand it from Williams, the revolution in the new productive means of circulation and replication meant the eventual creation of a culture of image multiplication.[25] Although humanism with its commitment to the unique individual would prefer to de-emphasize human reproduction as multiplication, the fact is that the human body *is* the great machine of mass production, a miraculous and amazing machine, especially in its *automatic* reproduction, and its production not only of distinctiveness but of species similarity. And it is here that the body reveals itself as the first mimetic technology. But it is not only that the body has the capacity to reproduce itself, like other natural phenomena, but that it produces bodies in the image of itself, that are like and not-like itself. Think of the myriad ways in which children mirror the traits of their parents—how obvious and how strange this taken-for-granted mimesis. As with that other mimetic technology, the cinema, resemblance is everything, as Bill Nichols once noted.[26]

Think now of the relevance of this understanding of the body as mimetic technology to the question of racial reproduction. The question of racial reproduction reminds Richard Dyer that the question is tied up with heterosexuality: "If race is always about bodies, it is also about the reproduction of those bodies through heterosexuality."[27] Heterosexuality is a prerequisite but not only a prerequisite; it is a presumption that heterosexual intercourse will produce more heterosexuals, that it will propagate heterosexuality (that normative practice that Judith Butler defines as an "incessant and panicked imitation of its own naturalized idealization)".[28] Not insignificantly, the homosexual would categorically fall in with the mythical mulatto whose crime was that it could not reproduce, only one more indication that procreation was an antebellum obsession. While one might think that homosexuality would be the furthest thing from the minds of the plantation patriarchs and their progeny, homosexuality was thus implicated in this question of racial reproduction. But homosexuality and racial difference, while they may confound the normative white human community, do not pose the same challenge as the human reproductive system, a system whose potential subversiveness we would do well to appreciate. For here is one of those situations in which biological functioning is radical because on one level *it doesn't know* racial distinctions. White people can produce black people and black people can produce white, for all it cares. Perhaps this is even one of those places where the biological escapes social construction, if only for a fleeting second—that second before the child is officially "birthed," that same moment before, as in the Althusserian moment, the girl is "girled" and the boy "boyed."[29]

But the moment of birth represents a very narrow window of opportunity for the biological body, a moment increasingly encroached on by the social, and it is the philosophical question of that which eludes social construction that is relevant here since the unconstructed also has its way of constructing things. As Judith Butler has argued, it is "as important to think about how and to what end bodies are constructed as it will be to think about how and to what end bodies are *not* constructed."[30] To review, on her list of those areas that constructivism must refute, and that may therefore represent the new frontier of the unconstructed, are the "reality of bodies, the relevance of science, the alleged facts of birth, aging, illness, and death."[31] These, the material sites of "enabling or constitutive exclusion," would seem, if nothing else, to lead us to a better understanding of the blanket of the social that appears to be so deferential to the untainted natural all the while it is constructing it.[32] There may be no better example of the problem of exclusion than the second at birth *before* the constitutive moment in which the child is "raced" as well as "gendered." One thinks here of George Schuyler's satire on this moment in the scene in the hospital in *Black No More* when Max Disher waits for the birth of his first child, a parody of parental trauma over racial uncertainty so determinedly resolved at birth.[33]

The body's reminder that it can and does elude social construction, if ever so slightly, is also dramatized in fiction in the reversal of parental expectations at the moment of birth, a reversal represented in the motion picture by the reaction shot of the parent from the point of view of the cradle and a marked withholding of the shot of the newborn infant. Perhaps best exemplified by the sequence in *Rosemary's Baby* in which Mia Farrow reacts to the sight of her devil infant that the camera never dares to show, this is a shot combination that signifies the discrepancy between the (constructed) expectation and the (unconstructed) issue of the body. Although the devil child is named into being, it is never shown on screen, can never be shown, like the dark baby born to the white plantation mistress who seduces the slave to spite her husband in *Mandingo*.[34] Parental expectation may construct the child as white even before it is born despite the in-vitro reality of the situation, by which I mean that since the baby has yet to be proclaimed either white or black, pre-birth it is *neither* white nor black. To date, no fetal test has been devised on the model of amniocentesis that would designate that which belongs so overwhelmingly to culture. Culture would reach into the womb if it could, but unconstructed nature holds out as long as it can. For these reasons and more, the illegitimate black baby born to the white mother is surely one of the most unrepresentable of objects, an object that would contradict the truth of the mimetic reproductive system at the same time that it absolutely confirms its biological neutrality. Herein lies the significance of the reverse shot that will always and ever be withheld: it represents the brief moment of the triumphant resistance of the biological before it is subdued as culture.

As we know, all depends on the utilization and the interpretation, and the biological, it is clear, must be bended to ideological needs. And so it has been that historically in the United States the definition of who is white and who is black has been stretched to fit local prerogatives, as in the section of Louisiana where the one-drop rule was reversed, producing black as white, or as I mentioned earlier, the parts of South Carolina where the rule didn't hold because so many were thought to have this drop that it would have precluded marriage between almost everyone who had been classified as white.[35] But the racial classification was never more illogical than in the attempt to actually breed color in or out, especially when one considers that the same intermixture encouraged in Brazil in an attempt to breed "out" blackness was used in the United States to breed it "in."[36] Ever before us now is the human toll taken in the translation of sexual intercourse into economic terms, a premise almost impossible to believe in the abstract and a practice ill-conceived from the start. Cedric Robinson lays it all out: "In Virginia, the heat of the sexual licence granted by slavery had eventually assumed a market function: slave breeding."[37] As is often said, the planters reproduced their labor forces with their own bodies—the most mechanical use of the reproductive function of the human body conceivable. But as they reproduced their labor force, they also undermined their own system for, as Winthrop Jordan writes, the planter "may have sensed that continual racial mix there would eventually undermine the logic of racial slavery . . . [for] mulattoes blurred . . . [the] essential distinction."[38] If some racial distinction could be bred in, too much intermixture could conceivably obliterate the difference between black and white. This may have been on the mind of Kentuckian Henry Clay, who is said to have predicted that "amalgamation" would produce the abolition of slavery.[39] Again, biology stubbornly resists—genetic mixing, another imperative of human reproduction (not to mention human survival), is here at odds with the ultimate needs of the slave-producing culture. I refer here to the need not just to produce labor but to produce black labor (i.e., slave labor).

My reader may wonder why in my discussion of interracial unions I have not once used the term "miscegenation," particularly since in recent U.S. history sexual intercourse between whites and nonwhites, especially nonwhites of African descent, has been uniformly understood with reference to the concept. However, usage has gathered under the same banner all unions, from those forced for the purposes of breeding to those that might have been consensual, making it difficult to consider historical variation. Given the history and associative baggage that the concept carries, it is virtually impossible to use it descriptively. Clearly, "miscegenation" is not a neutral term, even though today it is frequently used in a scientific way in social science contexts. That miscegenation still has contemporary currency is remarkable since the word is so arcane and obviously dated. First coined in conjunction with the 1864 presidential campaign in a pamphlet supporting racial "blending," "miscegenation" was advocated in an attempt to embarrass and discredit the Lincoln effort. Written as an attack on Lincoln's Republican party, the term "miscegenation" was thus never neutral and came quite quickly to have sinister connotations.[40] The fiction of the "frenzy of love in the white woman for the Negro," in the words of the pamphlet, was the country's worst nightmare in this period, although today it is difficult to imagine that this political hoax was ever taken seriously, so exaggerated is its mock advocacy. Miscegenation, from the Latin *miscere*, meaning "to mix," was thus coined to suggest the act of interracial intercourse it referenced as a kind of disgusting pollution, the very pronunciation of it in English connoting a corruption through illicit sexuality, the word (sounded in the mouth) passing judgment on the act. Thus in an attempt to refuse judgmental connotations, I have scrupulously avoided the use of "miscegenation."

Others before me have faced this dilemma. Considering the problem of terminology in her important historical study of sexual relations between white women and Negro men in the United States before the Civil War, Martha Hodes, who also rejects "miscegenation," explains her preference for understanding these relations as occurring across the "color line," a usage derived from W. E. B. Du Bois who, it is well known, located the problem of the twentieth century as one of dividing lines.[41] The notion of relations occurring across this imaginary line even has the advantage over "interracial," she says, which is always susceptible to a naturalization.[42] Like so many other contemporary critics, Robert Young, in his overview of desire in the colonial context, is partial toward variations on the concept of the "hybrid," especially as it serves the dual purpose of standing for the mixture of other cultural forms.[43] My own preference for "mixed-blood relations" in the context of this study is intended to avoid the above-stated pitfalls of "miscegenation" as a concept as well as to sidestep the vogue in studies of the "hybrid."[44] In the long run, "mixed blood" invokes the period, thus helping us to get increased distance on the mythology of the blood or the "blood fictions" of race relations, fictions critic Lisa Jones references in her satirical use of the "raging bloods" and the warring "bloods" thought to characterize the old tragic mulatta, internally divided by her dual origins.[45]

My interest is in the invisible referent that courses through the body, in the hereditary "blood" so difficult if not impossible to represent in relation to its purported manifestations, if for no other reason than to understand the success of the one drop (of blood) rule and its inverse, the conditions of possibility for passing.[46] For it can be seen that whereas *as much as* one drop is interpreted as black, *as little as* one drop can secure whiteness. The "blood" metaphor works *because* the process of genetic transmission is microscopic and mysterious. While the bloodline is thought to be in evidence on the body, it is truly a metaphor without an image, which is why its powers to mystify are so great. Further complicating this difficult problem in representation, racial markers as natural signs always throw up resistance to arguments about the constructedness of race. The "blood" is a great naturalizer of social relations and has historically made a significant contribution to the ideology of the natural, that widely embraced view of things that has done so much to help establish institutionalized racism.[47] In the end, of course, there is nothing more overdetermined than genetic makeup, and the idea that black and white are singly determined by a substance that is red in color is hopelessly simplistic if not ludicrous.

Blood-mixing is also useful to me as a starting point for situating desire in relation to reproduction. Robert Young is right that a theory of desire always seems implicit in theories of race, seems always to be lurking as an explanation for how it is that peoples came to exist here as opposed to there, or looking like this as opposed to that.[48] And no narrow sense will finally do here, as in the reading of mixed bloods as a "visible symbol of lust," or even as in Eric Lott's identification of "yaller" as a "signifier of racial trespass."[49] Resisting that smaller sense of a sexual draw, we need to again import Hegel's enlarged sense of Desire, that Desire that wants to "encompass the external world," that is, to embrace it but also to spread oneself over it entirely. How better to "encompass" the world than to literally produce it? One thinks here of the imperializing gesture that could manifest itself in the personal reproduction of one's own permanent labor force. Desire for, of, and through the other is a desire for expansion.

Yet again I want to draw my parallel with motion pictures, here emphasizing less the face-to-face encounter of the exhibition hall that characterizes the function of the othering machine that encourages ones to circle back to themselves via others. The reproductive aspect of cinema, manifested in the photographic foray into the world beginning with the travels of the Lumière cameramen, is undoubtedly an imperializing function.[50] To borrow from Gilles Deleuze and Félix Guattari, the imperializing function is also a facializing one, and their "abstract machine of faciality" asks to be explored as it metamorphoses into the motion picture apparatus.[51] And I will suggest, following Richard Dyer, that the apparatus has its racial affinities. If, as in Deleuze and Guattari, the black hole in the white wall is the camera and the facializing mission is the drive to produce an all-white cinema, what we have is nothing more nor less than the reproduction of the white race on a silver screen or a white sheet.[52] And yet the apparatus does not eternally and exclusively reproduce the white race. Consider the facializing mission of race movies, a drive that was not necessarily imperializing, a use of the new motion picture technology that would give a "face to the race" that is not-white.

But what exactly did motion picture technology have to give race movies? What kind of a face would this machine reproduce when it was turned by the black subject onto the black subject? Here I want to return once more to the phenomenon I discussed in chapter 4 as color coding, now with the emphasis on the capabilities of the photographic apparatus. Over the last decade, film theorists have argued that the motion picture apparatus is not ideologically neutral and that, most importantly, it has built into it a view of the world that reinstates the singular individual (the focal point of Western culture) with every screening.[53] Given the immense theoretical significance of the assertion of this ideological function (the contribution the motion picture makes to the production of the ideal bourgeois subject), it is surprising that no equivalent move has been made to rethink the role of the machine in the equally ideological production of the raced subject, and this has been my recurring lament. While we are wondering about the shortsightedness of this influential theory in relation to the raced subject, it may also occur to us that the oversights of this theory are not limited to its focus on the view of the single subject seated in the theater. Its exclusive location of the ideological function in the perspective relations produced by photographic lenses meant that other material aspects of the technical production of motion pictures were overlooked. When we start to examine the conventions of lighting, the scientific development of film stock and processing techniques as well as exposure time and makeup styles, the question of racial representation immediately arises, and it becomes clear that historical practices have racial proclivities. Other scholars have noted this, and one by one they are beginning to ask questions about the apparent technological preference for some flesh tones over others.

In an early article Brian Winston confirms our suspicions that motion picture color film stock does not represent dark skin tones with the same ease that it represents the light tones that it also measurably improves. He finds irrefutable evidence of white-skin color bias in the evolution of photographic practices.[54] Expanding on these findings, Richard Dyer discovers in the history of motion picture lighting technology an entire system of approaches to illuminating figures, which, as he says, has always assumed a "special affinity between [whites] and light."[55] The measure of the ideal, as Dyer describes it, has been Griffith's lighting of Lillian Gish who, through the use of close-up shots employing side-lighting, soft focus, and gauzes in films such as *Hearts of the World* (1918) and *Way Down East* (1920), comes to standardize the "characteristic glow of white women."[56] It is as though in the history of cinema all lighting decisions were thenceforth made with Lillian Gish in mind. Thus it is that the race bias, Dyer argues, is not articulated as such but is a consequence of this privileging of white women, which has the effect of producing the nonwhite or less white as a problem. One example of such a problem that confronts the cinematographer is the difficulty of shooting light- and dark-skinned people when they are positioned in the same frame. Because of the wide differential between the Caucasian face and the black face measured in what is called the "percentage of reflectance," a problem arises for the lighting crew called on to attempt to compensate for their difference.[57] A Lasky Studios "electrical illuminating engineer," writing in 1921, describes how in such a situation "much care must be exercised in so regulating the light that it neither 'burns up' the light make-up nor is of insufficient strength to light up the dark make-up."[58]

The material difference between light and dark figures was a recurrent challenge that filmmakers in the silent era faced daily, but not necessarily because of the need to place actors with a wide variety of skin and hair color tones within the same frame. Filmmakers shooting in black and white had to think constantly about color balance because of the basic limitations of orthochromatic film stock. As the standard in the industry from around 1913 to 1925, orthochromatic film was understood and accepted as unable to render red and yellow as anything but black, that is, it was virtually insensitive to these areas of the color spectrum. In addition, there were further trouble areas, and a chief complaint about the stock had to do with the difficulty of rendering blondes as blonde. Blonde hair photographed too dark and blue eyes washed out to white.[59]

That complaints were registered about blondes but not about brunettes might suggest a bias based on a hierarchy of expectation and valuation, but it also suggests a caveat that we should add to Dyer's argument about the way whiteness has been privileged, and that is this. At some points, the new reproductive technology (here the technology of the image produced when light hits a chemically treated strip of celluloid) *is oblivious to human hierarchies based on racial distinctions.* How could it know that orthochromatic film could make blue-eyed blondes look like zombies? Of course, creative technicians rush to compensate for such mechanical indifference, rush to highlight an actor or to stop down the lens, building cultural preferences into conventions. And new, improved processes are produced based on race-sensitive expectations, as the history of the perfection of flesh tones in color photography attests.

What do we do in this regard with the industry move from orthochromatic to panchromatic film late in the silent era, a move embraced by the industry because panchromatic film achieved the sensitivity to the entire spectrum of light (eliminating the problem of red and yellow)? What does this mean in terms of racial representation? In order to answer these questions, we need to think of the challenges of rendering figures on the screen as the silent filmmakers thought of them, not necessarily in terms of the rendering of black or white people but of the overall aesthetic look for which they strove, and here they would have been involved largely with white hired cameramen who brought industry standards and expectations with them to the shoot.[60] The challenge in the silent era was to translate the color spectrum into the widest possible range of *shades of gray.* And while the advantage of panchromatic film was that the relative valuation of shades to each other was more "lifelike," orthochromatic film, with careful compensations, could also be made to represent a range of color in amazing shades of gray.[61]

Given that they could reproduce this pleasing range of gray tones with orthochromatic film, how did the makers of race movies utilize the technological capabilities of this film stock that penalized whiteness and rendered red and yellow as black? First, let us raise the question of the existence of "black" and "white" people. This question of black and white film stock dramatizes the impossibility of "black" or "white" people. We need to raise an objection to these "color words" that, Naomi

Zack reminds us, no American could "approximate in appearance without being badly burned or suffering massive blood loss." Additionally, she says, the words used to refer to people of mixed race are not necessarily improvements, asking us to consider the futile approximation of "coffee," almond," "almond shell," "piney," "honey," "ivory," "mahogany," and "tan."[62] But assuming the unavoidable principle of approximation, let us consider the fortunate advantage of orthochromatic film stock. It seems reasonable to hypothesize that orthochromatic film might have offered a certain, perhaps accidental, advantage to the makers of race movies since they would be striving for the ideal range of gray tones, that is, representing brown-skinned actors in shades of gray. To be sure, striving for what I am calling *racial realism* might have meant that actors wore makeup that ensured against midnight-black lips or chalk-white faces, an acknowledgment of the worry about the "racially wrong look," as Dyer refers to it.[63] But the beige tonalities of the light-skinned race movie actors would have met with no serious resistance from orthochromatic stock. Also, to the contemporary eye, racial realism might also have been signified by the aesthetically pleasing gray palette of orthochromatic film, the simulation of color so exquisite that we forget that it is only approximating color values. Then as now, we appreciate the black and white aesthetic on its own terms, and rather than an absence of color see the presence of grain and gray gradation.

This hypothesis, however, will be difficult to test if for no other reason than the unfortunate condition of the surviving prints of the films produced by the race film pioneers in the silent and especially into the sound era. Many of the sound-era race movies we view are contrasty 16mm prints or videotapes made from these prints, meaning that they are characterized by the extremes of black and white, with detail either washed out or blacked out and loss of middle or gray tones, a condition resulting from the production of duplicate films from positive prints rather than original negatives. Film scholars and archivists have placed a premium on restoring as many of these films as possible, a restoration that has often involved a return to the look of the original film through the production of prints struck from the original orthochromatic negative.[64] That such prints of Micheaux's *Within Our Gates* and *The Symbol of the Unconquered* have recently been made available for public viewing means that we can finally begin to take the question of the gray tonalities of race movies seriously.

My point is twofold. First, I want to argue against the rule of the automatic bias of the apparatus and for the mechanical exception, the bonus produced because of the automatic function of the untutored machine. The bonus may be in the unforeseen scientific offshoot or in science out of control or just in the fact of mechanical reproduction where, as I have been arguing, the machine body can be oblivious of social stigma. The racial score is evened, for instance, in contrasty film that is not kind to either the very white-skinned or the very dark-skinned actor. As we have seen, in the history of race movies the same technology that produces the bourgeois subject and has historically enshrined whiteness could be made (against unbelievable odds) to serve the interests of oppositionality—here an all-black cinema. Second, when I refer to racial realism I am referring to a functioning misconception. Mine is a reference with all of the contemporary suspicion of the notion of realism behind it. I am referring to all of the baggage carried by any expectation of likeness that would come to a head in considerations of how to light the human figure in order to make it look like an assumption. *Racial realism is an approximation of an assumption.* And there is no place where realism wreaks more havoc than in the question of family resemblance.

Family Resemblance

Family resemblance is shocking. To see oneself reflected in the faces of one's children is to witness an effortless mirroring that is astounding and almost beyond comprehension. Similarities between the one and the other tend to amaze and intrigue, possibly because of the mystery of reproduction itself, possibly because there is something inherent in similitude at which we always stand aghast. "Is not any resemblance," asks Foucault, "both the most obvious and the most hidden of things?"[65] Stunning similarities between faces produce a response in us not unlike our reaction to the achievement of photographic realism. We are often dumbfounded, momentarily confused, a state that renders us particularly susceptible to its strategy. As Umberto Eco describes the way in which we are *struck* by this realism: "Confronted with a conventionalization so much richer, and hence a formalization so much subtler than anything else, we are shocked into believing we stand before a language which restores reality to us."[66] Certainly it is this sense of the impossibility, the improbability that there could be two of a kind, that strikes us in the resembling face as well as in the resembling photograph—the twin phenomena, an original and its copy. There are further commonalities, the first being the semiotics of similitude, the process that Foucault has identified as signifying "exactly in so far as it resembles what it is indicating," thus always a reference back.[67] But relevant to us, these images of an originary reality, the resembling child and the photographic image, are also analogizable because of their causal connection to an original, a causality that brings them into being, a thin connection in the case of the photograph "caused" by the world it copies, but the defining connection for the offspring.[68]

It is this presumed causal connection in the version of human reproduction in which parents "make" babies by spitting them out that supports the custom of examining early the face of the young child for signs of parental likeness. Commonsense knowledge has its insightful but misguided version of this causality as evidenced in the phrase "spitting image," a phrase that both captures the precision of lookalikeness and describes the process of its biological production. [69] The "spitting image" is shorthand for the folk wisdom that describes the production of likeness and the production of offspring as a process of spitting out, as in, "How can they deny that the child is his when she looks just like he spit her out?" The folk insight explains likeness in terms of an analogy between saliva and sperm, a comparison that belies a naive notion of where babies "come from," the mouth hopelessly confused with the vagina, the directionality of the sperm reversed, or the mouth too literally the penis and an even more fantastic version of how babies are made.

Note also in this blindsided wisdom the stubborn insistence on causality. It is no wonder that there is so much invested in the practice of looking for family likeness. This is the exercise in which it is determined who "takes after" whom, an obligatory study in the reproducibility of traits but also a lesson in interpretation, in how faces can be "read" one way or another when so much is at stake. Gender enters with a vengeance at this stage to introduce the age-old fallacy to which I have referred, the fantasy, actually, that men produce men and women produce women.[70] Never mind that women bear all of the children or that these children may be as unlike their parents as they are alike, or that on the faces and bodies of children the heritable traits mingle and modify one another in unpredictable ways, surfacing and receding in the early years. The game of "look and see if you can tell" who "fathered" (or less commonly who "mothered") is still played incessantly.

If a child is thought to have mixed-race parentage, entire societies will play this game, and societies have historically looked to try to find evidence of dubious deeds past and deeds future—looked more for evidence of the *black* portion than the white. Indeed, much of the case for establishing that Sally Hemmings was Thomas Jefferson's slave mistress relies on the documented accounts of visitors to Monticello as well as Jefferson's grandson who observed Hemmings's children. According to these accounts, her children all resembled Jefferson and one of her sons had a particularly strong resemblance.[71] Given the one-drop rule, it would seem that the black part overrules and overwhelms the white, but this is in theory, of course, because actual faces tell significantly different tales. With all of this conjecture, however, and particularly during key periods in American history, very little has been written of a serious nature undertaking what might be called the "close analysis" of the mixed-race face, this aside from the copious work on craniology and other pseudoscientific ventures.[72] Such study would at least have to begin with the larger problem of *why* the face, which might immediately lead on to the postindustrial development in which human faces have come to seem increasingly like the very photographs that frame them, cropped off from the rest of the body and expressively set.

Although the work of Deleuze and Guattari is well known and their theorization of the facializing imperative instrumental, it is important to recall the indebtedness of their schematization to Hungarian film theorist Béla Balázs, who first published his study of the silent film in 1924. The seeds of what would become their "white wall, black hole" system might be found in Balázs's basic understanding of the totalizing function of the physiognomy, which has not a Christianizing but an anthropomorphizing drive in which everything in the world gets a human face.[73] It is difficult to miss the correspondence between the Hungarian theorist's notion of landscape as physiognomy and Deleuze and Guattari's curious concept of "landscapification" so crucial to their understanding of the territory of the motion picture close-up.[74] And it is perhaps as crucial to point out that the linkage between the facializing close-up and the racializing tendency that the closeup has been made to serve was made first by Balázs. Thus it could be said that in the first theorization of the motion picture close-up we find a nascent attempt to think about racial characteristics in relation to the photographic image. Admittedly, Balázs is more interested in the "class physiognomies" of Eisenstein's revolutionary cinema, an interest that leads him to consider the racial aspect of the face of the English aristocrat, even the degeneracy of it. The face is unexplored territory to the film theorist, he goes on, and "[o]ne of the tasks of the film is to show us, by means of 'microphysiognomics,' how much of what is in our faces is our own and how much of it is the common property of our family, nation or class."[75]

But Balázs opens the door to the complexity and difficulty of reading the territory of the face only to close it with an unexamined assumption about the typicality of racial traits. The Negro, grouped with the Chinese and the Eskimo, is part of a predictible class with recognizible "group physiognomies."[76] The close-up individuates or, in other words, adds another mask to the underlying one: "In the mingling of the individual and racial character two expressions are superimposed on each other like translucent masks."[77] But that does not alter in any way the racial givens, which is to say that they are inalterable. In answer to this, one could assert the subversive potential of the existence of the mulatto, asserting "race" characteristics not as givens but as shifting and malleable, and since in the United States the same people have been able to belong to the white *and* the black racial group, it would seem that the idea of a fixed and hereditary group is nullified with every change.[78]

There is yet another challenge to the hardness of the racial category, even a challenge to the theory and practice of rape and concubinage that for so many years has been credited with the reproduction of children of mixed blood. This is the challenge of the historical existence of the interracial family. Some may argue that there never was such a family. Right when the protest arises that this family did not exist historically, however, a photograph of just such a family emerges, forcing us to rethink old positions. In an image taken by the black photographer Richard S. Roberts in the 1920s, John Hiller and his wife Alice Johnson Hiller sit for their portrait with their four children, Simmie, Bernice, Samuel, and Benjamin. Here is a studio-style family portrait of father standing and mother seated, flanked by their children, carefully posed and arranged. We have to look twice, and what we notice first are the father's ears. Pointed and jutting out from the side of his head like two horns, they are the unmistakable ears of a white man. It is these elfin ears that encourage the speculation about the distribution of racial traits among the children, traits distributed from the parents and divided equally or unequally, it is difficult if not impossible to tell. Still, one is intrigued, and returned for a moment to the familiarity of that old custom of searching the faces of the young for the iteration of parental traits. This is different, however, because in scrutinizing this territory of the faces of the offspring of a mixed-race union, the viewer of the photograph is positioned as the community that sat in racial judgment. We turn from the comparison between sets of ears to the comparison between noses and discover that the father's nose does not appear exactly on any of his children, although whereas Benjamin and Simmie appear to have inherited their mother's nose, Bernice and Samuel have noses that, although similar, are unlike the noses of either their mother or their father. Yet we might pose a theory of modification whereby the hereditary contribution of one partner alters the gift of the other. Clearly, there are entirely too many familial similarities within the differences to discount the contribution of either parent.

John Hiller (standing center) and Alice Johnson Hiller (seated center) with their children
Simmie, Bernice, Samuel, and Benjamin in Columbia, South Carolina
(photographer: Richard S. Roberts, 1920s)

But what variety and randomness in the distribution of traits, and
how difficult to translate six arrangements of ears, noses, and eyes into
racial groupings! Do we see a white man and his black family? Do we
see a white man with his black wife and their four children who are neither white nor black but an entirely other group within or without the
black or the white group? Does the portrait strike us as odd because the
white patriarch is present instead of absent? Does his presence make him
appear more or less responsible? Or does he seem more incongruous
than responsible? John Hiller is seen here in marked contrast to the paternity that refuses to see itself in the other. Still, if there is something

"wrong with this picture," it is his presence. And yet he might as well be there. After all, he is the source of the middle class respectability of this family. He may be why his sons wear suits. And why when many free black men would have been wearing suits for several generations in this country, does the black man in a suit in the 1920s still look like a novelty? Why do the two brothers wear their stiff suits as though they had been borrowed, submitting to the choke-hold of collar studs, a question to which we must return in relation to the way black male characters in race movies and in all the Harlem portraits of James Van Der Zee wore their clothes, their uniforms of the middle class, wore them with such relish, such cheerful tolerance of the discomfort, as though to counter the prevalent attitude that a black man does not belong in a suit.[79] Are we caught in a wrong racial assumption? Many white as well as black men looked as though they had been stuffed into their suits in all of the photographic sittings from the first century of the invention.

The intact interracial family thus calls precious convictions into question: it dissolves dividing lines, muddies distinctions, and softens categories. The mere existence of such families in the 1920s went a long way toward refuting the mythology of promiscuity and illicit interracial coupling. But what if, after this exercise in reading this photograph as troubling to the racial status quo in Columbia, South Carolina, in the 1920s, we hear that this is the portrait of John Hiller with his black family taken outside his house the very day that he was photographed with his white family inside the same house? Does the doubleness of the situation explain the expression of exhausted resignation on his "wife" Alice's face? If we think of this as John Hiller's parallel family, does the pose take on a fictional aspect? Does this mean that for each sister and brother in this secondary family there may be a white equivalent, a further dispersal and dilution of John Hiller's features?[80]

Despite the trouble it makes for the categories, there are ways in which the interracial family may be nothing more than a microcosm of the larger society, meaning that stratification and classification start at home. Filmmaker Kathe Sandler has written penetratingly about the relativity of color within the black family, looking more closely at her own after seeing the photograph titled "Newly Freed Slaves." In this 1863 portrait she saw the full range of complexions that have historically been understood as part of black America, from the darkest to the whitest. Considering her position as the lighter of two daughters, she faces the contradictoriness, treated as the good daughter no matter what her behavior.[81] She "looks" white but she thinks of herself as black. What does it mean to maintain and assert a black identity in spite of the testimony of one's own physical features, which cue others to think "white"? How can one "look" white and "be" black? The double meaning of "looks" that bell hooks plays on in the title of her book, *Black Looks*, draws our attention to the wide discrepancy between the active and passive forms of "looking."[82] To receive "looks" and to appear or to "look" one way or another is always to be culturally framed. We always need to wonder about the light-skinned mulatta, "she 'looks' white to whom"? And what if she "manages" her black looks as Simmie and Bernice Hiller appear to have done in the family photograph? Does such "management," as evidenced in hair straightening, for instance, signal an attempt to appear more white or just less black?

Family resemblance is terrifying. There is something ghostly about the Hiller family portrait, in the tracings of the two races (the one foregrounded and the other managed into the background), in the strange superimpositions on the faces of the children, almost as though the mother's face was printed over the father's. One thinks of Lillian Smith's observation about the three ghost relationships that "haunted the mind" of the American South: "the white man and the colored woman, white father and colored children, white child and his beloved colored nurse."[83] Are the ghost relationships really printed on the faces of those who signify the intermingling or are we imagining things? Are we imagining the resemblances between six distinct and separate persons merely because they are photographed together? They are as different as they are alike, and the likeness is so fleeting, a likeness amounting to an expression, a close-mouthedness, a firm closure that guarantees that no secrets will slip out. What is terrifying is that for their sitting, these family members all wear the same expressionless expression: they all wear the same family mask. And yet the illusion of familial sameness is interrupted by the stark difference between John and Alice. Even the mother—the only family member who presumably has no whiteness in her—may indeed, as is so often said, "have some white blood," as though that were either discernable or important. The question arises not because it ultimately matters in the larger scheme of things but because it matters in the local scheme where the mother is seen as "wearing" her African-like face.

If the black face is a strange mask, strange because it is a face not because it is black, the white face is an absolutely horrifying mask. Thinking of the white face, the paradigm of the close-up, Deleuze and Guattari say, "The face, what a horror." As a close-up, the "naturally inhuman face" is a "monstrous hood."[84] In order to see this hood, however, one needs some distance on the white face close-up. Knowingly, Micheaux examines the "monstrous hoodedness" of the white face in his fourth film, *The Symbol of the Unconquered* (1920), a narrative about legacies— the legacy of land ownership, the legacy of passing, and, most memorably, the legacy of the white night riders, the Ku Klux Klan. And it is within this film that Micheaux presents a new enigma to critics and historians who have been recently focused on the blackface performance that has come to assume a certain theoretical fashion in recent years. Because in this film the director turns blackface inside out, using black actors to play white characters. What do we call it, then, when black people play white people? Is this "whiteface"? But there is no concealed envy here, no fascination, as Eric Lott finds in the phenomenon of "blackface," that backhanded compliment whites paid to blacks in their enthusiasm for the minstrel show.[85] Not only does Micheaux mine the doubleness of black-as-white in at least one scene in this film, but he accelerates the irony. He intensifies the irony to the point where, we suspect, not only does he place a black character passing as a white within the ranks of the Klan but, since it was his practice to use as many black actors as possible, he most likely sheeted up black actors to play the epitome of the horror of the white face: the pillow-faced Klan member. Micheaux also makes subtle trouble by casting light-skinned actresses as white. Another generation of scholars will inevitably research the racial identities of these double-passers.[86]

The Symbol of the Unconquered (1920)

Eve Mason (played by Iris Hall), the light-skinned heroine, is left a legacy by her dying grandfather, and she sets out to find and claim his cabin in the northwestern woods. At night, she enters a hotel run by the villain Jefferson Driscoll (Lawrence Chenault), another light-skinned black, but one who is passing as white. (Title: "One of the many mulattoes who concealed their origins.") Identifying Eve as black (Title: "But if her skin is white, yet eyes betray her origins.") Driscoll cruelly refuses to let her stay in his hotel, sending her to the barn to sleep on a cold and storming night. In the barn, Eve is "startled" by Abraham, a peddler, who has earlier been turned out by Driscoll and is also seeking shelter in the barn. Awakened by the storm just in time to see her fall in the mud as she runs, frightened, from the barn, Driscoll jumps gleefully in his bed, a scene that underlines his heartless cruelty toward members of the black race. (Title: "His ferocious hatred for his own race.") In an early flashback we see Driscoll reject and deny his own dark-skinned mother who exposes his race when she interrupts his courtship of a white woman (who in all likelihood is played by a black woman). (Title: "Cursed moment—reason for his hatred.")

Lost after the storm, Eve is rescued by the light-skinned hero Hugh Van Allen (Walker Thompson), who is prospecting nearby and who takes her to find the cabin. But danger lurks; in an adjacent cabin two more villains, August Barr, a former clergyman, and Tugi, a "fakir" Indian, are torturing the prospector Philip Clark who they are forcing to steal certain documents once in the possession of Eve Mason's grandfather, which they believe to be secreted in the old prospector's cabin where Eve is now staying. Van Allen becomes a target of Driscoll's duplicity when the schemer sells him two stolen Arabian horses (an echo of Micheaux's repeated problems with horse traders in his autobiographical novels). A fight ensues in a saloon, and Driscoll is badly beaten by Van Allen, a humiliation that causes the villain to swear revenge. We have already seen that the villains are working as a gang and that their opportunity for profit arrives when Driscoll accidentally finds a letter dropped by the postal service informing Van Allen of the worth of his land. The gang members conspire to force him to sell his land with threatening letters and when they don't succeed, they prepare to ride as "The Knights of the Black Crow," a secret society of men covered in sheets with an uncanny likeness to the riders of the Ku Klux Klan. We see Driscoll, who is passing, hesitate before the ride, but the assumption is that he will ride because he is part of the group. Here Driscoll's race betrayal is magnified, his treachery to the race epitomized by his membership in the Klan.

It is the female characters who discover the plot and, betraying the men, decide to warn Van Allen. Eve jumps on a spirited horse and, in a scene crosscut with the ride of the Black Crow, rushes to sound the alarm. In this scene Micheaux once again turns the tables on custom and expectation, playing up the anomaly—a black woman in buckskin riding against the Klan on her thundering steed! Our assumption is that the gang is thwarted because we see a single iris shot of Driscoll sprawled out on a rock. The intertitle in the restored print next tells us that a section of the film is missing and that a review in the *New York Age* at the time of the film's release describes how a "colored man with bricks" helped to "annihilate" the Klan.[87] The identity of this character remains a mystery, but since one would assume that the reviewer would credit the hero Van Allen if it had been he who had routed the Klan, this leaves perhaps one other good black male character who might have been turned into a hero—the ever-present Abraham, played by E. G. Tatum, the actor who Micheaux used as Ephrain, the tattletale butler in

The Symbol of the Unconquered (dir. Oscar Micheaux, 1920)

"One of the many mulattoes who concealed their origins"
Jefferson Driscoll (Lawrence Chenault)

"But if her skin is white, yet eyes betray her origins," Eve Mason (Iris Hall)

"The Knights of the Black Crow"

"What! You! Of the black race!" Eve Mason and Hugh Van Allen (Walker Thompson)

Within Our Gates, a character whose function in the early scenes of *The Symbol of the Unconquered* appears to be nothing more than comic relief. After the clarifying title card, the film cuts to two years later when Eve surprises Van Allen in the offices of the Van Allen Corporation, a visit she pays on behalf of the Committee for the Defense of the Race. The two profess the love they have had for one other over the years, he confessing that it was fear of her possible rejection that kept him from revealing his feelings.

This conclusion, almost an epilogue, depicting the reunion of the lovers after the passage of time, implies that they were separated because he did not know that she, too, was black. (Title: "What! You! Of the black race!") She, however, knows that he is "of the black race," else why would she be soliciting him for help in the "defense of the race"? It would seem that since *we* know, he must know too, and the movement toward intimacy between the two in the film has already suggested that they were "of the same race." But how can the hero be so oblivious? Was it only in Micheaux's fantasy (and in his fantasy territory, the American West) that in 1920 a white woman could fall asleep in a wagon with her head on a strange black man's shoulder?[88] Racial recognition and misrecognition are, as I have noted, an important concern in both Micheaux's literary and cinematic fictions, and the most obvious theory to advance here is that Micheaux wants to delay recognition until the end of his narrative, using it as a device to first separate and then reunite the heroine and the hero, using the discovery of the heroine's "true" racial identity as a reward to the black hero for being deferential to what Micheaux would call the "custom of the land."

That same hero, however, has also challenged that custom by loving the heroine anyway, even when he thought she was a white woman, making the same forgivable mistake that the hero of *The Homesteader* had made. In Micheaux, the heroine's actual blackness is the hero's reward for *not seeing race,* for not seeing it as a reason to *not love.* The paradox is remarkable. Love should *not know* racial difference but it cannot find happiness unless it does. In the relationship between the hero and the heroine who see each other without beholding racial markers, Micheaux is refuting the whole ideology of telltale signs. It is the yellow-bellied Driscoll who is aligned with the position of the self-evidence of the seen, and he has been discredited from the start because of his rejection of his own mother who by her very existence threatens his attempt to pass, a reference to that deep division of family members in the black community, to brothers and sisters, parents and children separated by their own variety.

But this still leaves contemporary viewers with the question why would Driscoll, the villain, be able to see Eve as black when Van Allen, the hero and lover, *cannot* see her as black? A contemporary reviewer for *The New York Age* also noticed this enigma and commented, "As in nine cases out of ten Negroes instinctively recognize one of their own, some are apt to wonder why he did not learn the truth sooner."[89] Van Allen's myopia is even more puzzling when one considers whether Eve recognizes Driscoll and sees through his deception at the moment that he "reads" her as black. In the charged encounter between the two in the hotel the shot/reaction shot pairing suggests that this is a moment of dual recognition, that, in Eve's eyes (as in our own, as viewers), Driscoll is not just a white bigot but a black man in the guise of a white, acting out both white bigotry and race betrayal. As Pearl Bowser and Louise Spence have probed Driscoll's motives, they stress his own "dread of discovery."[90] This is a discovery that could bring about financial as well as personal ruination since Driscoll, owner of the Driscoll Hotel and later the Driscoll Real Estate Company, exemplifies that group of blacks who used the cover of whiteness to pursue business avenues not as easily open to them as blacks. But Micheaux gives Driscoll another motive for his race hatred in the "cursed moment" when his mother appears, jeopardizing his suit with a white woman who "recognizes" Driscoll through his mother.

Clearly, Driscoll, who rejects his race, is finally ruined because he read everything in racial terms, and consequently expires on a rock, unmasked. In contrast, Van Allen is rewarded for not seeing everything in racial terms, and he is portrayed as one of the successful oil kings, as signified by the panoramic view of his developed land, his impressive office, and the cigar in his mouth. It would be a mistake to simply argue that one man "can tell" while the other "can't tell," since this would be to ignore the difference in the heroine's relationships between the two men, the one bent on misreading her blackness as the threat of his own exposure and the other reading her black self as pure goodness. The curious difference between Eve's encounters with Driscoll and Van Allen is given further complexity in the African American jazz legend Max Roach's score for *The Symbol of the Unconquered*.[91] This all-percussion score, performed on the solo drumset, assigns rhythmic leitmotifs or "rhythmic signatures" to each character in much the same way that classical scoring for narrative fiction films has used the motive to characterize and classify.[92] The significant difference in Max Roach's approach, which makes it boldly antithetical to the Hollywood score, is its unrelenting modernism, its management of narrative ideas without recourse to the melodic, and its use of the gaping hole of silence. This is the silence that produces almost a gasp at the moment that we learn that the Klan is gearing up, a silence that would produce the worst nightmare of the television producer, a dead sound track on the broadcast.

Roach's score is perhaps most compelling in its development of what Malcom Miranda-Monsman has called the "Tension Motive," a rhythmic cell that develops into Driscoll's "Hate Motive," a signature "sizzling" effect produced by the cymbals. That the metallic sound with its connotations of anxiety and what he calls an "unnatural tension" are attached both to Driscoll, consumed with hate, and to the scenes involving Hugh Van Allen and Eve Mason suggests that something is unresolved.[93] In this case, the key narrative enigmas are racially unresolved and the "shimmering" cymbals invest moments of uncertainty, the suspension between recognition and nonrecognition, with enormous importance, as though everything is hanging in the balance as we anticipate the outcome of a raced identity question.

I opened this chapter with the question of racial recognition and misrecognition, asking, in effect, "Why does Arnold Girdlestone not recognize his own daughter?" Put differently, why does he not see himself in her? The white patriarch, as we know, is categorically unable to see himself in his mixed-blood offspring. But how is his *not* seeing (his own) whiteness different from Van Allen's inability to see blackness? The asymmetry stings. In the one case whiteness recedes, in the other blackness, but not for the same reasons. If we were to draw any conclusion from the situations of Sylvia and Eve, we would have to note once again the absolute absurdity of racial readings. No one gets it right. Skin color is no measure of anything and should be seen through and beyond. At the same time, however, race pride wins the day through recognition and the consequent resolution.

This problem in this history of the mimetic technology (nothing more nor less than the human body) has another facet to which I now want to turn—the oblique relation of this body to the mimesis of the screen. As a technology producing bodies that could conceivably reproduce the social unrest that looked just like the trouble on the screen, the motion picture was often demonized in this period, as we will see. For the reproductive technology could not show these stories of racial resemblance. As a consequence, one could see everywhere the faces that "told," but nowhere could one see the stories of interracial mixing on the screen.

$\mathscr{R}ace / \mathscr{R}iot / \mathscr{C}inema$

Of all the offending scenes in *The Birth of a Nation*, the "Gus chase" scene has perhaps stirred the strongest reactions, beginning with the year of the film's release. From all accounts, local censorship boards or city hall representatives consistently required Griffith to cut this scene before they would issue the necessary license to exhibit the picture, and some of the most vivid accounts of the heated response to the film in 1915 are the descriptions of the audience reaction to this scene. Opening at the Liberty Theatre in New York on March 3, 1915, the film created an immediate sensation and divided critics and supporters into armed camps. The city was in turmoil over the controversy by the end of the month, particularly when it became clear that the National Board of Censorship, asked to reconsider their earlier decision to approve the film, voted to pass the film but with required cuts.[1] The vote was unanimous, and the strong denunciations of the film by dissenting voters were quoted in the press.[2]

Two days after the report in the press, trouble broke out at the Liberty Theatre. During the "Gus chase" scene culminating in "Little Sister's" suicidal leap from the cliff, spectators in the front rows of the theater threw eggs at the screen. As the *New York Times* reported the incident, when policemen and private detectives rushed to the front and grabbed the leaders, "two eggs splattered over the screen, blotting out portions of a picture showing a white Southern girl in the act of leaping off a cliff to escape from a negro pursuer. As one of the men was escorted from the theatre he was heard to shout out 'Rotten, rotten.' After his arrest, Howard Schaeffle, a white man, admitted throwing the eggs and when searched, a bag containing more eggs was found in his pocket. In his defense, he asserted, 'I am a Southerner and a libertarian, and I believe in the education and uplifting of the negro. It made my blood boil to see the play and I threw eggs at the screen.' "[3]

In what might have been a copycat action in Boston, other angry spectators singled out the same scene to "egg." As Thomas Cripps describes the tense situation at Boston's Tremont Theatre, two hundred police interrupted when blacks tried to buy tickets. Editor and founder of the important black newspaper the *Guardian,* William Monroe Trotter, who the next day would lead a crowd in a famous protest march to the steps of the Massachusetts State House, railed against the film in the lobby, but when a policeman hit him, others entered and arrested ten blacks.[4] Although Trotter and other blacks were turned away at the box office, some were able to get into the theater. Again, as in New York, the "Gus chase" scene was a target. This time a black man in the audience stood up, and according to a newspaper account, "spattered a very ancient egg by a well-directed shot over the exact middle of the white screen." Charles Ray was charged with malicious mischief.[5]

The Egging of *The Birth of a Nation*

Cripps has not been the only film historian to mention the egging of *The Birth of a Nation.* Referring to the instance of egg-throwing at the Liberty Theatre, Janet Staiger restores to history the fact that whites as well as blacks disrupted the early screenings of the film with politicized, antisocial actions. But more significantly, Staiger gives us an extremely thorough and critically informed account of the political complexities of the reception of Griffith's epic, an account that is open to seeing a range of social interventions as interpretative acts. "Although violence—such as throwing eggs at the screen—occurred," she says, "public safety alarmists" observed that the protesters seemed aware of the way in which particular tactics could hurt their cause.[6] It suits my purpose in this chapter, where ultimately I want to look at the paranoia that produced the connection between motion pictures and race riots, to think of these protesters as political strategists and to consider egg-throwing as a hermeneutic act. In this context we will need to consider the *mimetic spectator,* a variant of which is the rowdy egg-thrower whose reaction to the screen confirms the worst suspicions of the moral reformers who see only the antisocial act and miss the critical and analytical dimension of the well-placed egg. So, too, the critical component of the race riot would be easily missed, and the stage is set for the local hysteria that blames the image for social atrocities, a pattern that continues into the present, a formation learned by the culture in this troubled period between the 1915 release and the 1924 rerelease of *The Birth of a Nation.*

In contemporary culture, terror of images is often accompanied by what could be called *violence discourse*. In mainstream-media discourse, decrying "violence" in the society is a lament that often has no particular point of reference, a complaint that effectively lumps together a wide spectrum of acts ranging from youthful vandalism to first-degree murder to mob destruction. Then there is the related problem of violence discourse that puts the antisocial at arm's length. In its skittishness about the bodily, the (often white) discourse on violence does not help us understand the difference between egg-throwing, protesting, and rioting in 1915 but, even more important, such discourse does not answer the question, "Whose violent acts against whom or what?" Neither does violence discourse make a distinction between people and property, and agency often disappears (as in the passive tense when violence is said to have "broken out"). Further, this particularly obtuse discourse cannot imagine either revolutionary moments (situations in which brutal reprisals are necessary) or the use of force in righteous struggle. And, finally, violence discourse is unable to conceptualize the crucial difference between realistic representations of historic events and flesh-and-blood brutalities, since "violence on the screen" is often given the same discursive weight as the real historical events to which the screen image refers. In retrospect, it would seem that the stage was set in 1915 for the encouragement of contemporary fears about the possible violent "effects" of the new spectacular "real-seeming" moving image on the mass public, and unfortunately the terms of the public debate about these effects have changed little since that time.

A new approach might bring the "violent" act and the perpetrating text closer together, in effect considering the antisocial act as a flagrant act of interpretation, a precise interpretative tactic. Here the key questions are seen in concentrated form in the egg-throwing incident. We wonder first about the basic apprehension of the cinematic signifier. We wonder if as late as 1915 we have an actual case of the naïveté about the screen summed up in the early *Uncle Josh at the Moving Picture Show* (1902), a comedy about a rube who jumps on stage and tries to intervene in the on-screen drama.[7] We wonder if the egg-throwers, like the backward Uncle Josh, mistook the screen for real life or if they were throwing eggs at the representation they *knew* to be a representation. Is the protest a protest against the black-and-white luminous image of Gus and "Little Sister" or against the connotation that black men had raped or killed innocent white women? Does the protest target the signifier or the signified? Or is such protest semiotically "on target," hitting the sign right where the signifier and the signified come together, and if this is the case, is the egg-thrower *less* the literal-minded Uncle Josh and more the sophisticated semiotician? And, finally, does this example mean that the imaginariness of the signifier is not at all daunting to the patron who throws things at the screen?

The separation between the world of the audience and the world of the screen is dramatized by the egg that is directed at race hatred in the world but hits the motion picture screen instead. Thus it is the social change trajectory of the egg that concerns us here. Historically, it has been radical filmmakers who have urged the relation between screen realism and social change, filmmakers who made us think about screen effects in a more productive and expansive way. But I am not thinking of filmmakers here, and I want to take the question of social intervention in another direction—to ask about the other ways in which groups or institutions intervene in the world of the text in order to effect change in the other world, also the world of the text. I am thinking of an institution that has not been historically associated with protest and social change, perhaps because of its association with social maintenance and petty bureaucracy. But in the case of *The Birth of a Nation*, censorship has been understood as on the side of people's struggles. Francis G. Couvares, arguing for a more complex approach to censorship, would understand such efforts as "good" censorship, a movement with a goal of protecting subordinate groups from the potential harm of the social repercussions of representation. But he also notes the way "good" censorship can quickly become "bad" when protection turns into repression.[8]

In Annette Kuhn's reconsideration of censorship, she asks that we begin to think less of a singular institution and more of the relations of power and their interplay, spread over a field of intersecting forces. As in Michel Foucault, it is in the "tension" produced between groups and in the "exercise" (rather than in the having) of power that the forces felt as censorship are brought to bear on culture.[9] While this definition has distinct advantages for our approach, the prevalent understanding in film industry studies has depended on an important separation between the *censorship* that involves the intervention of the state and the *self-regulation* that the American industry attempted, beginning in 1909 and thereafter, to stave off industry criticism as well as official censorship.[10] And although we will be speaking about, for instance, the censoring gaze, we may be speaking about an unofficial as well as an official criticism that hovers over the text; nonetheless, when we are talking about cuts in the film ordered by local authorities, we are speaking of an official act of censorship.[11] The term censorship not only carries the connotation "official," but it has become associated with the kind of prohibition that is intolerable in a free society, and it is therefore difficult to conduct any discussion of the censorial without calling up connotations of unwanted intervention. And since it is generally conservative moral crusaders and political opportunists who have historically found representations of sexuality to be offensive (thus defining the limit test of censorship), it is difficult to now offer censorship as any kind of critically interesting invervention or even as an instrumental act of interpretation as I am attempting to do here. Clearly, we need to move toward an understanding of the censorial as a network of forces exerted on the text, as Kuhn recommends.

Not surprisingly, the campaign to ban *The Birth of a Nation* has remained immune to the associations of censorship with intolerance and seems to exist in U.S. history as an exception to the belief that constraint on cultural expression is dangerous. As we will see, NAACP warrior W. E. B. Du Bois had later thoughts along these lines about the political implications of the organization's struggle to stop the hate campaign of Thomas Dixon, the author of *The Clansman* and *The Leopard's Spots*, with whom the NAACP was familiar from earlier skirmishes around the theatrical performance of the play adapted from *The Clansman*.[12] There are reasons to rally behind *The Birth of a Nation* struggle, a fight that made heroes of Rabbi Stephen Wise, Oswald Garrison Villard, Walter White, William Monroe Trotter, Mary White Ovington, Jane Addams, and Frederic Howe, head of the National Board of Censorship of Motion Pictures, among others in local government and NAACP chapters.[13] We continue to learn about the ways in which the NAACP campaign galvanized the local chapters, helping them to sharpen their skills in the war against racism, which would translate into the struggle to integrate the schools, the police force, and often the motion picture theaters as well.[14] In such a case, when the call to censor is simultaneously a struggle for social equality and a campaign for race consciousness and against marginalization, we have to consider how censorship empowers those groups who have no claim on power.[15] Achieving the moral high ground in the context of people's struggles, censorship loses its connotations of intolerance and conservatism and is understood as a righteous movement against vilification and hatred.

But in the force field of censorship, the troublesome text functions as a kind of magnet for unanticipated local power, for outlaw as well as legitimate discourses. And *The Birth of a Nation* attracted dense and contentious discourses, even beyond the obvious sides—the Griffith and Dixon camp that consistently faced off against the NAACP organization and its liberal followers. Perhaps it is another tribute to the success of the NAACP campaign that we find it so difficult to attempt to change the

Peoria, Illinois, 1916

terms of the discussion of the historical reception of this film. But here I am suggesting that we think about the spectrum of interpretative response, from the way the film helped to resurrect a modern Ku Klux Klan to the way it encouraged paranoia about motion pictures themselves, animosity toward the teeming masses of viewers, and disgust and contempt for interracial sexuality in addition to the offspring of such unions. The interpretation of the film was not only split along racial lines but along regional ones, and in addition to the predictable North/South split, some states such as Ohio supported a consistent prohibition of the exhibition of the film where other states vacillated and the position for or against exhibition varied from town to town. For every mayor who banned the film out of respect for local blacks and desire to keep the peace, there would be another who did so out of opposition to the representation of interracial sex. It is finally almost impossible to identify all of the official pressures on this text, but suffice it to say that they are perhaps as varied as the communities where the film was exhibited or banned.[16]

The force field of censorship is defined by the intersections of power but also pleasure, and contemporary feminist considerations of sexualized imagery have so transformed this question of the censorial that we no longer understand the prohibition in isolation from the transgression it produces. In the Foucauldian sense, censorship produces the proliferation of the desires that it would repress; the constraint effects the increase, the multiplication of the very deeds that it would inhibit or eradicate. Janet Staiger, preferring the concept of regulation to that of censorship, asks, "Who is getting what pleasures from each instance of self-regulation?"[17] Thus it is that many contemporary considerations of censorship begin with the acknowledgment of the futility of the exercise.

And it is here that we seem to be the furthest away from the conventional approach to *The Birth of a Nation,* for to suggest that the censorship of this film produced the desire to see it, even encouraged the fascination with its own prohibited status and fantasies of the black bodies deleted from it, would seem to challenge the validity of the effort to protest the film's exhibition. Have we focused on the NAACP attack on the film at the expense of looking at this phenomenon? Consider, for instance, the outcome of the New York attempts to censor the film. According to the report of NAACP national secretary Mary Childs Nearney, only the most "vulgar" parts had been cut out after meetings with the mayor, and the highly objectionable "Gus chase" scene still remained. The film was breaking all of the city records for length of run and attendance.[18] The enormous popularity of the film needs to be considered in these terms, and the time has come to look at the way the censored portions drew spectators to it.

In at least one case, a mayor refused to ban the film because he said he had caught on to the way theater managers would use the suppression of the film to get more publicity in the next city.[19] The evidence indicates that showmen took advantage of the way censorship and protest could produce the desire to see the controversial text. Both *The Birth of a Nation* and the earlier theatrical production of *The Clansman* in 1906 were also associated with faked insurgence when exhibitors, convinced of the publicity value of controversy, attempted to hire blacks to stage protests.[20] No one, however, better understood the use of censorship to produce the desire to see than Oscar Micheaux, who is legendary for his opportunistic use of the trouble he encountered in one community as an advertisement for his film in the next. In the end, more than anything else, it is Micheaux's experience with countless censorship boards in film after film during this early period that has influenced my reconsideration of the censorial gaze. The censorial gaze is a group gaze, going

beyond the individual outburst and seeking its influence in official reprisals. This gaze is an expression of power that has its eye more on the
world than on the screen.

Official censoring power wants nothing more than to have its way
with the world. Censorship, whether of pornography or racist abomina-
tion, whether from the moral majority Right or the NAACP Left (and
Center), is an attempt to intervene in both the world and the text. Curiously, censorship actually bridges the screen–world divide and hopes
that it can fix the text, and in fixing it, repair the world. Consider, for instance, the way in which the protest against the "Gus chase" scene pres-
sured censors to cut the text; consider further the reconstruction of the
text after subsequent screenings as a response by other, different, fac-
tions urging the return of scenes previously removed. Censorship allows
communities a way into the text as well as giving them a foot into the
world by way of the protested text. The community, via the censor, exerts its influence over others by means of the text.

According to Annette Kuhn, this screen–world divide is just as
much a problem for film studies as it is for the frustrated protester. Censorship, as I have said, spans this divide. In her discussion of censorship
in early British cinema, Kuhn remarks about the difficulty of studying
censorship as anything more than an institutional history precisely because the screen–world split also corresponds with a disciplinary division. Where the realm of the text is the domain of critical theory and semiotics, the study of the social institutions outside the text, the crucial
production, distribution, and exhibition factors, is the purview of social
science. Separate methodologies and terminology work, as she says, to
"police the boundaries between disciplines." Most problematic in her estimation, however, is the tendency to completely relegate texts to the unreal "cultural" realm as opposed to the "real" space of institutions.[21] Certainly, important theoretical attempts have been made to bridge this
methodological divide, and one of the most productive of these has been
the use of concepts that analogize the economic and the cultural, concepts such as the "economy of the text" or the "production of meaning,"
concepts often utilized in order to stress inside–outside correspon-
dences. Still, in these examples the text remains extremely abstract and
not of this world, and the textual economy, losing its industrial base,
seems "only" a metaphor. But this criticism of the separateness of disciplines momentarily forgets that Marxist cultural theory has historically
defined itself as dedicated to the very problem of the interpenetration
of real historical forces and cultural forms that so stubbornly separate at

every opportunity. More than anything, the following is another effort to resist this inevitability.

The Effect of the Text

Following Kuhn's lead, it would seem that the narrowly institutional approach to cinema censorship that only sees federal and local governments regulating culture could be challenged by an approach that factors the resistance to that regulation into the equation, or that allows for *The Birth of a Nation* model of censorship-as-resistance. This would lead us to the highly charged force field of censorship crossed with erratic surges of power instead of the more linear version of censorship that leads to the dead end of "free speech" issues and predictable concerns about the mutilation of an author's work.[22] This, then, is not another discussion of the way censorship threatens art or speech. Given the phenomenon of censorship and banning in film history, I want to know what such social stigmatization *does* to texts, does to them structurally.

Far more theoretically productive than free speech questions, I am arguing, is the discussion of the way in which censorship and active protest produce a tangible reconstruction of works of culture in the open space of the public sphere.[23] Under these circumstances, rather than seeing the film as a completed authorial work, we see it instead as a work subject to compulsory public rewritings. It is "submitted," in a sense, for community approval. Add to this community pressure on the offending text the stress of the threat of social upheaval plus the pressure of the future unrest that looms as a potential effect of the text. The case of the NAACP's objection to *The Birth of a Nation* is a case of protest that not only read the film as racist but that attempted to effect a complete rewriting of the text by asking for deep cuts. For the NAACP, such incisive incursions into *the text of the film* at the level of cinematic signs were political acts, political strategy writ large—a case of genuinely social semiosis. Certainly both the NAACP and the local authorities they successfully influenced, as well as those with whom their campaign failed, were deeply concerned with textual "effects." Widely cited was the case of the white man in Lafayette, Indiana, who shot and killed a young Negro boy after exiting from a screening of *The Birth of a Nation*, an incident that clearly invited speculation about "effects."[24] But poststructuralism has quickly inserted itself before such a case can arise with its eerie question, "Do signs follow bodies or do bodies follow signs?"[25] What, if anything, does the presumed mimetic status of language have to do with mimetic acts?

This question of the power of the highly mimetic motion picture to produce immediate "effects" will raise some theoretical red flags, simultaneously returning us to the critique of realism as well as to the much maligned "media effects" approach to popular film and television. While we might want to believe that texts can have effects, following poststructuralist theory we might *not* want to argue that there is a real world on which the text can have its effect. Again, the disciplinary division asserts itself. While critical theory understands "effects" in relation to "ideological effects" (with all of the possibilities of praxis as well as the consequences of consciousness), media effects studies have to do with measuring behaviors, a dubious project from the perspective of critical theory.[26] Confronting again the question of effects, however, we are once more reminded why it is that we finally care about them. In mainstream social science as well as in Marxist theory, "effects" implies social actors and social acts, whether measurable or immeasurable. Thus it is that the question of textual effects dramatizes as it figures the screen–world divide.

Offering a way of straddling both worlds, Pierre Macherey reminds us that the text's relation to external reality is built up by degrees and starts at the level of language: "It might be said that the language spoken by the work is not answerable to any external meaning or reality; however, it will later be seen that there is no first, independent, innocent language."[27] It is not just that at the level of the referent the text draws on the historical moment, but that the very signs that the text uses are the stuff of social history. By no means pure in relation to the world outside the text, these already tainted and experienced signs *are*, however, "answerable" to the social reality to which they may not always defer but to which they still belong. Historical signs come to the text already used and are reused in ways that reveal their deep indebtedness.

The question would thus seem (given the indebtedness of signs) to pertain to the rules to which the motion picture text is subject. Which rules? Is the popular film subject to the laws of society or to the laws of art? On the one hand, it would be foolish to try to argue that the film's first allegiance is to anything other than the conventions that define it as narrative fiction or even documentary (the form that is thought to have such a special relationship with the real historical event). But, on the other hand, to claim (as formalism in its ascendence seemed to imply) that the cultural sign was never subject to any other rules or conventions would be going too far.[28] Poststructuralism, as I have mentioned, has had its own way of discouraging further inquiry into the text–world relation, and in answer to poststructuralism I would say that while we acknowledge that reality only comes to us via signs, we would also want to acknowledge that it comes again and again. Over and over, the realist text takes something *out of* and returns something *to* the historical moment to which it refers, and thus it is that the text can be said to be "answerable." For if a text is semiotically answerable to external meaning, is it not also socially answerable? Is it not finally responsible to the source of the signs that constitute it?

This question of answerability has particular ramifications for censorship, that supercritical stance that always starts from the premise that texts will have effects on the real world (without, of course, ever offering any explanation as to precisely how this happens). Further, as an offshoot of the unrivaled success of cinematic realism, protest against a text (protest for censorship of it) also assumes that there is a continuity between the world of the protesters and the world of the text, even if the text is set in an earlier time period. In fact, one might say that the protest against the inflammatory text, a position of refusal to see the point where the world leaves off and the text begins, constitutes a strategy that takes on its own reality. Or, to the egg-thrower, the space of the screen and the lived conditions of racism may be separate, but the worlds in which the film and the conditions exist are one. Hence my question: "Is it the film or the world of the film?"

The world is somehow attached to the signs that constitute the moving picture. To test this assertion, we need look no further than the stubborn *perception* of similarity between the world and the text. Audiences repeatedly make this connection. But the text is especially real and has real effects on the strength of the interpretation of those who *act on* the perception of similarity. Following from this premise, protest against a text that is not recognizable as part of the protester's world is pointless. Thus it is that aesthetic realism can be seen as advancing politics.[29] The degree to which the realist text (even in a fantasy genre) is perceived as similar to the familiar world (and even issuing from it) is the degree to which the text is treated as subject to the rules of the society. This perception of similarity is encouraged by little more than the effortless *lookalikeness* of the cinematic text, a remarkable family resemblance between the world and the film. The premise that world and text are somehow alike has political potential as it dramatizes social imperatives, but close likeness also produces serious misreadings, the best example of which is censorship itself. Censorship is, of course, a thoroughly bureaucratic act of interpretation, and censors, if they "read" a text at all, do not read well.

This question of censorship as interpretation urges us to rethink the protest around *The Birth of a Nation* in terms that draw the color lines in new ways. Clearly, this struggle has been fundamentally understood as the fight taken up by the fledgling NAACP as national leaders (including the staff of *The Crisis*) and local chapters urged the National Board of Censorship, followed by local governments and community censor boards, to either refuse the film a license or to require cuts before it could be exhibited. Although careful not to align themselves against the First Amendment, the NAACP (made up of both black and white members at the time) did ask the predominately white censor boards to ban the film outright. In many cases, such as in New York, as we have seen, the NAACP settled for cutting out specific scenes when it failed to secure an outright ban.[30] But the NAACP never did *win* the battle to suppress the incendiary film, and it was exhibited in hundreds of communities in the early years of its release.

In these communities, numerous arguments made against the film emphasized the defamation of the Negro through stereotypage. Despite this emphasis, the most frequently used "official" argument against its exhibition was that it constituted a threat to the peace, that under the law it was a "public nuisance."[31] After a concentrated struggle in the early years after the release of *The Birth of a Nation* and after continued skirmishes up until the 1960s, the NAACP had only limited success with its attempts to either alter or to stop the screening of Griffith's film. In the end, however, it could be argued that the NAACP won the publicity war, evidence of which is the fact that the 1915 public interpretation of the film as viciously racist has remained the dominant interpretation. And this is the interpretation that has marked the text for life—a strange case in which the historical intervenes at every subsequent exhibition.[32] Summing up the outcome of the hard-fought campaign, *The Crisis* editor W. E. B. Du Bois reported, "While the NAACP has failed to kill *The Birth of a Nation* it succeeded in wounding it."[33]

The Censor's Cut

Although Du Bois might have meant that the NAACP campaign, which succeeded in getting the film banned in eighteen states and numerous cities, damaged the reputation and consequently had a negative effect on the box office for *The Birth of a Nation*, he could also be interpreted as meaning that the group's efforts significantly scarred the text. This raises for us the issue of what it is that the censor's cut actually does to the film text. Does it, for instance, permanently injure the text (to continue Du

Protest against exhibition of *The Birth of a Nation*, 1947

Bois's metaphor)? How exactly does the censor deform the offending text?

I am arguing that censors do not read closely, yet, superficial reading that it is, the censor's reading is a deeply committed and antagonistic (as opposed to an oppositional) reading since it is a reading with the goal of deleting or outright banning of certain scenes.[34] The censorial reading is a reading-with-a-purpose—the purpose of suppressing or cutting—but unlike the classical film editor's reading, which is a close analysis in an attempt to produce smoothness and continuity, the censor's reading is indifferent to the whole of the text and overfocused on the part. The censor's cut, therefore, produces discontinuity, but a discontinuity that may or may not be perceived as incoherence.[35] Audiences, looking for the cut in the expurgated text, view the gap that can't be seen and produce their own continuity. The censor's intentional and instrumental reading is an inadvertent (albeit compulsory) rewriting but a rewriting that often produces a limp and tepid text. What matters to the censor is the offending scene, a scene that throbs with too much meaning, and this meaning, to the censor, is always a singular meaning. Censorship can construct film texts as "carriers of fixed meanings," says Annette Kuhn.[36] And the censor's cut, assuming a fixed meaning, also assumes that the cut "fixes" the troublesome text, as I am arguing.[37] Most important for our purposes is to see film censorship, particularly in the wake of *The Birth of a Nation*, not only as an attempt to "fix" the text so that it would not cause trouble, but as a project of "elimination," to use the terminology of the censor boards—an official public elimination of offending scenes.

My readers may worry that in my criticism of the censorship of *The Birth of a Nation* I have not been hard enough on the racist project of the film's supporters. There is no denying that history will not let up on these individuals. But is it now or will it ever be possible to separate the racism of the groups who rallied around the film from what might be called the racism of the film? Ever cautious about the charge of "racism" as well as the charge of "homophobia," Anthony Appiah has argued that a work of art is not racist in the same way that a person might be a racist in thought and deed, and that what we need to look at is the contribution that a particular film might make to the production of a more racist culture.[38] This sounds reasonable. But the more we think about it, the more we wonder about the incremental production of a more or less racist culture. What is to be the measure of this? And another issue arises. If racism doesn't inhere in the film itself, would it then be possible to use an analysis of *The Birth of a Nation* to make an antiracist statement?[39] Has showing the film always automatically reproduced racism? And what about the effect of the climate of censorship on other films? Did the fear of trouble from films about race have an effect on the production of race movies? This questioning leads us back to the NAACP's soul-searching moment, to Du Bois's second thoughts on the campaign, and to the struggles of filmmaker Oscar Micheaux, forced to negotiate a hostile gauntlet of censor boards, local committees whose point of critical reference was always and inevitably *The Birth of a Nation*.

W. E. B. Du Bois's complete statement on the NAACP decision to boycott the film is not well known, and it reveals a premonition of struggles ahead for African Americans. This "fight," he says, is illustrative of the "peculiar contradictoriness" of the "Negro problem," a compromised situation in which those people who would love liberty and freedom were put in the position of recommending the opposite—constraint on actions and expression. Reflecting back on the organization's strategy in a memo to NAACP head Walter White, Du Bois concludes that the campaign against *The Birth of a Nation* was a "special case," justified, he says, by an unprecedented emergency situation, and the film was not opposed as a work of culture but rather as, in his words, a "public menace." To support his assertion that the historical situation was exceedingly incendiary, he cites statistics:

> In 1914, 60 Negroes were lynched; in 1915, 99; in 1916, 65, and the number of lynchings per year kept on at the rate of at least one per week from 1915 until 1922. More Negroes were lynched in 1915 than in any other year since the beginning of the century.

Du Bois next notes that it was in 1915 that Thomas Dixon's *Clansman* was, as he puts it, "picturized." What DuBois does here is subtle—wrapping the film up in the culture of lynching. Note how he stops short of drawing a cause-and-effect relation between the "picturization" of *The Birth of a Nation* and the atrocities that were, as he says, so repeatedly defended with recourse to the fiction of attacks on white women by black men.[40] His analysis is bold and important, standing out in this period as a lone attempt to draw connections, to *implicate* the film in the culture of lynching without saddling it with the entire blame.

In the force field of censorship, in contrast, attempts were made to severely scrutinize and restrict *The Birth of a Nation* as well as other films with racial subjects on the assumption that these works tended to "incite to crime." An early example of the legislative attempt to formulate a rationale for banning films with racial topics is the Illinois state legislature's bill introduced months after the East Coast premiere of *The Birth of a Nation*, a bill to ban either a film or pictorial drawing that "tends to incite race riot, or race hatred or that shall represent or purport to represent any hanging, lynching, or burning of any human being incited by race hatred."[41] The language of incitement tends to criminalize the work of culture, to justify swift and unyielding action against it in defense of the community. If there is a theme and a recurring modus operandi in the history of *The Birth of a Nation*, it is the defense of the community against unknown terrors, a theme that plays from 1915 to the 1970s through over 350 actions having to do with the right to screen the film and at least a 120 controversies over censorship.[42] Only in recent years have we come to understand the way this fight touched nearly every town and city in the United States, communities made vulnerable because motion picture censorship has historically been a local matter.

Over the years, political progressives may have applauded the boycott against D. W. Griffith in the name of racial harmony. This same community-safety theme played in defense of the ban on *The Birth of a Nation*, however, sounds quite different when played as justification for censoring Oscar Micheaux's films, none of which posed the kind of threat to public order represented by Griffith and Dixon's epic of hate.[43] Since the history of Micheaux's struggles with censor boards, most notably in New York, Chicago, and Virginia, have just recently come to light, scholars are only now beginning to weigh the significance of the massive resistance and naked hostility the filmmaker encountered when he tried to secure licenses to exhibit nearly every one of his films produced in the 1918 to 1930 period.[44] The list of titles we know to have been either banned or cut by censor boards, beginning with Micheaux's first film, *The Homesteader* (1919), includes *Within Our Gates* (1920), *The Brute* (1920), *The Symbol of the Unconquered* (1920), *Deceit* (1923), *The Gunsalus Mystery* (1921), *The Dungeon* (1922), *The Virgin of the Seminole* (1922), *Birthright* (1924), *Body and Soul* (1925), *The House behind the Cedars* (1924/25), *A Son of Satan* (1924), *The Spider's Web* (1926), and *The Millionaire* (1927). Striking are not only the number of titles and the number of roadblocks to exhibition represented by each but the transparency of the censor boards' objections.

Consider, for instance, the New York State Commission's first denial of a license to *Body and Soul* because of the representation of the minister as forcing the daughter to steal her mother's savings kept in her Bible as well as the "betrayal" of that girl, representations that they found "sacrilegious, immoral" and likely to "incite to crime."[45] One has to ask when one looks at the list of objectionable action sequences in Oscar Micheaux's films whether it is these particular deeds (drinking, gambling, stealing, wielding knives) that offend or the fact that it is blacks who are engaged in these questionable activities. Is the all-black-cast action film a nightmare inversion from the point of view of the white censor? As Thomas Cripps suggests, in reference to *Body and Soul*, a reedited version had "white fingermarks" all over it by the time it was exhibited.[46]

One could hypothesize that all race movies had to pass a special white test before they could be exhibited—and this test was erratic and unpredictable, the cuts required differing from city to city (although, as we will soon see, blacks were more involved in this process than previously understood). When *A Son of Satan* was rejected in New York, the reason given was that "the leader of a 'hooded organization' was killed," but Virginia gave more elaborate and complicated reasons for its refusal of the license, never mentioning the killing of the leader. That board objected to the villainy of the main character, a mulatto, particularly because his criminality was attributed not to his black, but to his white inheritance, and it took exception to the film's "unwholesome" references to miscegenation as well as to the representation of race riots "incited" by the mulatto villain.[47] In other cases, boards acted predictably in concert, as in the elimination in both New York and Chicago of Micheaux's militant intertitle from *Birthright*, the kind of outburst that summed up the rigged system of the censor boards themselves: "Legal—hell—anything a white man wants to pull over on a nigger is legal."[48]

Of all of the ways *Birthright* is linked with Griffith's dangerous epic, this censorship connection is the most subtle, for it is almost as though the scenes cut from *The Birth of a Nation* show up in inverted form in Micheaux's films of the silent era, from the sadistic lynching sequence in *Within Our Gates* to the defiant *Birthright* intertitle. Publically eliminated in Griffith, these scenes return in Micheaux as historical "corrections," only to be eliminated again by Micheaux's censors. And it is this legacy of the Micheaux censorship battles that leads me to a new view of *The Birth of a Nation* struggles, a view that considers the everyday racism of the local censor. While the Left has been focused on the liberal support of the NAACP battles, and on leaders such as Jane Addams in the major cities, there is the distinct possibility that the film was banned in many towns not because of its ideological message but because of general white distaste for and paranoia about anything black. In other words, the racism that the NAACP was fighting led not to the support of the film, as one might expect, but to the opposite—the total ban and selective elimination of scenes from the print.

The scenes excised in *The Birth of a Nation* are well known, having a life and a notoriety quite apart from the rest of the film. They circulate now as relics—once inflammatory material now cooled down by time and rendered indistinguishable from the rest of the film. Yet reconsidering these rejected scenes, now returned to the original, their offense seems in danger of drying up along with their privileged relation to the historical real. Thus it is important that their animosities toward the Negro must be periodically revisited. What was it about these scenes that presented such a threat to public order in 1915? What was it about these scenes that, as William Monroe Trotter predicted, would "make white women afraid of Negroes and . . . have white men stirred up on their account"?[49] And finally, what, if anything, do these scenes have in common?

A list of cuts required by the National Board of Censorship, the very board whose second meeting preceded the "egging" of the screen at the New York exhibition, appeared in detail in one publication, *The Survey*, that first week in April 1915. As *The Survey* describes the required eliminations: "These [alterations] are said to have been chiefly a substantial reduction in the details of the chase of the white girl by the renegade

Negro, which in the original is said to have been the most dreadful portrayal of rape ever offered for public view [the "Gus chase" scene]; the insertion of various soothing captions, such as 'I won't hurt you, little Missy'; the entire excision of a lynching [the "castration" scene]; and a toning down of the scene in which the mulatto all but marries a white girl by force [Sylas Lynch forces himself on Elsie Stoneman]."[50] Griffith supporter Seymour Stern's language is vivid as he years later describes "flashes of screaming white girls being whisked by Negro rapists into doorways in back-alleys of the town." However, Stern also recalls in detail the infamous deportation epilogue, "Lincoln's solution," including "full-scale images of the deportation of masses of Negroes from New York harbor to the (filmed) jungles of Liberia," even though scholars have no definite evidence of the existence of such a sequence.[51]

For this and other reasons, we may have reason to question Stern's minutely detailed recollection of the most gruesome but least discussed sequence—Gus's castration. This recollection includes a description of the rhythmic cutting of the castration scene to Beethoven's *Pastorale* "Storm" music, which Stern says comes up after the title "Guilty" in the contemporary version. It is the material between the title and the medium long shot of Gus's body thrown across the Clansman's horse that Stern recalls, including the cutting on the movement of the Clansman-executioner's sword striking to the beat of Beethoven's thunder crashes, the "moaning strings and agonized woodwinds," a cut to Gus in close-up ("mouth flowing blood, the eyes rolling white in agony, the head falling back"), flash-cuts of accelerated sword-plunging, and a final flash of "the castrated Negro's pain-racked face and body."[52] Consider these segments together: the Gus "rape" scene with its long chase; the forced "marriage" between Elsie Stoneman and the mulatto Sylas Lynch; and the short castration sequence, which Stern tells us was only shown in the midst of opposition in the first five or six weeks after the opening at New York's Liberty Theatre but shown without objection for the first five years in the South.[53]

The Fear of Interracial Lust

In a film filled with images that vilified the Negro, many of which contributed to the diabolical vision of the South under Negro rule, why were these images singled out above all others as the most dangerous? What was the threat to public order posed by these particular scenes? Putting on hold the question of the now-lost castration sequence, which requires its own serious study, let us consider the sequences that have so often been understood as representing black lust for whites—Gus chasing Flora Cameron, and Lynch pressing himself on Elsie Stoneman, to which could be added the encounter between Senator Stoneman and his mulatta housekeeper Lydia, a scene singled out elsewhere by censors. Confirming this reading of black lust is the often-cited interview with Thomas Dixon quoted in the Boston NAACP's pamphlet, "Fighting a Vicious Film: Protest against *The Birth of a Nation*." As recalled by Rolfe Cobleigh, associate editor of *The Congregationalist* and *Christian World*, Dixon's comments about the danger to white women and girls posed by Negro men resonate with these scenes:

> He emphasized the alleged dominant passion of colored men to
> have sexual relations with white women and said that one pur-
> pose of his play was to create a feeling of abhorrence in white peo-
> ple, especially white women against colored men. Mr. Dixon said
> that his desire was to prevent the mixing of white and Negro
> blood by intermarriage.[54]

Dixon's views, often summarized by quoting his reference to the NAACP as a "Negro Intermarriage Society," were well known.[55] While Dixon's commitment to preventing intermarriage is often stressed in the literature on the reception of *The Birth of a Nation*, the possibility of achieving this by producing fear in white women, predicted by William Monroe Trotter, has received little, if any, comment. But the possibility that the film would "produce" fear and abhorrence in impressionable white women is hardly sufficient grounds for declaring it a public nuisance.

It is difficult to probe the white paternal mind on this issue. Were the interracial "marriage" scenes censored because they were seen as having a particular (dangerous) influence on white women? Then why, given what we know about the more notorious opposition to interracial sexual unions in the South, did *The Birth of a Nation* continue to play there without opposition? Was it that white city fathers might actually have approved scenes in a film that would "teach" their daughters abhorrence of black men? Could it be (since we know that the film, including the castration scene, met with no resistance in the South) that southern fathers *wanted* their daughters to witness these scenes?[56] The South, as we recall, is the place where women and children participated in lynchings.

What about opposition to interracial sexual union, cloaked in the euphemism "marriage"? Does such opposition explain the cuts any better, particularly since "intermarriage" would have been universally opposed by blacks as well as whites in this period? Oscar Micheaux's opposition to intermarriage would have been fairly typical within the black community. Still, however morally opposed he might have been, the showman in him was willing to use an interracial attraction as a titillating narrative device.[57] But what exactly is the interracial scenario feared most by these censorship boards? Cindy Patton illuminates this question in her discussion of the assumptions about social crimes that underwrote the Motion Picture Production Code of 1930, a code that traces its ancestry back to the 1915 censorship boards. The Code, she says, divides the representation of sex acts from violent acts. The representation of violent acts, seen as crimes against human law, are thought to produce imitation, whereas sex acts, crimes against natural law, are associated with "lowered defenses." The Code assumes that while it is only the criminal who will imitate the criminality he sees represented, representations of sexuality on screen influence virtually everyone. Everyone is susceptible to these images since everyone has lustful emotions that could be aroused, and here interracial lust is one such emotion that could be "unleashed."[58]

The concern about the possible social damage that could be caused by images of interracial sexuality is interesting for its extremity in the face of the unfoundedness of such fears. For all of the protest against *The Birth of a Nation* based on historical inaccuracies, no protest was registered against the fallacy that sexual unions between blacks and whites during Reconstruction were on the rise. Granted, the three examples of interracial coupling in the film did offer scenarios of extremity—a sinful union out of wedlock and two attempted rapes—exaggerating black "desires." "Marriage" between blacks and whites was, strangely, both imaginable and unimaginable—imaginable enough for the Klan to use it as the trumped-up reason for lynching thousands of black men between 1865 and 1915, but unimaginable because the legitimacy was withheld by law while the occurrence was denied through censorship. In 1915 interracial marriage was illegal in most states, and the situation remained unchanged until well into the 1960s.[59]

Not only illegal, interracial sexuality was considered the epitome of salaciousness and degradation. The degree to which these connotations were successfully borrowed by D. W. Griffith is indicated by one contemporary account of the "Gus rape" scene:

> Encouraged by the black leader, we see Gus the renegade hover about another young white girl's home. To hoochy-coochy music we see the long pursuit of the innocent white girl by this lust-maddened Negro, and we see her fling herself to death from a precipice, carrying her honor through "the opal gates of death."[60]

Much has already been said about the exaggeration of Flora Cameron's fears in the face of Gus's awkward "proposal" and about the extreme "better dead than raped" implications of her tragic suicide, all of which produces the Negro as nothing more nor less than a sexual monster. But this contemporary recollection, which mentions the "hoochy-coochy" music played over the silent image in at least one of the performances in the early months of the film's release, suggests that Gus's desire is to be read as cheap and tawdry. Again, the "mistake" of interracial sexual desire is associated with the carnival and the sideshow. (The act is once more withheld from view, and the audience is left to imagine the perversity of the coupling.) Any possibility of understanding the scene as Flora's tragedy would seem to be undermined and canceled by the music that interprets the chase as lurid entertainment, that encourages ogling rather than shock.[61]

Interracial sexuality in *The Birth of a Nation* thus represented a come-on as well as a terror, almost as though the producers were trying to formulate unformulated and amorphous fears as one might do in the design of a horror film. After all, one of the intents was to frighten white women. There is an inverse relationship, however, between the mythic proportions of the fear of interracial sexuality and the reality of the situation, for as the historical record shows, beginning in the Reconstruction period, interracial unions (with or without the benefit of marriage) were in decline. Although there was an overall lightening of the population, a production of mulattoes in such great numbers that the mulatto would be more apparent, this lightening was produced, according to some theories, as I have mentioned, by the marriage of light-skinned blacks within the black community rather than by sexual unions between blacks and whites.[62]

The "Gus chase" scene has been read in countless ways—as a brutal rape, a salacious stalking and pursuit, a tentative proposal of marriage, a tragic death of an innocent, and, as I am now suggesting, a horrific warning with a tawdry twist.[63] In another discussion elsewhere, I also conclude that Flora Cameron "dies both instead of and because of the rape," and in a close study of this scene have compared the blood that trickles from Flora's adolescent mouth to menstrual blood wiped away by her terrified brother with the corner of the Confederate flag or, alternatively, in hurling herself off the cliff, Flora aborts the black fetus.[64] Ben Cameron is left to mop up the "afterbirth of the nation." But all the close analysis in the world will never help us to finally understand the telescopic antagonism of the censorial gaze. For the censorial gaze is a scrutiny that sees only what it "wants to see." What it sees does not

Ben Cameron (Henry Walthall) and Flora Cameron (Mae Marsh)
The Birth of a Nation (dir. D. W. Griffith, 1915)

ultimately depend on the image on the screen, and often film censorship has been advocated by individuals and groups who have never viewed the film in question at all. The censorial gaze does not look. In their campaign against *The Birth of a Nation,* even members of the NAACP were on occasion guilty of attacking the film before they had seen it, which is not to detract from the importance of the organization's political struggle, but rather to emphasize that the censorial gaze is a very particular point of view putting the interpretation before the image in such a way that the interpretation stands on its own quite apart from the scenes themselves. Thinking of the situation of the censor who leaps before he looks, J. M. Coetzee has observed that "[t]he censor acts, or believes he acts, in the interests of a community. In practice he often acts out the outrage of that community, or imagines its outrage and acts it out; sometimes he imagines both the community and its outrage."[65]

It is difficult to think of another emotional force as feared as interracial lust in 1915, but in the minds of community fathers the motion picture itself (regardless of its subject) was also just such a bottomless source of emotion, and therefore the motion picture was a cause of great community trepidation. There is no better evidence of the generalized paranoia about motion pictures than the findings of the Ohio Supreme Court in its decision to uphold the right of the state of Ohio to ban *The Birth of a Nation.* Finding in *Mutual v. Ohio* that motion pictures were not protected speech like newspapers but were rather a business for profit, the high court went on to describe a version of motion pictures as dangerous. Analogous to other "spectacles," motion pictures, in their "attractiveness and manner of exhibition," were "capable of evil," the court agreed.[66] What censors really saw themselves as controlling, then, were not only suggestions of lurid sexuality but a dangerous and irresistible new force that could *produce* the same emotions that it *represented.* In yet another version of the confusion between the world and the screen, censors seem to have been convinced by cinematic realism that "if it was seen on the screen it would appear in the world." How the contents of the image actually came to be manifested in the world was another question.

Within Our Gates and Race Struggle

Was the censorial gaze white or black? It would be a mistake to give the impression that only whites or only blacks advocated censorship of racialized images in this period, although it is true that the members of the censorship boards themselves were largely white and male, with some interesting exceptions. Charlene Regester refers to the Harvard-educated black conservative Reverend A. J. Bowling, who served on the Chicago Board of Censors beginning in 1915 when he opposed the exhibition of *The Birth of a Nation.* Several years later, he also expressed disapproval of *The Symbol of the Unconquered.*[67] As we have seen in chapter 5, opposition to Micheaux's *Within Our Gates* in Chicago came from white as well as black ministers in the community, and it was the lynching sequence that we know gave blacks the most concern. Considering the earlier opposition to the film on the part of black ministers in Chicago, it is not surprising that George P. Johnson would have had similar difficulties with the film when he tried to book it for a second run at the Loyal Theatre in Omaha in August 1920, the summer after January's Chicago premiere.[68] Writing to Micheaux, Johnson requested that the director "kindly eliminate from the second reel all the objectionable lynchings" that had "caused trouble in other communities."[69] After the screening Johnson wrote again, chastising Micheaux for not cutting enough of the scene, and telling him bluntly that people had walked out.[70]

Later, Johnson would send correspondence referencing the difficulties Micheaux was encountering in his effort to distribute the film around the country to Robert Vann, the wealthy corporation lawyer in Pittsburgh who, you will recall, had been interested in helping to launch Lincoln Motion Pictures and an even larger company that could have included the Micheaux organization. Johnson, as I am suggesting, saved and filed documentation showing that the film had been refused exhibition in Shreveport and that the run had been canceled in New Orleans.[71] Johnson further reported to Vann that he had also seen *Within Our Gates* in Kansas where the exhibitor asked to have his $230 in rental fees rebated after the screening.[72]

While the ever-cautious George Johnson may have had many reservations about the picture, the militant *Chicago Defender* gave Micheaux's most controversial work a thorough endorsement, championing the film for the issues it boldly faced (and echoing Micheaux's own press package): "while it is a bit radical, it is withal the biggest protest against Race prejudice, lynching, and 'concubinage' that was ever written or filmed."[73] However, the *Defender*, with its impressive circulation (estimated at between 160,000 and 250,000 in 1920) and its commitment to reporting racial strife, did not necessarily represent the views of the entire black middle class.[74] Johnson and his friend Vann are here representative of those who did not want to make an issue of lynching, and as Kevin Gaines tells us, the tendency to "downplay" lynching was probably more typical within the black middle class leadership than we would like to think.[75] Perhaps Micheaux has given us a representative of this position in Dr. Vivian, who in the *Within Our Gates* epilogue tells Sylvia to "forget" the episode in her past and by implication to suppress a whole terrible chapter in American history. Also note that it is a woman (Sylvia's counsin Alma) who, in the tradition of Ida B. Wells, tells the lynching story.[76]

Micheaux's narrative of white brutality, however, parallels the reports of journalist Wells as well as the facts circulated in the more radical newspapers like the *Defender*. Thus one way of looking at the lynching sequence is as a newsreel—the newsreel that no other film company dared to produce and exhibit. Reporting lynching as the southern injustice that it was, Micheaux not only corrected Griffith's fictional representation of Gus's lynching as justice, but indicted the very vigilantes who were going unpunished for lynchings and other crimes against the black community in 1920. In his screen version of the attempt to hang an entire Negro family, Micheaux gives the white perpetrators the faces that so many conspiracies of anonymity, the *most* conspiratorial of which was Klan membership, withheld from view. Where Griffith and Dixon avoid the imagery of hanging in *The Birth of a Nation*, even trying to lay the blame for the practice of lynching on Negroes by the curious device of naming the mulatto villain Sylas "Lynch," Micheaux recreates the contemporary scene of lynching, as I have argued earlier, with documentary attention to detail.

There *is* a sense in which Micheaux can be said to have turned the spectacle of lynching back on those who created a circus sideshow of lynching, making visible the scenario of white revenge and scapegoating as nothing more nor less than the murder of innocent families. That his reenactment of a horrific crime is billed as entertainment is to his credit, not his detriment, for he put his showmanship to work in the interests of a crucial political project. It is all the more interesting in this regard to consider how the lynching sequence was designed in such a way that it could be cut completely and still leave the uplift narrative intact. In addition, as I have discussed, the lynching sequence, in the existing print, is crosscut with the attempted rape. Although the techniques of film editing would make it possible to cut out either the rape or the lynching scene and still leave the other scene, the two controversial scenes, standing as they do for inflammatory issues, could be seen as a complete package. One could speculate, however, that this removable or collapsible sequence with its double moral infraction almost invited the censor's intervention, since it is so clearly demarcated from the rest of the narrative in the surviving film. From the reports in the *Chicago Defender* of the 1,200 feet cut in the first screening in the city and the same footage immediately restored for the second screening, one gets the impression of the mobility of the parts (in technical terms, the "cut-outs").[77] It was not long, however, before Micheaux learned from this experience (and perhaps from Griffith's censorship battles as well) that censored footage cut in and cut out of a film is a public fascination, even an object of desire as I earlier suggested.[78]

But intriguing evidence of the existence of yet another scene, perhaps as troublesome to censors as the lynching sequence, challenges this hypothesis that the sequence was a removable package. In a series of interviews in the *Pittsburgh Courier,* actress Evelyn Preer, looking back at her career, describes the scene in which, as Sylvia, she is accosted by Arnold Girdlestone. The scene she describes closely follows the scene from the surviving print, which shows Sylvia followed into her house by the white-haired man who chases her around the room until, at the climax, she jumps up on a table and throws a vase at him. But here Preer recalls a part of the scene that has since disappeared. Although in the surviving print Sylvia is spared by luck, in an earlier version she is saved by a black hero. The extant print intertitles, as we have seen, tell the story of a white father who discovers that he has been attacking his own daughter. But in the scene that Preer recollects, Girdlestone locks the door behind him, and Sylvia is saved by a black man who breaks down the door and takes on the white man in a fight. Preer thus describes this scene that was originally shot and that was apparently shown at least once, as indicated by her reference to the animated audience response:

> I ran across the room and leaped upon a small table before the mantel and grabbed a vase and had drawn back to crown the villain when up leaped the man in the audience yelling "kill him!" . . . But I really wasn't in such great danger after all, for at this point my lover broke down the door and leaped on the villain's back and there took place one of the most realistic fights I witnessed since being in the movies.[79]

The first question that arises for the viewer who has seen the surviving version of *Within Our Gates* is the question of the identity of the suitor who fights Girdlestone, since in this print there are four male characters who profess interest in Sylvia, and all of them enter her life subsequent to the period in which the lynching flashback is set (presumably the period of her early youth). Further questions arise about the fate of the fight scene with censors, who no doubt would have had little tolerance for a scene in which a black man gives a white man a bad beating. The cultural attraction to and terror of the interracial fight on film had already been rehearsed in the years leading up to the milestone "fight of the century" between the white champion Jim Jeffries and the black champion Jack Johnson in Reno, Nevada, on July 4, 1910. Almost half of the fight films produced between 1900 and 1915 featured an interracial match, seen as early as Edison's *A Scrap in Black and White* (1903), which, Dan Streible suggests, "lays bare the true motivation for the interest in the boxing film cycle."[80] Opposition began in the states (which had banned boxing films unevenly) and culminated in the 1912 Sims Act prohibiting interstate traffic in prizefight films, ostensibly because of the brutality and possible damage to children.

But it was also clear, particularly with the popularity of Johnson's filmed matches, that the concern arose in the double-edged fear of the racial violence that could be triggered and the consequent need to suppress the powerful images of blacks.[81] Cedric Robinson urges a fuller understanding of Jack Johnson's threat to white male supremacy, a direct challenge represented by his public association with white women as well as by his tempestuous marriages—to four white women in a row.[82] It is tempting to note the similarities between interracial sexuality and interracial fighting on film, analogous visions of racial mixture as attraction and repulsion. In developing our theory of the mind of the censor in this early period, we now have at least two categories to consider based on an analysis of excised scenes in *The Birth of a Nation* and *Within Our Gates:* interracial sexuality and interracial fighting. Working back from the scenes to the consciousness of the censor, it would be moments such as the one in *Within Our Gates,* which stirred the man in the audience to jump up and yell "kill him," that would be so worrisome to local censor boards. The leap between the spontaneous reaction in the theater and mob action in the street can be seen as no leap at all. The stage was set, certainly as early as 1912 and probably earlier, for a firm linkage between motion pictures and race riots—a linkage both real and totally fantastic.

Micheaux's second film drew deeply from the historical moment, drew from the outrage against the medieval tortures still occurring in the South and from the determination of the black middle class to move up in spite of the virulence of white opposition to their success. His original story would have also absorbed some of the racial turmoil in Chicago where the film was shot in 1919, the very year of one of the most infamous of U.S. race riots. On the theory that the motion picture text is relatively porous because it is a popular form, we can assume that the extant version of *Within Our Gates* retains at least something from the tumultuous moment of its conception, something that can be detected even today. Here the relation between text and history formulated by the great Marxist literary critics of the twentieth century may be found wanting since they only show an interest in high culture texts and grand historical patterns. And if we look to film criticism for the theory we need that could rise to this political occasion, though we find a vast body of literature as well as a subgenre of radical film informed by the work of revolutionary filmmaker-theorist Sergei Eisenstein, we still do not receive any assistance with the problem of the fiction film that emerges from the blood and trouble of an abbreviated race war.

One of the difficulties we face in analyzing Micheaux's text by reading it for "signs of struggle" is that these signs have been obliterated or blurred by the very struggle that *would have* made its historical mark on the film. In other words, the film that grew out of the race riot was censored because of the fear of further rioting. Thus, as in the case of *The Birth of a Nation,* the film is rewritten as an act of official public excision. An instrumental reading is performed on the text, a reading that rewrites by cutting. And from all accounts, censorship was the catalyst for reshaping Micheaux's film much more thoroughly than Griffith's as well as for keeping it in a relatively fluid state throughout the single year of its U.S. distribution. This is not to say that Griffith did not also reedit *The Birth of a Nation* in response to public pressures, that it did not become a veritable sieve from all of the puncture holes produced by reediting. The enormous difficulties of establishing a definitive version is testimony to this. The evidence of the addition of the philanthropic Hampton Institute epilogue, if nothing else, attests to the fact that the film was restructured in an attempt to change the direction of its meaning.[83]

In contrast, Micheaux's text was even more fully impacted by racial tension. Race struggle produced it, rewrote it until it became nearly incoherent, and finally exiled it. It is clear that in the Spanish language print the mysterious mistakes—the upside-down shot, the intertitles that don't quite agree with the images—are the indelible signs of this struggle.[84] The existence of such a film, forged in and through race struggle, calls for a radically different theory of the text. Its gaps are entirely too literal to be understood as the throbbing "unsaid" of poststructuralist theory; it is not that the film is silent on the question of its own making but that it was *silenced* at the moment of its conception. And yet there is one advantage to viewing *Within Our Gates* as a text so full of literal gaps, fault lines, and crevices: it would seem to be easier to *see through it* historically, to peer through its holes to look at the events of 1919.

The Chicago Race Riot of 1919

In 1919 Carl Sandburg was a reporter for the *Chicago Daily News*, and in his capacity as reporter he wrote a series of articles on the race riots of that year, later published as a book. He thus opens his coverage:

> The so-called race riots in Chicago during the last week of July, 1919, started on a Sunday at a bathing beach. A colored boy swam across an imaginary segregation line. He was drowned. Colored people rushed to a policeman and asked for the arrest of the boys throwing stones. The policeman refused. As the dead body of the drowned boy was being handled, more rocks were thrown, on both sides. The policeman held on to his refusal to make arrests. Fighting then began that spread to all the borders of the Black Belt.[85]

It is difficult from the poet's cryptic journalism to tell much about the temperature of this moment that ignited the worst riot of the troublesome 1915–1919 period. Sandburg's short sentences mock the staccato rhythm of a police investigation, telling us that he is reporting facts but also telling us in his tight control of the facts that he knows that it is all in the reporting. Here he identifies the germ of the conflict: the policeman refused to make an arrest. However, in order to fully understand the dynamics of the race war that ensued, the reader has to supplement much of what Sandburg only cautiously implies: the *white* policeman refused to arrest the *white* boys who threw the stones that caused Eugene Williams to drown in Lake Michigan that hot Sunday afternoon, at the 29th Street beach, on the dividing line between white and black Chicago.

Sandburg jumps quickly from the policeman's adamant refusal to arrest anyone to the fighting that "spread to all the borders of the Black Belt," the section of Chicago's South Side where blacks, newly arrived in the city, were concentrated. It is a characteristic leap, a leap "over" the difficult middle area where actions are no longer single but multiple, where stories are overlapping and atrocities compounded, where it is not possible to find and unravel a single story. Causality can't be traced, culpability can't be assigned. Social scientists as well as journalists leap over the chaotic middle of social unrest onto solid ground—the reports, after so many days, of the dead and injured, the estimated cost of damages. After four days, twenty-three blacks and fifteen whites were killed in Chicago, and 536 people were injured.[86]

The middle ground, however, is important not only for correct political analysis but also, as is our purpose, for understanding the connection between race riots and motion pictures, a connection assumed but unfathomed by public officials. And perhaps it is W. E. B. Du Bois who, in turning his sociologist's eye on the July 1917 riots in East St. Louis, takes us into the center of the Chicago race battlefield. Here is poetry that surpasses Sandburg, and analysis that anticipates the consensus of political scientists in the 1960s:

So hell flamed in East St. Louis! The white men drove even black union men out of their unions and when the black men, beaten by night and assaulted, flew to arms and shot back at the marauders, five thousand rioters arose and surged like a crested storm-wave, from noonday until midnight; they killed and beat and murdered; they dashed out the brains of children and stripped off the clothes of women; they drove victims into the flames and hanged the helpless to the lighting poles. Fathers were killed before the faces of mothers; children were burned; heads were cut off with axes; pregnant women crawled and spawned in the dark, wet fields; thieves went through houses and firebrands followed; bodies were thrown from bridges; and rocks and bricks flew through the air.

The Negroes fought. They grappled with the mob like beasts at bay. They drove them back from the thickest cluster of their homes and piled the white dead on the street, but the cunning mob caught the black men between the factories and their homes, where they knew they were armed only with their dinner pails. Firemen, policemen, and militiamen stood with hanging hands or even joined eagerly with the mob.[87]

What Du Bois has compressed here are the themes replicated in Chicago two years later: the racial strife within labor unions, the brutality toward women and children, the close correlation between rioting and lynching in the image of helpless victims "hanged to the lighting poles." But it is the observation "The Negroes fought" that becomes the refrain of mainstream social scientists, at least one of whom would classify the Chicago conflict as an "ideal" riot on this basis: *the blacks fought back.*[88]

In this analysis, Chicago is a turning point in the way it gave clarity to a surging that could only be understood as the movement by blacks to end their subordinate status, the first major movement since Emancipation.[89] Much more was clarified as the racial lines in the conflict were delineated. Whereas in the South, blacks struggled against the white anonymity of the Klan, in the Chicago struggle the white perpetrators begin to be identified more precisely. Although it would still be possible to hide behind gang identification, in the Chicago conflict the white gangs, who called themselves "athletic clubs," were located by territory and named by their all-American code words: the "Ragen Colts," the "Hamburgers," the "Dirty Dozen," "Our Flag," the "Sparklers," and the "Standard."[90] The white gangs' attempt to cover their bloody campaign of race hatred in the signs of American popular culture and patriotism should bring to mind H. Rap Brown's rejoinder, "Violence is necessary and it's as American as cherry pie."[91] So the blacks fought back.

And in fighting back against whites, blacks in Chicago, as well as in the other towns and cities where race riots broke out in 1919, have given us the closest thing to a revolutionary tradition that we have had historically in the United States. In his essay on American violence, historian Richard Hofstadter concludes that American history is characterized by a great deal of violence but no revolutionary tradition.[92] Citing Barrington Moore's caution about the discrepancy between classical revolutionary conditions and revolutionary theory—"revolutionary rhetoric outruns the real possibilities inherent in a given historical situation"—

Hofstadter warns about inflating the word "revolution" in such a way that it applies to all manner of change and conflict.[93] But the consequence of downgrading the race riot from a "truly revolutionary situation" to a lesser conflict is also the downgrading of these events in historical importance. It should indeed be difficult to dismiss the racial outbreaks within that five-month period in 1919, outbreaks that numbered as many as twenty-five, seven of which were full-fledged riots that took place, in addition to Chicago, in Longview, Texas, Washington, D.C., Knoxville, Charleston, Omaha, and Phillips County, Arkansas. Some of these conflagrations grew out of lynchings as in the case of the Longview riot where the male Negro lynched on July 4 was accused of the rape of a white woman. When an article in the *Chicago Defender* reported that the young woman had been in love with the Negro and that she was unconsolable after his death, the white community went on a deadly rampage against the local teacher who contributed to the *Defender* and was part of the organized black community. As would happen in Chicago later that month, the black community retaliated.[94]

This bloody time period that James Weldon Johnson referred to as the "Red Summer of 1919," the period in which whites initiated violence and blacks fought back, illustrates the kind of reciprocity of violence that Fanon identified in the colonial situation.[95] It is even so symmetrical as to be seen as a counterbalancing: "The violence of the colonial regime and the counter-violence of the native balance each other and respond to each other in an extraordinary reciprocal homogenity."[96] We return through a circuitous route to one of the themes of this book, the way the one is paired with the other through whom he becomes himself. What he is, does, becomes, begins with the other. The one's violence begins with the other: "The practice of violence binds them together as a whole . . . a violent link in the great chain, a part of the great organism of violence which has surged upward in reaction to the settler's violence in the beginning."[97] Certainly, says Jean-Paul Sartre in his preface to Fanon, "for at first it is not *their* violence, it is ours, which burns back on itself and rends them."[98] Fanon's colonial mirror that shows us the structure of crimes answering crimes takes us beyond any random retaliation theory of the race riot and still insists on the question, whose violence? In answer, Frederick Douglass, without missing a beat, gives us an image: "Think of the American woman . . . mingling with the howling mob . . . with her own hand applying the torch to the faggots."[99] This is the woman who appears again in Micheaux's *Within Our Gates* for the briefest second, this time toting a rifle as she stands prepared to shoot at the black family on the run from the lynch mob.

Mimesis and Motion Pictures

From the boxing films of the early teens to the Rodney King videotape, pictures in motion have been implicated in U.S. racial unrest. Fighting images, as we have seen, have been historically legislated against and blocked by communities that feared these images. And yet the relationship between moving pictures and social and political unrest remains an unresolved problem in reception, and today the potentially incendiary film or videotape is caught between the unfounded fears of the Right and the unfounded claims of the Left—the one terrified of social change and the other perhaps too optimistic about the power of the image to single-handedly bring about that change. The popular conception that the image produces "effects" on viewing subjects is in need of reconsideration in light of the new theoretical positions that understand the body as produced by the machine and discourse as having the power to produce its own "effects."[100] In order to push these questions into new terrain, I want to consider the possibilities beyond the old cause-and-effect relationship in which films "incite" or "stimulate" social subjects to act. Although we are talking about apparently unlike phenomena—moving picture stories on the one hand and antisocial group actions on the other—one can't help noticing the way motion pictures have been closely aligned with and even analogized with riots, particularly during the early decades of cinema.

To begin with, movies and riots are seen to both rise out of and to speak to the masses. In this public dimension, both the runaway box-office success and the race riot demand immediate interpretation as monumental public signs—to be read by the community as well as by politicians, journalists, and social scientists. To the politicized eye, however, the popular outbreak produces not chaos but focus. Social scientists Omni and Wishart, for instance, observed of the 1992 Los Angeles uprising that it was an "immanent critique of the mainstream political process," a critique laid out on the wide screen of the city.[101] Carrying over their bad reputation from the early days of the nickelodeon, the movies would not lose this reputation quickly or easily even after the attempts to associate motion picture entertainment with respectability in the teens.[102] Even the motion picture industry's own code, produced in 1930, is deeply concerned about uncontrollable emotion and resorts to the unpredictable psyche of the mass audience as a way of explaining the perceived emotions held by the motion picture itself. The Production Code explains that the film goes beyond the theatrical play, "[b]ecause of the larger audience of the film, and its consequently mixed character."

And this "mixed character" audience is particularly susceptible to the image: "Psychologically, the larger the audience, the lower the moral mass resistance to suggestion."[103] In the Code, however, "mass" is a code word for "others." In her analysis of the Production Code as a backdrop to the censorship of Twentieth Century-Fox's *Pinky* (1949), Cindy Patton identifies the "others" who, in the words of the Code, are thought to have a "lower resistance to suggestion." Merging the audiences most likely to respond to "violent images" and "steamy plots" produces a grouping of women, children, and blacks. White middle class men, she concludes, must then be unaffected, must be the group that is least vulnerable to suggestion.[104]

So motion pictures and race riots epitomize the greatest fears of white city fathers: uncontrollable passions, feelings run wild, bodily pleasures, revolts against their authority. Like women and dark others, motion pictures and race riots are both the trouble itself and the cause of the trouble. Mary Ann Doane has investigated the analogy between white women and blackness, beginning with Freud's reference to the "dark continent" of woman, that vast space of unexplored emotionality and inexplicable sexuality. On and off the screen, the white woman and especially the black man are too much in and of the body; both are plagued with a tendency to too much embodiment. The white woman, says Doane, in her "unknowability and sexual excessiveness" has a "close representational affiliation with blackness."[105] The censorship of both *The Birth of a Nation* and *Within Our Gates* was an attempt to reduce this excess of image produced by the new motion picture feature with its overabundance of appeals—too many black bodies with white women in Griffith's film and too much fire and desire in Micheaux's. But it is finally the combination of volatile bodies on- as well as off-screen that is so potentially explosive, and here it is the theoretical companion to overpresence that explains the real trouble: overidentification.

In feminist film theory, overidentification with the image explains the problem the female spectator has with the image from which she cannot attain distance because, as Doane has argued, "she *is* the image."[106] For feminists, this concept productively addresses both the impossibility of voyeurism for women as well as the female attraction to the melodrama "weepie." But with the black spectator (male or female) who is perceived by whites as especially "susceptible" to violent images on screen, overidentification has its own particular bodily correlate: imitation. For imitation is the lowest form of identification, an identification that knows no limits to incorporation, an identification that incorporates everything in sight. Given their concern about law and order, it is not surprising that this very identification–imitation relation is assumed by film censors. Thus, as Anne Friedberg has observed, "All demands for film censorship stem from the position that cinema encourages imitation/mimetic incorporation of the harmful, illegal, or immoral actions of a character, actor, or star. In short, a fear of identification."[107]

Returning, then, once again to our thesis that one goes through the other on the way to establishing one's own identity, that difference is transformed into identity, we are struck here with the community opposition to using the other as a route to the self, the opposition to identification with the image of the other. Censoring motion pictures here becomes a method of quelling black urban uprisings that are actually nascent expressions of group identity and solidarity. The fiction film in this analysis had to be historically censored because the black bodies exposed to it could, by means of mimic operations, carry the images they saw into the streets. What was believed was that through the incorporation of the image into the black body, the criminal violence (coupled with taboo sexuality) on the screen would be replicated in the wider society. The black body, in its remarkable capacity to reproduce images, then, is not only the screen but the projector as well. If, as in Metz, the desiring machine is a "precision tool" like the human body, the human body is a "robust mechanism" like the cinema, able to record and recreate the images it stores.[108]

Mimesis and Militant Action

Let us not deny either that the mimic machine imitates or that it is imitated. Perhaps one of the reasons that the mimetic aspects of motion pictures have received so little attention is that attempts to look at the apparatus as a copy machine are at odds with the need to establish high art credentials for cinema. But cinema *does* give us a miraculous copy of the world. And mimesis itself as a critical concept has not been fully developed in critical theory, which has meant that concepts such as "representation" have had to assume too much of the burden of standing for all of the things that signs do. In his important rehabilitation of the concept of "mimesis," anthropologist Michael Taussig remarks on this neglect, which he attributes to the "facile use of terms such as identification, representation, expression [that] . . . depend on and erase all that is powerful and obscure in the network of associations conjured by the notion of the mimetic."[109] But to even conceive of mimesis as in competition with "identification" or "representation" is to miss the concept's fascinating legacies, which recommend it all the more to film studies.[110]

In recent years, a few scholars have made significant attempts to re-habilitate the mimetic mode as a way of intervening in the world, even a "way of knowing," an active, expressive intelligence. Michel Foucault has reminded us that for the seventeenth century, resemblance and similitude were bona-fide modes of scholarly inquiry and investigation; scientific engagement with the natural world meant seeing and replicating, striving for likeness.[111] Clearly, cinema can be seen as the culmination of a centuries-long fascination with the visible resemblances between things, with echoes and imitations. More recently, Taussig has reconsidered ancient mimesis, which he observes in South American cultures outside the influence of the First World. Mimesis, he says, is the "art of becoming something else, of becoming Other."[112] And it is magical. Sympathetic magic, in fact, effects that bodily incorporation that seems impossible from a Western scientific standpoint. Worlds away from the Western psychoanalytic theory of identification, imitation rites celebrate subject–object unification, reminding us that notions of mimesis predate Freud as explanations for the phenomenon post-Freudians have talked about as projection. Particularly relevant to discussions of cinema and other mimetic machines is Taussig's emphasis on the way sympathetic magic reverses the terms of art's intervention in the world. As the antithesis of the fear that art has the power to "make people do things," to make them imitate and replicate in their bodies and lives, sympathetic magic flaunts the power of the image, based as it is on the possibility that the "soulful power that derives from replication" will thoroughly transform things.[113]

The awesome potency of the mimetic effect is based on a relationship between that which is represented and its representation, in which the effigy or "copy" comes to have the same powers as the original and, in addition, power *over* the original. In this magical practice, the copy or image takes on the properties of the represented.[114] This principle has particular implications if one wants to "manipulate reality by means of its image." The effigy or likeness is created to influence persons or control events—to have command over things.[115] Notice here how sympathetic magic reverses the epistemology of Western rationality: "instead of moving from fact to thought, from things to image, magic moves from image to thing, from thought to fact."[116] The copy in this schematic is not degraded but has more power than the original, but only because it derives its power from the original without actually being that original.

Translate this tension between the copy and the original into the epistemological question of the photographic image and the world of which the photograph is so often said to be "only" an image. Suddenly it would seem that all of the censors' worst fears about the power of motion pictures are confirmed. The motion picture *does* have its influence over the world that it has apparently copied. But the motion picture has this power only because it derives its power from that world. It stops short of being the world itself. Reality is here "manipulated" by means of the image of that reality. Motion pictures, those mimetic machines, are censored because (like sympathetic magic) they *do* have the power to produce compelling similarities, in one's body (through imitation) and consequently between the film and the world. Immediately the problem produced by the epistemology of cause and effect seems insignificant if the fiction film works back on the world from which it emerges only to emerge again. Screen images and "life" images here eternally "mimic" one another.

In this "sympathetic" relationship, bodies on screen have their concrete connection with bodies in social space, whether those screen bodies are seen as performing the ideal or enacting the taboo. Certainly I am recommending another way of formulating the mass culture/society relationship so often dealt with by means of those inadequate metaphors of reflection: the mirror and the window. The problem with reflection, as Brecht reminded us, was that it was always more accurately selective reflection that described the art–life relation. Seeing a "sympathetic" relationship between the world and the wide screen, however, takes us out of the realm of the mirror image, past the mechanical, behavioral connection, and into the realm of unpredictability, giving us more room for mysticism and paranoia, but also more room for miraculous transformation.

However, if we are going to attribute this transformative power to the motion picture, we will have to attribute it to films with agendas as different as *The Birth of a Nation* and *Within Our Gates.* In retrospect, and particularly from the point of view of the NAACP and its supporters, the hatred of the one film turns into the possibilities of the other, the film that wasn't allowed to "stir a continent." If we want to make a case for magical mimesis, we will have to concede the turbulent power of Griffith's film in its service as a recruitment tool for the Ku Klux Klan in 1915 and later in the early 1920s at the time of the film's rerelease.[117] Conversely, we will need to imagine the potential of Micheaux's film to bring about transformation and race progress through mimesis.

Race movies in their day were monumental attempts by blacks to "image back," to return the image of themselves given them by whites, to "face off" against white-produced "blackface." And, as I have argued elsewhere, it is in the project of "imaging back" that we see the mimetic faculty in all of its genius.[118] In Micheaux's case, to show the brutal acts that whites have historically perpetrated against blacks is to "manipulate reality by means of its image," to use imitation in an attempt to magically influence present and future events. Here it is that we see the mimetic powers of the body extended to those of the cinema where the projective powers of the machines of repetition throw up their imitations again and again and again. Race movies, which we have seen as an elaborate paralleling of things white, can also be understood according to Taussig's definition of mimesis as "slipping into Otherness, trying it on for size."[119] Race movies were a *magical* inhabitation of white forms, deriving their power from that which blacks were not, using that power to become what they wanted to be. Black race movie pioneers brought about change by means of an imaginative incorporation, not a simple assimilation.

If the production side of the mimetic faculty is the power to "image back," what is the reception side? Here is where we come to the question of what the film "makes the body do."[120] Emphasizing the generic expectations of the spectator as much as any notion that popular films automatically produce predictable effects is important here since what sets these genres apart from others is a willing, knowing, and expectant audience. The fear of deleterious effects approach presumes an unformed sponge. I have considered before the question of how to adapt the concept of the body genre to political documentary in relation to its ideal audience—the audience that sees the film as it sees the world, the audience that is radicalized by the film that claims "this is how things are." It is these specialized audience members on whose bodies the radical documentary will ideally produce "involuntary mimicry," the *sympathetic* replication of acts of protest recorded on film. Another way of putting this is that, like the other body genres, the radical documentary (with its footage of strikes, marches, and riots) has the potential to "make the body do things"—to yell, kick, and shout, to fight back by whatever means. Sensationalized bodies on-screen sensationalize the politicized spectator. The radical documentary is the film that makes you want to do things, not because of what you see on the screen but because the infuriating conditions depicted on the screen have their correlation in the conditions of the world of the film.[121] The radical film that "makes the body do things" is, of course, the censor's worst nightmare.

Consider, however, the problems that arise when we shift from the question of radical documentary filmmaking within a tradition of media activism back to the controversy surrounding *The Birth of a Nation*, a work of fiction. There is no doubt that Griffith and Dixon's film made viewers want to yell, kick, and shout. We know that angry viewers threw eggs at the screen during the Gus chase scene, and that the day after the Boston egg-throwing incident, NAACP supporters at the Tremont Theatre marched up the street to the state house singing "Nearer My God to Thee" to protest the film's exhibition in that city.[122] We also know that at the revival of the same film in New York in 1922, members of the Ku Klux Klan in the audience cheered when the white-sheeted night riders appeared on the screen.[123] Even as the Klan learned to use the film as an organizing tool, protests against the film continued into the 1920s.[124] So which is it? Did the film historically produce revolutionary effects or reactionary effects? I would hope that it would be possible to avoid any conclusions along the lines of "bad film–good protest" and "good film–bad protest" here, particularly since it is so difficult to be precise about the political ingredients of the struggles along the protest–race riot continuum. In theories of class struggle, protest can be important as an indicator of evolving class consciousness, and therefore we want to keep it in the equation in our discussion of race riots. Yet the protest around *The Birth of a Nation* as well as *Within Our Gates* gives evidence of variations that complicate traditional approaches to peoples' struggles, the most difficult having to do with understanding censorship as protest. More important, and not surprisingly, the difference between a protest and a race riot was also a class dividing line within the black community in the 1915 to 1919 period. Protest was the black middle class solution to staving off full-fledged riots in which lower class black "others" might fight back as they had done in Chicago in their struggle to keep their jobs and to defend their homes against white enemy gangs.

But in radical film theory, revolutionary effects have been translated into aesthetic effects. When we consider the excitability factor in Griffith's crosscut chase scenes, we are not such a far cry from the montage effect that Sergei Eisenstein described as "excited emotional speech," the revolutionary Soviet aesthetic that, as film historians know, took its inspiration from none other than Griffith.[125] I have discussed elsewhere the impossibility of permanently assigning a political valence to an aesthetic form, which is one of the reasons that the "effects" of any one text always need to be seen as overdetermined, as I explained in chapter 5. But if we subscribe to a theory of the multiply determined or overdetermined event, does this contradict any theory of politicized "involuntary mimesis" based on the idea that the politically incendiary film can make the body do things? No claim has yet been made for behavioral predictability, and "involuntary mimesis" belongs more to the realm of the utopian possible than to the empirical realm of the probable. Note also that here we are seeking to expand the theoretical vocabulary for discussing the question of the politicized body of the spectator rather than searching for empirical proof that films can produce angry actions in spectators, angry actions that can accelerate into the mass expressions of racial rage that we understand as race riots. In addition, we are countering the negative "effects" fear of the involuntary with an anticipatory notion of irresistability. We are reversing the fear of effects by asking "why the fear?"

In this regard, probably the most important aspect of the race riot–cinema association to address first is the way in which lower class blacks are seen as perpetrators and imitators. To some degree, in U.S. culture the notion of the mimetic already carries with it a lower class racial association, synonymous with mindless imitation, copycat criminality, and animality, or what Todd Boyd has called the "monkey see, monkey do" effect.[126] Even Homi Bhabha's notion of "colonial mimesis" borrows something from the darker race overtones in the imitative mode, although he has productively incorporated these connotations into a powerful critical concept.[127] Further, mindless imitation gets easily linked with naïveté about the screen, giving us the copycat who also is unable to distinguish real worlds from fictional worlds. But the *mimetic spectator* we are describing here is discriminating. The spectator who yelled "kill him" to the Evelyn Preer character when she aimed a vase at her white attacker in *Within Our Gates*, the protesters who threw eggs at *The Birth of a Nation* screen, and even possibly the naïf (Uncle Josh) who jumped up on the stage have in common the *refusal* to recognize the conventional difference between the screen world and the material world. Knowing the difference, the mimetic spectator parodically rejects the difference. In contrast with the social science approach that might worry about this highly involved viewer, a new theory of mimesis would valorize this spectator. Here, the apparent *inability* to distinguish the real from the imagined is the *ability* to imitate. And it is this reversal that returns us to Taussig's anthropological observation: mimesis is a body-first way of knowing.[128]

Mixed-Race Movies

Sympathetic magic is a way of knowing, and the spectator who yells "kill him" is not carried away by the machinery, not carried "away from reality," as is often implied in the notion that the reader-spectator is lost to the world in the fiction. The power of the image is derived from the world (the original) and not from itself, and the *mimetic spectator* who yells "kill him" understands and enjoys these distinctions. But let us remind ourselves here that these issues of the confusion between fiction and reality would not continually arise if it were not for the remarkable capacity of the motion picture to resemble.[1] We are faced with the undeniable and persistent *lookalikeness* of the image, that same tendency that continues to embroil the media in questions of causality.

Pinpointing the source of the fiction–reality confusion as well as its possibilities, Tom Gunning has remarked on the way motion pictures are characterized by an "excess of mimesis over meaning."[2] This surplus mimesis, this supraresemblance, always implies a particular spectator. So often the very lookalikeness of the image implies the gullible spectator, who film theorists at one time worried might be experiencing representations as perceptions and even confusing the sign with that which it represents.[3] One wonders what was at stake for French theorists in their characterization of the spectator as so thoroughly mistaken. But the question of the spectator's confusion of the screen with the world was actually given a fuller theorization fairly early on by Jean-Louis Comolli, who argued that in spite of its impressive "reality effects," the cinema always "gives itself away." And it is the spectacular success of the delusion that the spectator relishes because "it is precisely *for that* that he or she came."[4] Comolli's identification here of the spectator's happy complicity in his or her own "fooling" addresses the paradox that inspires so many homegrown theories about cinematic realism: the very unreality of cinema works to make the fiction real.[5] Or the fictionality of the cinematic signifier increases the belief in the reality of the fiction. And it is this paradox that also encourages the familiar fear that the representation may become *more* real than the real thing, once again the universal apprehension of the censor.

Many aesthetic realisms, recourses to "the real," and invocations of "reality" have been important in the history and criticism of cinema. Sometimes, as in the above, the aesthetic has been wrapped up in the question of the look of the world, and at other times the realist aesthetic is further linked to the question of "the truth about the world." Then there is the adjacent question of the devices that deliver the impression. For several decades in film theory, these questions were simplified with reference to what has been called either the classic realist text or classical Hollywood cinema. The great success of this cinema, it was said, was its ability to signify "the real" by means of a few key strategies, only the first of which is its apparently effortless use of photographic realism to produce its signature "realistic effect."[6] And it is this successful mimesis, referenced in my concept of lookalikeness, that I would want to retain above others. Recently, it is important to note, at least one critic has challenged earlier formulations of classical realism in cinema not only for their tendency to attribute too much to realism (at the expense of overlooking the antirealist devices employed in the same text) but also for the way in which textual realism has been so automatically aligned with the concept of ideology.[7] Perhaps the problem lies in the way it was said so prescriptively in 1970s film theory that "reality is nothing more nor less than the prevailing ideology."[8] Still, this concept taught us caution in relation to versions of the world that passed themselves off as "the real" all the while advancing a particular political agenda.

This is not the time to abandon the concept of ideology, the lone concept that has historically referenced and continues to stand for the realm of the social, particularly when we need it to talk about the representation of race.[9] We need a concept that alerts us to another, deeper "realism," to a way of thinking that operates to deliver premises that "ring true" to the culturally initiated, a reflex of thought that governs the probable and consequently the possible. And it is *this* "realism" as nothing more than the familiar and the habitual that underwrites the false obviousness of racialized imagery. Not surprisingly, as Homi Bhabha explains how this obviousness works, it is a matter of the "knowability, visibility of the 'Other' [that] employs a system structurally similar to Realism."[10] This is the structural "realism" that says, "That is the way it is, isn't it?" This is the "realism" that offers the self-evidence of the seen as proof of how things "actually are," a pattern, a habit that leads us to suspect that there is always some necessary redundancy supporting the structure. And this is the realism that I want to invoke in the following discussion of stereotypage and that I am calling *racial realism.*

But what we may also be actually talking about is the self-evidence of empiricism at its most self-serving, an empiricism that has served the cause of essentialist arguments in the contemporary period. I am even wondering, then, if this redundant, self-evident realism is that same realism used by the NAACP in the justification for their protest against Griffith and Dixon's defamation of the Negro, a strange mirroring of the very ideological strategy that has historically been used against black people, and it is this possibility to which I want to finally turn. That is, I want at last to look more closely at the terms under which *The Birth of a Nation* has been studied, discussed, and condemned over the better part of the past century.

Stereotypes and the NAACP

What every American history student who studies *The Birth of a Nation* first learns is that the NAACP fought against a racist film, opposing it largely because of the stereotypical depiction of the characters. This familiar approach to the film holds that broad types such as the comic mammy, the faithful manservant, and the black beast have historically misrepresented "real" black people. Here, the objection is often to the fixity of the "unreal" type that never appears to change or grow, and the racist hand that always selects the most degrading, untrue characteristics to foreground. This argument has had tremendous staying power, particularly as it has been adapted to serve other minority groups, notably women, gays, and Asian Americans in their attacks on mainstream constructions of minority characters, attacks that I have discussed as the politics of mirroring.

Recently, however, major challenges have been mounted against this approach to protesting stereotypes by Michelle Wallace and Sander Gilman.[11] Ann duCille's analysis is also notable in the way she provides a fuller articulation of African American criticism of popular imagery that was for so many years locked in one gear. Her objection is to the overwhelming burden of representation borne by each black person in U.S. culture where "any black is every black." Growing up, says duCille, she was every black to the extent that, looking at the offensive screen, no matter how accomplished she was, "I was those ignorant darkies and they were me."[12] And it was not that the most proud black child was unable to define and defend himself or herself against these images but that these images became white people's select reality: "That white folks were watching was the issue."[13] We are reminded that in racialized U.S. society white people have historically been overseers and overlookers, and overlooking in two senses, both the supervisory as well as the unseeing and noncomprehending sense. White people have looked to censor, as we have noted, and overlooked in seeing only what they wanted to see. But the "my reality–your reality" question cuts both ways, and it is for this reason that I want to finally revisit the invocation of reality in the traditional criticism of stereotypage.

From the standpoint of film studies, one of the most compelling critiques of the mode of criticism of stereotypes can be found in the context of Steve Neale's discussion of *The Birth of a Nation,* an analysis that owes much to the reconsideration of the theoretical concept of "difference." For critical theorists, Neale's analysis is particularly satisfying for the way its poststructuralist premises so neatly identify the rhetorical flaws in the protest against stereotypes. Stereotypes, he says, seem always to be measured against "the real": "Stereotypical characters are evaluated negatively to the extent that they are not like 'real people,' to the extent that the characters do not appear as complex individuals living complex lives in a complex society."[14] And here is where I find that the argument used by those who have been "misrepresented" against the very stereotypes that misconstrue and misunderstand can be seen to borrow the same ideological strategy so often used against themselves. To argue that "real people are not like that" is to answer one empirical claim (the self-evidence of racial characteristics) with another (the self-evidence of how black people really are). Or one empiricism is pitted against another empiricism.[15] But it is finally not empirical people after all who underwrite the most potent antidote to the stereotype. It is instead an imaginary group.

Stereotypes may appear to be measured against the "real," but, says Neale, they are actually measured against the "ideal." That is, objectionable types are not measured against real people at all; rather, they are compared with a characterization that could serve as a "positive" image for the minority group (as opposed to a "negative" one). It is this "positive" image that is an idealization. Here the rhetorical flaw is in the assumption that the "positive" image is not itself also a stereotype—that somehow it is exempted from criticism because it is not pejorative (another problem arising from the situation in which "stereotype" has become synonymous with "pejorative" even when stereotypes can as easily be laudatory). Neale observes: "What in fact is being demanded is the replacement of one set of stereotypes by another."[16] It is almost as though "positive" has taken on the connotation of "real and true," a move that fosters a compatibility between two positions that should be incompatible—the constructed "ideal" and the unconstructed "real." While we would certainly want to allow for the political efficacy of any argument by marginalized groups on behalf of "real people and real lives," a cause that verges on what Gayatri Spivak at one time called "strategic essentialism," one has to wonder why the inconsistency in these two positions never seems obvious in political contexts, particularly when the "recourse to the real" and the "recourse to the ideal" are used almost interchangeably by the same groups.[17]

Finally, Neale points out that the focus on stereotypes, particularly in the NAACP formulation, is basically about identification, and he sees identification as fundamentally conservative as it holds up role models for emulation.[18] Another way of looking at the NAACP-inspired attack on stereotypes, then, would be as the perfect inverse of the fear of identification—the *hope* that identification with positive images will produce a new breed of minority citizens who have modeled their behavior after that of the heroic and idealized types they view on the larger-than-life screen. But contemporary black critics have swiftly dismissed the Pollyanna standpoint of "positive images," which could be construed as an uplift mission out of touch with the times. Kobena Mercer, for one, sees the motive behind the minority advocacy of positive images as nothing more nor less than "behavioral engineering."[19] Dismissing the NAACP "Image Awards," Anthony Appiah asserts that there is "no evidence that a good Negro could change the mind of a single bigot."[20]

And yet the rhetoric of the real, interchangeable with the appeal to the positive, has had its political victory. One could observe in the struggles around racial realism in the first two decades of the twentieth century the opportunism of the concept of realism. Then, as now, there are as many realisms and realities as political positions espousing change. Reality is invoked to instill the fear of reality that that reality would unleash. Returning to the virulence of the public censorship campaigns against D. W. Griffith as well as the quieter censorship of race movies with this critique in mind, one cannot miss the inconsistency of the recourse to realism and its companion, the charge of falsehood. While one side wants a ban on images because what it sees represented is *not* reality, the other defends the representation on the basis of reality. One group urges censorship because what it sees is too close to reality and the other justifies the representation on grounds of truth, or adherence to reality. The NAACP challenged *The Birth of a Nation* on the basis of its "not enough reality," and forces opposing Micheaux's films in the silent era essentially banned and cut merely because what was represented was taken to be the "wrong reality." At some point, however, this rhetorical strategy will box us into a corner since we will always need some concept of the real—yet another real, beyond the one in question.[21] Criticizing *The Birth of a Nation* campaign is to highlight the instability of "reality" and the double edge of recourse to racial realism, running the risk of appearing to dismiss the veracity of the very historical conditions that we need to remember as *having really happened.*

The critical legacy of the protest surrounding *The Birth of a Nation* is a mixed legacy. On the one hand, the NAACP campaign was a model of political organizing that galvanized new local chapters during the crucial early years. On the other hand, the focus on this film was at the expense of focus on films produced by African Americans themselves, perhaps the most important of which was Micheaux's small masterpiece, *Within Our Gates.* But as we have seen, race movies were an outcry against Griffith and Dixon that was soon silenced as these films were shunted away. Rectifying the historical record involves not only retrieval but an analysis that appreciates the phenomenon of race movies in all of its doubleness.

The Identity of Difference

"Difference, difference worth talking about, can only exist on the basis of some identity. And identity conversely can only exist on the basis of difference."[22] C. L. R. James summarizes Hegel in a kind of tutorial on the dialectic where he shows himself to be a most enthusiastic Hegelian. The self, we learn from all of the Hegelian systems, is constituted in differentiation and similitude. Paradoxically, the self is constituted through the not-self, thus going counter to common sense, which would have the self as so much of an island that it cannot conceive of an other, let alone an other that is essential to its production. We see the major historical scenarios of the last three centuries in Hegel's encounter between the master and the slave: the imperialism of the one "taking over" the other, the revolution of the other "overthrowing" the one, and even the cooperative democracy of each "containing" the other.

And we wonder if C. L. R. James is imagining the racial ramifications of the philosophical principle he asserts. Is the difference between peoples secured by their identity, their commonality? And is their identity their very difference? Is the one who she is because of the other and the other because of the one? Does difference based on identity describe

Du Bois's formulation? Du Bois thinks of the "twoness" of double consciousness not as symmetrical and reciprocal but as asymmetrical, for it is the two "unreconciled strivings" that define not only the tension within each black American, but stand for the antagonism between black and white that describes the nation in the period we are considering.[23] And we have tried to remember the qualification in Du Bois throughout, particularly as we have analyzed the asymmetry of the uplift project that held some up and kept some down, that tempered and modified the utopian aspiration associated with liberation and world improvement. For it is the "two things at once" (an American, a Negro) that defines the conflicted consciousness of race movies. As Ron Green has argued, the work of Oscar Micheaux is characterized by this impossible "twoness."[24]

This political drama of the one and the other is reenacted within the historically specific concept of identification, which, after so many attempts to explain and capture its function, can be found to be reducible to a *position* in relation to another. Making less of the concept instead of more, Roland Barthes has argued that identification "is not a psychological process; it is a pure structural operation: I am the one who has the same place I have."[25] And yet the becoming of myself raises many issues, at least one of which is defined for Barthes in the rivalry that follows from the production of each as identical, a chaotic production that sets off a chorus of "Mine! Mine!"[26] Me and mine, me and mine. Is this where the historic dawning of self-consciousness as described by the philosopher has led us? For identification at this time in history can be described as the tendency to see oneself everywhere, in everything and everyone, and hence to displace the other and replace him with one's self, the ultimate hegemonic act.

To emphasize the "me" and the "mine" is to stress what is perhaps the most reactionary side of the cube of identification, the side that looks only at and to its own, eschewing others. That this deadly aspect of similitude is involved in the brutal exclusions of segregation is undeniable, and we still need to understand how the motion picture works in extreme cases to confirm the one as the "we." With reference to Freud's analysis of the malevolent organization of social groups, Julia Kristeva describes how this organization of exclusion "binds the identity of a clan, a sect, a party, or a nation." And, she goes on, it is this separation that produces the persecution of others, the very separation that provides the "pleasure of identification," a perverse pleasure it would seem. This is an identification that works through the most linear of similitudes in which the self finds itself in the selfsame: " 'this is what *we* are, therefore it is what *I* am.' "[27] We need to consider further how the "I am / we are" conjunction is magnified by films such as *The Birth of a Nation,* perhaps the first successful example of the mass media production of a group identity through exclusion and scapegoating. Here the literal production of a new Ku Klux Klan, resurrected with the release and the rerelease of Griffith and Dixon's epic, is tied to *The Birth of a Nation.*[28] As film historian Terry Ramsaye summarized the situation, "The picture . . . and the K.K.K. secret society, which was the afterbirth of a nation, were sprouted from the same root."[29]

Film theory has historically had an ambivalent relationship to the concept of identification, divided between the Brechtian condemnation of the identification that sucks us in and the Metzian fascination with psychological mechanisms. But lately some film theorists have begun to reverse these positions. Critiquing the hostility toward identification of an earlier film theory, Kaja Silverman suggests that "political cinema for today must be one which, rather than lamenting the identification at the center of the cinematic experience, seizes upon it as a vehicle for taking the spectator somewhere he or she has never been before, and which discourages the return journey."[30] Identification may be a matter of seeing ourselves in places we would least expect to find recognition, just as James Baldwin, for instance, saw his own face in the face of Bette Davis. And if we are finding ourselves in strange places, what about white people who see themselves in race movies, who, after the contemporary rediscovery of these films, can now (almost) see themselves *as blacks*?[31] Identification, as we have seen, may be conservative as it supports the sociology of role modeling and, in the case of gays and lesbians, politically problematic as it fails altogether, but progressive as it is an invitation to imagine other selves, other positions.[32]

A reconsideration of identification also allows us to see in *The Birth of a Nation* much more than the pleasures of reactionary white identification, for illusionistic as it is in form and style, its image produced among black and even some white viewers the very critical capacity advocated by Brechtians. But this critical capacity was never produced by the film alone but was rather produced as its overconfident realism backfired. As the history of the NAACP protest against the film demonstrates, in the black community the most perfect illusion only produced a radical refusal of the film's inducements. The othering machine that shows ones to others is not inherently reactionary nor can we expect it to be always progressive. (And here I want to reiterate that perhaps race movies are the example that best challenges the rule of the thorough ideological saturation of the motion picture apparatus.) The machine has its duality, especially as we also understand it as the desiring machine that meets that other desiring machine, the subject who wants something of himself or herself reflected back. Sometimes the subject seizes the self or selves from the image. Since the screen is never a true mirror, selves will always be formulated through, across, and between others. Identification, if nothing else, is an invitation to be other than.

For *wanting something back* from the image has the potential to be one of the most radical demands that has ever been made on the cinema, and this I would assert in spite of my criticism of the politics of mirroring and its expectation of an impossibility: pure reflection and positive images. A theory of spectatorship that is concerned about the viewer who *wants something back* is presented with a special challenge. If the viewer simply wants confirmation of who he or she is, why not just look in the mirror? One does not really go to the cinema to see only oneself. Is it that the viewer wants himself or herself *as* another, in the guise of the larger-than-life screen figure? And which others? Some, but not others? The screen is full of others.

In addition, there are so many relations between spectator and screen, only a few of which we have touched on here. Who is the viewer who wants something back? The white censor who watched race movies? The black viewer who wanted to see more of Noble Johnson on the screen? The black censor who recommended cuts in *The Birth of a Nation*? George Johnson who wanted Micheaux to cut the lynching sequence in *Within Our Gates* before it was screened in Omaha, Nebraska? The white as well as the black man who threw eggs at Griffith's screen? The spectator (race and gender unknown) who yelled "kill him" as Arnold Girdlestone cornered Sylvia Landry in *Within Our Gates*? And what about Jimmy Baldwin whose several identities in apparent conflict were formulated across and through white movie stars? Let us not forget Ann duCille who, in wanting to be Shirley Temple, expressed the desire *for* as well as the right *to* so much seductive power. Perhaps the radical possibilities of *wanting something back from the image* are best seen in aspirations for a cinema of one's own, the impulse that led feminists in the 1970s to produce as well as to theorize feminist film and video works, and Third World peoples to start their own national cinemas as a counter to Hollywood. There is no doubt that the race movie pioneers from William Foster to Oscar Micheaux, in their wish to produce the image of the race *for* the race, were working along these lines.

Thinking about race movies means that we cannot leave spectatorship where we found it. What is also wanted at this time in history, however, is a better recipe for mutuality, a theory or theories that offer us a way around the dichotomized antagonism of gendered as well as raced relations, a tall order, it would seem. Some would recommend the influence of the ethical philosophy of Emmanuel Levinas, which has begun to interest film studies scholars, particularly in his theorization of the face to face, an approach that builds in commitment and obligation.[33] This is a phenomenology of the face that attaches responsibility to recognition, a phenomenology concerned with relationality above all. In Levinas's account of the relation between the self and the other, the starting point as well as the end point is coexistence. The glue that holds entities together is ethical obligation, still strangely ethereal for film studies, an approach that has been so productively designed around the materialist paradigm with its checks and balances in the economic.

What is suggestive for film theory, however, is the "conjuncture of the same and the other," a proximity manifested in the "*direct* and *full face.*"[34] The facing of the other puts the one under an obligation that shifts the outcome of the encounter away from the self and toward the other, a decided difference from the Hegelian outcome that Levinas characterizes as "for-itself."[35] But the ethical obligation would seem to obtain in the realm of real historical relations rather than the realm of representation and substitution. It would appear that the ethical command is contingent on the existence, the presence of the other. In the movie theater we sit face to face not with others but with images of faces. And yet the identity transactions we engage in there are significant, take on significance in the social realm. As Seán Hand understands Levinas, an ethical politics holds the promise of the elimination of concepts like assimilation and identity, the tension between which is so definitive of the modern moment.[36] Clearly, much is at stake, but still we wonder about the problem of that other proximity, not of physical entities to each other but of the human body to the machine body.

Vivian Sobchack's phenomenological exploration of what she calls the film's body as distinct from the human body works out the problem of the fundamental incongruence between the body of the film and the body of the human actor on camera. Although hers is an exhaustive exploration of the analogy between the human body and the body of the cinematic apparatus, this exercise is suggestive for us. And reading Sobchack, we become intrigued with the problem of the differences between our own bodies and the "nonhuman lived-body" that is the film. It is the very difference between the functioning body of the film and our own that makes the experience of engagement so like what we are considering as identification possible: "Nonetheless, insofar as the film's material conditions for providing access to the world, accomplishing the commutation of perception and expression, and constituting or signifying a coherence are *different* from our own, they provide us actual and possible modes of becoming other than we are."[37] So the very distinction, the division between ourselves and the film (a strange other), two unlike bodies, suggests, encourages, facilitates the process of becoming ourselves by means of the other, another. Sometimes that other through which we become ourselves is embodied in a character on-screen and sometimes the other is none other than the body of the film itself.

The othering machine that presents ones to others in search of identity is itself an other. And yet not in the same way as in the face-to-face encounter where the ethical principle governs. Some modifications of the master–slave paradigm that we have explored here are in order, and what we would retain from Hegel is the idea that one *receives* oneself from the other, that, paradoxically, one can only become oneself by becoming another. And this would mean that it is possible to yet see the one in the other, a halfway state perhaps between identity and assimilation with assimilation that dubious ideal in which the one is *not seen* in the other. There is no doubt that during the 1910s and 1920s the othering machine functioned as an assimilation machine, facilitating the production of likeness out of difference. Strangely enough, if we were looking for a better classical definition of identification, we would be referred to assimilation, the process of absorption that leaves no trace of the original, the merger of cultural forms that dissolves the one into the other. We have already noted Alexander Kojève's fondness for the concept. But we also find the use of the term elsewhere, where we would least suspect, innocent of the political connotations the concept would later develop. To make his case that identification was more than imitation, Freud described this unconscious process as "assimilation on the basis of a similar aetiological pre-tension," a taking in of the other that effects a transformation in the direction of likeness or resemblance.[38]

Clearly, the question of identification has been and continues to be politically sensitive for U.S. minorities. For American blacks during the silent film era there would always be this danger from the othering machine, this machine designed to overcome otherness, in its invitations and inducements promising the dissolution that was assimilation. But Freud's terminology plays a trick on us, and we momentarily conflate the psychological with the sociological. The othering machine does not assimilate in the same way that, for instance, intermarriage does, intermarriage another othering machine, perhaps the most mechanical of approaches to race intermixture. But even intermarriage and biological reproduction do not guarantee either cultural incorporation or full absorption of one group into another. Here, my example of the interracial family and their uneven lookalikeness speaks of the inevitable lumpiness of cultural mixture. And what of race movies? Race movies, as we have looked at them here, have a disjunctive relation to the premise of assimilationism in which black people are both *already* "just like" and *can be* like whites. In their eagerness to show that black people are "just as" good as whites in every way, race movies confirmed the premise, but in their enthusiasm they also negated it. Race movies went far beyond the "just as" assumption. The race movie anthem was that blacks were better than whites. Both a vision of assimilation in which all blacks are white-like and a defiance of assimilation in their race pride and aspiration, race movies overshot the ostensible target. They could certainly not be counted on to turn black people into white.[39]

Here I have wanted to argue the relative race neutrality of the othering machine that could conceivably show every kind of folk to anyone who wanted to see, although, as we know, everybody was *not* shown to everybody. Exhibition practices being what they were during the Jim Crow period, race movies showed black faces to black faces, but light-skinned black faces to audiences that were largely darker than the actors on the screen—a strange practice, eventually criticized by the black press, but justified by black showmen as a perhaps necessary evil. In order for these new entrepreneurs to succeed in business, they could not buck the white-like aesthetic. For these showmen, the middle class vision would have been a means to an end, a temporary becoming of the other in order to become themselves. And this would have been a significant challenge to white society had it not been for the fact that the better society envisioned essentially looked the same as the exclusionary white one with the difference that it now included blacks. Race movies, in effect, since they featured apparently assimilated characters on the screen, could be seen as producing racial indistinguishability in a cinema that distinguished itself by its blackness as well as its separateness. All of the melodramatic dilemmas of passing, the familial misrecognition and racial renunciation, seem concentrated in this historical and sociological phenomenon: the inability to tell.

The Mise-en-scène of Mixture

Race movies, as we have understood them, were a product of the irrationality of U.S. capitalism, a society and a system torn between profit and prejudice, unable to determine whether segregation or market expansion was in its best interests. Hence the short segregation windfall that black business experienced in the years following Reconstruction and into the early 1920s, a golden era in the history of African American enterprise.[40] One of the great achievements of race cinema in the silent era was its institution of an exhibition network that took advantage of this prosperity, a network with hubs in the areas that offered the greatest density of opportunity for African Americans in these years: Chicago, New York, New Orleans, Tulsa, Memphis. The other achievement was the wholesale evacuation of white people from the screen that they had so far dominated. On the one hand, an apparent acceptance of the principle of segregation, and on the other hand, a calculated oblivion of it, race movies created a racially specialized space. If race cinema mirrored back segregation, it was not as separation but as a self-contained world in which blacks were the majority and whites were the marginal few.[41] And in this, they were positively utopian.

Race cinema was a thorough re-facialization of the space of the screen, a replacement realism not meant to represent the entire spectrum of Americans at all, and in this practice strangely echoing the white cinema's exclusionary principle with the exception that there was no malice in the exclusivity. In this other cinema world, *all* of the important roles went to black actors. One hundred percent of the heroes and heroines were black in race movies, a cinema out of sight of white cinema and white people. And also out of sight of much of the black elite, which is why the race movie phenomenon fits so uneasily into discussions of the Harlem Renaissance literary and artistic tradition. Neither does it fit into the discussions of the political avant-garde, that is, the avant-garde as we have known it. Race cinema with its eye on Hollywood was undeniably an echo cinema. The world of the race movie, as I have argued, also looked just like the middle class white one, setting up equivalences and parallels while maintaining the principle of *all-black everything*. This, then, is the paradox of uplift.

But while race movies appeared on the surface, at the level of the mise-en-scène, to be less expensive copies of Hollywood, thematically they were a world apart. The same genres were emptied and filled with different issues and outcomes. Topical and frank, these films demonstrated how education lifted some up while others were left in the gutter. In the films of Oscar Micheaux in particular, a hypocritical black clergy was exposed, race betrayal through passing as white was punished, and lynching was portrayed as horrific with both blacks as well as whites shown to be complicit. Race films, while appearing to be turned inward in their consideration of black community problems and black aspirations, were simultaneously running commentaries on the white world that remained off-screen. While whites were never seen pulling the strings, they exerted a mysterious force that might work through a villainous "yellow" character, best exemplified by Micheaux's use of the actor Lawrence Chenault, who exhibited a streak of white treachery.

In Chenault's intentional, purely calculated passing, we see him as two-faced as well as two-raced, the latter attributable to the former, almost like the duplicitous mulattoes in Griffith's *The Birth of a Nation,* but with the notable difference that in *The Symbol of the Unconquered,* the Jefferson Driscoll character's race hatred is attributed to a trauma, which, while an excuse, is still an attempt to explain his behavior rather than to attribute it to a racially flawed nature. And note that Driscoll's villainy is canceled by the virtue of the light-skinned Eve Mason, mistaken for white by her own would-be suitor. Passing here is a paradigm for exposing; it is about exposure, about seeing and unseeing, even about overlooking, here in the sense of the inability to see the one race in the other. It is at this point that passing presents itself as a paradigm for spectatorship, for if the practice of passing involves overlooking blackness, viewing race movies as black culture entails overlooking whiteness. But unlike the unseeing looks of the deceived (whites) who fail to recognize passing, race movie viewers overlook in a perhaps political, perhaps blindsided way. Because to overlook the whiteness in race movies may be to claim them for a pure but impossible blackness. And yet this is understandable because by definition race movies overlook their own whiteness.[42]

If this represents a significantly different approach to what Micheaux's critics identified as the problem of the light-skinned, white-like aesthetic, it is because it lays the groundwork for a hard-edged critique. Just as the existence of the mulatto/a has been discovered as a critique of racial classification, the phenomenon of race movies presents the opportunity for a double-barreled challenge to whiteness as well as blackness. As I have noted, whiteness is critiqued by exclusion, but also whites are attacked, by implication, as the original perpetrators of racial mixing, the evidence of which is held before us, held before our eyes in the faces of the actors, players who might have been cast for no reason other than their lightness. If whiteness is critiqued by exclusion, blackness is problematized by impurity. Race movies, in their racial mixedness, in their reliance on combination, speak to the tendency to essentialize blackness, which is to intentionally overlook but also to override the not-black—the one-drop rule applied, this time in favor of the black portion. Race movies, considered closely, should thwart attempts to form essentialized identities, identities that could be formed only by completely overlooking the look of these films.

Thus I would argue that these films are the most subversive in the very way that they have been claimed to be the most reactionary. While we might want race movies to be both authentically black and formally experimental (the fondest hopes of the writers for *Close-up*, as I discussed in the introduction), if they are politically avant-garde, indeed even subversive, it is at the level of the white-like aesthetic, the same aesthetic for which they were so sharply criticized in their time. This is the aesthetic that reintroduces the problem of skin color with every attempt to claim race movies for black culture. But this is surely a contemporary attempt, informed by the politics of looking for the "black" part, an approach that is beyond the wildest dreams of the original race movie audience.

And even today, we are witnessing another development.We can't ask about the "black" part without also asking another question. Where exactly is the "white" in race movies? One could easily say that white society is there in the mixed-race character since nearly all of the actors in race movies appeared to be "of mixed race." One could even argue that the dark-skinned actors such as Paul Robeson (in *Body and Soul*) and E. G. Tatum, who played Ephrain in *Within Our Gates* and the traveling salesman in *The Symbol of the Unconquered*, were "of mixed race," if one wanted to make a point about the prevalence of race mixing in U.S. culture. It is tempting to push aside this question of the mixedness of race movies with the assertion that these films are an important aspect of black culture, allowing the "black" umbrella to cover the variations in skin color as well as cultural reference. But race movies really do force the issue of the old one-drop rule, exposing the sexual practices of an earlier century, and thus finally returning us to the historical question of slavery that injected itself into the first decades of the twentieth century. Because race movies tell these stories by utilizing light-skinned actors who present us with a gray and cream-toned vision of everything, the very mise-en-scène of these films is mixture. Race movies were aesthetic impurities in every sense. But turning this around, Stuart Hall has recently argued for the possibility in impurity: "The future belongs to the impure. The future belongs to those who are ready to take in a bit of the other, as well as being what they themselves are."[43] The fact is that there is no pure all-black America—not then and not now. Even that warm and wonderful separate community and enclave for which we all long is a mixed space, crossed with other cultural influences. The lightness of the race movie actors is not a preference for whiteness but rather the emblem of cultural confluence, the sign of intersections both consensual as well as forced. Race movies are really mixed-race movies.

Notes

Introduction

1. Kenneth Macpherson, "As Is," *Close-up* 5, no. 2 (August 1929): 90. The importance of the journal *Close-up* to the development of the international avant-garde film as well as sophisticated film criticism has been demonstrated by the publication of James Donald, Anne Friedberg, and Laura Marcus, eds., *Close-up, 1927–1933: Cinema and Modernism* (London: Cassell, 1998). This collection includes critical sections and reprints of many of the journal's more significant articles.

2. Robert Herring, "Black Shadows," *Close-up* 5, no. 2 (August 1929), continues:

> But one wishes . . . there were young Negroes who could and would get together and make their films, and let us in to see them perhaps, but *make* them anyway, and make them black. One wishes, when one turns over in one's mind the richness laid there by Negro writers and singers, and then one looks at the screen as it is and wonders why all this world finds no place there. All this world whose speed and sensitiveness and saltness and—ironically—freedom, is locked in the word "black."

3. Ibid., 99.

4. See Thomas Cripps, *Slow Fade to Black: The Negro in American Film 1900–1942*, 2d ed. (New York: Oxford University Press, 1993), chap. 10; Arthur Knight, *Dis-integrating the Musical: African American Musical Performance and American Musical Film, 1927–1959* (Durham: Duke University Press, forthcoming).

5. Harry A. Potamkin, "The Aframerican Cinema," *Close-up* 5, no. 2 (August 1929): 108, reprinted in *The Compound Cinema: The Film Writings of Harry Alan Potamkin*, ed. Lewis Jacobs (New York: Teachers College Press, 1977); Donald, Friedberg, and Marcus, eds., *Close-up, 1927–1933*.

6. Geraldyn Dismond, "The Negro Actor and the American Movies," *Close-up* 5, no. 2 (August 1929): 93. The author passes on the rumor that Johnson

owned a good deal of Universal Film Company stock and mentions that the studio used the actor for "all parts calling for a swarthy skin."

7. Ibid., 96. He also mentions Liberty Photoplays, Inc., a Boston company, but says he has seen no pictures from this company. Furthermore, he reports the rumor that the new "all-Negro" Tono-Film Company was in the process of organization and that Paul Robeson was among its directors and officers.

8. Ibid.

9. Ibid. On the black press, see Charlene Regester, "The African American Press and Race Movies," in *Oscar Micheaux and His Circle: African American Filmmaking and Race Cinema of the Silent Era*, ed. Pearl Bowser, Jane Gaines, and Charlie Musser (Pordenone-Sacile, Italy: Giornate del Cinema Muto, forthcoming). The *Close-up* evaluation of "race movies" appears to have been taken as the final word in Britain as Peter Noble, *The Negro in Films* (London: S. Robinson, 1948), 98, pretty much repeats the earlier consensus on black independent films: "It is a regrettable fact, however, that none of these has been outstanding; indeed most of them have been mediocre." Noble later mentions Micheaux Pictures, but the only films he specifically cites are *The Wages of Sin* and *The Broken Violin;* referencing The Colored Players of Philadelphia, he cited only *Ten Nights in a Barroom* with Charles Gilpin. Perhaps Noble's limited information is drawn from *Close-up*. His summation of these "inferior" films is thus: "They were shown largely in Negro cinemas and their only usefulness was in putting before the public some indications of the possibilities of the Negro in films" (p. 100).

10. As contemporary critics have argued, the POOL group that published *Close-up*, of which photographer Macpherson was a member along with the poet H. D. (Hilda Doolittle), was perhaps "part of the problem." (The group came to be named after a collection of poems they wrote entitled "Pool.") Macpherson's experiment with Paul and Eslanda Goode Robeson, while intending to illustrate the inherently photogenic qualities of the Negro, may have confirmed as well assumptions about nascent sexuality. See Jean Walton, " 'Nightmare of the Uncoordinated White-Folk': Race, Psychoanalysis, and *Borderline*," *Discourse* 19, no. 2 (winter 1997): 88–109, for a discussion of aesthetics and racial politics as well as background on the POOL group's interest in psychoanalysis. Richard Dyer, *Heavenly Bodies: Film Stars and Society* (London: British Film Institute, 1987), 130–133, discusses the way Macpherson and his collective used Robeson as a passive image. It does not seem to have occurred to the POOL group members that they could have put their espoused politics into practice by asking the Robesons to write and direct their own film. See also Anne Friedberg, "Approaching *Borderline*," in *H.D., Woman and Poet*, ed. Michael King (Orono, Maine: National Poetry Foundation, 1986); Donald, Friedberg, and Marcus, eds., *Close-up: 1927–1933*, part 5, 212–238; Cripps, *Slow Fade to Black*, 208–211.

11. For an overview of these debates, see Judith Williamson, "Two Kinds of Otherness," in *Black Film/British Cinema*, ed. Kobena Mercer (London: Institute

of Contemporary Arts, 1988); see also Tommy L. Lott, "A No-Theory Theory of Contemporary Black Cinema," *Black American Literature Forum* 25, no. 2 (summer 1991): 221–236, reprinted in *Representing Blackness: Issues in Film and Video,* ed. Valerie Smith (New Brunswick, N.J.: Rutgers University Press, 1997); Coco Fusco, *Young, British and Black: The Work of Sankofa and Black Audio Film Collective* (Buffalo, N.Y.: Hallwalls / Contemporary Arts Center, 1988); Kobena Mercer, "Diaspora Culture and the Dialogic Imagination: The Aesthetics of Black Independent Film in Britain," in *Blackframes: Critical Perspectives on Black Independent Cinema,* ed. Claire Andrade-Watkins and Mbye B. Cham (Cambridge: MIT Press, 1988).

12. Herring, "Black Shadows," 104.

13. Ibid., 100.

14. Ibid., 101. For a fresh approach to Carl van Vechten's connoisseurship of the new black arts in the 1920s, see James Smalls, "Public Face, Private Thoughts," *Genders* 25 (spring 1997): 145–186.

15. An example of such Negro essentialism in its application to theater arts might be Jessie Fauset in "The Gift of Laughter": "All about him and within him stalks the conviction that like the Irish, the Russian and the Magyr he has some peculiar offering which shall contain the very essence of the drama." Reprinted in *Within the Circle: An Anthology of African American Literary Criticism from the Harlem Renaissance to the Present,* ed. Angelyn Mitchell (Durham: Duke University Press, 1994), 45. Originally published in Alain Locke, ed., *The New Negro: An Introduction* (1925; reprint, New York: Arno Press, 1968).

16. Clyde Taylor, *The Mask of Art: Breaking the Aesthetic Contract—Film and Literature* (Bloomington: Indiana University Press, 1998), 6–7.

17. Charles Musser, "To Redream the Dreams of White Playwrights: Reappropriation and Resistance in Oscar Micheaux's *Body and Soul,*" in Bowser, Gaines, and Musser, eds., *Oscar Micheaux and His Circle,* argues that "Oscar Micheaux was not there for the dress rehearsal of the Harlem Renaissance in 1924." Further, in note 1 he documents the paucity of references to film in the work on this period. In contrast, Richard J. Powell, *Black Art and Culture in the 20th Century* (London: Thames and Hudson, 1997), arguing from the point of view of art history, includes Oscar Micheaux in his discussion of the "New Negro," finding in his work the message of "rediscovery, growth, and rebirth." The main problem with Powell's argument is that his single example, Micheaux's *The Homesteader* (1919), is thought to be "lost," presenting an insurmountable problem for its inclusion in a survey of the visual culture of the period. Further questions arise when one considers the inclusion of the segment from Micheaux's *Within Our Gates* in the important "Rhapsodies in Black" tour organized by the Hayward Gallery in London in 1997–1998. The curators' inclusion of Micheaux is provocative since it considerably enlarges as it redefines the Harlem Renaissance. But the most important question has to do with whether such an inclusion redefines the Harlem Renaissance "up" (toward high art) or "down" (as it democratizes an elite arts movement). See also Jeffrey C. Stewart,

"Paul Robeson and the Problem of Modernism," *Rhapsodies in Black: Art of the Harlem Renaissance,* ed. David A Bailey and Richard J. Powell (Berkeley: University of California Press, 1997), 93, which makes a case for seeing *Body and Soul* (1925) as formally modern because of its flashback and dream sequence. Many film scholars, however, would not see it as modernist on this basis, particularly since the most conventional Hollywood narratives may contain flashback structures. Stewart makes a more convincing point in his assertion that the film is modern in the way it breaks with the "black Victorian" commitment to positive images. Hazel Carby, *Race Men: The Body and Soul of Race, Nation and Manhood* (Cambridge: Harvard University Press, 1998), 69–70, should be mentioned for her significant contribution to Micheaux scholarship with her discovery that *Body and Soul* is an adaptation of *Roseanne,* a popular play by white playwright Nan Bagby Stephens.

18. Cornel West, *Race Matters* (New York: Vintage Books, 1994), 8.

19. See, for instance, my discussion of the videotape *The Birth of a Nation*4*29*1992* produced in the political climate surrounding the Rodney King verdict: "Political Mimesis," in *Collecting Visible Evidence,* ed. Jane Gaines and Michael Renov (Minneapolis: University of Minnesota Press, 1999).

20. Juli Jones, Jr., "*The Birth of a Nation* Runs Up against a Submarine—in Hon. Wm. Hale Thompson, the Mayor of Chicago," *Chicago Defender,* 22 May 1915, as quoted in J. Ron Green, "Micheaux v. Griffith," *Griffithiana* 60/61 (October 1997): 37. Juli Jones was the pen name for William Foster, whose *The Railroad Porter* (1913) was probably the first black-produced motion picture; see chapter 3 for further details. For examples of the more restrained attacks from white as well as black NAACP members, see *Focus on "The Birth of a Nation,"* ed. Fred Silva (Englewood Cliffs, N.J.: Prentice Hall, 1971).

21. *Within Our Gates,* formerly *La Negra* (with intertitles in Spanish) was returned to the Library of Congress from the Filmoteca Española in Madrid, the National Film Archive of Spain, in an exchange for a print of the Bela Lugosi version of *Dracula* (1931). For more, see Jane Gaines, "Micheaux's *Within Our Gates:* Now Available on Videotape," *Oscar Micheaux Society Newsletter* 3 (summer 1994). See also chapter 5, note 3, and chapter 3, note 46, regarding the dating of Micheaux's films and other early motion pictures. *The Symbol of the Unconquered* was returned from the Cinémathèque Royale / Koninklijk Filmarchief, the National Film Archive of Belgium, to the Museum of Modern Art. In 1998 the French and Flemish intertitles were translated into English when a new 35mm print was struck. See Jane Gaines, "*The Symbol of the Unconquered* Restored by Turner Classic Movies," *Oscar Micheaux Society Newsletter* 5 (summer 1998). See also chapter 6, note 87 and chapter 7, note 84. The question as to how Micheaux's films came to be distributed in Europe has not yet been satisfactorily answered. The evidence indicates that he was thinking about going abroad as early as January 1920, and that by August of the same year he was trying to arrange for someone else to travel abroad in order to arrange for world distribution. See *Chicago Defender,* 31 January 1920, 8; Oscar Micheaux to George P.

Johnson, 14 August 1920, in George P. Johnson Collection, Department of Special Collections, Young Research Library, University of California, Los Angeles, hereafter GPJC.

22. Green, "Micheaux v. Griffith," 47. See also J. Ron Green, *Straight Lick: The Cinema of Oscar Micheaux* (Bloomington: Indiana University Press, 2000). In addition to Green's long-awaited *Straight Lick*, the first of two volumes on Oscar Micheaux's cinema to be published by Indiana University Press, other notable forthcoming scholarship on Micheaux includes the much anticipated book by Pearl Bowser and Louise Spence, *Writing Himself into History: Oscar Micheaux, His Silent Films, and His Audiences* (New Brunswick, N.J.: Rutgers University Press, 2000). See also, as cited earlier, *Oscar Micheaux and His Circle: African American Filmmaking and Race Cinema in the Silent Era,* ed. Bowser, Gaines, and Musser, a catalog designed to accompany a touring package of 35mm race movies from the silent era, which includes essays by most of the scholars now working on Micheaux.

23. The one book that has done the most for African American film history is Thomas Cripps, *Slow Fade to Black,* originally published in 1977. Almost as significant has been the detailed reference book, Henry T. Sampson, *Blacks in Black and White: A Source Book on Black Films* (1977; 2d ed., Metuchen, N.J.: Scarecrow Press, 1995), and the essential filmography by Phyllis Klotman, *Frame by Frame: A Black Filmography* (Bloomington: Indiana University Press, 1979), as well as *Frame by Frame II: A Filmography of the African American image, 1978–1994* (Bloomington: Indiana University Press, 1997). Another study from the 1970s, Daniel J. Leab, *From Sambo to Superspade: The Black Experience in Motion Pictures* (Boston: Houghton Mifflin, 1975), is important for its accessibility and deserves mention here. Still, Cripps's *Slow Fade to Black,* for all its virtues as a history, did not achieve the integration of this history into the rest of film history. A model of how this could be achieved is Cripps's *Hollywood's High Noon* (Baltimore: Johns Hopkins Press, 1997). Until very recently, the standard film histories included neither chapters nor sections on African American film in the silent period. The situation is beginning to change gradually. See David A. Cook, *History of Narrative Film,* 3rd ed. (New York: W. W. Norton, 1996); Robert Sklar, *Film: An International History* (New York: Prentice Hall, 1993), 122; Geoffrey Nowell-Smith, ed., *The Oxford History of World Cinema* (London: Oxford, 1996); and David Bordwell and Kristin Thompson, *Film History: An Introduction* (New York: McGraw Hill, 1994), 181. Another recent example, David Parkinson's *History of Film* (London: Thames and Hudson, 1995), includes a still from Micheaux's *Body and Soul* (1925) and a long caption detailing his career (p. 46). Important early scholarship by African Americans on race movies and race film pioneers includes Donald Bogle, *Toms, Coons, Mulattoes, Mammies and Bucks: An Interpretative History of Blacks in American Film* (1973; reprint, New York: Continuum, 1994); Jim Pines, *Blacks in Films* (London: Studio Vista, 1975), chap. 3; James Murray, *To Find an Image: Black Film from Uncle Tom to Super Fly* (Indianapolis: Bobbs-Merrill, 1963).

More recently, work in what could be called the Second Wave of African American film scholarship has begun to appear. See bell hooks, "Micheaux: Celebrating Blackness," *Black American Literature Forum* 25, no. 2 (summer 1990): 351–360; Jacqueline Bobo, "The Subject Is Money: Reconsidering the Black Film Audience as a Theoretical Paradigm," *Black American Literature Forum* 25, no. 2 (summer 1990): 422–425; Mark A. Reid, *Redefining Black Film* (Berkeley: University of California Press, 1993), chap. 1; James Snead, *White Screens/Black Images* (New York: Routledge, 1994), 107–114. Other important historical work has been done by established African American film scholars Michelle Wallace, Clyde Taylor, Gloria Gibson-Hudson, and Pearl Bowser. The most prolific new African American film historian is Charlene Regester, whose work I quote throughout this study. Other significant scholarship since the late 1980s includes Richard Grupenhoff, *The Black Valentino: The Stage and Screen Career of Lorenzo Tucker* (Metuchen, N.J.: Scarecrow Press, 1988), and J. Ron Green and Horace Neal, Jr., "Oscar Micheaux and Racial Slur: A Response to 'The Rediscovery of Oscar Micheaux,'" *Journal of Film and Video* 40, no. 4 (fall 1988): 66–71. The most comprehensive overview of Micheaux scholarship is J. Ron Green, "The Reemergence of Oscar Micheaux: A Time Line and Bibliographic Essay," in Bowser, Gaines, and Musser, eds., *Oscar Micheaux and His Circle.*

24. Rudolf Arnheim, *Film as Art* (1933; reprint, Berkeley: University of California Press, 1966). For instance, Robert Herring warns in his review of *Hearts in Dixie* that as audiences learn to follow talk, they are "losing their picture sense." "Black Shadows," 162.

25. Peter Brooks, *The Melodramatic Imagination: Balzac, Henry James, Melodrama and the Mode of Excess* (New Haven: Yale University Press, 1976), 57.

26. Ibid., 72. Micheaux's *The Exile* (1931) is believed to be the first black "talkie." I thus date 1931 as the end of the silent era in race movies to call attention to the difference between the black and white silent eras. When historians identify 1927 as the end of the silent era, they are not taking into account that minority cinemas in the United States and Third World film industries in such countries as India would have continued silent production for a longer period because of the higher costs involved in producing a sound film.

27. See, for instance, Michele Wallace, *Invisibility Blues: From Pop to Theory* (New York: Methuen, 1990); Manthia Diawara, ed., *Black American Cinema* (New York: Routledge, 1993); Ed Guerrero, *Framing Blackness* (Philadelphia: Temple University Press, 1993); Jacqueline Bobo, *Black Women as Cultural Readers* (New York: Columbia University Press, 1995); bell hooks, *Reel to Real: Race, Sex, and Class at the Movies* (New York: Routledge, 1996); Todd Boyd, *Am I Black Enough for You? Popular Culture from the 'Hood and Beyond* (Bloomington: Indiana University Press, 1997); and, as already cited, Taylor, *The Mask of Art*, Reid, *Redefining Black Film*, and Snead, *White Screens/Black Images.*

28. Judith Mayne, *Cinema and Spectatorship* (London: Routledge, 1993), 155.

29. Mayne, Ibid., 154–155, says, "What I, as a white critic writing about race and whiteness might say, is different from what a black critic writing

about race and black spectatorship might say," but she makes this statement in the context of arguing that the model of black spectatorship will not necessarily follow from the model already established in "white film theory."

30. Ann duCille, *Skin Trade* (Cambridge: Harvard University Press, 1996), 80.

31. The reference is to West, *Race Matters*, but also to the important "Race Matters Conference" held at Princeton University, the papers from which are published in Wahneema Lubiano, ed., *The House That Race Built* (New York: Vintage Books, 1998). Toni Morrison, "Home," in Lubiano, ed., 9, discusses this place where "race both matters and is rendered impotent," referring as well to her experiments in "race-specific, race-free language." Morrison here confirms my sense of how, as I put it, race does / doesn't matter.

32. A number of white feminist film critics have called for more feminist work dealing with race, particularly in relation to black diasporic culture. A few have made significant forays into the field. I would list here Gwendolyn Audrey Foster, *Women Filmmakers of the African and Asian Diaspora* (Carbondale: Southern Illinois University Press, 1997); Sheila Petty, ed., *A Call to Action: The Films of Ousmane Sembene* (Westport, Conn.: Greenwood Press, 1996); Lola Young, *Fear of the Dark: "Race," Gender and Sexuality in the Cinema* (London: Routledge, 1996); Sharon Willis, *High Contrast: Race and Gender in Contemporary Hollywood Film* (Durham: Duke University Press, 1997); E. Ann Kaplan, *Looking for the Other: Feminism, Film, and the Imperial Gaze* (New York: Routledge, 1997); and Linda Williams, *Playing the Race Card: Melodramas of Black and White from Uncle Tom to O. J. Simpson* (Princeton: Princeton University Press, forthcoming).

33. Jane Gaines, "White Privilege and Looking Relations: Race and Gender in Feminist Film Theory," *Cultural Critique* no. 4 (1986): 59–79, revised and reprinted, *Screen* 29, no. 4 (1986): 12–27, reprinted in *Visual Culture: The Reader*, ed. Jessica Evans and Stuart Hall (London: Sage, 1997) and *Film Studies: A Reader*, ed. Joanne Hollows, Mark Jancovich, and Peter Hutchings (London: Arnold, 1999).

34. The seminal work in feminist film theory to which I refer is Laura Mulvey, "Visual Pleasure and Narrative Cinema," *Screen* 16, no. 3 (1975): 6–18. This is not to say that productive new approaches did not grow out of the limitations of the model in question here, as exemplified by Mulvey's own reconsideration of her earlier essay. See Laura Mulvey, "Afterthoughts on 'Visual Pleasure and Narrative Cinema' Inspired by *Duel in the Sun*," *Framework* 6, nos. 15–17 (1981), reprinted in *Feminism and Film Theory*, ed. Constance Penley (New York: Routledge, 1988).

35. S. I. Hartman and Farah Jasmine Griffin, " 'Are You as Colored as That Negro?' The Politics of Being Seen in Julie Dash's *Illusions*," *Black American Literature Forum* 25, no. 2 (summer 1991): 361–373.

36. Ralph Ellison, "The Shadow and the Act," in *Shadow and Act* (New York: Vintage Books, 1953), 276. Hartman and Griffin critique Ellison in similar terms: "However, *shadow* and *act* reduce questions of representation to considerations of accurate or distorted reflections. Images do not simply fulfill desires;

they create desires and identities." " 'Are You as Colored as That Negro?' " p. 364.

37. See Diane Waldman, "There's More to a Positive Image Than Meets the Eye," in *Jump Cut: Hollywood, Politics, and Counter-Cinema,* ed. Peter Steven (New York: Praeger, 1985).

38. W. E. B. Du Bois, *The Souls of Black Folk* (1903; reprint, New York: Penguin Books, 1982), 45. Mayne, *Cinema and Spectatorship,* 155, also recommends this as a starting point, as does Kaplan, *Looking for the Other,* 8.

39. John Berger, *Ways of Seeing* (London: Penguin, 1972), chap. 3; Jean Paul Sartre, *Being and Nothingness* (1956; reprint, New York: Simon and Schuster, 1966); Simone de Beauvoir, *The Second Sex,* trans. and ed. H. M. Parshley (New York: Knopf, 1953).

40. Frantz Fanon, *Black Skin, White Masks* (New York: Grove Press, 1967), 110. In contrast, Richard Dyer, *White* (London: Routledge, 1997), 51, argues that "white is virtually unthinkable except in opposition to black." But Diana Fuss disagrees in *Identification Papers* (New York: Routledge, 1995), 143, adding that conversely the white man is not white in relation to the black man because white "exempts" itself from this structure. While this may hold true philosophically, we still need to recall the way ethnic groups emigrating to the United States had to "learn" to be white. See Cornel West, "The New Cultural Politics of Difference," in *Marginalization and Contemporary Cultures,* ed. Martha Gever, Russell Ferguson, Trinh T. Minh-ha, Cornel West (New York: MIT Press, 1990), 29.

41. Bertell Ollman, *Alienation* (London: Cambridge University Press, 1971), 14–15.

42. See my "Women and Representation: Can We Enjoy Alternative Pleasure?" in *American Media and Mass Culture: Left Perspectives,* ed. Don Lazere (Berkeley: University of California Press, 1987), and in *Sexual Stratagems: Issues in Feminist Film Criticism,* ed. Patricia Erens (Bloomington: Indiana University Press, 1990).

43. Nick Browne, "Race: The Political Unconscious in American Film," *East-West Film Journal* 6, no. 1 (January 1992): 8.

44. See Richard C. Lewontin, "Of Genes and Genitals," *Transition* 69 (1996): 178–193.

45. Anthony Appiah and Amy Gutmann, *Color Conscious: The Political Morality of Race* (Princeton: Princeton University Press, 1996), 37.

46. Hortense Spillers, "All the Things You Could Be by Now, If Sigmund Freud's Wife Was Your Mother: Psychoanalysis and Race," in *Female Subjects in Black and White,* ed. Barbara Christian, Elizabeth Abel, and Helene Moglen (Berkeley: University of California Press, 1997), 137.

47. Hazel V. Carby, "The Multicultural Wars," in *Black Popular Culture,* ed. Gina Dent (Seattle: Bay Press, 1992), 193–194.

48. Here I date the silent era in race movies as beginning in 1913 to include the first black-produced film, William Foster's *The Railroad Porter,* and in order

to encompass the output of production companies such as the Lincoln Motion Picture Company and others that predated Micheaux. See chapter 3.

49. Joel Williamson, *New People: Miscegenation and Mulattoes in the United States* (New York: Free Press, 1980).

50. For an earlier overview of the appearance of the mulatto in American literature, see Judith Berzon, *Neither White Nor Black: The Mulatto Character in American Fiction* (New York: New York University Press, 1978). More recently, Werner Sollors, *Neither Black Nor White Yet Both* (New York: Oxford University Press, 1997), has produced the most exhaustive study. Sterling Brown analyzed this character before African American studies programs and departments existed, and Barbara Christian's early work on the figure is notable. See Sterling Brown, *The Negro in American Fiction* (1937; reprint, New York: Atheneum, 1969); Barbara Christian, *Black Women Novelists: The Development of a Tradition, 1892–1976* (Westport, Conn.: Greenwood Press, 1980). However, it was Hazel Carby who offered the new rationale and the paradigm for a theoretical consideration of the type, particularly as she understands how the character offers an analytical entry point into white as well as black culture. See *Reconstructing Womanhood: The Emergence of the Afro-American Woman Novelist* (New York: Oxford University Press, 1987). For a more recent development of the theoretical possibilities of the mulatto, see Walter Benn Michaels, *Our America: Nativism, Modernism, and Pluralism* (Durham: Duke University Press, 1995).

51. See Naomi Zack, *Race and Mixed Race* (Philadelphia: Temple University Press, 1993), for this argument.

52. See, for example, Mike Hill, ed., *Whiteness: A Critical Reader* (New York: New York University Press, 1997); Ruth Frankenberg, ed., *Displacing Whiteness* (Durham: Duke University Press, 1997); Daniel Bernardi, ed., *The Birth of Whiteness: Race and the Emergence of U.S. Cinema* (New Brunswick, N.J.: Rutgers University Press, 1996). See also the special issue of *American Quarterly* on "White Studies" edited by George Lipsitz (1995). Important precursors of "White Studies" were Vron Ware, *Beyond the Pale: White Women, Racism, and History* (London: Verso, 1992), and Ruth Frankenberg, *White Women, Race Matters: The Social Construction of Whiteness* (Minneapolis: University of Minnesota Press, 1993).

53. See also Mab Segrest, *Memoir of a Race Traitor* (Boston: South End Press, 1994).

54. Walter Benn Michaels, "Autobiography of an Ex-White Man," *Transition* 73 (1998): 130.

55. Ibid.

56. Michael Taussig, *Mimesis and Alterity* (London: Routledge, 1993), 49.

Chapter One

1. Christian Metz, "The Imaginary Signifier," *Screen* 16, no. 2 (1975): 54.

2. For a good discussion of the use of high theory in African American literary criticism, see Diana Fuss, *Essentially Speaking* (New York: Routledge, 1990),

82–83. Also pertinent in this context is Trinh T. Minh-ha, who understands theory as a kind of writing "which does not translate a reality outside itself but, more precisely, allows the emergence of a new reality." See *Woman, Native, Other* (Bloomington: Indiana University Press, 1989), 22. A useful overview of the politics of theoretical writing is Henry Giroux and Stanley Aronowitz, "The Politics of Clarity," *Afterimage* (October 1991): 5, 17.

3. Anne Friedberg, "A Denial of Difference: Theories of Cinematic Identification," in *Psychoanalysis and Cinema*, ed. E. Ann Kaplan (New York: Routledge, 1990), also notes that Metz appears to assume that Lacan's mirror has all of the functions of an empirical mirror (p. 40).

4. Metz, "The Imaginary Signifier," 48.

5. Umberto Eco, *Semiotics and the Philosophy of Language* (Bloomington: Indiana University Press, 1986), 207.

6. Joan Copjec has pointed out that film theory has often misunderstood Lacan, particularly when conceiving of the screen as a mirror. I am less concerned here about misconstrual of Lacan and more interested in the fascination that film theory has had with the mirror metaphor. See Copjec, *Lacan against the Historicists* (Cambridge: MIT Press, 1995), 15–16, 21–22.

7. Metz, "The Imaginary Signifier," 49.

8. Ibid., 48–49.

9. Friedberg, "A Denial of Difference," 40.

10. Isaac Julien and Kobena Mercer, "Introduction: De Margin and De Centre," *Screen* 29, no. 4 (1988): 9.

11. Mary Ann Doane, *Femmes Fatales* (New York: Routledge, 1991), has argued that psychoanalysis is "radically destabilized by those excluded" (p. 211). Lillian Smith, *Killers of the Dream* (New York: W. W. Norton, 1949), notes the "dual relationship which so many white southerners have had with two mothers, one white and one colored and each of a different culture centered in different human values, which makes the Oedipus complex seem by comparison almost a simple adjustment" (p. 131). For a discussion of the radical difference of childrearing under the "peculiar institution" of slavery, see Hortense J. Spillers, "Mama's Baby, Papa's Maybe: An American Grammar Book," *Diacritics* 17, no. 2 (summer 1987): 65–81.

12. I have been influenced here by Kwame Anthony Appiah and Henry Louis Gates, Jr., "Introduction: Multiplying Identities," *Critical Inquiry* 18 (1992): 625–629.

13. Stuart Hall, "Minimal Selves," in *Identity: The Real Me*, ICA Document 6 (London: The Institute of Contemporary Arts, 1987), 45.

14. James Baldwin, *The Devil Finds Work* (New York: Dell, 1976), 3–4. Hereafter page numbers are noted in the text.

15. Very special thanks to Tom Doherty, who astutely pointed out Baldwin's error as well as my own and generously loaned me a tape of *Laughing Sinners*.

16. Michelle Wallace, "Race, Gender, and Psychoanalysis in Forties Film:

Lost Boundaries, Home of the Brave, and *The Quiet One,"* in *Black American Cinema,* ed. Manthia Diawara (New York: Routledge, 1993), 264.

17. Also struck by Baldwin's eyes, Hinton Als, looking over old photographs of the writer, describes "his enormous eyes, like dark poppies in bloom, raised in mock or serious consternation." Als, "The Enemy Within: The Making and Unmaking of James Baldwin," *The New Yorker,* 16 February 1998, 72.

18. Eric Lott, *Love and Theft: Blackface Minstrelsy and the American Working Class* (New York: Oxford University Press, 1993), 197.

19. Kobena Mercer, "Skin Head Sex Thing: Racial Difference and the Homoerotic Imaginary," in *How Do I Look? Queer Film and Video,* ed. Bad Object Choices (Seattle: Bay Press, 1991), 207.

20. The reference is to Judith Butler's provocative suggestion that gender is a "fabrication." See Butler, *Gender Trouble: Feminism and the Subversion of Identity* (New York: Routledge, 1990), 136–137, where it is clear that the origin of the concept of gender as "worn" is certainly in Esther Newton's groundbreaking anthropological definition of drag as both distance and costume. Newton, *Mother Camp: Female Impersonators in America* (Chicago: University of Chicago Press, 1972), 109.

21. As quoted in Kendall Thomas, "Ain't Nothin' Like the Real Thing," in *The House That Race Built,* ed. Wahneema Lubiano (New York: Vintage Books, 1998), 121.

22. Ibid., 130.

23. José Muñoz, "Photographs of Mourning: Melancholia and Ambivalence in Van Der Zee, Mapplethorpe, and *Looking for Langston,"* In *Race and the Subject of Masculinities,* ed. Harry Stecopoulos and Michael Uebel (Durham: Duke University Press, 1997), 351. See also José Muñoz, *Disidentifications: Queers of Color and the Performance of Politics* (Minneapolis: University of Minnesota Press, 1999); Kobena Mercer, *Welcome to the Jungle* (London: Routledge, 1994), chap. 6.

24. José Esteban Muñoz, "Famous and Dandy Like B. 'n' Andy: Race, Pop, and Basquiat," in *Pop Out,* ed. Jonathan Flatley, Jennifer Doyle, and José Esteban Muñoz (Durham: Duke University Press, 1996), 146.

25. See, for instance, Eve Kosofsky Sedgwick, "Across Gender, Across Sexuality: Willa Cather and Others," *Displacing Homophobia: Gay Male Perspectives in Literature and Culture,* ed. Ronald R. Butters, John M. Clum, and Michael Moon (Durham: Duke University Press, 1989).

26. Eve Kosofsky Sedgwick, *Tendencies* (Durham: Duke University Press, 1993), xii.

27. Muñoz, "Famous and Dandy," 147–148. See also Michel Pecheux, *Language, Semantics, Ideology* (New York: St. Martin's Press, 1982), 158–159, who understands disidentification as related, among other things, to the effect of "proletarian political practice" on the subject.

28. Stuart Hall, "Notes on Deconstructing 'The Popular,'" in *People's History and Socialist Theory,* ed. Raphael Samuel (Boston: Routledge and Kegan Paul, 1981).

29. Frantz Fanon, *Black Skin, White Masks* (New York: Grove Press, 1967), 152–153.

30. Toni Morrison, *The Bluest Eye* (New York: Plume Book, 1994).

31. Ann duCille, "The Shirley Temple of My Familiar," *Transition* 73 (1998): 21.

32. Judith Butler, *Bodies That Matter* (New York: Routledge, 1993), 219.

33. Muñoz, "Famous and Dandy," 152.

34. Probably the best basic definition of camp is the one that Esther Newton draws from the subjects of her early ethnography: "Camp is not a thing. Most broadly it signifies a *relationship between* things, people, and activities or qualities, and homosexuality" (p. 105). She finds her most vivid examples of camp juxtapositions in apartments decorated by her subjects: "One queen said that *TV Guide* had described a little Mexican horse statue as campy. He said there was nothing campy about this at all, but if you put a nude cut-out of Bette Davis on it, it would be campy." Newton, *Mother Camp*, 107.

35. One of the earliest discussions of this phenomenon in relation to film stars is Jack Babuscio, "Camp and the Gay Sensibility," in *Gays and Film*, ed. Richard Dyer (New York: Zoetrope, 1984), 44–47.

36. See Richard Dyer, *Heavenly Bodies: Film Stars and Society* (London: Macmillan, 1987), chap. 3, for the definitive discussion of Judy Garland as epitomizing this too-close relation between role and self that gives itself away. Alex Doty begins to rethink the now commonplace discussion of gay men and film stars in relation to queer theory in *Making Things Perfectly Queer: Interpreting Mass Culture* (Minneapolis: University of Minnesota Press, 1993), 6–16.

37. See note 20. Again, the reference is to Judith Butler's use of the concept that gender is "fabricated." As Esther Newton sketched out the paradigm in relation to the concept of drag: "The drag concept implies distance between the actor and the role or 'act.' But drag always means 'costume.'" Newton, *Mother Camp*, 109.

38. It was not until after Baldwin's death in 1987 that Marlon Riggs would proclaim that "Negro faggotry is in fashion." See Riggs, "Black Macho Revisited: Reflections of a SNAP! Queen," as well as Joseph Beam, "James Baldwin: Not a Bad Legacy, Brother," and Carlyle R. Black, "James Baldwin (1924–1987)," in *Brother to Brother: New Writings by Black Gay Men*, ed. Essex Hemphill (Boston: Alyson Publications, 1991). The Riggs quotation appears on page 253 of this collection.

39. Arthur Knight, "Star Dances: African-American Constructions of Stardom, 1925–1960," in *Classic Hollywood; Classic Whiteness*, ed. Daniel Bernardi (Minneapolis: University of Minnesota Press, forthcoming).

40. Jacqueline Bobo, *Black Women as Cultural Readers* (New York: Columbia University Press, 1995).

41. On how white culture finds itself in African Americans, see Clyde Taylor, *The Mask of Art: Breaking the Aesthetic Contract—Film and Literature* (Bloomington: Indiana University Press, 1998), 121; Cornel West, "The New Cultural

Politics of Difference," in *Out There: Marginalization and Contemporary Cultures,* ed. Martha Gever, Russell Ferguson, Trinh T. Minh-ha, Cornel West (New York: MIT Press, 1990), 29; Toni Morrison, *Playing in the Dark: Whiteness and the Literary Imagination* (Cambridge: Harvard University Press, 1992).

42. Perhaps it is just assumed that racial crossing over, one way or the other, is part of the queer appropriation of female stars that always enhances the fascination. Alex Doty refers to "even less-analyzed queer readership positions formed around the nexus of race and sexuality, or class and sexuality, or ethnicity and sexuality, or some combination of gender / race / class / ethnicity and sexuality" and footnotes the work of Richard Fung, Kobena Mercer, Essex Hemphill, Marlon Riggs, Isaac Julien, and one black lesbian, Jackie Goldsby. Doty, *Making Things Perfectly Queer,* 7, 108. But note that Doty's comprehensive list of the spectacular female personalities around whom gay male cults have grown includes a mix of white and black women, from Maria Callas to Beverly Sills and from Bette Davis and Joan Crawford through Bette Midler and Barbra Streisand to Diana Ross (p. 6). One would assume that it is not just that gay male fascination knows no bounds but that the cross-race dimension contributes to glamor-as-danger.

43. Baldwin refers to his "young white school teacher who was a Communist" in his conversations with Margaret Mead. James Baldwin and Margaret Mead, *A Rap on Race* (New York: Laurel Books, 1971), 22. David Leaming, in his biography of Baldwin, identifies Orilla Miller as the daughter of a Farmer's Cooperative organizer who attended Antioch College until forced to leave school because of the Depression. She later married Evan Winfield, a seaman she met in New York during a strike, and the couple periodically continued to pull Baldwin into their radical activities for the short time they lived in New York before moving to Los Angeles. Leaming, *James Baldwin: A Biography* (New York: Alfred Knopf, 1994), 14–15.

44. James Baldwin, "Everybody's Protest Novel," in *Notes of a Native Son* (1955; reprint, New York: Beacon Press, 1984), 13–23.

45. Stuart Hall, "Gramsci's Relevance for the Study of Race and Ethnicity," *Journal of Communication Inquiry* 10, no. 2 (1986): 24.

46. Marxist theorists have tended to put class first, on top of race. An interesting example is Eugene Genovese's theorization in *Roll, Jordan, Roll: The World the Slaves Made* (New York: Random House, 1976), where he says that racial subordination "rendered its fundamental class relations more complex and ambiguous; but they remained class relations" (p. 3). Ruth Frankenberg, in *White Women, Race Matters: The Social Construction of Whiteness* (Minneapolis: University of Minnesota Press, 1993), uses the concept "race-as-class" and suggests that race privilege must always be seen as "crosscut by other axes of difference and inequality: class, culture, ethnicity, gender, and sexuality" (p. 1).

47. Toni Morrison, "Unspeakable Things Unspoken: The Afro-American Presence in American Literature," *Michigan Quarterly Review,* 28, no. 1 (1988): 3.

48. Frantz Fanon, *Toward the African Revolution,* trans. Haakon Chevalier

(New York: Monthly Review Press, 1967), 18. Albert Memmi, *Dominated Man* (New York: Orion Press, 1968), gives this example of the way race works ideologically: "The black man is labeled congenitally good-for-nothing so that he can be kept in economic bondage; the colonized is tagged as unfit to handle anything technical so that colonization can last; the proletariat as politically and socially childish so that the domination of the property-owning classes can continue unchallenged" (p. 194).

49. Barbara Fields, "Slavery, Race, and Ideology in the U.S. of A.," *New Left Review* 181 (1990): 106.

50. Kwame Anthony Appiah, *In My Father's House* (New York: Oxford University Press, 1992), 44. Elsewhere Appiah writes "races are like witches: however unreal witches are, *belief* in witches, like belief in races, has had—and in many communities continues to have—profound consequences for human social life." Appiah, "Race," in *Critical Terms for Literary Study*, ed. Frank Lentricchia and Thomas McLaughlin (Chicago: University of Chicago Press, 1987), 177.

51. Anthony Appiah, "The Uncompleted Argument," in *"Race," Writing, and Difference*, ed. Henry Louis Gates, Jr. (Chicago: University of Chicago Press, 1986), 35–36.

52. Houston Baker, "Caliban's Triple Play," in *"Race," Writing, and Difference*, 384–385.

53. W. E. B. Du Bois, *Dusk of Dawn: An Essay toward an Autobiography of a Race Concept* (1940; reprint, New York: Viking, 1986), 153.

54. Adolph Reed, Jr., "Skin Deep: The Fiction of Race," *Village Voice*, 24 September 1996, 22.

55. In "Race, Culture, Identity: Misunderstood Connections," in Anthony Appiah and Amy Gutmann, *Color Conscious: The Political Morality of Race* (Princeton: Princeton University Press, 1996), Appiah talks about this phenomenon in terms of "ascription": "ascription of racial identities—the process of applying the label to the people, including ourselves—is based on more intentional identification and . . . there can be a gap between what a person ascriptively is and the racial identity he performs" (p. 79).

56. Joyce Joyce, "The Black Canon: Reconstructing Black American Literary Criticism," *New Literary History* 18, no. 2 (1987): 333–344.

57. See Stuart Hall, "The Whites of Their Eyes," in *Silver Linings*, ed. Rosalind Brunt (London: Lawrence and Wishart, 1981).

58. Gates, *"Race," Writing, and Difference*, 5. A useful overview of these debates is Fuss, *Essentially Speaking*, chap. 5.

59. Butler, *Bodies That Matter*, 10.

60. Ibid., 5.

61. Ibid.

62. W. E. B. Du Bois, "The Conservation of Races," *W. E. B. Du Bois Speaks: Speeches and Addresses, 1890–1919*, ed. Philip S. Foner (New York: Pathfinder Press, 1970), 75, as quoted in Appiah, "The Uncompleted Argument," 23.

63. See Colette Guillaumin, "Race and Nature: The System of Marks," *Feminist Issues* 8, no. 2 (fall 1988): 33–34.

64. Further commenting on this development in which the child takes the race of the mother, Barbara Fields notes, "Paternity is always ambiguous whereas maternity is not." Fields, "Slavery, Race, and Ideology," 107. See also chapter 6, note 16.

65. See Martha Hodes, *White Women, Black Men: Illicit Sex in the Nineteenth-Century South* (New Haven: Yale University Press, 1997), on the history of white women who had children by black (slave) men.

66. James F. Davis, *Who Is Black? One Nation's Definition* (University Park: Pennsylvania State University Press, 1991), 45. A South Carolina judge in the 1850s also balked at applying the one-drop rule, declaring a person to be white because he was accepted by whites as white (p. 35). Davis observes that although whites certainly were responsible for devising the one-drop rule in order to uphold Jim Crow segregation and to protect the institution of slavery, these original reasons for inventing the rule no longer matter to most blacks (p. 138). One could argue in response to this that the black community may have turned this rule to their political advantage, but the question remains as to what the reversal does to the history of the practice.

67. Hortense Spillers, "Notes on an Alternative Model—Neither/Nor," in *The Difference Within: Feminism and Critical Theory*, ed. Elizabeth Meese and Alice Amsterdam (Philadelphia: A. J. Benjamin, 1989), 165.

68. Here I am obviously falling back on "intermarriage" as the old euphemism for "interbreeding." The alternatives, such as "breeding" or "sexual reproduction," seem to exclude the cultural dimension here, and "unions" seems oblivious to the sexual dimension.

69. Joel Williamson, *New People: Miscegenation and Mulattoes in the United States* (New York: Free Press, 1980), 25–26, 63–64, 32–42. This is a major challenge to the sociological findings of Edward Reuter, *The Mulatto in the United States* (Boston: Gorham Press, 1918). Reuter has been further taken to task for resurrecting the myth of the superiority of the mulatto with his statistics on mulatto achievement. See Patricia Morton, "From Invisible Man to 'New People': The Recent Discovery of American Mulattoes," *Phylon* 46, no. 2 (1985): 117.

70. Nahum Chandler, "The Economy of Desedimentation: W. E. B. Du Bois and the Discourses of the Negro," *Callaloo* 19, no. 1 (1996): 82.

71. Aristotle, *Aristotle's Metaphysics*, trans. Hippocrates G. Apostle (Grinnell, Iowa: Peripatetic Press, 1979).

72. Chandler, "The Economy of Desedimentation," 85, says that the "African American subject is quite often 'both/and' as well as 'neither/nor.' "

73. Ben Nightingale, "A Matter of Black and White," *Today* (*The Philadelphia Inquirer Magazine*), 27 April 1980, 12–17. Thanks to Pearl Bowser and Clyde Taylor for this reference.

74. Ibid., 15.

75. Ibid., 12.

76. Ibid.

77. Attempts to think about a black aesthetic include Trey Ellis, "The New Black Aesthetic (N.B.A.)," *Callaloo* 12, no. 1 (winter 1989): 233–247, and Houston A. Baker, *Blues, Ideology, and Afro-American Literature: A Vernacular Theory* (Chicago: University of Chicago Press, 1984). See also Taylor, *The Mask of Art*, 6–7.

78. Appiah, "The Uncompleted Argument," 55.

79. Nightingale, "A Matter of Black and White," 17.

80. James Baldwin, *Nobody Knows My Name*, as quoted in ibid., 6.

81. Baldwin, as quoted in ibid., 17.

82. Hall, "Minimal Selves," 45.

83. Baldwin, *Notes of a Native Son*, 6–7.

84. See, for instance, my "Scar of Shame: Skin Color and Caste in Black Silent Melodrama," in *Imitations of Life*, ed. Marcia Landy (Detroit: Wayne State University Press, 1991), 344, where I argue that "[f]or black readers, then, domestic melodrama would have made the cruel irrationality of social and political disenfranchisement seem manageable; cast in personal terms, injustice could almost seem to be dealt with finally and absolutely."

85. Baldwin, *Notes of a Native Son*, 14.

86. The Lafayette Theatre opened in 1912 and was the first theater in New York to desegregate after a campaign led by Lester Walton in the pages of the *New York Age*. For more on early film exhibition in Harlem, see Alison Griffiths and James Latham, "Early Cinema and Ethnic Identity in Harlem before 1915," paper presented at "Hollywood and Its Spectators: The Reception of American Films, 1895–1900" (London, 1998).

87. It is interesting to compare Baldwin with Metz on the difference between film and theater. And here one begins to see that Metz's theorization of the absence of the signifier in cinema is also a comparison with the theater where the actor is "physically present, in the same space as the spectator." Metz, "The Imaginary Signifier," 62. Because of this absence, the film spectacle, in Metz, is "more radically ignorant of its spectator," more, that is, in contrast with theater (p. 64). For all the cinema cares, the spectator is not there.

Chapter Two

1. This is somewhat the idea informing André Gaudreault, "Showing and Telling: Image and Word in Early Cinema," in *Early Cinema: Space/Frame/Narrative*, ed. Thomas Elsaesser (London: British Film Institute, 1990). Tom Gunning, *D. W. Griffith and the Origins of American Narrative Film* (Urbana: University of Illinois Press, 1991), 17, points out that in contrast with literary language, film can "show more immediately than it can tell."

2. For the textbook approach to *The Great Train Robbery*, see *The Cinema Book*, ed. Pam Cook (London: British Film Institute, 1985), 208–211. *Life of an American Fireman* is perhaps a more interesting example of the "problem of the

evolution" of crosscutting because of the existence of two versions—an earlier version not crosscut and a later crosscut version, apparently reedited. See André Gaudreault, "Detours in Film Narrative: The Development of Cross-Cutting," *Cinema Journal* 19 (fall 1979): 39–59, reprinted in Elsaesser, ed., *Early Cinema;* Charles Musser, "The Early Cinema of Edwin S. Porter," *Cinema Journal* 19 (fall 1979): 29–31; Charles Musser, *Before the Nickelodeon: E. S. Porter and the Edison Manufacturing Company* (Berkeley: University of California, 1991), 232–233.

3. Lynne Kirby, *Parallel Tracks: The Railroad and Silent Cinema* (Durham: Duke University Press, 1997). In her brilliant reading of this film, Kirby suggests a different way of understanding the racial component: she reads the black leader as "the alternating obscurity of film's repressed other," this blackness between the frames ultimately threatening continuity (p. 126).

4. See Noel Burch, *Life to Those Shadows,* trans. Ben Brewster (Berkeley: University of California Press, 1990), 268, for a summary of this thesis.

5. See Tom Gunning, "The Cinema of Attractions: Early Film, Its Spectator and the Avant-Garde," *Wide Angle* 8, no. 3/4 (fall 1986), reprinted in Elsaesser, ed., *Early Cinema,* for his extremely influential reconsideration of Sergei Eisenstein's concept of the "cinema of attractions."

6. Musser mentions Ferdinand Zecca's *Flirt en chemin de fer* (1901) and Sigmund Lubin's *Love in a Railroad Tunnel* (1902). See Musser, *Before the Nickelodeon,* 262–263.

7. Ibid., 263. See "A Tunnel Mystery," *New York Journal,* 31 March 1898, 12, for the gag.

8. Lauren Rabonivitz, in *For the Love of Pleasure: Women, Movies, and Culture in Turn-of-the-Century Chicago* (New Brunswick, N.J.: Rutgers University Press, 1998), 86, describes two variations on what she calls the "racist joke" in *What Happened in the Tunnel—The Mis-Directed Kiss* and *A Kiss in the Dark,* both produced by American Mutoscope and Biograph in 1904, a year after *Tunnel.* Peter Noble, in *The Negro in Films* (London: Skelton Robinson, 1948), 28, also describes "race change" as the basis of the joke in *The Masher* (1907), in which the "masher" lifts the veil of the woman he has been flirting with and is horrified to find that she is black rather than white.

9. Kirby, *Parallel Tracks,* 99, 247.

10. Kirby, ibid., 46, says that Hale's Tours, first appearing in Kansas City in 1905, "consummated" what could be called the "perpetual marriage of the railroad and the cinema." Musser, in *Before the Nickelodeon,* says that we do not know whether *What Happened in the Tunnel* was shown in Kansas City that first summer (p. 264). The film would have been shown in subsequent years at other Hale's Tours sites, however. For more on Hale's Tours, see Raymond Fielding, "Hale's Tours: Ultrarealism in the Pre-1910 Motion Picture," *Film before Griffith,* ed. John Fell (Berkeley: University of California Press, 1983), 116–130; Charles Musser, *The Emergence of Cinema: The American Screen to 1907* (Berkeley: University of California Press, 1990), 429–431.

11. See Gunning, "Cinema of Attractions," 65, on the connection between the evolution of cinema and the appearance of the big amusement parks such as Coney Island. See also John Kasson, *Amusing the Millions: Coney Island at the Turn of the Century* (New York: Hill and Wang, 1978), 74.

12. See, of course, Sigmund Freud, *Jokes and Their Relation to the Unconscious,* ed. and trans. James Strachey (1900; reprint, New York: Norton, 1963).

13. Judith Mayne, *The Woman at the Keyhole* (Bloomington: Indiana University Press, 1990), 168. See also Judith Mayne, "Uncovering the Female Body," in *Before Hollywood: Turn-of-the-Century Film from American Archives,* ed. Jay Leyda and Charles Musser (New York: American Federation of Arts, 1986).

14. See Tom Gunning, " 'Primitive' Cinema—A Frame-up? Or The Trick's on Us," *Cinema Journal* 28 (winter 1989): 3–12, reprinted in Elsaesser, ed., *Early Cinema,* 95–104.

15. See R. Bruce Brassell, "A Seed for Change: The Engenderment of *A Florida Enchantment,*" *Cinema Journal* 36, no. 4 (1997): 3–21, for a thorough analysis and industry study of the film.

16. The best formulation of this is Chris Straayer, *Deviant Eyes, Deviant Bodies* (New York: Columbia University Press, 1977), chap. 3, "Redressing the 'Natural': The Temporary Transvestite Film."

17. Miriam Hansen, in *Babel and Babylon: Spectatorship in American Silent Film* (Cambridge: Harvard University Press, 1991), 39, reads the maid's direct look at the camera as a knowing look suggesting that *she* might have been responsible for the trick.

18. Mayne, *The Woman at the Keyhole,* 174.

19. See Laura Mulvey, "Visual Pleasure and Narrative Cinema," *Screen* 16, no. 3 (1975): 6–18; E. Ann Kaplan, *Women and Film: Both Sides of the Camera* (New York: Methuen, 1983). Kaplan's chapter "Is the Gaze Male?" exemplifies the way the "male look" took hold and came to be synonymous with the "male gaze." Mulvey's influential article was reprinted over ten times in the first ten years after its initial publication and still continues to be widely cited in several disciplines.

20. Homi Bhabha, "The Other Question: The Stereotype and Colonial Discourse," *Screen* 24, no. 6 (1983): 18–36, reprinted in *The Location of Culture* (New York: Routledge, 1994).

21. Ibid., 19, 29.

22. Notable exceptions are Ella Shohat, "Gender and the Culture of Empire: Toward a Feminist Ethnography of the Cinema," *Quarterly Review of Film and Video* 13 (1991): 45–84 and Kobena Mercer, "Imaging the Black Man's Sex," in *Photography/Politics: Two,* ed. Patricia Holland, Jo Spence, and Simon Watney (London: Comedia, 1986), 61–69.

23. See, for instance, Mitsuhiro Yoshimoto, "The Difficulty of Being Radical: The Discipline of Film Studies and the Postcolonial World Order," *boundary 2: An International Journal of Literature and Culture* 18, no. 3 (fall 1991): 242–257.

24. See, for instance, Lola Young, *Fear of the Dark: "Race," Gender and*

Sexuality in the Cinema (London: Routledge, 1996); E. Ann Kaplan, *Looking for the Other: Feminism, Film, and the Imperial Gaze* (New York: Routledge, 1997).

25. Examples include Matthew Bernstein and Gaylyn Studlar, eds., *Visions of the East: Orientalism in Film* (New Brunswick, N.J.: Rutgers University Press, 1997); Gina Marchetti, *Romance and the "Yellow Peril": Race, Sex, and Discursive Strategies in Hollywood Fiction* (Berkeley: University of California Press, 1993); and John King, Ana Lopez, and Manuel Alvarado, eds., *Mediating Two Worlds: Cinematic Encounters in the Americas* (London: British Film Institute Publishing, 1993).

26. Michelle Wallace, *Invisibility Blues* (London: Verso, 1990), 227.

27. Trinh T. Minh-ha, *When the Moon Waxes Red* (New York: Routledge, 1991), 185, summarizes her impossible position: "The story of otherness and marginality has recently become so central to theoretical discussion that it is difficult both to respond satisfactorily to the demand and to take on the dubious role of the Real Other to speak the 'truth' on otherness."

28. Mary Ann Doane, *Femmes Fatales: Feminism, Film Theory, Psychoanalysis* (New York: Routledge, 1991), chap. 11, "Dark Continents: Epistemologies of Racial and Sexual Difference in Psychoanalysis and the Cinema." See also Kaplan, *Looking for the Other*, 62.

29. Linda Gordon, "On 'Difference,'" *Genders* 10 (spring 1991): 91, dramatizes the gap between the now-established American academic feminism and the rest of the women in the United States in that "gains for academic women now coexist with one of the worst periods of immiseration for the urban and rural poor, particularly for African-Americans and Puerto Ricans, ever in U.S. history."

30. Derek Attridge, "Innovation, Literature, Ethics: Relating to the Other," *PMLA* 114, no. 1 (January 1999), 21, remarks that *"The other* is an overworked phrase in current academic discourse."

31. Mayne, *The Woman at the Keyhole*, 180–182. See Janet Staiger, *Interpreting Films: Studies in the Historical Reception of American Cinema* (Princeton: Princeton University Press, 1992), chap. 5.

32. Christian Metz, "The Imaginary Signifier," *Screen* 16, no. 2 (1975): 14–76.

33. Robert Stam, Robert Burgoyne, and Sandy Flitterman-Lewis, eds., *New Vocabularies in Film Semiotics: Structuralism, Post-structuralism, and Beyond* (London: Routledge, 1992), 167.

34. Burch, *Life to Those Shadows*, 249–250 (emphasis in the original).

35. See my *Contested Culture: the Image, the Voice, and the Law* (Chapel Hill, N.C.: University of North Carolina Press, 1991), 30–32, for a discussion of the problem of the concept of the "subject" as used across disciplines. The question as I phrased it was whether or not different discursive systems (cultural studies, legal studies) were assuming the same subject, in effect drawing from the same philosophical reservoir.

36. See Stuart Hall, ed., *Representation: Cultural Representations and Signifying Practices* (London: Sage, 1997), 56–61, for a practical demonstration of how the concept of the subject has been used to understand the ideological working of visual representation.

37. Jean-Paul Sartre, in *Being and Nothingness: An Essay on the Phenomenological Ontology*, trans. Hazel E. Barnes (New York: Pocket Books, 1956), 786–787, does, in fact, situate his concept in relation to the Platonic "other" within Plato's *The Sophist*.

38. G. W. F. Hegel, *Phenomenology of Spirit*, trans. A. V. Miller (1807; reprint, Oxford: Oxford University Press, 1977).

39. Judith Butler, *Subjects of Desire: Hegelian Reflections on Twentieth-Century France* (New York: Columbia University Press, 1987), 31, 44.

40. Ibid., 6.

41. Judith Butler, *Gender Trouble* (New York: Routledge, 1990). See also Judith Butler, *The Psychic Life of Power: Theories in Subjection* (Stanford: Stanford University Press, 1997), 34–37, in which she reads Hegel's *Phenomenology* in relation to scenarios of subjection.

42. This theory of the mutuality between master and slave would seem to reappear in Eugene Genovese's controversial argument about the mutual responsibilities of master and slave in *Roll, Jordan, Roll: The World the Slaves Made* (New York: Random House, 1976).

43. Albert Memmi, *The Colonizer and the Colonized*, trans. Howard Greenfeld (Boston: Beacon Press, 1967).

44. Butler, *Subjects of Desire*, 78. See Hegel, *Phenomenology of Spirit*, 117, on how servitude turns into its opposite.

45. Alexander Kojève, *Introduction to the Reading of Hegel*, trans. James H. Nichols, Jr. (Ithaca: Cornell University Press, 1969), 4.

46. Fredric Jameson, in "Third-World Literature in the Era of Multinational Capitalism," *Social Text* (fall 1986): 85, gives us one of the most colorful versions:

> Two equals struggle each for recognition by the other: the one is willing to sacrifice life for this supreme value. The other, a heroic coward in the Brechtian, Schweykian sense of loving the body and the material world too well, gives in, in order to continue life. The Master—now the fulfillment of a baleful and inhuman feudal-aristocratic disdain for life without honor—proceeds to enjoy the benefits of recognition by the other, now become his humble serf or slave. But at this point two distinct and dialectically ironic reversals take place: only the Master is now genuinely human, so that "recognition" by this henceforth sub-human form of life which is the slave evaporates at the moment of its attainment and offers no genuine satisfaction.

47. Hegel, *Phenomenology of Spirit*, 111.

48. Edward Said, *Orientalism* (New York: Pantheon Books, 1978).

49. Sartre, *Being and Nothingness*. For Sartre's critique of Hegel, see 320–324, 331.

50. Ibid., 482.

51. Sartre, ibid., 515, almost seems to define desire for heterosexual intercourse as the epitome of desire, but then he takes this back, opting instead for the pleasure of deferral: "But the full pressing together of the flesh of two people against one another is the true goal of desire. Nevertheless desire is itself doomed to failure. As we have seen, coitus, which ordinarily terminates desire, is not its essential goal. . . . But pleasure is the death and the failure of desire. It is the death of desire because it is not only its fulfillment but its limit and its end."

52. See Fredric Jameson, "Imaginary and Symbolic in Lacan: Marxism, Psychoanalytic Criticism, and the Problem of the Subject," *Yale French Studies*, no. 55/56 (1977): 379, on the way the Hegelian paradigm has been extended through *Being and Nothingness* to Fanon where it contributes to the development of the "psychopathology of the colonized and the colonial order."

53. Mikkel Borch-Jacobsen, in *Lacan: The Absolute Master*, trans. Douglas Brick (Stanford: Stanford University Press, 1991), 4, recommends *Introduction to the Reading of Hegel* as the starting point for understanding Lacan, and notes that Alexander Kojève was the only "master" Lacan ever acknowledged.

54. Gayatri Spivak, "Translator's Preface," *Of Grammatology* (Baltimore: Johns Hopkins Press, 1974), lxviii.

55. Metz, "The Imaginary Signifier," 19.

56. Gilles Deleuze and Félix Guattari, in "Balance Sheet—Program for Desiring-Machines," *Semiotext(e)* 2, no. 3 (1977): 117, refer to the complementary controls of the "foreign market of capitalism" and the "home market of psychoanalysis." That they are thinking specifically of cinema at several points in this essay is made clear by the references to Buster Keaton, "one of the greatest artists of desiring-machines" (p. 130), whose vision of the electric house gone haywire in *The Scarecrow* (1920) epitomizes their vision of gadget and fantasy under the influence of capital and the oedipal (p. 120). A more comprehensive introduction to their concept of the "desiring-machine" can be found in Gilles Deleuze and Félix Guattari, *Anti-Oedipus: Capitalism and Schizophrenia*, trans. Robert Hurley, Mark Seem, and Helen R. Lane (Minneapolis: University of Minnesota Press, 1983), part I.

57. Metz, "The Imaginary Signifier," 54.

58. See Stam et al., *New Vocabularies in Film Semiotics*, 160.

59. Metz, "The Imaginary Signifier," 60.

60. Elizabeth Cowie, *Representing the Woman: Cinema and Psychoanalysis* (Minneapolis: University of Minnesota Press, 1997), 99. Linda Williams, in *Hard Core: Power, Pleasure, the "Frenzy of the Visible"* (Berkeley: University of California Press, 1989), 44, explains the "imaginary signifier" as a reference to the "paradoxical combination of the illusion of reality with the radical absence of the object represented."

61. Metz, "The Imaginary Signifier," 75.

62. The articles that deal with some aspect of voyeurism in cinema are too numerous to list. But it is interesting to note the number of books on feminist film theory with "desire" in the title: Sandy Flitterman-Lewis, *To Desire Differently* (Urbana-Champaign: University of Illinois Press, 1990); Mary Ann Doane, *The Desire to Desire* (Bloomington: Indiana University Press, 1987); Joan Copjec, *Read My Desire* (Cambridge, Mass.: MIT Press, 1994).

63. Metz, "The Imaginary Signifier," 61.

64. Ibid., 62.

65. Orgasm, conspicuously missing in Laura Mulvey's account of voyeurism, figures at this point in Metz, who gives us a modified version of the popular Freudian account of the function of sexual arousal in relation to the "looking drive." The gap between subject and object *could* be filled, but this is threatening to the subject and finally the subject retreats into fantasy where orgasm is the "suppression of the gap," yet another move that serves to postpone satisfaction or gratification. Mulvey, "Visual Pleasure and Narrative Cinema," *Screen* 16, no. 3 (autumn 1975): 61.

66. Teresa de Lauretis, "Film and the Visible," in *How Do I Look? Queer Film and Video*, ed. Bad Object-Choices (Seattle: Bay Press, 1991), 253.

67. The exception is feminist work on pornography. See, for example, Williams, *Hard Core*; Laura Kipnis, *Bound and Gagged: Pornography and the Politics of Fantasy in America* (Durham: Duke University Press, 1999).

68. Linda Williams, "Corporealized Observers: Visual Pornographies and the 'Carnal Density of Vision,'" in *Fugitive Images: From Photography to Video*, ed. Patrice Petro (Bloomington: Indiana University Press, 1995), 14.

69. A particularly dramatic example of this proliferation is Catherine A. Lutz and Jane L. Collins, *Reading National Geographic* (Chicago: University of Chicago Press, 1993), chap. 7, titled "The Photograph as an Intersection of Gazes." For an extremely provocative analysis of the intersecting gazes of the photographic subject and the viewer, see Alan Trachtenberg, *Reading American Photographs: Images as History, Matthew Brady to Walker Evans* (New York: Hill and Wang, 1989), 53–60. Trachtenberg analyzes the photographs of African-born slave subjects taken in 1850 by J. T. Zealy in Columbia, South Carolina, for the use of Harvard scientist Louis Agassiz. The photographs were found at Harvard in 1976 at the Peabody Museum where they had been stored. Trachtenberg analyzes the photographs, drawing on the master–slave dialectic, in terms of the impossibility of reciprocity.

70. See Bob Stam and Ella Shohat, *Unthinking Eurocentrism: Multiculturalism and the Media* (New York: Routledge, 1994), 322–333. Important early thinking on the relation between cultural dominance and looking can be found in Ella Shohat, "Gender and the Culture of Empire," *Quarterly Review of Film and Video* 131, nos. 1–2 (spring 1991): 45–84, and Ella Shohat, "Imaging Terra Incognita: The Disciplinary Gaze of Empire," *Public Culture* 3, no. 2 (spring 1991): 41–70. Drawing on

this work, Ann Kaplan has productively refined her concept of the "male gaze" to suggest that it "intersects with the imperial gaze." E. Ann Kaplan, *Looking for the Other: Feminism, Film, and the Imperial Gaze* (New York: Routledge, 1997).

71. See Mulvey, "Visual Pleasure and Narrative Cinema," 6–18. By my count, Mulvey only uses the word "gaze" four times in this essay: the "controlling and curious gaze" (p. 8); the "male gaze" (p. 11); Hitchcock's "uneasy gaze" and "cinematic codes create a gaze, a world, an object" (p. 17). This would lead us to the conclusion that the concept was developed by others in subsequent work. See E. Ann Kaplan, *Women and Film: Both Sides of the Camera* (London: Routledge, 1983), chap. 1, "Is the Gaze Male?"

72. Jacques Lacan, *The Four Fundamental Concepts of Psycho-Analysis,* trans. Alan Sheridan, ed. Jacques-Alain Miller (London: The Hogarth Press and the Institute of Psychoanalysis, 1977), 75, 77. In the same essay Lacan is impressed and fascinated by experiments in perception reported in Merleau-Ponty, his fascination producing a phenomenological detour that leads him to also suppose that the gaze is an instrument or a medium of light (p. 106).

73. Kaja Silverman, *The Threshold of the Visible World* (New York: Routledge, 1996), 167, suggests that Alan Sheridan's translation of Lacan's *Four Fundamental Concepts* uses "the gaze" for *le regard* consistently as a strategy to get around any attempt to connect the concept too narrowly to seeing. The dilemma arises, as she explains, because where there is only one word in French for vision, *le regard,* in English one might use "look" or "gaze."

74. Lacan, *Four Fundamental Concepts,* 73, 78.

75. Ibid., 73.

76. Copjec, *Read My Desire,* 35.

77. Sartre, *Being and Nothingness,* 363.

78. Ibid., 475, 529.

79. Silverman, *Threshold of the Visible World,* 166. In one of the few extensive discussions of the relationship between Sartre's theorization and Lacan's, Silverman finds Lacan preferable, judging Sartre's formulation too "anthropomorphically inflected" as well as too "personalistic." She goes on in her analysis: "although his insistence upon the eye's embodiment and specularity is of inestimable value to all feminist attempts to divest the male look of its false claim to be the gaze, Sartre reduces that organ to the status of a lackey or slave, devoid of power."

80. Fredric Jameson, *Marxism and Form: Twentieth-Century Dialectical Theories of Literature* (Princeton: Princeton University Press, 1971), 301.

81. Stuart Hall, David Held, and Tony McGrew, eds., *Modernity and its Futures* (London: Polity Press, 1992), 288. Making this more clear in their introduction, the editors say: "Meaning arises in the relations of similarity and difference which words have to other words within the language code. We know what 'night' is because it is *not* 'day.'"

82. Claudia Tate, *Psychoanalysis and Black Novels* (New York: Oxford Univer-

sity Press, 1998), 16. She goes on: "psychoanalytic practice relegates the bleak material circumstances of real lives to the background and blames the dysfunction on personal or familial deficiency. No wonder scholars of African American literature and culture shun this model and instead enforce materialist analyses of black novels, for mainstream psychoanalysis effaces racism and recasts its effects as a personality disorder caused by familial rather than social pathology."

83. See Elizabeth Abel, Barbara Christian, and Helene Moglen, eds., *Female Subjects in Black and White* (Berkeley: University of California Press, 1997). In their introduction to their collection based on a 1992 conference on Psychoanalysis in African American Contexts, the editors present the essays from the conference as "a series of dialogues rather than reconciliations, between feminist psychoanalysis and African American representations of female subjectivity" (p. 1). Later they ask: "Does psychoanalytic criticism, rarely practiced by black feminists, entail conscription to dominant cultural discourses?" (p. 3). Kaplan, *Looking for the Other*, 128, in her consideration of the productive uses of psychoanalysis as an approach to understanding the constitution of raced as well as gendered subjectivity, concludes, "I do not think psychoanalytic theory is yet equipped to answer this question definitely." E. Ann Kaplan, in "The Couch-Affair: Gender, Race and the Hollywood Transference," *American Imago* (winter 1993): 481–514, presents a strong case for the compatability between psychoanalysis and questions of raced identity and suggests some of the rich theoretical possibilities.

84. Noël Carroll, "Prospects for Film Theory: A Personal Assessment," in *Post-Theory: Reconstructing Film Studies,* ed. David Bordwell and Noël Carroll (Madison: University of Wisconsin Press, 1996), 61–66, presents a lively case for the use of cognitive theory as opposed to psychoanalytic theory in film studies, ending his list of what's wrong with psychoanalysis with the charge that psychoanalytic theorists are "confecting theories, but with no empirical constraints" (p. 66).

85. Mary Ann Doane, *Femmes Fatales: Feminism, Film Theory, Psychoanalysis* (New York: Routledge, 1991), 211.

86. Ibid. Doane quotes Freud's "The Question of Lay Analysis: Conversations with an Impartial Person," in which she has also discovered his reference to woman as the "dark continent": Among races at a low level of civilization, and among the lower strata of civilized races, the sexuality of children seems to be given free rein. This probably provides a powerful protection against the subsequent development of neuroses in the individual. But does it not at the same time involve an extraordinary loss of the aptitude for cultural achievements?" *The Standard Edition of the Complete Psychological Works of Sigmund Freud,* vol. 20, trans. and ed. James Strachey (London: Hogarth Press, 1953), 212.

87. Elizabeth Abel, "Race, Class and Psychoanalysis? Opening Questions," in *Conflicts in Feminism,* ed. Marianne Hirsch and Evelyn Fox Keller (New York: Routledge, 1990), 189. See also Hortense J. Spillers, "Changing the Letter:

The Yokes, The Jokes of Discourse, or, Mrs. Stowe, Mr. Reed," in *Slavery and the Literary Imagination*, ed. Deborah E. McDowell and Arnold Rampersad (Baltimore: Johns Hopkins University Press, 1989), 25–61.

88. Lillian Smith, *Killers of the Dream* (1949; reprint, New York: W. W. Norton, 1961), 131.

89. Hortense J. Spillers, "Mama's Baby, Papa's Maybe: An American Grammar Book," *Diacritics* 17, no. 2 (summer 1987): 77.

90. Harriet A. Jacobs, *Incidents in the Life of a Slave Girl* (Cambridge: Harvard University Press, 1987).

91. Melton A. McLaurin, *Celia, A Slave* (New York: Avon, 1993).

92. Deleuze and Guattari, *Anti-Oedipus*, 170.

93. Kwame Anthony Appiah, *In My Father's House: Africa in the Philosophy of Culture* (New York: Oxford University Press, 1992), 56.

94. Homi Bhabha, "What Does the Black Man Want?" *New Formations* 1 (spring 1987): 118–124; Henry Louis Gates, Jr., "Critical Fanonism," *Critical Inquiry* 17, no. 3 (spring 1991): 457–470. For more discussion of this point, see my "Who Is Reading Robert Mapplethorpe's Black Book?" *New Formations* 16 (summer 1992): 24–39.

95. Diana Fuss, *Identification Papers* (New York: Routledge, 1995), 157.

96. Doane, *Femmes Fatales*, 222.

97. Frantz Fanon, *Black Skin, White Masks* (New York: Grove Press, 1967), 156. Doane, *Femmes Fatales*, 221, is admirably restrained: "This analysis clearly rests on a serious confusion between rape and sex with which feminists of any color might take issue."

98. Hortense Spillers, "All the Things You Could Be by Now, If Sigmund Freud's Wife Was Your Mother: Psychoanalysis and Race," in Abel et al., eds., *Female Subjects in Black and White*, 135. A longer version has been published in *boundary* 2 (fall 1996): 75–141, and a portion of that essay in *Critical Inquiry* 22 (summer 1996): 712–734.

99. Ibid., 139, 140.

100. Ibid., 140.

101. Ibid., 138.

102. This question continues to arise in feminist film theory. Kaplan, *Looking for the Other*, 295, has expressed concern about my argument that psychoanalysis is unequipped to deal with questions of race. I would slightly revise this earlier argument to the effect that there is no area of human interest that psychoanalysis cannot be made to say something significant about. If white feminists in their development of film theory dealt with questions of gender to the exclusion of race, this had to do with a number of factors, not the least of which was the current vogue of those questions in intellectual circles in the 1970s. To hold psychoanalysis accountable for "not seeing" race is really to ask about the political and intellectual climate, particularly in Europe and England, during those years that were so formative in the development of psychoanalytic film theory, to call attention to what had become an exclusive approach to film. See

my "White Privilege and Looking Relations: Race and Gender in Feminist Film Theory," *Cultural Critique* no. 4 (1986): 59–79, revised and reprinted in *Screen* 29, no. 4 (autumn 1988): 12–27, reprinted in *Visual Culture: The Reader,* ed. Jessica Evans and Stuart Hall (London: Sage, 1999), and in Joanne Hollows, Mark Jancovich, and Peter Hutchings, *Film Studies: A Reader* (London: Arnold, 1999).

103. Georg Wilhelm Friedrich Hegel, *Lectures on the Philosophy of History,* trans. J. Sibree from third German ed. (London: G. Bell & Sons, 1894), 103.

104. Ibid., 99, 100, 103. Charles T. Davis and Henry Louis Gates, Jr., in "Introduction," *The Slave's Narrative* (Oxford: Oxford University Press, 1985), xxvii, identify Hegel along with Kant and Hume as a purveyor of the idea that Africa had no history. In Hegel's pronouncement, "civilization" can be substituted for "history": "What we properly understand by Africa, is the Unhistorical, Undeveloped Spirit, still involved in the conditions of mere nature, and which had to be presented here only as on the threshold of the World's History" (p. 103).

105. David Brion Davis, *The Problem of Slavery in the Age of Revolution, 1770–1823* (Ithaca: Cornell University Press, 1975), 564, concludes his book with the observation that "[i]t was Hegel's genius to endow lordship and bondage with such a rich resonance of meanings that the model could be applied to every form of physical and psychological domination."

106. Paul Gilroy, *Black Atlantic: Modernity and Double Consciousness* (Cambridge: Harvard University Press, 1993), 54.

107. Ibid., 50.

108. As Robert Young, *White Mythololologies: Writing History and the West* (New York: Routledge, 1990), 3, puts it, the problem is always with the dialectic itself:

> The real difficulty has always been to find an alternative to the Hegelian dialectic—difficult because strictly speaking it is impossible, insofar as the operation of the dialectic already includes its negation. You cannot get out of Hegel by simply contradicting him, any more than you can get out of those other Hegelian systems, Marxism and psychoanalysis, by simply opposing them: for in both your opposition is likewise always recuperable, as the workings of ideology or psychic resistance.

Others might disagree with him about Marxism, which, it could be argued, is a Hegelian system that broke with Hegel; also, the difficulties in getting outside of it have to do with its attempt to account for everything.

109. Fanon, *Black Skin, White Masks,* 161.

110. Homi Bhabha, in "What Does the Black Man Want?" *New Formations* 1 (spring 1987): 123–124, one of the essays that helped put the reconsideration of Fanon on the map, pulls the two together with this quotation from Lacan's *Four Fundamental Concepts:* "In the case of display . . . the play of combat in the form

of intimidation, the being gives of himself, or receives from the other, something that is like a mask, a double, an envelope, a thrown-off skin, thrown off in order to cover the frame of a shield. It is through this separated form of himself that the being comes into play in his effects of life and death."

111. Metz, "The Imaginary Signifier," 28. It is also interesting to recall that at this same point in the essay Metz expresses the opinion that psychoanalysis will always need to be used in conjunction with other discourses such as linguistics.

112. See Stam et al., eds., *New Vocabularies in Film Semiotics,* 139.

113. For a tough critique of the use of the concept of subject position as well as the argument that in film theory "all of the processes of representation" are "lumped" under identification as a concept, see David Bordwell, "Contemporary Film Studies and the Vicissitudes of Grand Theory," in Bordwell and Carroll, eds., *Post-Theory,* 17. This is not to say that there haven't been some important attempts to set out a theory of identification that was not psychoanalytic. Richard Dyer's *Stars,* 2d ed. (London: British Film Institute, 1998), 96–97, 125, contains the seeds of an important theorization. Jackie Stacey, *Star Gazing: Hollywood Cinema and Female Spectatorship* (London: Routledge, 1994), 170–175, contains an excellent critique of cinematic identification to date. She also makes important distinctions between cinematic and "extra-cinematic" identification, the fan's use of the star identity outside of the film viewing experience (p. 171).

114. Manthia Diawara, "Black Spectatorship: Problems of Identification and Resistance," *Screen* 29, no. 4 (1988): 68, reprinted in *Black American Cinema,* ed. Manthia Diawara (New York: Routledge / American Film Institute, 1993).

115. bell hooks, "The Oppositional Gaze: Black Female Spectators," in Diawara, ed., ibid., 293.

116. Sigmund Freud, "New Introductory Lectures on Psycho-Analysis" (1933), in *The Standard Edition of the Complete Psychological Works,* vol. 22, at 63.

117. However, Charles Affron, in "Identifications," in *Imitations of Life: A Reader in Film and Television Melodrama,* ed. Marcia Landy (Detroit: Wayne State University Press, 1991), 102, takes the remark "I liked it because I identified with the characters" and does more with it than I imagined possible.

118. In Lacanian psychoanalysis the child's mirror recognition is a "misrecognition" because of the disjuncture between the way the child imagines his perfect mirror image to be and the way he actually is at this stage of development. Mary Ann Doane, in "Misrecognition and Identity," *Cine-tracts* 3, no. 3 (fall 1980): 28, suggests that "misrecognition" is also a basic paradigm for cinema spectatorship; in classical narrative, confusion between the screen fiction and reality is a "misrecognition."

119. The reader will wonder why I have not emphasized characters more. Perhaps this is an attempt to shift the focus away from the more traditional approach, working our way through questions of space and relationality, of eyes

and ears and bodies. In this regard, one of the most provocative theorizations of the space of spectatorial identification is still Jean Mitry's:

> thanks to the mobility of the camera, to the multiplicity of shots, I am everywhere at once. . . . I *know* that I am in the movie theatre, but *feel* that I am in the world offered to my gaze, a world that I experience "physically" while identifying myself with one or another of the characters in the drama— with all of them, alternatively. This finally means that at the movies I am both *in* this action and *outside* it, *in this space and outside of this space.* Having the gift of ubiquity, I am everywhere and nowhere.

Esthétique et psychologie du cinéma: I. Les structures, trans. Charles Affron, in Affron, "Identifications," 104.

120. Elizabeth Cowie, *Representing the Woman,* 75. Cowie further argues that Metz's distinction between primary and secondary identification is not compatible with generally accepted psychoanalytic notions of primary and secondary identification. She suggests a shift from psychological identity construction to fantasy and the many positions it offers (p. 102). See also Jacques Aumont, *The Image,* trans. Claire Pajackowska (London: British Film Institute, 1997), 81–82.

121. Cowie, *Representing the Woman,* 105, also states what we assume would be the case—that the full face in close-up "invokes identification."

122. Gilles Deleuze and Félix Guattari, *A Thousand Plateaus: Capitalism & Schizophrenia,* trans. Brian Massumi (Minneapolis: University of Minnesota Press, 1987), chap. 7, "Year Zero: Faciality." See also Gilles Deleuze, *Cinema 1: The Movement-Image,* trans. Hugh Tomlinson and Barbara Habberjam (Minneapolis: University of Minnesota Press, 1986), 88.

123. Anne Friedberg, "The Denial of Difference: Theories of Cinematic Identification," in *Psychoanalysis and Cinema,* ed. E. Ann Kaplan (New York: Routledge, 1990), 36, 40.

124. This is, of course, the disavowal of Freud's boy child, a child so traumatized by the difference between his having and his mother's not having that he must deny what he sees.

125. Jacqueline Rose, *Sexuality in the Field of Vision* (London: Verso, 1986), 202, has significantly challenged the use of the concept of disavowal in Metz ("The Imaginary Signifier") as well as in Jean-Louis Comolli. See Comolli, "Machines of the Visible," in *The Cinematic Apparatus,* ed. Teresa de Lauretis and Stephen Heath (New York: St. Martin's Press, 1980), 121–142. The problem as she defines it is in Metz's insistence on a dependence on the concept as referring only to things at the perceptual level. "The paradox is that the instance of disavowal only has meaning in relation to the question of sexual difference but is used within the theory only in relation to the act of perception itself." In other words, she is objecting to the divorce of the concept of disavowal from the original Freudian scenario of the denial of castration with its concomitant implica-

tions for a theory of sexual difference as well as a theory of the function of the unconscious.

126. Michèle Barrett identifies Difference I, II, and II, probably irreconcilable positions in feminism, in "The Concept of 'Difference,'" *Feminist Review* no. 26 (1987): 29–41.

127. Hall, ed., *Representation*, 238. For another critique, see Hazel V. Carby, "The Multicultural Wars," in *Black Popular Culture*, ed. Gina Dent (Seattle: Bay Press, 1991), who argues that the "paradigm of difference is obsessed with the construction of identities rather than relations of power and domination and in practice concentrates on the effect of this difference on a (white) norm."

128. Barbara Johnson, "Thresholds of Difference: Structures of Address in Zora Neale Hurston," in *"Race," Writing, and Difference*, ed. Henry Louis Gates, Jr. (Chicago: University of Chicago Press, 1985) 323.

129. Butler, *Subjects of Desire*, 9.

130. C. L. R. James, *Notes on Dialectics: Hegel and Marxism* (Detroit: Friends of Facing Reality Publications, 1966), 85.

131. Ernst Bloch, *The Principle of Hope*, vol. 1, trans. Neville Plaice, Stephen Plaice, and Paul Knight (Oxford: Basil Blackwell, 1986), 412.

132. Rosalind Coward, *Female Desire: Women's Sexuality Today* (London: Granada Publishing, 1985), 95, 96. For further on the kiss, see Virginia Wexman, *Creating the Couple: Love, Marriage and Hollywood Performance* (Princeton: Princeton University Press, 1993).

133. Some will recognize the reference to Erica Jong, *Fear of Flying* (New York: Rinehardt and Winston, 1973), which made this rather improbable idea popular.

134. Musser, *The Emergence of Cinema*, 118, describes how the short film, taken from a scene in the popular musical comedy, *The Widow Jones*, was the Edison company's most popular film that year. See "The Anatomy of a Kiss," *New York Herald*, 24 April 1896, 11, reprinted in Charles Musser, *Edison Motion Pictures, 1890–1900* (Washington, D.C.: Smithsonian Institution Press, 1997), 197–201.

135. bell hooks, *Black Looks* (Boston: South End Press, 1992), 24, 25.

136. Ibid., 38.

Chapter Three

1. Hayden White, *The Content of the Form: Narrative Discourse and Historical Representation* (Baltimore: Johns Hopkins University Press, 1987), 57.

2. Ibid., 21.

3. See "The Real Returns," my introduction to *Collecting Visible Evidence*, ed. Jane Gaines and Michael Renov (Minneapolis: University of Minnesota Press, 1999), in which I further discuss the theoretical dilemma for documentary film and video of the retrieval of a highly problematic "reality" thought to be before the camera.

4. For more on the press and public fascination with black films "lost and found," see Pearl Bowser and Jane Gaines, "New Finds/Old Films," *Black Film Review* 7, no. 4 (1992): 2–5.

5. White, *The Content of the Form,* 21.

6. White, ibid., 10, uses the metaphors so often employed to discuss classical editing techniques in both film theory and film practice:

> Every narrative, however seemingly "full," is constructed on the basis of a set of events that might have been included but were left out; this is as true of imaginary narratives as it is of realistic ones. And this consideration permits us to ask what kind of notion of reality authorizes construction of a narrative account of reality in which continuity rather than discontinuity governs the articulation of the discourse.

7. Ibid., 5.

8. Here I am indebted to Charlene Regester, "The African American Press and Race Movies," in *Oscar Micheaux and His Circle: African American Filmmaking and Race Cinema of the Silent Era,* ed. Pearl Bowser, Jane Gaines, and Charles Musser (Pordenone-Sacile, Italy: Giornate del Cinema Muto, forthcoming).

9. There is every indication that the many African Americans who had the experience of going to race movies kept the memory alive. Further, those who have more recently viewed race movies from the 1930s on BET (Black Entertainment Television) have been intrigued and impressed. Much more research needs to be done on the way black communities have kept such specialized histories alive.

10. The two most detailed histories have since been reprinted. See Henry T. Sampson, *Blacks in Black and White: A Source Book on Black Films,* 2d ed. (1977; Metuchen, N.J.: Scarecrow, 1995); Thomas Cripps, *Slow Fade to Black: The Negro in American Film 1900–1942,* 2d ed. (1977; New York: Oxford University Press, 1993). Three excellent reference works should encourage future scholarship: Alan Gevinson, ed., *Within Our Gates: Ethnicity in American Feature Films, 1911–1960* (Berkeley: University of California Press, 1997); Phyllis R. Klotman, *Frame by Frame: A Black Filmography* (Bloomington: Indiana University Press, 1979), and *Frame by Frame II: A Filmography of the African American Image, 1978–1994* (Bloomington: Indiana University Press, 1997). See also the appendix in Bowser, Gaines, and Musser, eds., *Oscar Micheaux and His Circle.*

11. Bill Nichols, *Representing Reality: Issues and Concepts in Documentary Film* (Bloomington: Indiana University Press, 1991), 17.

12. Cripps, *Slow Fade to Black,* 79–80. Cripps also says that Foster "began in 1912" and that he tried to raise funds from the NAACP in 1929 after moving to Los Angeles (p. 179). Sampson, *Blacks in Black and White,* says that Stepin Fetchit starred in the musical shorts that Foster produced there (p. 176). According to Cripps, Pathé hired Foster to produce a series with vaudevillians Buck and Bubbles (p. 224). See Mark A. Reid, *Redefining Black Film* (Berkeley: University of California Press, 1993), 7–9.

13. Sampson, *Blacks in Black and White*, 172–176, dates the production of *The Railroad Porter* as 1913. Cripps confirms that Foster was a sportswriter for the *Chicago Defender* and says that Juli Jones was the name he used as an actor. At some point he went into the sheet music business and even sold Haitian coffee. *Slow Fade to Black*, 79–80.

14. *The Indianapolis Freeman*, 20 December 1913, as quoted in Sampson, *Blacks in Black and White*, 174.

15. Sampson, ibid., 174–175.

16. See Cripps, chap. 10, "Black Music, White Movies," in *Slow Fade to Black*, and Arthur Knight, chap. 4, "Black Folk Sold: Hollywood's Black Cast Musicals," in *Dis-integrating the Musical: African American Musical Performance and American Musical Film, 1927–1959* (Durham: Duke University Press, forthcoming).

17. One of the strongest statements of this is Clyde Taylor, "Crossed Over and Can't Get Black: The Crisis of 1937–39," *Black Film Review* 7, no. 4 (1993): 22–27.

18. Sampson, *Blacks in Black and White*, 181.

19. Ibid., 208.

20. Cripps, *Slow Fade to Black*, 72–75; Thomas Cripps, "*The Birth of a Race* Company: An Early Stride toward a Black Cinema," *Journal of Negro History* (January 1974): 28–37; Thomas Cripps, "*The Birth of a Race*: A Lost Film Rediscovered in Texas," *Texas Humanist* (March / April 1983): 10–11.

21. Cripps, *Slow Fade to Black*, 71; Thomas Cripps, "The Making of *The Birth of a Race*: The Emerging Politics of Identity in Silent Movies," in *The Birth of Whiteness: Race and the Emergence of U.S. Cinema*, ed. Daniel Bernardi (New Brunswick, N.J.: Rutgers University Press, 1996).

22. Cripps, *Slow Fade to Black*, 68–69; *Crisis* (November 1915): 36; *Crisis* (December 1915): 76–77.

23. Sampson, *Blacks in Black and White*, 182.

24. The Library of Congress has incomplete prints of *The Birth of a Race* in both 16mm and 35mm. Six of the original twelve reels can be viewed at the Motion Picture, Broadcasting, and Recorded Sound Division Archive in Washington, D.C. For more on the Library of Congress holdings in African American film history, see *The African American Mosaic* (Washington, D.C.: The Library of Congress, 1993), 205–211. See also Klotman, *Frame by Frame*, 48.

25. See Sampson, *Blacks in Black and White*, chap. 5, for the most comprehensive and well-organized overview of these companies, although the thumbnail sketches here should be considered invitations to further research.

26. "Noble Johnson," typescript (available on microfilm) in George P. Johnson Collection, Department of Special Collections, Young Research Library, University of California, Los Angeles, hereafter GPJC. The typescript written by Noble's brother George refers to the injury of one of the actors during the filming of *The Eagle's Nest* (1914). Noble Johnson applied for the part and was hired to play an Indian. More recently, Cecilia Rasmussen, in "Brothers Became Film

Pioneers," *Los Angeles Times,* 13 September 1998, explains Noble's career break as the consequence of the help of Lon Chaney, a former classmate in Colorado Springs. Although the typescript biography mentions that Lon Chaney and Noble Johnson attended the same school, Romaine Fielding and the Lubin Company are credited with Noble's start in the business. The Lubin Company, founded in Philadelphia in 1897, also had a company of actors it employed for all-black-cast productions, but these films were exceedingly insulting to blacks. See Sampson, *Blacks in Black and White,* 28.

27. Noble Johnson went on to costar in such Universal films as *The Lure of the Circus* (1919) and *The Adventures of Robinson Crusoe* (1922, in which he played Friday), as well as in the popular serial *The Bull's Eye* (1918). In later years, after the advent of sound and until 1950, Johnson appeared in about 150 film productions. "Noble Johnson's Entrance into Films," typescript in GPJC; Cripps, *Slow Fade to Black,* 130–131; Sampson, *Blacks in Black and White,* 529–533. On the question of D. W. Griffith's casting, Clyde Taylor, in *The Mask of Art: Breaking the Aesthetic Contract—Film and Literature* (Bloomington: Indiana University Press, 1998), 114, reminds us that the director's excuse for using whites in the roles of blacks in *The Birth of a Nation* (1915) was that he couldn't find "qualified Negro performers" in the Los Angeles area.

28. Jesse Rhines, *Black Film/White Money* (New Brunswick, N.J.: Rutgers University Press, 1996), 23. For a short history of the Lincoln Motion Picture Company, see Sampson, *Blacks in Black and White,* chap. 3, especially on the resignation of Noble Johnson, 132–138; Cripps, *Slow Fade to Black,* 75–89. James Snead, in *White Screens, Black Images* (New York: Routledge, 1994), 111, notes that William Foster and Noble Johnson both left their own companies for Hollywood, an early example of career "crossover" before the phenomenon became as widespread as it is today.

29. "Minutes," Lincoln Motion Picture Company, Inc., 22 April 1919, and Noble Johnson contract excerpt, both in GPJC. See my *Contested Culture: The Image, the Voice, and the Law* (Chapel Hill: University of North Carolina Press, 1991), chap. 5, on star contracts.

30. Sampson, *Blacks in Black and White,* 138, 140.

31. Muskogee, Oklahoma flyer in GPJC.

32. Sampson, *Blacks in Black and White,* 172.

33. Ironically, during a short window of time from Reconstruction until the 1920s, segregation created opportunities for black capital. See Robert H. Kinzer and Edward Sagarin, *The Negro in American Business: The Conflict between Separation and Integration* (New York: Greenberg, 1950); John Sibley Butler, *Entrepreneurship and Self-Help among Black Americans* (New York: State University of New York Press, 1991); Manning Marable, *How Capitalism Underdeveloped Black America* (Cambridge, Mass.: South End Press, 1983). Dan Streible, in "The Harlem Theater: Black Film Exhibition in Austin, Texas: 1920–1973," in *Black American Cinema,* ed. Manthia Diawara (New York: Routledge, 1993), 232, discusses the way in which the Harlem Theatre was a "creation of segregation."

34. For an account of the difficulties these early black theaters had staying in business in Lexington, Kentucky, between 1907 and 1916, and especially the way they were plagued by white competition, see Gregory A. Waller, *Main Street Amusements: Movies and Commercial Entertainment in a Southern City, 1896–1930* (Washington, D.C.: Smithsonian Institution Press, 1995), chap. 7.

35. On vertical integration, see Tino Balio, ed., *The American Film Industry* (Madison: University of Wisconsin Press, 1985).

36. Mary Carbine, in " 'The Finest outside the Loop': Motion Picture Exhibition in Chicago's Black Metropolis, 1905–1928," in *Silent Film*, ed. Richard Abel (New Brunswick, N.J.: Rutgers University Press, 1996), 242, says that "[d]espite the support for black ownership of theaters in the press, the majority of theaters in the community were owned and operated—through not necessarily staffed—by whites." See Cripps, *Slow Fade to Black*, 80, on the Lincoln Company survey, which he calls "an imaginative tactic" that "outstripped white Hollywood in its search for a profile of its audience."

37. Palace Theatre to George P. Johnson, 31 May 1919, in GPJC.

38. Cripps, *Slow Fade to Black*, 80, 87. Thomas Cripps, in "Movies in the Ghetto, B.P. (Before Poitier)," *Negro Digest* (February 1969): 24, says that by the end of the 1920s it was estimated that there were over 700 ghetto theaters in the United States. Cripps adds that the growth was such that in 1927 the addition of three new movie houses in Chicago added a total of 8,000 seats. Contrast this figure with Richard J. Norman's estimates in 1921 and 1922. He writes in 1922 that "[t]here are about 354 Negro theatres in the United States (many now closed) scattered over 28 states. Eighty five percent of these theatres [showing race films] have an average seating capacity of but 250. We have been able to do business with 86 of these 354 theatres, a condition due to opposition and petty jealousy among the negro theatres." Matthew Bernstein and Dana F. White, " 'Scratching Around' in a 'Fit of Insanity': The Norman Film Manufacturing Company and the Race Movie Business in the 1920s," *Griffithiana* 62/63 (1998): 103. A year earlier Norman wrote to black actress Anita Bush that "[t]here are only 121 theatres that can use an exclusive colored product and 84% of these theatres have a small [250] seating capacity and many are closed at present." Bernstein and White, ibid., 123, note 57.

39. Sampson, *Blacks in Black and White*, 141.

40. Ibid.

41. Ibid., George P. Johnson biography, typescript in GPJC.

42. Cripps, *Slow Fade to Black*, 178.

43. For further on the Norman Company, see Gloria Gibson-Hudson, "The Norman Film Manufacturing Company," *Black Film Review* 7, no. 4 (1992): 16–20; Phyllis Klotman, "Planes, Trains, and Automobiles: *The Flying Ace*, the Norman Company and the Micheaux Connection," in Bowser, Gaines, and Musser, eds., *Oscar Micheaux and His Circle*; Bernstein and White, "Scratching Around," 81–127; Sampson, *Blacks in Black and White*, 215–217.

44. The exception to this pattern was Ebony Pictures where Luther J.

Pollard was both a spokesman and a film director and the only black in a white company that produced comedies that so offended the race movie audience that black theaters often refused to book its films. Sampson, *Blacks in Black and White*, 200, 204. Cripps, in *Slow Fade to Black*, calls Pollard the "black boss" and contrasts him with the "honest hustler" William Foster. On Reol, see Sampson, *Blacks in Black and White*, 214–215.

45. The two other films that Sampson lists as produced by the Colored Players of Philadelphia are *A Prince of His Race* (1926) and *Children of Fate* (1928).

46. Cripps, *Slow Fade to Black*, 195–198; Thomas Cripps, *Black Film as Genre* (Bloomington: Indiana University Press, 1978), 67; Stephen Zito, "The Black Film Experience," *American Film Heritage: Impressions from the American Film Institute Archives*, ed. Tom Shales and Kevin Brownlow et al. (Washington, D.C.: Acropolis Books, 1972), 65. In " 'Race Movies' as Voices of the Black Bourgeoisie: *The Scar of Shame*," in *Representing Blackness: Issues in Black Film and Video*, ed. Valerie Smith (New Brunswick, N.J.: Rutgers University Press, 1997), 54, Cripps describes Starkman as a "little Napoleon" who financed the Colored Players productions by selling his own theater and also by using his wife's inheritance as well as capital raised from South Philadelphia lawyers and hardware merchants. Cripps adds that Starkman wrote the scripts and went on the road hand-delivering prints to out-of-town bookings. The question of the date given for *The Scar of Shame* is illustrative of the challenge of doing accurate historical research on these films, which as a rule did not have the date of release on the prints. Films without dates have been "dated" by means of arduous checking of trade papers or, as in the case of race movies, by means of advertisements for shows placed in black newspapers. For many years, *The Scar of Shame* was listed as 1926. However, recent research indicates that although the film may have been several years in production, it had its first screening in April 1929 at the Odeon Theatre in New York, hence the corrected date of 1929. Thanks to Charles Musser for some remarkable research. See appendix in Bowser, Gaines, and Musser, eds., *Oscar Micheaux and His Circle*.

47. Both Oscar Micheaux and Richard J. Norman shared a skeptical view of Starkman's venture, Micheaux writing Norman that the investors expected to gross an unrealistic $175,000 to $200,000 per film. Bernstein and White, "Scratching Around," 123, note 48. Years later, Leonora Starkman shed some light on her father's motivations when in an interview she was quoted as saying: "My father was a crusader. Nobody played the black people as heroes and heroines. This fit in with his ethic. He felt the black people shouldn't be stepped on, that at the same time that he was making money he could glorify his position." Sampson, *Blacks in Black and White*, 218.

48. Bernstein and White, "Scratching Around," 107.

49. Homer Goins to George P. Johnson, 21 July 1920, gives his opinion of *The Brute* and closes with "afraid they might see this letter"; Telegram from Homer Goins to George P. Johnson, stating that he was quitting the Micheaux Company and citing Micheaux's "unbusinesslike behavior," n.d.; Typescript,

"Correspondence from two of Lincoln Film Agents Placed in Mitcheaux" [sic] lists Ira McGowan, George Johnson's brother-in-law, and Homer Goins of St. Paul, Minnesota. All documents appear in GPJC.

50. Bernstein and White, "Scratching Around," 123, note 57.

51. The best source of synopses in published form is Sampson, chap. 7, "Synopses of Black Films Produced between 1910 and 1950," in *Blacks in Black and White.*

52. One reel of the six original reels of *By Right of Birth* is located in the Library of Congress. Klotman, *Frame by Frame,* 88, lists it as a dramatic short, not a feature as the other Lincoln films had been.

53. Roland Barthes, *Image/Music/Text,* trans. Stephen Heath (New York: Hill and Wang, 1977), 123, 124 (emphasis mine).

54. See Tom Gunning, *D. W. Griffith and the Origins of American Narrative Film* (Urbana: University of Illinois Press, 1991), 17.

55. Jean-Paul Sartre, "Introduction" to Frantz Fanon, *The Wretched of the Earth,* trans. Constance Farrington (New York: Grove Weidenfeld, 1963), 17.

56. Ed Branigan, *Narrative Comprehension and Film* (New York: Routledge, 1992), 66.

57. Kevin K. Gaines, *Uplifting the Race* (Chapel Hill: University of North Carolina Press, 1996), xv.

58. Ibid., 74–75.

59. Paul Gilroy, *Black Atlantic: Modernity and Double Consciousness* (Cambridge: Harvard University Press, 1993), 236, note 26, updates this dilemma of the black middle class with reference to Trey Ellis, "The New Black Aesthetic," *Callaloo* (1989): 233–243, which profiles the coolness of the "NBA" (the new black aesthetic). It is, says Gilroy, a case of not just economic but cultural interdependence at this time, a case of a "small and isolated segment of the black middle class which has struggled with its dependence on the cultural lifeblood of the black poor."

60. T. S. Stribling, *Birthright* (1922; reprint, Delmar, N.Y.: Scholars' Facsimiles & Reprints, 1987).

61. Both Pearl Bowser and Charlene Regester have urged me to take note of this similarity between Alice and Louise. See my *"The Scar of Shame:* Skin Color and Caste in Black Silent Melodrama," *Cinema Journal* 26, no. 4 (summer 1987): 7, for a discussion of Louise Howard as having what the black community once called a "waste of color," in reference to the light-skinned advantage that could not be realized because of a woman's class position. Reprinted in Smith, ed., *Representing Blackness.*

62. David Gordon Nielson, *Black Ethos: Northern Urban Negro Life and Thought* (New York: Greenwood Press, 1977), 76, quotes Rayford Logan, "The Hiatus—A Great Negro Middle Class," *Southern Workman* 58 (December 1929): 53, on this phenomenon.

63. Thomas Cripps, "Response," *Cinema Journal* 27, no. 2 (winter 1988): 58, suggests that David Starkman's strategy in producing *The Scar of Shame* was

to attract a new black middle class audience to his theater, in effect "custom-designing" it to reach out to a new group. Cripps's argument depends on seeing the black moviegoing audience in this period as primarily "riffraff" rather than "respectable" blacks whose religion and sense of propriety were at odds with the low reputation of the movies. In this analysis, *The Scar of Shame* was an effort to convert the respectable blacks moving into the neighborhood of one of Starkman's white theaters to moviegoing. In a way, this effort is reminiscent of the larger-scale strategy on the part of nickelodeon operators in the period from 1907 to 1909 to appeal to middle class patrons. It has been argued that this appeal effected the transition of the movies from working class, immigrant diversion to middle class entertainment, although some scholars are dubious about this assertion. For a summary of these debates, see Janet Staiger, *Interpreting Films: Studies in the Historical Reception of American Cinema* (Princeton: Princeton University Press, 1992), 103. See Thomas Cripps, *Hollywood's High Noon* (Baltimore: Johns Hopkins University Press, 1997), 133–135, for more on the class composition of the race film audience. See also chapter 4, note 19.

64. Joseph Wilson, *Sketches of Higher Class of Colored Society in Philadelphia* (Philadelphia: Merrihew and Thompson, 1841), 66–67.

65. W. E. B. Du Bois, *The Philadelphia Negro: A Social Study* (1899; reprint, New York: Schocken, 1967), 317, 177.

66. Adrienne Rich, "Disloyal to Civilization: Feminism, Racism, Gynephobia," in *On Lies, Secrets, and Silence* (New York: W. W. Norton, 1979), 293. Written twenty years ago, this essay stood alone at the time of its publication in its focus on the historical separation of white women from black and the silence that surrounded the lives of black women and lesbians.

67. Kevin Gaines, *Uplifting the Race*, xiv.

68. Nielson, *Black Ethos*, 51, 53, 61, 76.

69. See Carbine, "The Finest outside the Loop," 9–41. Charlene Regester, in "Stepin Fetchit: The Man, the Image, and the African American Press," *Film History* 6, no. 4 (winter 1994): 504, tells us that in the 1920s Fetchit, whose real name was Lincoln Perry, worked as an entertainment reporter for the *Chicago Defender*.

70. Houston Baker, *Long Black Song: Essays in Black American Literature and Culture* (Charlottesville: University Press of Virginia, 1972), 4.

71. M. K. Johnson, " 'Stranger in a Strange Land': An African American Response to the Frontier Tradition in Oscar Micheaux's *The Conquest: The Story of a Negro Pioneer*," *Western American Literature* 33, no. 3 (fall 1998): 237, comments on the way the West is free from the racial discrimination of the East for Micheaux but simultaneously argues that his own characterization of the Sioux Indians reproduced the West as a territory based on such distinctions.

72. John W. Ravage, in *Black Pioneers: Images of the Black Experience on the North American Frontier* (Salt Lake City: University of Utah Press, 1997), offers

photographic evidence of the variety of roles blacks played in the western experience. See also William Loren Katz, *The Black West* (New York: Doubleday, 1971).

73. On the Lafayette Players, see Alex Albright, "Micheaux, Vaudeville, and Black Cast Film," *Black Film Review* 7, no. 4 (1992): 6–9, 36; Sister Francesca Thompson, "The Lafayette Players (1915–1932)," in Bowser, Gaines, and Musser, eds., *Oscar Micheaux and His Circle.*

74. "Oscar Mitcheux," typescript sketch, version 5, in GPJC.

75. Telegram, Oscar Micheaux to George P. Johnson, 30 March 1920, asking him to accept a position in the Micheaux organization; George P. Johnson to Oscar Micheaux, 22 September 1920, declining the offer, stating that he is "somewhat reluctant to give up my Government position." Both in GPJC.

76. Oscar Micheaux, *The Conquest: The Story of a Negro Pioneer* (1913; reprint, Lincoln: University of Nebraska Press, 1994).

77. "Oscar Mitcheux," typescript sketch, n.d., in GPJC.

78. "Oscar Mitcheux," typescript sketches, n.d.; "Mitcheaux, Oscar & Mitcheaux Film Corp.," typescript sketch, n.d. Both in GPJC.

79. "Oscar Mitcheux," version 3, in GPJC. See also Sampson, chap. 4, "Micheaux Film Corporation: Oscar Micheaux," in *Blacks in Black and White.*

80. Oscar Micheaux, *The Forged Note* (Lincoln: Western Book Supply Company, 1915).

81. Oscar Micheaux, *The Homesteader* (1917; reprint, Lincoln: University of Nebraska Press, 1994).

82. Oscar Micheaux, *The Wind from Nowhere* (New York: Book Supply Co., 1944).

83. George Johnson was not the only one who misspelled Micheaux's name. Charles Musser, in "Troubled Relations: Paul Robeson, Eugene O'Neill, and Oscar Micheaux," in *Paul Robeson: Artist and Citizen,* ed. Jeffrey C. Stewart (New Brunswick, N.J.: Rutgers University Press, 1998), 89, writes that when Micheaux's *Body and Soul* encountered trouble at the box office in New York, offending many members of the black community, the *New York Amsterdam News* referred to him satirically as "Mischeaux."

84. The most current filmography in print is Bernard L. Peterson, "A Filmography of Oscar Micheaux: America's Legendary Black Filmmaker," in *Celluloid Power: Social Film Criticism from The Birth of a Nation to Judgment at Nuremberg,* ed. David Platt (Metuchen, N.J.: Scarecrow Press, 1992), 113–141. However, other scholars have found this filmography inaccurate. On the problems of compiling a Micheaux filmography, see J. Ronald Green, "Toward a Definitive Listing of Oscar Micheaux's Films," *Oscar Micheaux Society Newsletter* 3 (summer 1994), 2–3, and Green's *Straight Lick: The Cinema of Oscar Micheaux* (Bloomington: Indiana University Press, 2000). See also Corey Creekmur, Charles Musser, Pearl Bowser, and Charlene Regester, "Oscar Micheaux Filmography," in Bowser, Gaines, and Musser, eds., *Oscar Micheaux and His Circle.*

85. "Oscar Mitcheux," version 5, in GPJC.

86. George P. Johnson to Western Book Supply Company, 7 May 1918, inquires about the rights to the book he has seen advertised in the *Chicago Defender;* Oscar Micheaux to Lincoln Motion Picture Company, 13 May 1918, replies confirming that he is sending Johnson a copy of *The Homesteader.* Both in GPJC. See Sampson, *Blacks in Black and White,* 149, for an account of the early negotiations between Johnson and Micheaux.

87. Learthen Dorsey, in "Introduction," *The Homesteader* (1917; reprint, Lincoln: University of Nebraska Press, 1994), 3, says that the contract between Micheaux and the Lincoln Company was canceled when, after Micheaux arrived in Los Angeles, he wanted to direct the film.

88. Oscar Micheaux to George Johnson, 3 June 1918, in GPJC.

89. Oscar Micheaux to Lincoln Motion Picture Company, 25 June 1918, in GPJC.

90. "Oscar Mitcheux," version 4, in GPJC.

91. "Oscar Mitcheux," version 5, in GPJC.

92. Typescript copy of letter from Johnson to Micheaux, n.d. (though it refers to *The Brute,* which was released in 1920), in GPJC.

93. Cripps, *Slow Fade to Black,* 83. See also "A Million Dollar Negro Film Deal Fell Through," typescript, in GPJC.

94. Bernstein and White, in "Scratching Around," 113, cite a further attempt by George Johnson to merge the interests of race film producers in March 1922, this time writing to Richard J. Norman with his suggestion. The authors cite Norman's skepticism of the "stock schemes" employed by Micheaux and Lincoln as a means of raising capital as a major reason for his reluctance to consolidate.

95. George Johnson secured information on Micheaux's stockholders by posing as R. R. Dale & Co., an Omaha stockbroker. He wrote Micheaux in Chicago, feigning interest in the purchase of stock in order to secure information about Micheaux's business; Swan Micheaux replied to R. R. Dale on August 19, 1920, listing seven stockholders, all of whom lived in either Sioux City, Nebraska, or Sioux City, Iowa, and filling out a form with information about authorized capitalization, dividends, and share value. In GPJC.

96. Richard Grupenhoff, *The Black Valentino: The Stage and Screen Career of Lorenzo Tucker* (Metuchen, N.J.: Scarecrow Press, 1988).

97. The other three are *The Case of Mrs. Wingate* (New York: Book Supply Co., 1945); *The Story of Dorothy Stanfield, Based on a Great Insurance Swindle, and a Woman! A Novel* (New York: Book Supply Co., 1946); *The Masquerade, an Historical Novel* (New York: Book Supply Co., 1947).

98. See P. T. Barnum, *Struggles and Triumphs: Forty Years of Recollections of P. T. Barnum* (1869; reprint, Harmondsworth: Penguin, 1981).

99. "Oscar Mitcheux," version 3, in GPJC.

100. "Regarding a Screen Version of 'The Homesteader,'" n.d., in GPJC.

101. Ibid.

102. Micheaux Book and Film Company form letter to exhibitors, March 1919, in GPJC.

103. "Booking Route," in GPJC. In addition, on this same tour *The Home-steader* played in Birmingham, Bessemer, Shreveport, and New Orleans. It was booked for three days in June and for a return engagement in July in Atlanta and at the famous Douglas Theatre in Macon, Georgia. In South Carolina it played at the Atlas in Spartansburg, the New Lincoln in Columbia, and the New Liberty in Greenville. In North Carolina the film completed its southern tour at the Gem in Reidsville and the Rex in Durham.

104. Martin Jay, in *Downcast Eyes: The Denigration of Vision in Twentieth-Century French Thought* (Berkeley: University of California Press, 1993), 463, puts the development succinctly when he says that the " 'death of the author' championed by Barthes and Foucault in literary and philosophical terms had its counterpart in the death of the *auteur* in film studies." See also John Caughie, *Theories of Authorship* (London: British Film Institute, 1981).

105. See Staiger, *Interpreting Films*, chap. 3, for an overview of the significance of reception studies in the development of film history and theory.

106. See Neil Harris, *Humbug: The Art of P. T. Barnum* (Boston: Little, Brown and Co., 1973).

107. Micheaux Book and Film Company form letter to exhibitors, in GPJC. See Charles Musser, "To Dream the Dreams of White Playwrights: Reappropriation and Resistance in Oscar Micheaux's *Body and Soul*," in Bowser, Gaines, and Musser, eds., *Oscar Micheaux and His Circle*, for evidence that Micheaux also used street exploitation, including a facsimile of the Sing Sing electric chair with an attention-attracting buzzer, in the New York exhibition of *Body and Soul*. Musser quotes the *New York Age:* "It is said that lurid and sensational canvases are stretched each Sunday, in front of the theatre, showing scenes from prisons, depicting the electric chair, escaping prisoners, shooting of guns, and other pictures calculated to excite and stir onlookers."

108. See my "From Elephants to Lux Soap: The Programming and 'Flow' of Early Motion Picture Exploitation," *The Velvet Light Trap* 25 (spring 1990): 31.

109. Ibid., 35.

110. As quoted in Bernstein and White, "Scratching Around," 99.

111. See James Hoberman, "A Forgotten Black Cinema Surfaces," *Village Voice,* 17 November 1975, 86; James Hoberman, "Bad Movies," *Film Comment* 14, no. 4 (1980): 11.

112. James Hoberman, "Race to Race Movies," *Village Voice,* 22 February 1994; Richard Grupenhoff, "Veiled Aristocrats Uncovered in Tennessee," *Oscar Micheaux Society Newsletter* 1 (February 1993): 2.

113. Theophilus Lewis, "The Harlem Sketch Book," *The New York Amsterdam News,* 16 April 1930, 10.

114. Ron Green, " 'Twoness' in the Style of Oscar Micheaux," in Diawara, ed., *Black American Cinema,* 26–39. See Cripps's reply to Green, "Oscar Micheaux: The Story Continues," in Diawara, ibid.

115. Daniel J. Leab, *From Sambo to Superspade: The Black Experience in Motion Pictures* (Boston: Houghton Mifflin, 1975), 81.

116. As quoted in Leab, ibid., 191.

117. Charlene Regester, "The Misreading and Rereading of African American Filmmaker Oscar Micheaux: A Critical Review of Micheaux Scholarship," *Film History* 7 (1995): 426–449.

118. John Harding, "Motion Picture Withdrawn after Protest in New York," *New York Age,* 10 May 1938, 4. For more, see chapter 5, note 46.

119. Ron Green, "Oscar Micheaux's Interrogation of Caricature as Entertainment," *Film Quarterly* 51, no. 3 (spring 1998): 16–30; Jeffrey C. Stewart, "Paul Robeson and the Problem of Modernism," in *Rhapsodies in Black,* ed. David A. Bailey and Richard J. Powell (Berkeley: University of California Press, 1997), 93.

Chapter Four

1. Henry Louis Gates, Jr., "The Trope of a New Negro and the Reconstruction of the Image of the Black," *Representations* 24 (fall 1988): 129.

2. Ibid., 130.

3. Gates, ibid., 144, cites W. H. A. Moore, writing in 1892, as having made the early argument that the literary work of Paul Lawrence Dunbar, Charles Chesnutt, and W. E. B. Du Bois would create the movement that would "recreate" the Sambo figure.

4. Ibid., 148.

5. It is interesting that Gates uses the term "effacement" in relation to the Harlem writers since it is well known that so many of them were light-skinned. Although it has been politically important in past decades to claim these writers for blackness, an argument could be made that they were already inside rather than outside white culture since they were as cultivated as they were light-skinned. Indeed, such an argument has almost been made in a book that takes a minority position on the subject. Naomi Zack, *Race and Mixed Race* (Philadelphia: Temple University Press, 1993), 101, argues that "[m]any of the Harlem Renaissance leaders were a breath away from redefining both themselves and the majority of Negroes as neither black nor white or as both, but they did not do so." In conclusion, she challenges prevalent practices: "So perhaps the time has come to reject the concept of a black American race, because that concept is coercive" (p. 165).

6. Diana Fuss, in *Identification Papers* (New York: Routledge, 1995), 151, asks, "But is it possible to separate so completely the imitation from what it imitates?"

7. Henry Louis Gates, Jr., *The Signifying Monkey: A Theory of Afro-American Literary Criticism* (New York: Oxford University Press, 1989).

8. Donald Bogle, *Toms, Coons, Mulattoes, Mammies and Bucks* (New York: Continuum, 1973), 163.

9. The theatrical melodrama version of *Ten Nights in a Barroom and What I*

Saw There by temperance advocate Timothy Shay Arthur opened in 1858 at New York's National Theatre and in its popularity rivaled *Uncle Tom's Cabin.* Film versions, starting with the 1909 Edison short directed by Edwin S. Porter, appeared in 1910, 1911, 1913, 1921, and 1926. In 1931 it was directed by William A. O'Connor and produced by Roadshow Productions.

10. John O. Thompson, "Screen Acting and the Commutation Test," *Screen* 19, no. 2 (summer 1978): 56–57.

11. Ibid., 59.

12. James Baldwin, *The Devil Finds Work* (New York: Dell, 1976), 48.

13. Richard Grupenhoff, *The Black Valentino: The Stage and Screen Career of Lorenzo Tucker* (Metuchen, N.J.: Scarecrow, 1988), 72.

14. Feminist film critics in the seventies argued provocatively that "woman as woman" was missing from mainstream cinema, even though those films were full of female characters. See Claire Johnston, "Women's Cinema as Counter-Cinema," in *Notes on Women's Cinema,* ed. Claire Johnston (London: British Film Institute, 1973), 26, reprinted in *Movies and Methods,* ed. Bill Nichols (Berkeley: University of California Press, 1976).

15. Joseph Beam, "James Baldwin: Not a Bad Legacy, Brother," in *Brother to Brother: New Writings by Black Gay Men,* ed. Essex Hemphill (Boston: Alyson Publications, 1991), 185.

16. W. E. B. Du Bois, *Darkwater: Voices from within the Veil* (1920; reprint, New York: AMS Press, 1969), 186–187.

17. Cornel West, "The New Cultural Politics of Difference," in *Out There: Marginalization and Contemporary Cultures,* ed. Russell Ferguson, Martha Gever, Trinh T. Minh-ha, and Cornel West (New York: The New Museum, 1990), 27–28.

18. See Thomas Cripps, *Slow Fade to Black: the Negro in American Film 1900– 1942,* 2d ed. (New York: Oxford University Press, 1993), 89, emphasizes the historical specificity of assimilationism, which constitutes his explanation of black "mirroring" of white, arguing that specific "dark reflections of white models [were] very much in line with the optimistic assimilationism abroad in the black ethos of the World War period." Further, he identifies the NAACP with assimilationism in this period (p. 170).

19. Film scholars have been less interested in the question of how immigrants "learned" than with the question of the point at which the class composition of the early nickelodeon theaters (a significant feature by 1907) began to change significantly once theater owners attracted middle class patrons in significant numbers. The thorough sociology of the phenomenon that will resolve some of these questions is yet to be done, and this question of assimilation would also seem to be on that agenda. Janet Staiger, in *Interpreting Films: Studies in the Historical Reception of American Cinema* (Princeton: Princeton University Press, 1992), 102–103, summarizes these issues and suggests a way in which the class composition of the audience could be read off the films themselves, considering the evolution of the form of narrative continuity after 1909, which she interprets as a sign of an expansion of the audience to include not only the

middle class but also rural audiences, immigrants, and the working class. While she is referring to developments that take place some years before race movies, her argument is suggestive, particularly as it might be adapted to a notion of cinema as an assimilation machine based not on cultural content but on cinematic form. See chapter 3, note 63.

20. Bogle, *Toms, Coons,* 163.

21. Ibid.

22. bell hooks, *Black Looks* (Boston: South End Press, 1992), 120.

23. Ibid., 119.

24. Christian Metz, "The Imaginary Signifier," *Screen* 16, no. 2 (summer 1975): 14–76.

25. Robert Stepto, *From behind the Veil: A Study of Afro-American Narrative,* 2d ed. (Urbana: University of Illinois Press, 1991), 56.

26. As quoted in ibid., 69.

27. William Loren Katz, *The Black West* (New York: Touchstone, 1996), 249. Katz goes on to detail the reversal of opportunity for blacks in the state of Oklahoma after statehood. In 1910 a "grandfather clause" written into the state constitution took the vote away from blacks on the basis of the slave status of their grandfathers who had not been allowed to vote. A 1914 Supreme Court ruling enforced segregation in the state, a decision that turned back the clock for black Oklahomans (p. 252).

28. Pamphlet, George P. Johnson Collection, Department of Special Collections, Young Research Library, University of California, Los Angeles, hereafter GJPC.

29. Ibid.

30. Jimmie Lewis Franklin, *Journey toward Hope* (Norman: University of Oklahoma Press, 1982), 23–27, confirms that not only in Muskogee but in Guthrie, Ardmore, Wagoner, and Oklahoma City blacks owned many businesses, and the professional classes (dentists, teachers, lawyers, doctors) numbered many blacks in the early years of the century. However, for a more complex account of life in these all-black towns, see John Hope Franklin and John Whittington Franklin, eds., *My Life and an Era: The Autobiography of Buck Colbert Franklin* (Baton Rouge: Louisiana State University Press, 1997). Buck Franklin, a lawyer, describes his life in the small all-black town of Rentiesville, Oklahoma, during the years just after statehood, recalling that the divisions among the people produced by rival churches made life in the town almost intolerable. He and his family moved to Tulsa.

31. Ernst Bloch, *The Principle of Hope,* vol. 1, trans. Neville Plaice, Stephen Plaice, and Paul Knight (Oxford: Basil Blackwell, 1986), 14.

32. Ibid., 412.

33. Michael Taussig, *Mimesis and Alterity* (London: Routledge, 1993), 33.

34. Bloch was approving of "On Dreamers and Dreaming" but critical of Freud's concept of sublimation. See *The Principle of Hope,* 94.

35. Ibid., 92.

36. Ibid., 95.

37. Paul Gilroy, *Black Atlantic: Modernity and Double Consciousness* (Cambridge: Harvard University Press, 1993), 56, 68.

38. Kevin K. Gaines, *Uplifting the Race* (Chapel Hill: University of North Carolina Press, 1996), xv.

39. Bloch, *The Principle of Hope*, 99.

40. Fredric Jameson, *Marxism and Form: Twentieth-Century Dialectical Theories of Literature* (Princeton: Princeton University Press, 1971), 139.

41. See my discussion in "*Within Our Gates:* From Race Melodrama to Opportunity Narrative," in *Oscar Micheaux and His Circle: African American Filmmaking and Race Cinema of the Silent Era*, ed. Pearl Bowser, Jane Gaines, and Charles Musser (Pordenone-Sacile, Italy: Giornate del Cinema Muto, forthcoming).

42. On *East Lynne*, see Guy Barefoot, "*East Lynne* to *Gaslight:* Hollywood, Melodrama, and Twentieth Century Notions of the Victorian," in Christine Gledhill, ed., *Melodrama: Theatre/Picture/Screen* (London: British Film Institute, 1994).

43. See my "The Queen Christina Tie-Ups: Convergence of Show Window and Screen," *Quarterly Review of Film and Video* 11, no. 4 (1989): 35–60, reprinted in *Feminist Cultural Studies*, ed. Terry Lovell (London: Edward Elgar Publishing, 1996).

44. Bloch, *The Principle of Hope*, 13.

45. Ibid., 412.

46. Richard Dyer, "Entertainment and Utopia," in *Movies and Methods II*, ed. Bill Nichols (Berkeley: University of California Press, 1985).

47. See J. Ronald Green, *Straight Lick: The Cinema of Oscar Micheaux* (Bloomington: Indiana University Press, 2000), for an analysis of Micheaux and the musical, and especially his excellent discussion of *Swing* (1938).

48. For a brilliant analysis of the mother's dream, see Richard Dyer, *Heavenly Bodies: Film Stars and Society* (London: Macmillan, 1987), 114–115.

49. Charles Musser, in "To Redream the Dreams of White Playwrights: Reappropriation and Resistance in Oscar Micheaux's *Body and Soul*," in Bowser et al., eds., *Oscar Micheaux and His Circle*, elaborates on his original thesis that *Body and Soul* was in dialogue with Robeson's performance in the play version of *The Emperor Jones*. Hazel Carby, in a brilliant piece of research, discovered the source of *Body and Soul* in Nan Bagby Stephens's play *Roseanne*. See Carby, *Race Men: The Body and Soul of Race, Nation, and Manhood* (Cambridge: Harvard University Press, 1998).

50. Kevin Gaines, *Uplifting the Race*, 6, refers to the "misplaced equation of race progress with the status of the family."

51. Ibid., 2.

52. Kevin Gaines, ibid., asks the most difficult question about the similarities as well as the differences between middle class whites and middle class blacks: "Given that racial uplift ideology constituted a complicated, contested

appropriation of dominant racial discourses, some readers will no doubt wonder what precisely is the difference between black middle-class ideology and that of Anglo-American elites. To be sure, I will argue that there were similarities, the crucial one being that both black and white elites spoke the same dominant language of race in defining their middle-class status. At the same time, obviously, there were crucial divergences. The unequal social positions and thus disparate experiences of blacks and whites made all the difference" (xix–xx).

53. Bloch, *The Principle of Hope*, 13.

54. Julia Lesage, "Hegemonic Fantasies in *An Unmarried Woman* and *Craig's Wife*," *Film Reader* 5 (1982): 83–94.

55. Stuart Hall, "Notes on Deconstructing 'The Popular,'" in *People's History and Socialist Theory*, ed. Raphael Samuel (Boston: Routledge and Kegan Paul, 1981).

56. See my "Dream/Factory," in *Film Studies*, ed. Christine Gledhill and Linda Williams (London: Arnold, 2000).

57. Fredric Jameson, "Reification and Utopia in Mass Culture," *Social Text* 1 (1979): 144.

58. Bloch, *The Principle of Hope*, 112.

59. Ibid., 159.

60. Another way of putting this is that black audiences would go to see a race movie even if it was a "bad" one. One of George Johnson's "plants" in the Micheaux Film Corporation in Chicago wrote to him that exhibitors had discovered that "the colored people will come to see a rotten negro picture as quick as they will to see the best one." Ira McGowan to George P. Johnson, 17 August 1921, in GPJC. See chapter 3, note 49.

61. For the original theorization of the "progressive text" in film studies, see Jean-Louis Comolli and Jean Narboni, "Cinema/Ideology/Criticism," in *Film Theory and Criticism*, ed. Gerald Mast, Marshall Cohen, and Leo Braudy (New York: Oxford University Press, 1992).

62. Bloch, *The Principle of Hope*, 156.

63. Ibid., 158.

64. Jack Zipes, "Toward a Realization of Anticipatory Illumination," introduction to Ernst Bloch, *The Utopian Function of Art and Literature: Selected Essays*, trans. Jack Zipes and Frank Mecklenburg (Cambridge: MIT Press, 1988), xxxvii.

65. Because Bloch's gentle criticism of socialism came to media studies in the West not directly but mainly through Hans Magnus Enzensberger's critique of "false needs," this connection between the utopian anticipatory consciousness and revolutionary consciousness seems to have been progressively weakened over the last decades. The crucial passage is this:

> The attractive power of mass consumption is based not on the dictates of false needs, but on the falsification and exploitation of quite real and legitimate ones without which the parasitic process of advertising would be

quite redundant. A socialist movement ought not to denounce these needs, but take them seriously, investigate them, and make them politically productive.

Hans Magnus Enzensberger, "Constituents of a Theory of the Media," in *The Consciousness Industry: Literature, Politics, and the Media* (New York: Continuum, 1974), 110.

66. Paul Gilroy, *There Ain't No Black in the Union Jack* (London: Hutchinson, 1987).

67. Stuart Hall, in "What Is This 'Black' in Black Popular Culture?" in *Black Popular Culture*, ed. Gina Dent (Seattle: Bay Press, 1992), says, "we are tempted to use 'black' as sufficient in itself to guarantee the progressive character of the politics we fight under the banner—as if we don't have any other politics to argue about whether something's black or not" (p. 30).

68. Bogle, *Toms, Coons*, 163.

69. As quoted in Richard Grupenhoff, *The Black Valentino*, 70.

70. See J. Hoberman, "A Forgotten Black Cinema Resurfaces," *The Village Voice*, 17 November 1975, 11, for a sense of how the Communist boycott has been understood. See also Daniel Leab, *From Sambo to Superspade: The Black Experience in Motion Pictures* (Boston: Houghton Mifflin, 1975), 191; chapter 3, note 118; chapter 5, note 46.

71. Green, *Straight Lick*.

72. J. Ronald Green, "Oscar Micheaux's Interrogation of Caricature as Entertainment," *Film Quarterly* 51, no. 3 (spring 1998): 31, note 12, states that in conversation with surviving Micheaux family members, he learned that Oscar, as well as most of his brothers and sisters, was "fair-skinned." See also J. Ronald Green and Horace Neal, Jr., "Oscar Micheaux and Racial Slur," *Journal of Film and Video* (fall 1988): 66–71.

73. Grupenhoff, *The Black Valentino*, 71.

74. James Snead, *White Screens/Black Images* (New York: Routledge, 1994), 146, notes that Bert Williams, Nina Mae McKinney, Fredi Washington, and Lena Horne were all required to darken their skins. To quote Snead, black skin had to be "as black as possible to eliminate ambiguity" (p. 145).

75. F. James Davis, *Who Is Black?* (University Park: Penn State University Press, 1991), 12, says that by 1920 the mulatto category was dropped in the census.

76. Snead, *White Screens/Black Images*, 5.

77. Kathy Peiss, *Hope in a Jar: The Making of America's Beauty Culture* (New York: Metropolitan Books, 1998). For more, see A'Lelia Perry Bundles, *Madame C. J. Walker, Entrepreneur* (New York: Chelsea House, 1991); Bettye Collier Thomas, "Annie Turno Malone," in *Notable Black American Women*, ed. Jessie Carney Smith (Detroit: Gale Research, Inc., 1992). See also the videotape *Madam C. J. Walker: Two Dollars and a Dream* (Stanley Nelson & Associates, 1988).

78. As quoted in Peiss, ibid., 204.

79. Ibid.

80. Peiss, ibid., 208, mentions the dark-skinned ideal promoted by Marcus Garvey's United Negro Improvement Association, and the Negro Universal Protective Association's denunciation of Madame Walker.

81. As quoted in Peiss, ibid., 210.

82. Bloch, *The Principle of Hope,* vol. 1, 412.

83. Peiss, *Hope in a Jar,* 226.

84. Ibid., 232.

85. Noliwe M. Rooks, *Hair Raising* (New Brunswick: Rutgers University Press, 1996), 4. See also Kathy Peiss, "Making Faces: The Cosmetics Industry and the Cultural Construction of Gender, 1890–1930," *Genders* (March 1990): 155–157, on the African American culturists.

86. *Chicago Defender,* 22 February 1919, as quoted in Henry T. Sampson, *Blacks in Black and White: A Source Book on Black Films,* 2d ed. (Metuchen, N.J.: Scarecrow, 1995), 252.

87. Oscar Micheaux, *The Homesteader* (1917; reprint, Lincoln: University of Nebraska Press, 1994); Oscar Micheaux, *The Wind from Nowhere* (New York: Book Supply Co., 1944).

88. *New York Amsterdam News,* 19 June 1948, as quoted in Sampson, 440. Micheaux's last film was not, however, a critical success; see "*Betrayal* Severely Criticized, a Bore," *Chicago Defender,* 10 July 1948, which has further denunciatory words: "*The Betrayal* is a betrayal and is pretty awful."

89. I raised this issue rather tentatively in "Who Is Reading Robert Mapplethorpe's Black Book?" *New Formations* 16 (summer 1992): 31.

90. Maurice Berger, "Interview with Adrian Piper," in *Art, Activism, and Oppositionality,* ed. Grant H. Kester (Durham: Duke University Press, 1996), 217.

91. Oscar Micheaux, *The Conquest* (1913; reprint, Lincoln: University of Nebraska Press, 1994).

92. For the most thorough analysis of Micheaux's novels to date, see Jayna Brown, "Black Patriarch on the Prairie: National Identity and Black Manhood in the Early Novels of Oscar Micheaux," in Bowser, Gaines, and Musser, eds., *Oscar Micheaux and his Circle.*

93. The classic model of this narrative is Frances E. W. Harper, *Iola Leroy* (1893; reprint, Boston: Beacon Press, 1987).

94. Charles Chesnutt, *The House behind the Cedars* (1900; reprint, New York: Collier Books, 1969). See Susan Gilman, "Micheaux's Chesnutt," *PMLA* 114, no. 5 (October 1999): 1080–1088, for fuller development of the parallel between Chesnutt and Micheaux, who both use the "classic passing plot of discovery," with particular reliance on Chesnutt's *The Marrow of Tradition.* For the details on Micheaux's elongated and complicated negotiations with Chesnutt over the rights to his novel, see Charlene Regester, "Oscar Micheaux the Entrepreneur: Financing *The House behind the Cedars,*" *Journal of Film and Video* 49, nos. 1–2 (spring–summer 1997): 17–27.

95. Eric J. Sundquist, *To Wake the Nations: Race in the Making of American Literature* (Cambridge: Harvard University Press, 1993), 394, refers to the journal entry Chesnutt made in 1875 to the effect that he was considering passing. In Sundquist's analysis, it was the "ambiguity of blackness" that Chesnutt was drawn to not only in *The House behind the Cedars* but in his color line stories.

96. Corey Creekmur, "Telling White Lies: Oscar Micheaux and Charles W. Chesnutt," in Bowser, Gaines, and Musser, eds., *Oscar Micheaux and His Circle.* For more on the relationship between Chesnutt and Micheaux, see also Regester, "Oscar Micheaux the Entrepreneur."

97. *Afro-American,* 21 March 1925, 5, as quoted in Charlene Regester, "Headline to Headlights: Oscar Micheaux's Exploitation of the Rhinelander Case," *The Western Journal of Black Studies* 22, no. 3 (1998): 200.

98. Earl Lewis and Heidi Ardizzone, "A Modern Cinderella: Race, Sexuality, and Social Class in the Rhinelander Case," *International Labor and Working-Class History* 51 (spring 1997): 129–147. See also Regester, "Oscar Micheaux the Entrepreneur," 24–25, for a discussion of the way Micheaux exploited the connection to the Rhinelander case in his promotion for *House behind the Cedars.*

99. Elaine K. Ginsberg, "Introduction: The Politics of Passing," in *Passing and the Fictions of Identity,* ed. Elaine K. Ginsberg (Durham: Duke University Press, 1996), 4.

100. Adrian Piper, "Passing for White, Passing for Black," in Ginsberg, ed., ibid., 246.

101. George P. Johnson, "Collector of Negro Film History," transcript of oral history conducted in 1967–1968 by Elizabeth I. Dixon and Adelaide G. Tusler, 246, 254, 258. Collection 300/71, Department of Special Collections, Young Research Library, University of California, Los Angeles.

102. Piper, "Passing for White, Passing for Black," 244.

103. Nella Larsen, *Quicksand* and *Passing* (New Brunswick, N.J.:Rutgers University Press, 1986); Fannie Hurst, *Imitation of Life* (1933; reprint, New York: Perennial, 1990); *Imitation of Life* (dir. John M. Stahl, 1934); *Imitation of Life* (dir. Douglas Sirk, 1959). See Valerie Smith, *Not Just Race, Not Just Gender: Black Feminist Readings* (New York: Routledge, 1998), for an extremely nuanced discussion of passing in relation to the two versions of *Imitation of Life,* a discussion that allows for both the conservative and the subversive aspects of the practice. She says, for instance: "The light-skinned black body thus both invokes and transgresses the boundaries between the races and the sexes that structure the American social hierarchy. It indicates the contradiction between appearance and 'essential' racial identity within a system of racial distinctions based upon differences presumed to be visible" (p. 40).

104. Hazel V. Carby, *Reconstructing Womanhood: The Emergence of the Afro-American Woman Novelist* (New York: Oxford University Press, 1987).

105. Naomi Zack, *Race and Mixed Race* (Philadelphia: Temple University Press, 1993), 83.

106. Peter Stallybrass and Allon White, *The Politics and Poetics of Transgres-*

sion (Ithaca: Cornell University Press, 1986), 5, are often quoted for having noted that the "socially peripheral is so frequently *symbolically* central."

Chapter Five

1. The reference is to the famous quote from Woodrow Wilson. For more on the full story of the president's unusual relationship to this film, see Michael Rogin, " 'The Sword Became a Flashing Vision': D. W. Grifith's *The Birth of a Nation*," *Representations* 9 (winter 1985): 150–195. See J. Ron Green, "Micheaux v. Griffith," *Griffithiana* 60/61 (October 1997): 33, for an intriguing theory of the derivation of the title *Within Our Gates* that links Micheaux with Griffith.

2. "Race Problem Play Raises Fuss in Chicago," *Chicago Defender*, 24 January 1920, clippings file, George P. Johnson Collection, Department of Special Collections, Young Research Library, University of California, Los Angeles, hereafter GPJC.

3. Ibid. There has been some confusion about the dating of Micheaux's films. In cases in which a film from this period is produced late in one year and released early in the next, some sources provide a double year. In the case of *Within Out Gates,* Micheaux may have produced the film in 1919, but it did not premiere until early in 1920. For more on the question of dating early motion pictures, see chapter 3, note 6, and "Note on Film Dates," xv.

4. See David Burner, Elizabeth Fox-Genovese, Eugene D. Genovese, and Forrest McDonald, *An American Portrait: A History of the United States,* vol. 2, 2d ed. (New York: Charles Scribner's, 1985), 595–597, for placement of the 1919 Chicago race riot in the context of the year of the "Red Scare." I refer here to a college textbook in an attempt to suggest something about the positioning of these events in U.S. history courses in recent years. See also Carl Sandburg, *The Chicago Race Riots: July, 1919* (New York: Harcourt, Brace and Howe, 1919). James Weldon Johnson's reference to the "Red Summer of 1919" may not necessarily be a reference to community organizing. He says in the next paragraph that "[d]uring the summer, bloody race riots occurred in Chicago, and in Omaha, in Longview, Texas, in Phillips County, Arkansas, in Washington and other communities." *Along the Way* (New York: Viking Press, 1933), 341.

5. Letter to D. Ireland Thomas, Jacksonville, Florida, from the manager of the Star Theatre, Shreveport, Louisiana, 19 March 1920, in GPJC. Harry T. Sampson, in *Blacks in Black and White: A Source Book on Black Films* 1st ed. (Metuchen, N.J.: Scarecrow, 1977), 47, says that the Star Theatre manager was white, and that his refusal to exhibit the film had to do with his receiving from the New Orleans superintendent of police a copy of a letter referring to the "execution by hanging of about nine negroes for absolutely no cause" in the film.

6. Letter to Oscar Micheaux, Chicago, Illinois, from George P. Johnson, Omaha, Nebraska, 10 August 1920, in GPJC.

7. Letter to Frank T. Monney, Superintendent of Police, from Capt. Theodore A. Ray, Special to Superintendent, New Orleans, Louisiana, 10 March

1920, in GPJC. This may be the letter that was copied and sent to the Shreveport theater manager. That copies of the letters from Shreveport and New Orleans found their way into the hands of George Johnson suggests that they may have circulated further.

8. The primary sources in the George P. Johnson Collection make numerous references to sections of *Within Our Gates* as either cut out or replaced for one showing or another. Charlene Regester, in "Lynched, Assaulted and Intimidated: Oscar Micheaux's Most Controversial Films," *Popular Culture Review* 5, no. 1 (February 1994): 48–49, quotes the *Chicago Defender* on how the 1,200 feet removed from the film after its first showing would be returned to the film for subsequent screenings in the city.

9. See my discussion in chapter 7 of the way in which protest created a desire to see the film. Thomas Cripps, in *Slow Fade to Black: The Negro in American Film 1900–1942*, 2d ed. (New York: Oxford University Press, 1993), 186, says that fears of a "race riot" contributed to the poor box office of the film.

10. Advertising cuts for *Within Our Gates*, clippings file, in GPJC. See also chapter 6, note 1, on the "Girdlestone" spelling.

11. On Harriet Beecher Stowe's novel as sentimental fiction, see Jane Tompkins, "Sentimental Power: *Uncle Tom's Cabin* and the Politics of Literary History," in *Feminist Criticism: Essays on Women, Literature, Theory*, ed. Elaine Showalter (New York: Pantheon Books, 1985).

12. Jacqueline Dowd Hall, *Revolt against Chivalry: Jessie Daniel Ames and the Women's Campaign against Lynching* (New York: Colorado University Press, 1979), 130–133.

13. See for the source of the concept of overdetermination, Sigmund Freud, "Jokes and Their Relation to the Unconscious," in *The Standard Edition of the Complete Psychological Works*, vol. 13, ed. James Strachey (London: The Hogarth Press, 1959), 163.

14. See Louis Althusser, *For Marx*, trans. Ben Brewster (London: New Left Books, 1977), part III, for the Marxist application of the concept of overdetermination.

15. Hall, *Revolt against Chivalry*, 141. For the most complete account of this historical phenomenon, see Arthur F. Raper, *The Tragedy of Lynching* (1933; reprint, New York: Negro Universities Press, 1969); Sampson, *Blacks in Black and White*, 1st ed., 46. The review is quoted in Sampson, *Blacks in Black and White: A Source Book on Black Films*, 2d ed. (Metuchen, N.J.: Scarecrow, 1995), 152.

16. Ida B. Wells-Barnett, "Southern Horrors: Lynch Law in All Its Phases," in *On Lynchings: Southern Horrors, A Red Record, Mob Rule in New Orleans* (1892–1900; New York: Arno Press, 1969).

17. Advertising cuts for *Within Our Gates*, clippings file, in GPJC.

18. Linda Williams, *Playing the Race Card: Melodramas of Black and White from Uncle Tom to O. J. Simpson* (Princeton: Princeton University Press, forthcoming). See my *"Scar of Shame:* Skin Color and Caste in Black Silent Melodrama," *Cinema Journal* 26, no. 4 (summer 1987) 3–21, reprinted in *Imitations of Life: A*

Reader on Film and Television Melodrama, ed. Marcia Landy (Detroit: Wayne State University Press, 1991). bell hooks, in "Celebrating Blackness," *Black American Literary Forum* 25, no. 2 (summer 1991): 351–360, reprinted in bell hooks, *Black Looks: Race and Representation* (Boston: South End Press, 1992), has also understood Micheaux in terms of melodrama.

19. See Andre Gaudreault, "Detours in Film Narrative: The Development of Cross-Cutting," in *Early Cinema: Space, Frame, Narrative,* ed. Thomas Elsaesser and Adam Barker (London: British Film Institute, 1990). The case of *The Life of an American Fireman* is significantly different, however, in that what is at stake in the Porter example is nothing less than the question of the origins of the practice.

20. Tom Gunning, "Weaving a Narrative: Style and Economic Background in Griffith's Biograph Films," in Elsaesser and Barker, *ibid.,* 341. Although I am stressing the assumption that crosscutting represents events occurring simultaneously, for purposes of my argument, in practice, temporal arrangements edited in this style tend to be much more approximate. Simultaneity is by no means a fast rule.

21. Harriet A. Jacobs, *Incidents in the Life of a Slave Girl* (1861; reprint, Cambridge: Harvard University Press, 1987).

22. Eric Bentley, *The Life of the Drama* (New York: Atheneum, 1964), 201.

23. Rick Altman, "Dickens, Griffith, and Film Theory Today," *South Atlantic Quarterly* 88, no. 2 (spring 1989): 342, reprinted in *Classical Hollywood Narrative: The Paradigm Wars,* ed. Jane M. Gaines (Durham: Duke University Press, 1992).

24. Tzvetan Todorov, *The Fantastic: A Structural Approach to a Literary Genre,* trans. Richard Howard (Ithaca: Cornell University Press, 1975), 166.

25. Gunning, "Weaving a Narrative," 342.

26. See, for instance, Russell Merritt, "D. W. Griffith's *The Birth of a Nation:* Going After Little Sister," in *Close Viewings: An Anthology of New Film Criticism,* ed. Peter Lehman (Tallahassee: Florida State University Press, 1990). For an important analysis of why the black spectator, although set up to view this scene as a "rape," might resist this reading, see Manthia Diawara, "Black Spectatorship: Problems of Identification and Resistance," *Screen* 29, no. 4 (autumn 1988): 67–70, reprinted in *Black American Cinema,* ed. Manthia Diawara (New York: Routledge, 1993).

27. Wells-Barnett, "Southern Horrors," 11.

28. Elizabeth Fox-Genovese, *Within the Plantation Household: Black and White Women of the Old South* (Chapel Hill: University of North Carolina Press, 1988), 101.

29. See Nick Browne, "Griffith's Family Discourse: Griffith and Freud," in *Home Is Where the Heart Is: Studies in Melodrama and the Woman's Film,* ed. Christine Gledhill (London: British Film Institute, 1987).

30. James Baldwin, "Everybody's Protest Novel," in *Notes of a Native Son* (1955; reprint, New York: Beacon Press, 1984), 14.

31. Sergei Eisenstein, *Film Form* (1949; reprint, New York: Harcourt Brace, 1977), 235.

32. Homi Bhabha, "The Other Question," *Screen* 24, no. 6 (November–December 1983): 32. Bhabha quotes Frantz Fanon, *Black Skin, White Masks*, trans. Charles Lam Markmann (New York: Grove Weidenfeld, 1967), 79: "the corporeal schema crumbled, its place taken by a racial epidermal scheme. . . . It was no longer a question of being aware of my body in the third person but a triple person. . . . I was not given one, but two, three places."

33. Eisenstein, *Film Form,* 233–235.

34. Eisenstein, ibid., 198, says:

> In order to understand Griffith, one must visualize an America made up of more than visions of speeding automobiles, streamlined trains, racing ticker tape, inexorable conveyor-belts. One is obliged to comprehend this second side of America as well—America the traditional, the patriarchal, the provincial. And then you will be considerably less astonished by this link between Griffith and Dickens. . . . The threads of both these Americas are interwoven in the style and personality of Griffith—as in the most fantastic of his own parallel montage sequences.

35. See Isaac Julien, as quoted in Coco Fusco, *Young, British, and Black: The Work of Sankofa and Black Audio Film Collective* (Buffalo, N.Y.: Hallwalls / Contemporary Arts Center, 1988), 32.

36. Paul Willemen, "The Third Cinema Question: Notes and Reflections," in *Questions of Third Cinema,* ed. Jim Pines and Paul Willemen (London: British Film Institute, 1989), 9. See also Kobena Mercer, "Diaspora Culture and the Dialogic Imagination: The Aesthetics of Black Independent Film in Britain," in *Blackframes: Critical Perspectives on Black Independent Cinema,* ed. Claire Andrade-Watkins and M. Bye Cham (Cambridge: MIT Press, 1988), 59; Julio Garcia Espinosa, "For an Imperfect Cinema," in *Twenty-Five Years of the New Latin American Cinema,* ed. Michael Chanan (London: British Film Institutes / Channel 4 Television, 1983).

37. Willemen, "The Third Cinema Question," 15.

38. For overviews of Micheaux criticism, see J. Ron Green, "The Emergence of Micheaux Scholarship: A Bibliographic Essay," in *Oscar Micheaux and His Circle: African American Filmmaking and Race Cinema of the Silent Era,* ed. Pearl Bowser, Jane Gaines, and Charles Musser (Pordenone-Sacile, Italy: Giornate del Cinema Muto, forthcoming); Charlene Regester, "The Misreading and Rereading of African American Filmmaker Oscar Micheaux," *Film History* 7, no. 4 (winter 1995): 426–449; Thomas Cripps, "Oscar Micheaux: The Story Continues," in Diawara, ed., *Black American Cinema,* an answer to J. Ronald Green, " 'Twoness' in the Style of Oscar Micheaux," in Diawara, ibid.

39. J. Hoberman, "A Forgotten Black Cinema Resurfaces," *Village Voice,* 17 November 1975, 86–87.

40. Richard Dyer, *Heavenly Bodies: Film Stars and Society* (London: Macmillan, 1987), 115, interprets the film this way.

41. Geneva Smitherman, *Talkin' and Testifyin': The Language of Black America* (Detroit: Wayne State, 1977).

42. This is one of the original themes of Ron Green's work on Micheaux. See J. Ronald Green, *Straight Lick: The Cinema of Oscar Micheaux* (Bloomington: Indiana University Press, 2000).

43. Willemen, "The Third Cinema Question," 9.

44. Joseph A. Young, *Black Novelist as White Racist: The Myth of Black Inferiority in the Novels of Oscar Micheaux* (Westwood, Conn.: Greenwood Press, 1989).

45. Hazel Carby, *Reconstructing Womanhood: The Emergence of the Afro-American Woman Novelist* (New York: Oxford University Press, 1987). Deborah McDowell, in her "Introduction," to Jessie Redmon Fauset, *Plum Bun* (1928; reprint, London: Pandora, 1985), xxii, analyzes Fauset in terms that might apply here to Micheaux: "It passes for conservative, employing 'outworn' and 'safe' literary materials while, simultaneously, remaining suspicious of them."

46. Hoberman, "A Forgotten Black Cinema Resurfaces," 88; Daniel Leab, *From Sambo to Superspade: The Black Experience in Motion Pictures* (Boston: Houghton Mifflin, 1975), 191. For another explanation of what has been perceived as Micheaux's negative images of blacks, see J. Ron Green. "Oscar Micheaux's Interrogation of Caricature as Entertainment," *Film Quarterly* 51, no. 3 (spring 1998): 16–20, where the author argues that Micheaux's caricature is a critique: "The cutting gaze is, however, a formal foundation for an intensely critical cinema, and as such, it contributes to uplift by criticizing the obstacles of uplift and figuratively suggesting their removal" (p. 20).

47. Cornel West, "The New Cultural Politics of Difference," in *Out There: Marginalization and Contemporary Cultures,* ed. Russell Ferguson et al. (Cambridge: MIT Press, 1990), 28; W. E. B. Du Bois, *The Souls of Black Folk* (1903; reprint, New York: Signet, 1969), 45.

48. See, for instance, Steve Neale, "The Same Old Story: Stereotypes and Difference," *Screen Education* nos. 32/33 (autumn/winter 1979–1980), discussed at length in my conclusion.

49. Stuart Hall, "Gramsci's Relevance for the Study of Race and Ethnicity," *Journal of Communication Inquiry* 10, no. 2 (summer 1986): 27. Albert Memmi articulated the concept of hegemony in his own way before Gramsci became fashionable. See *Dominated Man: Notes towards a Portrait* (New York: Orion Press, 1968), 20: "We have already met the well-behaved colonized, the Good Spirit. He becomes in reality, like them, an accessory after the fact of his own oppression."

50. Young is to my knowledge the first to go beyond the early condemnation of Micheaux through the use of Fanon's understanding of the colonized subject's alienated psyche. See *Black Novelist as White Racist,* 146.

· 51. Christine Gledhill, "The Melodramatic Field: An Investigation," in Gledhill, ed., *Home is Where the Heart Is,* 13.

Chapter Six

1. The Spanish language intertitle in the print from the Filmoteca Española does not stress Sylvia's legitimacy as does this new English translation of the Spanish (itself a translation of an earlier English): "Una cicatriz que tenia en el pecho la salvró de la des honora pues al descu brirla Gridlstone supo que Sylvia era hija suza habida en legitimo matrimonio con una mujer de su raza y luego adoptada por los Landry." Although the intertitle retains "Gridlestone" as the spelling from the Spanish language print, most scholars now use "Girdlestone," the spelling that Micheaux used in his publicity the year of the film's release in the United States. See introduction, note 21, for background on the Spanish revision.

2. Jane Gaines, "*The Birth of a Nation* and *Within Our Gates:* Two Tales of the American South," in *Dixie Debates: Perspectives in Southern Culture,* ed. Richard H. King and Helen Taylor (London: Pluto Press, 1995), 188.

3. See Valerie Smith, "Split Affinities: The Case of Interracial Rape," in *Conflicts in Feminism,* ed. Marianne Hirsch and Evelyn Fox Keller (New York: Routledge, 1990).

4. *Chicago Defender,* 7 February 1920, as quoted in Henry T. Sampson, *Blacks in Black and White: A Source Book on Black Films,* 2d ed. (Metuchen, N.J.: Scarecrow, 1995), 279.

5. Jayna Brown, "Black Patriarch on the Prairie: National Identity and Black Manhood in the Early Novels of Oscar Micheaux" in *Oscar Micheaux and His Circle: African American Filmmaking and Race Cinema of the Silent Era,* ed. Pearl Bowser, Jane Gaines, and Charles Musser (Pordenone-Sacile, Italy: Giornate del Cinema Muto, forthcoming).

6. See Roland Barthes, "The Rhetoric of the Image," in *Image/Music/Text,* trans. Ron Howard (New York: Hill and Wang, 1977), for the theory of the way linguistic signs limit the meaning of the image. Kristin Thompson discusses the transition between expository intertitles and dialogue intertitles in David Bordwell, Janet Staiger, and Kristin Thompson, *The Classical Hollywood Cinema: Film Style and Mode of Production to 1960* (New York: Columbia University Press, 1985), 186–188. This particular intertitle appears to have qualities of both.

7. Rudolph Arnheim, *Film as Art* (Berkeley: University of California Press, 1966), is the most extreme but eloquent example.

8. Mary Ann Doane, "The Voice in Cinema: The Articulation of Body and Space" *Yale French Studies,* no. 60 (1980): 33–60, reprinted in *Narrative/ Apparatus/Ideology,* ed. Philip Rosen (New York: Columbia University Press, 1986).

9. Helen Tunnicliff Catterall, ed., *Judicial Cases Concerning American Slavery and the Negro,* 5 vols. (1926–1937; reprint, New York: Octagon Books, 1968).

10. Frances E. W. Harper, *Iola Leroy* (1893; reprint, Boston: Beacon Press, 1987). Henry Wiencek, in *The Hairstons: An American Family in Black and White* (New York: St. Martin's Press, 1999), 121–122, describes how after Robert

Hairston died, having left his estate to his black daughter Chrillis, his family removed her to another plantation and changed her name to Elizabeth.

11. John D'Emilio and Estelle Freedman, *Intimate Matters: A History of Sexuality in America* (New York: Harper and Row, 1988), 103.

12. Martha Elizabeth Hodes, *White Women, Black Men: Illicit Sex in the Nineteenth-Century South* (New Haven, Conn.: Yale University Press, 1997). See also Carrie Allen McCray, *Freedom's Child: The Story of My Mother, a Confederate General's Black Daughter* (New York: Penguin Books, 1998), for yet another example of the phenomenon of the white master who continued a long-term relationship with his black mistress.

13. C. Vann Woodward, "History from Slave Sources," in *The Slave's Narrative,* ed. Charles T. Davis and Henry Louis Gates, Jr. (Oxford: Oxford University Press, 1985), 56.

14. See Joel Williamson, *New People: Miscegenation and Mulattoes in the United States* (New York: Free Press, 1980).

15. As quoted in Carter Woodson, "The Beginnings of the Miscegenation of the Whites and Blacks," *Journal of Negro History* 3, no. 4 (October 1918): 345.

16. Katherine Clay Bassard, " 'Beyond Mortal Vision': Harriet E. Wilson's *Our Nig* and the American Racial Dream-Text," in *Female Subjects in Black and White,* ed. Elizabeth Abel, Barbara Christian, and Helene Moglen (Berkeley: University of California Press, 1997), 195, excerpts the crucial passage from the Virginia state code:

> 1662. Act XII. Children got by an Englishman upon a Negro woman shall be bond or free according to the condition of the mother, and if any Christian shall commit fornication with a Negro man or woman, he shall pay double the fines of a former act.

17. Hortense J. Spillers, "Notes on an Alternative Model—Neither/Nor," in *The Difference Within: Feminism and Critical Theory,* ed. Elizabeth Meese and Alice Amsterdam (Philadelphia: A. J. Benjamin, 1989), 167.

18. Daniel Gerould, in "Russian Formalist Theories of Melodrama," in *Imitations of Life,* ed. Marsha Landy (Detroit: Wayne State University Press, 1991), 124, refers to the way melodrama often makes productive use of a secret.

19. Christian Vivani, "Who Is without Sin? The Maternal Melodrama in American Film, 1930–1939," trans. Dolores Burdick, in Landy, ed., ibid.

20. Kate Chopin, "Désirée's Baby," in *The Awakening and Selected Stories* (New York: Penguin, 1983), 189–193.

21. Here I am indebted to Susan Gubar, *Racechanges* (New York: Oxford University Press, 1997), who notes that the question of the heroine's race is never resolved (p. 209).

22. Barbara Fields, in "Slavery, Race and Ideology in the United States of America," *New Left Review,* no. 181 (1990): 107, notes that "[p]aternity is always ambiguous, whereas maternity is not."

23. Michael Moon, in "Coming Home to the Indian Territory: Washington

Irving's Unsettled Frontiers," an unpublished talk at Duke University, has
made this provocative point.

24. Michel Foucault, *History of Sexuality,* vol. I, trans. Robert Hurley (New
York: Random House, 1978), 139.

25. Raymond Williams, *The Sociology of Culture* (New York: Shocken Books,
1981), 101.

26. Bill Nichols, *Representing Reality: Issues and Concepts in Documentary*
(Bloomington: Indiana University Press, 1991), 28.

27. Richard Dyer, *White* (London: Routledge, 1997), 25.

28. Judith Butler, "Imitation and Gender Insubordination," in *Inside/Out,*
ed. Diana Fuss (London: Routledge, 1991), 23.

29. Louis Althusser, *Lenin and Philosophy, and Other Essays,* trans. Ben Brewster (New York: Monthly Review Press, 1972), 172–176.

30. Judith Butler, *Bodies That Matter* (New York: Routledge, 1993), 16.

31. Ibid., 10.

32. Ibid., 23.

33. George Schuyler, *Black No More: Being an Account of the Strange and Wonderful Workings of Science in the Land of the Free,* A.D. *1933–1940* (1931; reprint, Boston: Northeastern University Press, 1989), chap. 12. Werner Sollors, in *Neither
Black Nor White Yet Both* (New York: Oxford University Press, 1997), 74–75,
notes the similarity between *Black No More* and "Désirée's Baby," particularly
in the way the birth of the dark child throws the question of black blood back
onto parents who are then temporarily confused about each other. See also Jane
Kuenz, "American Racial Discourse, 1900–1930: George Schuyler's *Black No
More,*" *Novel* 30 (1997): 170–192.

34. Andrew Britton, "Mandingo," *Movie,* no. 22 (spring 1976): 1–22.

35. Patricia Morton, in "From Invisible Man to 'New People': The Recent
Discovery of American Mulattoes," *Phylon* 46, no. 2 (1985): 114, mentions the
Creoles living on the Cane River who interpreted their white ancestry to mean
that they were white people.

36. See Thomas E. Skidmore, *Black into White: Race and Nationality in Brazil-
ian Thought* (New York: Oxford University Press). Dyer, in *White,* 25–26, discusses this in terms of the assumption that since sexual reproduction could
achieve the desired whitening of the population, miscegenation should be encouraged.

37. Cedric Robinson, "In the Year 1915: D. W. Griffith and the Whitening of
America," *Social Identities* 3, no. 2 (1997): 183.

38. Winthrop Jordan, *White over Black: American Attitudes toward the Negro*
(Chapel Hill: University of North Carolina Press, 1968), 178.

39. William Wells Brown, *Clotel, or, The President's Daughter* (1853; reprint,
New York: University Books, 1969), 59.

40. Martha Hodes, "Sex across the Color Line: White Women and Black
Men in the Nineteenth-Century American South," Ph.D. diss. (1991), 190, later
published as *White Women, Black Men: Illicit Sex in the Nineteenth-Century South*

(New Haven: Yale University Press, 1997); David Croly and George Wakeman, *Miscegenation: The Theory of the Blending of the Races, Applied to the American White Male and Negro* (New York: H. Dexter, Hamilton & Co., 1894); Joel Williamson, *The Crucible of Race: Black–White Relations in the American South since Emancipation* (Oxford: Oxford University Press, 1984), 33.

41. Hodes, "Sex across the Color Line," 4–5. W. E. B. Du Bois, in *The Souls of Black Folk* (1903; reprint, New York: Signet, 1969), states, "The problem of the Twentieth Century is the problem of the color-line" (p. 78).

42. Hodes, "Sex across the Color Line," 5.

43. Robert J. C. Young, *Colonial Desire: Hybridity in Theory, Culture and Race* (London: Routledge, 1995), 9, notes that "hybrid" appears in the 1843–1861 period coincident with the idea that humans could be racial hybrids. The preferred term before "miscegenation" was, he says, "amalgamation."

44. The definitive theorization of the concept of the "hybrid" can be found in Homi K. Bhabha, *The Location of Culture* (New York: Routledge, 1994). The abolitionists placed emphasis on "mixed blood," but it has been suggested that this may have reflected their unfortunate assumption that the superiority of mulattoes had to do with the contribution made by their "white blood." See George M. Fredrickson, *The Black Image in the White Mind* (Middletown, Conn.: Wesleyan University Press, 1987), 97–129, on "mixed blood."

45. Lisa Jones, *Bulletproof Diva: Tales of Race, Sex and Hair* (New York: Doubleday, 1994), 51, 62.

46. Walter Benn Michaels, in "Autobiography of an Ex-White Man," *Transition* 73 (1998): 128, makes this point in the context of his critique of the social construction of race.

47. For a superb analysis of the logic involved here, see Colette Guillaumin, "Race and Nature: The System of Marks," trans. Mary Jo Lakeland, *Feminist Issues* 8, no. 2 (1988): 25–43. While the "sociosymbolic system of marks" is old and widespread, she says, the idea of naturalness is modern, belonging to the "industrial–scientific society" (pp. 30–31).

48. Young, *Colonial Desire*, 9.

49. John Mencke, *Mulattoes and Race Mixture: American Attitudes and Images, 1865–1918* (Ann Arbor: University of Michigan Press, 1979), 144; Eric Lott, "Love and Theft: The Racial Unconscious of Blackface Minstrelsy," *Representations* no. 39 (1992), 30.

50. Charles Musser, in "The Travel Genre in 1903–1904: Moving towards Fictional Narrative," in *Early Cinema: Space, Frame, Narrative,* ed. Thomas Elsaesser and Alan Barker (London: British Film Institute, 1990), 123, also refers to showman Lyman Howe's 1903 production featuring scenes of India, Japan, Arabia, and Africa along with Switzerland and England as well as the Edison Company interest in travel subjects. For more on early cinema in Africa, see Nwachukwu Frank Ukadike, *Black African Cinema* (Berkeley: University of California Press, 1994), 29–32.

51. Gilles Deleuze and Félix Guattari, *A Thousand Plateaus: Capitalism and*

Schizophrenia, trans. Brian Massumi (Minneapolis: University of Minnesota Press, 1987), 168.

52. Patricia Mellencamp, in *A Fine Romance: Five Ages of Film Feminism* (Philadelphia: Temple University Press, 1995), 225–226, discusses Deleuze and Guattari's relevance for theories of race and cinema, and especially notes the relevance of their insight for silent cinema. She says, "I see the race of 'early cinema' as a soft-focus close-up of a young, delicate white girl" (p. 226).

53. See Jean-Louis Baudry, "The Ideological Effects of the Basic Cinematographic Apparatus," trans. Alan Williams, *Film Quarterly* 28, no. 2 (1974–1975): 39–47, reprinted in Rosen, ed., *Narrative/Apparatus/Ideology.*

54. Brian Winston, "A Whole Technology of Dyeing: A Note on Ideology and the Apparatus of the Chromatic Moving Image," *Daedalus* 114 (fall 1985): 105–123.

55. Dyer, *White,* 84.

56. Ibid., 87.

57. Ibid., 89.

58. Frederick Mills, "Film Lighting as a Fine Art: Explaining Why the Fireplace Glows and Why Film Stars Wear Halos," *Scientific American* 124 (1921): 148, as quoted in Dyer, ibid., 89.

59. Kristin Thompson, "Major Technological Changes of the 1920s," in Bordwell, Staiger, and Thompson, *The Classical Hollywood Cinema, 282.*

60. Dyer, *White,* 98, quotes Ernest Dickerson, Spike Lee's African American cameraman, who has specialized in the problem of "correcting a white bias," which he explains as more than merely adding light, but a matter of an entire approach to exposure, subject, stock, and development. My point here is that the makers of race movies would not necessarily have worked with such a specialist.

61. Paolo Cherchi Usai, *Burning Passions: An Introduction to the Study of Silent Cinema* (London: British Film Institute, 1994), 12, says that panchromatic film "allowed for the reproduction of a much wider range of intermediate shades of gray." Also, since panchromatic film was more expensive than orthochromatic, it was not widely used when it was first introduced. Although the larger production companies adopted it late in the silent era, this does not mean that the smaller, more cost-conscious filmmakers (such as the race movie pioneers) would have discontinued use of orthochromatic film, even into the sound era when it was still available. More thinking should also be done about the cultural comparison between the photographic sepia tone and brown-skinned peoples, a comparison that would find its way into a popular film such as the all-black-cast *Sepia Cinderella* (1947).

62. Naomi Zack, *Race and Mixed Race* (Philadelphia: Temple University Press, 1993), 172.

63. Dyer, *White,* 92.

64. See Thompson, "Major Technological Changes of the 1920s," 281, for further explanation.

65. Michel Foucault, *The Order of Things* (New York: Vintage Books, 1970), 26.

66. Umberto Eco, "Articulations of the Cinematic Code," in *Movies and Methods I*, ed. Bill Nichols (Berkeley: University of California Press, 1976), 604.

67. Foucault, *The Order of Things*, 281.

68. See Victor Burgin, "Photographic Practice and Art Theory," in *Thinking Photography*, ed. Victor Burgin (London: Macmillan), 60–61, for further discussion of the way the photograph has been theorized in relation to its referent.

69. On commonsense knowledge, see Richard Dyer et al., eds., *Coronation Street* (London: British Film Institute, 1981).

70. Guillaumin, "Race and Nature," 29, is especially interesting on this point: "the sexed division of humanity is regarded as leading to and constituting two heterogeneous groups. The fantasy implies that men make men and women make women."

71. Annette Gordon-Reed, *Thomas Jefferson and Sally Hemmings: An American Controversy* (Charlottesville: University Press of Virginia, 1997), 217.

72. For some of the cultural history of racial classification based on body type, see Young, *Colonial Desire*, chaps. 3 and 4.

73. Béla Balázs, *Theory of the Film* (New York: Dover, 1970), 92, says, "Our anthropomorphous world-vision makes us see a human physiognomy in every phenomenon."

74. Ibid., 96–97; Deleuze and Guattari, *A Thousand Plateaus*, 175.

75. Balázs, 82–83.

76. Ibid., 81.

77. Ibid., 83.

78. See Guillaumin, "Race and Nature," 27.

79. It could be said that some of this historical incongruity between the black man and the suit is at work in Robert Mapplethorpe's infamous photograph, "Man in Polyester Suit." The definitive work on this photograph is in Kobena Mercer, *Welcome to the Jungle* (London: Routledge, 1994), chap. 6.

80. See Thomas L. Johnson, "Richard Samuel Roberts: An Introduction," in *A True Likeness: The Black South of Richard Samuel Roberts, 1920–1936*, ed. Thomas L. Johnson and Phillip C. Dunn (New York: Writers and Readers Publishing, Inc., 1994), 1–10. Johnson provides an overview of the career of the black photographer, who worked in Columbia, South Carolina, in the 1920s and 1930s. John Hiller is identified in the book as a farmer who lived around Lake Murray near Columbia (p. 84). The story about his two families is from Deborah Willis, "Framing Photography between the Wars: The Artist and Society," public lecture as part of "Rhapsodies in Black: Art of the Harlem Renaissance," The Corcoran Gallery of Art, Washington, D.C., May 2, 1998.

81. Kathe Sandler, "Finding a Space for Myself," in *Picturing Us*, ed. Deborah Willis (New York: New Press, 1994), 105–112.

82. bell hooks, *Black Looks: Race and Representation* (Boston: South End Press, 1992).

83. Lillian Smith, *Killers of the Dream* (1949; reprint, Garden City, New York: Anchor Books, 1963), 134–135.

84. Deleuze and Guattari, *A Thousand Plateaus*, 190.

85. Eric Lott, *Love and Theft: Blackface Minstrelsy and the American Working Class* (New York: Oxford University Press, 1993).

86. An excellent example of this kind of research already under way is Charlene Regester, "African American Extras in Hollywood during the 1920s and 1930s," *Film History* 9 (1997): 95–115.

87. The story of the discovery of *The Symbol of the Unconquered* in Europe is a companion to the repatriation story of *Within Our Gates*. In this case, however, Micheaux's lost film was discovered at the Cinémathèque Royale / Koninklijk Filmarchief in Brussels, another clue that he had distributed his films outside the United States when they met with resistance here. The film was returned from the Belgian Film Archive to the Museum of Modern Art around 1990, and in 1998 the intertitles (in both French and Flemish) were translated into English. Where the film appeared to be missing a section, a portion of a description of the sequence from a *New York Age* review was substituted as an intertitle. Pearl Bowser and Louise Spence, in "Identity and Betrayal: *The Symbol of the Unconquered* and Oscar Micheaux's 'Biographical Legend,'" in *The Birth of Whiteness: Race and the Emergence of U.S. Cinema,* ed. Daniel Bernardi (New Brunswick, N.J.: Rutgers University Press, 1996), 79, note 69, point out that the Museum of Modern Art print is only 3,852 feet, which means that the film material in this only known print may be around half of its original seven-reel length, the length that was advertised when the film was released in 1920. For more, see *"The Symbol of the Unconquered:* Restored by Turner Classic Movies," *The Oscar Micheaux Society Newsletter* 7 (summer 1998): 1–2. See also introduction, note 21, and chapter 7, note 84.

88. See Pearl Bowser and Louise Spence, *"The Symbol of the Unconquered:* Text and Context," in Bowser, Gaines, and Musser, eds., *Oscar Micheaux and His Circle,* for the important theme of Micheaux's West in this film. See also Pearl Bowser and Louise Spence, *Writing Himself into History: Oscar Micheaux, His Silent Films, and His Novels* (New Brunswick, N.J.: Rutgers University Press, 2000).

89. As quoted in Bowser and Spence, "Identity and Betrayal," 78, note 52.

90. Ibid., 69.

91. The score was performed live by Roach at the premiere of the new restoration of the film at the Apollo Theatre in Harlem on July 7, 1998, after the July 1 television premiere on Turner Classic Movies, kicking off a month of programming featuring early black cinema.

92. Malcom Miranda-Monsman, *"The Symbol of the Unconquered:* Rhythmic Leitmotifs and Perspectives on Max Roach's Musical Score," *The Oscar Micheaux Society Newsletter* 8 (spring 2000): 3–4.

93. Ibid.

Chapter Seven

1. "Films and Births and Censorship," *The Survey*, 3 April 1915, 4, gives the best account of the history of the first vote as well as the second vote and the cuts stipulated by the National Board of Censorship at its second meeting. Explaining the ramifications of the decision, the article explains, "While the board is purely a voluntary body without actual power of stopping any motion picture, its decisions are so widely accepted that disapproval of a film debars it from 80 per cent of the motion picture houses in the country." See Francis G. Couvares, "The Good Censor: Race, Sex, and Censorship in the Early Cinema," *Yale Journal of Criticism* 7, no. 2 (1994): 233–236, for a careful reconsideration of the NAACP campaign against *The Birth of a Nation*, particularly at the outset. Here he asserts that "little new has been added to the controversy over free expression" (p. 233).

2. *The New York Times*, 31 March 1915, p. 9, col. 2, quotes Rabbi Stephen Wise as saying:

> If it is true that the Mayor has no power to stop this indescribably foul and loathsome libel on a race of human beings, then it is true that Government has broke down. The Board of Censors which allowed this exhibition to go on is stupid or worse. I regret I am a member.

Oswald Garrison Villard, vice president of the NAACP, is quoted as saying that in his opinion the film was "improper, immoral and unjust."

3. The original article, "Egg Negro Scenes in Liberty Film Play," *New York Times*, 15 April 1915, p. 1, col. 2, is interesting for the use of "egg" as a verb. See also Janet Staiger, "*The Birth of a Nation*: Reconsidering Its Reception," in *The Birth of a Nation*, ed. Robert Lang (New Brunswick, N.J.: Rutgers University Press, 1994), 203. Raymond Cook, in "The Man behind *The Birth of a Nation*," *North Carolina Historical Review* 39, no. 4 (1962): 543, describes the scene: "As egg yolks oozed down the face of the screen and spectators took short cuts over the backs of seats, it became apparent that the sacred injunction of 'the show must go on' would be violated that night."

4. Thomas Cripps, *Slow Fade to Black: The Negro in American Film 1900–1942* (New York: Oxford University Press, 1977), 59–60. Stephen R. Fox, in *The Guardian of Boston: William Monroe Trotter* (New York: Atheneum, 1970), 193, quotes the Boston newspaper account to the effect that at the point when the young woman is about to leap from the cliff a Negro "spattered a very ancient egg by a well-directed shot over the exact middle of the white screen."

5. Fox, *The Guardian of Boston*, 193; " 'Birth of a Nation' Came Near Causing a Riot in a Boston Play House," *Philadelphia Tribune*, 24 April 1915, 1.

6. Staiger, "*The Birth of a Nation*: Reconsidering Its Reception," 198.

7. *Uncle Josh at the Moving Picture Show* has become a metaphor for discussing the relationship between the spectator and the illusion in film theory. See Judith Mayne, *The Woman at the Keyhole* (Bloomington: Indiana University

Press, 1990), 31–33; Miriam Hansen, *Babel and Babylon: Spectatorship in American Silent Film* (Cambridge: Harvard University Press, 1991), 25–28. Vance Kepley, in "Whose Apparatus? Problems of Film Exhibition and History," in *Post-Theory: Reconstructing Film Studies,* ed. David Bordwell and Noël Carroll (Madison: University of Wisconsin Press, 1996), 533, uses the film as a way of talking about the possibility that spectators were anything but naïve, that they may have been thoroughly aware of the projector in the theater and other devices that produced the illusion.

8. Couvares, "The Good Censor," 237. Citing the attempts of the National Board as well as local censor boards in the 1910s and 1920s to regulate ethnic images, he concludes, "Over and again, standards that might have seemed designed to protect disempowered groups from defamation became grounds for stifling all discussion of sensitive interethnic—and intraethnic—issues" (p. 238).

9. Annette Kuhn, *Cinema, Censorship and Sexuality, 1909–1925* (New York: Routledge, 1988), 7. Kuhn offers Michel Foucault's definition of power, from *Discipline and Punish: The Birth of the Prison* (Harmondsworth: Penguin, 1977), 26: "a network of relations, constantly in tension, rather than a privilege that one might possess. . . . In short, this power is exercised rather than possessed."

10. See Janet Staiger, *Bad Women: Regulating Sexuality in Early American Cinema* (Minneapolis: University of Minnesota, 1995), 54–61, on the early development of a self-regulating industry board as well as the practices of local regulation, which included seizing films in the theaters. See ibid., 196, note 1 for the basic distinction.

11. Marx argued for seeing censorship in close relation to criticism. See Sue Curry Jansen, *Censorship: The Knot That Binds Power and Knowledge* (New York: Oxford University Press, 1988), chap. 5, for the utility of Marx's analysis as well as a critique of it.

12. Thomas Dixon, *The Clansman: An Historical Romance of the Ku Klux Klan* (New York: Grosset & Dunlap, 1905); Thomas Dixon, *The Leopard's Spots: A Romance of the White Man's Burden, 1865–1900* (New York: Doubleday, 1902).

13. Thanks to Thomas Cripps for urging me to think about the way that the leaders who took up the cause against *The Birth of a Nation* were then and have continued to be considered heroic.

14. Carrie Allen McCray, in *Freedom's Child: The Story of My Mother, A Confederate General's Black Daughter* (New York: Penguin Books, 1998), chap. 26, describes her mother's involvement in both the struggle to integrate the Claridge Theatre in Montclair, New Jersey, and in the protest there against *The Birth of a Nation* at the time of the 1924 rerelease. Charles Flint Kellogg, in *NAACP: A History of the National Association for the Advancement of Colored People,* vol. 1, 1909–1920 (Baltimore: Johns Hopkins Press, 1967), 145, concludes that while the fight may have publicized the film, it also publicized the goals and aims of the NAACP.

15. Charles Lyons, "The Paradox of Protest: American Film, 1980–1992," in

Movie Censorship and American Culture, ed. Francis G. Couvares (Washington, D.C.: Smithsonian Institution Press, 1996), 280. Lyons mentions *The Birth of a Nation* in the context of important contemporary protests by coalitions of Puerto Ricans, Cuban Americans, Italian Americans, and Asian Americans against films such as *Fort Apache, the Bronx* (1981), *Scarface* (1983), *The Godfather* (1972), and *The Year of the Dragon* (1985).

16. Nickieann Fleener-Marzec, *D. W. Griffith's The Birth of a Nation: Controversy, Suppression, and the First Amendment As It Applies to Filmic Expression, 1915–1973* (New York: Arno Press), 97 (on the prohibition in Ohio). In the years the author studied, eighty-four municipal bodies were asked to censor the film. Twelve mayors indicated concern that the film would incite race prejudice as the reason for censoring the film. The first to do so, the mayor of Cedar Rapids, Iowa, agreed to ban the film in 1915 after he had heard from a delegation of five black citizens (pp. 216–217). NAACP committees exerted successful influence on the mayors of Louisville, Kentucky, and Gary, Indiana (p. 221). In Richmond, Virginia, the mayor responded not to the NAACP but to prominent citizens and to protesters who feared that the film would "stir up race feeling" and that it was "a reproduction of the Ku Klux days following the Civil War in which the intermarriage between negro and white is portrayed" (p. 218).

17. Janet Staiger, "Self-Regulation and the Classical Hollywood Cinema," *Journal of Dramatic Theory and Criticism* 6, no. 1 (1991): 224. Staiger's article, which challenges us to consider these pleasures produced by censorship, is a provocative beginning to a more comprehensive theory. She concludes after a close analysis of reviews of censored films from the 1930s, "What was regulated was not necessarily what the censors thought ought to be. What was consumed was not always 'inside' the text" (p. 225).

18. Fleener-Marzec, *D. W. Griffith's The Birth of a Nation*, 224.

19. Fleener-Marzec, ibid., 224–225, quotes the mayor of Oakland, California, who, concerned about the influence that his ban would have on showings in San Francisco, said, the film "would therefore get a thousand times more publicity than if permitted to run its course."

20. Cripps, *Slow Fade to Black*, 61, 64. Booker T. Washington, however, used the fact that protests had been simulated as an argument against involving his organization in the NAACP's attempts to stop the exhibition of the film (p. 61). Fleener-Marzec, *D. W. Griffith's The Birth of a Nation*, 49, note 103, cites the recollection of Bill Keefe, a Los Angeles reporter who says in his oral history that he hired sixty blacks to protest the opening of *The Birth of a Nation* at what would have been the March 1915 premiere in that city.

21. Kuhn, *Cinema, Censorship and Sexuality*, 5–6.

22. Ibid., 4. It is well known that among Griffith's several articulated defenses of *The Birth of a Nation* was a free speech defense. See D. W. Griffith, "The Rise and Fall of Free Speech in America," in *The Movies in Our Midst: Documents in the Cultural History of Film in America*, ed. Gerald Mast (Chicago: University of Chicago Press, 1982), 132–135. See, on the problem with the recourse

to "freedom of speech," Stanley Fish, "There's No Such Thing as Free Speech and It's a Good Thing, Too," in *Debating P.C.: The Controversy over Political Correctness on College Campuses,* ed. Paul Berman (New York: Dell, 1992).

23. See Hansen, *Babel and Babylon,* chap. 3, for the most important discussion of early cinema in relation to the concept of the public sphere. Adapting the theoretical work of Oskar Negt and Alexander Kluge, she imagines the possibilities (existing in theory) for seeing the new sphere produced under capitalism (the "industrial commercial public sphere") as "indiscriminately *inclusive*" (p. 92). It is relevant to recall here that it was the public debate around *The Birth of a Nation* that not only produced wide public awareness of the NAACP but provided the opportunity for black middle class entry into this space.

24. Kellogg, *NAACP,* 143. See also Mary White Ovington, *The Walls Came Tumbling Down* (New York: Harcourt & Brace, 1947), 127.

25. Judith Butler, *Bodies That Matter* (New York: Routledge, 1993), 30, lays out this quandary as resolved by poststructuralism: "If the body signified as prior to signification is an effect of signification, then the mimetic or representational status of language, which claims that signs follow bodies as their necessary mirrors, is not mimetic at all. On the contrary . . . it [language] is productive, constitutive."

26. The most important Marxist theorization of the "ideological effect" is still Stuart Hall's "Culture, the Media, and the Ideological Effect," in *Mass Communication and Society,* ed. J. Curran et al. (London: Edward Arnold, 1977), important in that it allowed a more precise use of the Marxist notion of ideology, a pinpointing that would be significant in the development of cultural studies. For an introduction to the early challenge to "effects studies" from the point of view of Marxist cultural studies, see Paddy Whannel, "Foreward," in André Glucksmann, *Violence on the Screen* (London: British Film Institute, Education Department, 1971).

27. Pierre Macherey, *A Theory of Literary Production* (London: Routledge and Kegan Paul, 1978), 45. See also Pierre Macherey, "Problems of Reflection," *Literature, Society and the Sociology of Literature,* ed. Francis Barker et al. (Proceedings of the University of Essex Conference, 1976).

28. For a relevant overview of the political implications of formalism, see Bill Nichols, "Form Wars: The Political Unconscious of Formalist Theory," in *Classical Hollywood Narrative: The Paradigm Wars,* ed. Jane Gaines (Durham: Duke University Press, 1992).

29. Alex Juhasz, in "They Said We Were Trying to Show Reality—All I Want to Show Is My Video: The Politics of the Realist Feminist Documentary," in *Collecting Visible Evidence,* ed. Jane M. Gaines and Michael Renov (Minneapolis: University of Minnesota Press, 1999), makes this point about the political uses of aesthetic realism as opposed to aesthetic modernism in her discussion of the feminist realist debates of the 1970s.

30. On the censorship struggles around the film, see Richard Schickel, *D. W. Griffith: An American Life* (New York: Simon and Schuster, 1984), 281–288;

Cripps, *Slow Fade to Black,* chap. 2, especially 56–64. Fleener-Marzec, *D. W. Griffith's The Birth of a Nation,* 214, summarizes the advice that the NAACP gave to its local chapters as they urged them to take legal action: (1) find a lawyer, preferably white, and study local ordinances that might be used against the films; (2) in the event that there is an ordinance, urge black as well as white organizations to protest the film's screening to mayors, police commissioners, and censorship boards; (3) in the event that there is no local ordinance, take steps to seek legislation; and (4) after these alternatives have been exhausted, attempt "to try to have the worst scenes eliminated." The NAACP national office identified the "most objectionable" scenes as the scene in which Gus pursues Flora and the scene in which Sylas Lynch attempts to force marriage on Elsie Stoneman.

31. In many cities such as New York, Philadelphia, and Des Moines, censorship was attempted through the invocation of antiriot ordinances. By the end of 1915, however, Griffith and his lawyers were successful against the NAACP, and it was clear that the film could be shown in most cities and towns where distributors wanted to exhibit it. Cripps, *Slow Fade to Black,* 63–64.

32. As recently as 1993, the film stirred controversy when it was exhibited at the Library of Congress. See J. Hoberman, "We Must Remember This," *Village Voice,* 30 November 1993, 2–4; "Cancellation of a 'Nation,' " *Variety,* 31 May 1989, 7 (on the NAACP pressure exerted against screening the film at Brown University); "Violence Causes Cancellation of Film Classic," *San Francisco Chronicle,* 13 June 1980 (on the vandalism at the Richelieu Cinema caused by Berkeley graduate student members of INCAR, the International Committee Against Racism). All available in Museum of Modern Art, New York, clippings file.

33. As quoted in Leonard C. Archer, *Black Images in the American Theatre* (Brooklyn: Pageant-Poseidon, 1973), 197.

34. J. M. Coetzee, *Giving Offense: Essays on Censorship* (Chicago: University of Chicago Press, 1996). Thinking of the censorship of his own writing, Coetzee considers that the censor is "an intrusive reader, a reader who forces his way into the intimacy of the writing transaction, forces out the figure of the loved or courted reader, reads your words in a disapproving and *censorious* fashion" (p. 35).

35. Fleener-Marzec, *D. W. Griffith's The Birth of a Nation,* 30, refers to the recollection by the historian of the NAACP Mary White Ovington that, because both the beginning and the end of the pursuit were missing from the Gus chase scene, the audience was left to wonder why Flora was discovered dead. Parker Tyler, in *Sex, Psyche Et Cetera in the Film* (New York: Horizon Press, 1969), 139, says that the result of cutting was that some sequences in the original print looked "absurd."

36. Kuhn, *Cinema, Censorship and Sexuality,* 129.

37. Kuhn also reminds us of the problems endemic to the anticensorship position. In addition to the alignment with the single-minded free speech position, anticensorship can be associated with a form of naive realism, espe-

cially when the censor is seen as intervening between the "real" world and the world of the text in such a way that the process of reflection is inhibited. Here the fear would be that the censored text could no longer be "true to life." *Cinema, Censorship and Sexuality*, 2.

38. Anthony Appiah, in " 'No Bad Nigger': Blacks as the Ethical Principle in the Movies," in *Media Spectacles*, ed. Marjorie Garber, Jann Matlock, and Rebecca L. Walkowitz (New York: Routledge, 1993), 85, says that

> to call a film racist or homophobic suggests that there is something wrong with it, in the way that there is something wrong with a person who is racist. Like it or not, terms like "racist" and "homophobic" are moralizing. But we need to be clear about *what* the wrong is. If the film reflects a racist or homophobic culture, then what's wrong is that the culture is racist or homophobic: the film's just a symptom and boycotting it is like blowing smoke when we should be dousing the fire. If a film reinforces racism, then what's wrong is that it makes the culture more racist than it would have been otherwise.

See also my "Who Is Reading Robert Mapplethorpe's Black Book?" *New Formations* 16 (summer 1992): 24–39, for a discussion of the problem of taking the racist temperature of cultural texts.

39. Appiah, "No Bad Niggers," 84, gives a dramatic example of the way a film produced by and through a culture of fascism does not necessarily reproduce itself ideologically when he describes Leni Riefenstahl's *Triumph of the Will* as a film "whose effect now is not to encourage Nazism but to chill the blood."

40. As quoted in Fleener-Marzec, *D. W. Griffith's The Birth of A Nation*, 8.

41. *Chicago Defender*, 22 May 1915.

42. Fleener-Marzec, *D. W. Griffith's The Birth of A Nation*, 38. To list only some of the significant struggles that Fleener-Marzec has documented: in addition to the well-known difficulties that the film encountered in the year of its release in New York, Boston, Chicago, Philadelphia, Atlantic City, Wilmington, Delaware, Charleston, West Virginia, Baltimore, Newark, and St. Louis, as well as in the states of Kansas and Ohio, there were struggles during the revivals in Philadelphia in 1931 and in New York in 1942, 1946, and 1947, as well as in Atlanta in 1959.

43. Micheaux said in a letter to the Virginia Censorship Board that had required cuts in *The House behind the Cedars*, "There has not been but one picture that incited the colored people to riot, and that still does, that picture is the BIRTH OF A NATION." Oscar Micheaux to Virginia Motion Picture Censors, 13 March 1925, Virginia Division of Motion Picture Censorship, Virginia State Library and Archives.

44. This important research, conducted primarily by Charlene Regester, reveals a treasure trove of information about the organization of the state and city

censor boards as well as their particular treatment of Micheaux. See, for instance, Charlene Regester, "Lynched, Assaulted, and Intimidated: Oscar Micheaux's Most Controversial Films," *Popular Culture Review* 5, no. 1 (February 1994): 49–51; Cripps, *Slow Fade to Black,* 189, 192. See also Charlene Regester, "Oscar Micheaux on the Cutting Edge: Films Rejected by the New York State Motion Picture Commission," *Studies in Popular Culture* (spring 1995): 61–72; Charlene Regester, "Black Films, White Censors: Oscar Micheaux Confronts Censorship in New York, Virginia, and Chicago," in Couvares, ed., *Movie Censorship.*

45. Regester, in "Oscar Micheaux on the Cutting Edge," analyzes the records of the New York State Motion Picture Commission, a three-person commission established in 1921. On the basis of correspondence between Micheaux and the Commission, it would seem that Micheaux was required to make many "eliminations" in the films he produced and attempted to exhibit in New York in the 1920s. Since the majority of titles dealt with in the correspondence are not extant, it is difficult to determine the nature of the imagery the board took exception to. One could conjecture that the board was applying a double standard of approval in their required "elimination" of scenes such as "sisters fight" and "Evelyn enters with a knife to stab father" in *Deceit* (1923) (p. 64).

46. Cripps, *Slow Fade to Black,* 192.

47. Regester, "Black Films, White Censors," 176–177.

48. Ibid., 174–175. In Chicago the title was worded somewhat differently: "Legal—hell—everything a white man wants to put over on a spade is legal."

49. Fox, *The Guardian of Boston,* 193.

50. "Films and Births and Censorship," *Survey,* 3 April 1915, 4–5.

51. Seymour Stern, "*The Birth of a Nation*," *Cinemages,* no. 1 (1955): 9, as quoted in Staiger, "*The Birth of a Nation*: Reconsidering Its Reception," 198, note 13. Robert Lang, in "History, Ideology, Narrative Form," in *The Birth of a Nation,* ed. Robert Lang (New Brunswick, N.J.: Rutgers University Press, 1994), 11, note 26, says that he has found no evidence that the film ever contained a scene of the black deportation to Africa, although there is evidence that it contained an intertitle ("Back to Liberia!") that refers to the famous "Lincoln's solution."

52. Seymour Stern, "Griffith: *The Birth of a Nation,* Part I," *Film Culture* no. 36 (spring–summer, 1965): 123–124. Stern is a strange figure in the history of D. W. Griffith's archive. In 1930 he was a Leftist, who with Lewis Jacobs, David Platt, and Harry Alan Potamkin started the progressive journal *Experimental Cinema.* By 1940 he was a rabid anti-Stalinist and fierce apologist for D. W. Griffith. His 1965 *Film Culture* description of the "castration" scene is, to my knowledge, the only detailed description in print, and efforts to find the footage and the more or less complete print he describes seeing in 1933 have not met with success. See Staiger's important overview of Stern's political vacillation as it relates to his alliance with Griffith in the director's later years. "*The Birth of a Nation*: Reconsidering Its Reception," 207–212. Linda Williams, in *Playing the Race Card: Melodramas of Black and White from Uncle Tom to O. J. Simpson* (Princeton:

Princeton University Press, forthcoming), is equally dubious about Stern's account. Clearly there is a lot riding on the discovery of this missing footage.

53. Stern, section on "The Film's Score," in "Griffith: *The Birth of a Nation,* Part I," 123.

54. Boston Branch, National Association for the Advancement of Colored People, "Fighting a Vicious Film: Protest against 'The Birth of a Nation,' " in Mast, ed., *The Movies in Our Midst.* See also Thomas Dixon, "Fair Play for *The Birth of a Nation,*" *Boston Journal,* 26 April 1915, reprinted in *Focus on The Birth of a Nation,* ed. Fred Silva (Englewood Cliffs, N.J.: Prentice Hall, 1971), in which Dixon says that "[t]he plain truth is that every Negro associated with Mr. Storey [Morefield Storey] in the Intermarriage Society, which is conducting this persecution, hates *The Birth of Nation* for one reason only—it opposes the marriage of blacks to whites" (p. 95).

55. "Fighting a Vicious Film," as analyzed by Francis Hackett, in Mast, ed., *The Movies in Our Midst,* 127. Dixon's characterization of the NAACP as the "Intermarriage Society" is a reference to its organized and effective campaign against state laws that made intermarriage illegal, a campaign that was successful in Ohio, Wisconsin, and New York. Schickel, *D. W. Griffith,* 287.

56. Stern, "Griffith: *The Birth of a Nation,* Part I, " 123, estimates that the castration scene was shown at the Liberty Theatre in New York in the first five or six weeks after its premiere (March through early April 1915) and in the South for fifty years. Michael Rogin, in " 'The Sword Became a Flashing Vision': D. W. Griffith's *The Birth of a Nation,*" *Representations* 9 (winter 1985): 174, takes Stern at his word and gives more emphasis to the deletion of "Gus's castration" than any other contemporary commentator. John Hammond Moore, in "South Carolina's Reaction to the Photoplay, *The Birth of a Nation,*" *Proceedings of South Carolina Historical Association* 33 (1963): 30–40, suggests that the enthusiasm for the film was not as uniform in the South as one might expect it to be, especially considering the feud between Dixon and the press in South Carolina that began the year that *The Clansman* was published.

57. In proposing a publicity approach, Micheaux wrote, "Nothing would make more people as anxious to see a picture than a litho reading: SHALL THE RACES INTERMARRY?" Oscar Micheaux to the Lincoln Motion Picture Company, 25 June 1918, in George P. Johnson Collection, Department of Special Collections, Young Research Library, University of California, Los Angeles, hereafter GPJC.

58. Cindy Patton, "White Racism/Black Signs: Censorship and Images of Race Relations," *Journal of Communication* 45, no. 2 (1995): 71. See also Motion Picture Producers and Distributors of America, "The Motion Picture Production Code of 1930," in Mast, ed., *The Movies in Our Midst,* 321–333. The relevant rule is "No. 6. MISCEGÉNATION (sex relationship between the white and black races is forbidden)" (p. 333).

59. Naomi Zack, *Race and Mixed Race* (Philadelphia: Temple University Press, 1993), 77, says that when the U.S. Supreme Court struck down the laws

against interracial marriage in 1967 in *Loving v. Virginia,* fifteen states in addition to Virginia still had miscegenation laws on the books, and as many as thirty-eight states had passed such laws before 1967.

60. Boston Branch, NAACP, "Fighting a Vicious Film," in Mast, ed., *The Movies in Our Midst,* 126.

61. See Jane Gaines and Neil Lerner, "The Orchestration of Affect," in *The Sounds of Early Cinema,* ed. Richard Abel and Rick Altman (Bloomington: Indiana University Press, forthcoming), for a discussion of the "Barbarism motif" in the Joseph Carl Breil score for the film, particularly relevant to this sequence. Martin Marks, *Music and the Silent Film: Contexts and Case Studies, 1895–1924* (Oxford: Oxford University Press, 1997), is the definitive source for information on the Breil score for *The Birth of a Nation.* See Marks, chap. 4.

62. Joel Williamson, *New People: Miscegenation and Mulattoes in the United States* (New York: Free Press, 1980), 127.

63. Rogin, "The Sword Became a Flashing Vision," 174, describes how Gus "foams at the mouth" as he chases Flora, but argues that "in the original version he probably raped her" since that is what happened in the novel, *The Clansman.* But this is problematic. Does he mean that the longer version of the film without cuts *represented* a "rape"? We would not want to get involved in a debate as to whether Gus did or didn't rape Flora; it is a matter of the use of imagery that stands for "rape." More recently, Cedric Robinson has shed new light on the sequence with his suggestion that the 1913 Leo Frank lynching case is influential here, particularly since the prosecutor in that case described the thirteen-year-old victim, Mary Phagan, as having chosen death instead of rape, a formulation of Flora's dilemma. Cedric Robinson, "In the Year 1915: D. W. Griffith and the Whitening of America," *Social Identities* 3, no. 2 (1997): 177–78.

64. See my *"Birth of a Nation and Within Our Gates,"* in *Dixie Debates: Perspectives in Southern Culture,* ed. Richard H. King and Helen Taylor (London: Pluto Press, 1995), and "Birthing Nations," in *Cinema and Nation,* ed. Matte Hjort and Scott Mackenzie (London: Routledge, 2000).

65. Coetzee, *Giving Offense,* 8.

66. *Mutual Film Corporation v. Industrial Commission of Ohio,* 236 U.S. 244 (1915).

67. Regester, "Black Films, White Censors," 170.

68. George P. Johnson to Oscar Micheaux, 13 August 1920, in GPJC.

69. George P. Johnson to Oscar Micheaux, 4 August 1920, in GPJC.

70. George P. Johnson to Oscar Micheaux, 10 August 1920, in GPJC.

71. Superintendent Monney to Captain Ray, 19 March 1920, in GPJC.

72. George P. Johnson to Robert Vann, undated letter, in GPJC.

73. As quoted in Regester, "Lynched, Assaulted, and Intimidated," 49. It is interesting to note that the *Defender* has integrated the wording from Micheaux's own publicity, "the biggest protest against Race prejudice, lynching, and, 'concubinage,' " a common practice in the early decades of cinema,

especially in the case of small-town newspaper reviews, which were often taken verbatim from material provided in the Hollywood press books that began to appear around 1913. Henry T. Sampson, *Blacks in Black and White: A Source Book on Black Films*, 2d ed. (Metuchen, N.J.: Scarecrow Press, 1995), 279, quotes the Omaha, Nebraska *Daily:*

> This is the picture that required two solid months to get by the censor board and it is the claim of the author and producer that while it is a bit radical it is also the biggest protest against race prejudice, lynching and "concubinage" that was ever written or filmed and that there are more thrills and gripping, holding moments than ever seen in any individual production.

74. James Grossman, *Land of Hope* (Chicago: University of Chicago Press, 1989), 79.

75. Kevin K. Gaines, *Uplifting the Race* (Chapel Hill: University of North Carolina Press, 1996), 88.

76. Ida Wells-Barnett, *On Lynching: Southern Horrors; A Red Record; Mob Rule in New Orleans* (1892–1900; reprint, New York: Arno Press, 1969).

77. Regester, "Lynched, Assaulted, and Intimidated," 49.

78. Linda Williams, in *Hard Core: Power, Pleasure, and the "Frenzy of the Visible"* (Berkeley: University of California Press, 1989), 11, confirms this from the standpoint of the pornography industry, arguing the futility of censorship on the theory that the "censored text becomes immediately desirable."

79. As quoted in Sampson, *Blacks in Black and White*, 557.

80. Dan Streible, "A History of the Boxing Film, 1894–1915," *Film History* 3 (1989): 243.

81. Ibid., 247.

82. Robinson, "In the Year 1915," 176–177. While Robinson offers the case of Jack Johnson as motivation for Griffith and Dixon's individualized tirade against the threat of black sexuality, I am more inclined to consider Johnson's relationships as another lightning rod for the public terror of interracial lust.

83. Nickie Fleener, "Answering Film with Film: The Hampton Epilogue, a Positive Alternative to the Negative Black Stereotypes Presented in *The Birth of a Nation*," *Journal of Popular Film and Television* 7, no. 41 (1980): 400–425.

84. See my "Micheaux's *Within Our Gates*: Now Available on Videotape," *Oscar Micheaux Society Newsletter* 3 (summer 1994): 1–2, in which I detail the history of the discovery of this film in the Spanish Film Archive in Madrid and its repatriation to the United States. Identified in the late 1970s by Thomas Cripps, the film, then titled *La Negra*, was acquired by the Library of Congress in a trade for a print of the Bela Lugosi version of *Dracula* (1931). The upside-down frames in the Spanish print were reversed when the 35mm film was restored and translated into English by Scott Simmon with the aid of an earlier translation by Kathleen Newman. See introduction, note 21; chapter 6, note 87.

85. Carl Sandburg, *The Chicago Race Riots* (New York: Harcourt, Brace and Howe, 1919), 1.

86. Arthur I. Waskow, *From Race Riot to Sit-In: 1919 and the 1960s* (Garden City: Doubleday & Co., 1967), 10; Lee E. Williams and Lee Williams II, *Anatomy of Four Riots* (Hattiesburg: University and College Press of Mississippi, 1972), 76.

87. W. E. B. Du Bois, *Darkwater: Voices from within the Veil* (1920; reprint, New York: AMS Press, 1969), 94–95.

88. Waskow, *From Race Riot to Sit-In*, 10.

89. Ibid.

90. William M. Tuttle, *Race Riot: Chicago in the Red Summer of 1919* (New York: Atheneum, 1970), 33.

91. As quoted in Richard Hofstadter, "Reflections on Violence in the United States," in *American Violence: A Documentary History*, ed. Richard Hofstadter and Michael Wallace (New York: Alfred Knopf, 1970), 35. See also ibid., 245–249, on the 1919 riots in Chicago.

92. Ibid., 10.

93. Ibid., 31–32; Barrington Moore, "Thoughts on Violence and Democracy," *Proceedings of the Academy of Political Science,* 29 (1968): 6–7.

94. Waskow, *From Race Riot to Sit-In*, 12.

95. James Weldon Johnson, *Along This Way* (New York: Viking Press, 1933), 341.

96. Frantz Fanon, *The Wretched of the Earth,* trans. Constance Farrington (New York: Grove Weidenfeld, 1963), 88.

97. Ibid., 93.

98. Jean-Paul Sartre, preface to *The Wretched of the Earth,* ibid., 18.

99. Frederick Douglass, "Lynch Law in the South," *North American Review* 155 (July 1892): 2.

100. Linda Williams, in "Corporealized Observers: Visual Pornographies and the 'Carnal Density of Vision,'" in *Fugitive Images: From Photography to Video,* ed. Patrice Petro (Bloomington: Indiana University Press, 1995), 20, says that "the body moves, and is in turn moved by, the machine." See also Jonathan Crary, *Techniques of the Observer: On Vision and Modernity in the Nineteenth Century* (Cambridge: MIT Press, 1995).

101. Michael Omni and Howard Wishart, "The Los Angeles 'Race Riots' and U.S. Politics," in *Reading Rodney King/Reading Urban Uprising,* ed. Robert Gooding-Williams (New York: Routledge, 1993), 100.

102. Hansen, *Babel and Babylon,* chap. 2.

103. "Motion Picture Production Code of 1930," in Mast, ed., *The Movies in Out Midst,* 323.

104. Patton, "White Racism/Black Signs," 73.

105. Mary Ann Doane, "Dark Continents: Epistemologies of Racial and Sexual Difference in Psychoanalysis and the Cinema," in *Femmes Fatales: Feminism, Film Theory, Psychoanalysis* (London: Routledge, 1991), 213. Clyde Taylor, in *The Mask of Art: Breaking the Aesthetic Contract—Film and Literature* (Bloomington: Indiana University Press, 1998), 98, discusses the way this formulation excludes black women. While white women bear the burden of the gaze, he says, non-

white women make this "burden" almost "bearable," located as they are as the "aesthetic others" of white women; in turn, the white woman's aesthetic has been cruelly "turned against" black women.

106. Mary Ann Doane, "Film and the Masquerade," *Screen* 23, nos. 3–4 (September–October 1982): 74–87, reprinted in *The Sexual Subject* (London: Routledge, 1992).

107. Anne Friedberg, "The Denial of Difference: Theories of Cinematic Identification," in *Psychoanalysis and Cinema,* ed. E. Ann Kaplan (New York: Routledge, 1990), 44.

108. Christian Metz, "The Imaginary Signifier," *Screen* 16, no. 2 (1975): 54.

109. Michael Taussig, *Mimesis and Alterity* (London: Routledge, 1993), 21.

110. See Miriam Hansen, "Benjamin, Cinema and Experience: The Blue Flower in the Land of Technology," *New German Critique* 40 (winter 1987): 179–224, for a discussion of Walter Benjamin's understanding of mimesis as mystical.

111. See Michel Foucault, *The Order of Things* (New York: Vintage, 1973), chap. 2.

112. Taussig, *Mimesis and Alterity,* 36.

113. Ibid., 2.

114. Ibid., 47.

115. Ibid., 57.

116. Ibid., 49.

117. See Maxim Simcovitch, "The Impact of Griffith's *Birth of a Nation* on the Modern Ku Klux Klan," *Journal of Popular Film* 1, no. 1 (1972): 45–54.

118. For further on the application of the concept of "imaging back," see my "Political Mimesis," in Gaines and Renov, eds., *Collecting Visible Evidence.*

119. Taussig, *Mimesis and Alterity,* 33.

120. Linda Williams, in "Film Bodies: Gender, Genre, and Excess," *Film Quarterly* 44, no. 4 (summer 1991): 4, identifies three "body genres": horror, melodrama, and pornography. To summarize her provocative analysis: horror makes you scream, melodrama makes you cry, and pornography makes you "come." Body genres feature a sensationalized on-screen body and "produce," on the bodies of spectators, an "almost involuntary mimicry of emotion or sensation of the body on screen." The germ of this idea can be found in Richard Dyer, "Gay Male Porn: Coming to Terms," *Jump Cut: A Review of Contemporary Media,* no. 30 (March 1985): 27–29.

121. See my "Political Mimesis," in Gaines and Renov, eds., *Collecting Visible Evidence.*

122. Cripps, *Slow Fade to Black,* 60.

123. Simcovitch, "The Impact of Griffith's *Birth of a Nation,*" 46.

124. Ibid., 49.

125. For a recent discussion of the Soviet "debt" to Griffith, see Yuri Tsivian, "Homeless Images: D. W. Griffith in the Eye of Soviet Filmmakers," *Griffithiana* 60/61 (October 1997): 51–75.

126. Todd Boyd, "Put Some Brothers on the Wall: Rap, Rock, and the Visual Empowerment of African American Culture," in *Shared Differences: Multicultural Media and Practical Pedagogy*, ed. Diane Carson and Lester Friedman (Urbana: University of Illinois Press, 1995).

127. See Homi K. Bhabha, *The Location of Culture* (New York: Routledge, 1994), especially chap. 4, "Of Mimicry and Man."

128. See Taussig's brilliant reading of Charles Darwin's account of his "first contact" with the people of Tierra del Fuego in his 1832 diary of the voyage of the *Beagle* where he describes the extraordinary mimetic capabilities of the Fuegians, who "mime the sailors' language by deadly accurate copying." *Mimesis and Alterity*, 80.

Conclusion

1. Pierre Macherey, in "Problems of Reflection," in *Literature, Society and the Sociology of Literature*, ed. Francis Bacon et al. (Essex: Proceedings of the Conference at the University of Essex, 1976), 42, returns us to an old formulation that lurks behind these questions of what the text "makes the spectator do." He asks, "In what sense does art reflect reality?" and answers, "In that it cannot be understood as in isolation from the material conditions which produce it."

2. Tom Gunning, *D. W. Griffith and the Origins of American Narrative Film* (Urbana: University of Illinois Press, 1991), 17. See also Gunning's "An Aesthetic of Astonishment: Early Film and the (In)Credulous Spectator," in *Viewing Positions: Ways of Seeing Film*, ed. Linda Williams (New Brunswick, N.J.: Rutgers University Press, 1994), 115, which refers provocatively to the "reality-testing abilities" of the early film viewer.

3. Jean-Louis Baudry, "The Apparatus: Metapsychological Approaches to the Impression of Reality in Cinema," in *Narrative/Apparatus/Ideology*, ed. Philip Rosen (New York: Columbia University Press, 1986), 314. On the reconsideration of the passivity of the spectator who, as implied in this characterization, only experiences with "his" eyes, see Linda Williams, "Introduction," in *Viewing Positions*.

4. Jean-Louis Comolli, "Machines of the Visible," in *The Cinematic Apparatus*, ed. Teresa de Lauretis and Stephen Heath (New York: St. Martin's Press, 1980), 139. The entire statement is crucial and worth quoting in full:

> The spectacle, and cinema itself, despite all the *reality effects* it may produce, always gives itself away *for what it is* to the spectators. There is no spectator other than one *aware* of the spectacle, even if (provisionally) allowing him or herself to be taken in by the fictioning machine, deluded by the simulacrum: it is precisely *for that* that he or she came.

5. Ibid.

6. Roland Barthes, "The Reality Effect," in *The Rustle of Language*, trans. Richard Howard (New York: Hill and Wang, 1986).

7. Christopher Williams, "After the Classic, the Classical and Ideology: The

Differences of Realism," *Screen* 35, no. 3 (1994): 275–292, challenges the concepts of the classical realist text (see, for example, Colin MacCabe, "Realism and the Cinema: Notes on Some Brechtian Theses," *Screen* 15, no. 2 (1974): 7–27), and classical Hollywood cinema as developed in David Bordwell, Janet Staiger, and Kristin Thompson, *The Classical Hollywood Cinema: Film Style and Mode of Production to 1960* (New York: Columbia University Press, 1985); David Bordwell, *Narration in the Fiction Film* (London: Methuen, 1985); and the basic textbook for so many courses in the United States, David Bordwell and Kristin Thompson, *Film Art: An Introduction*, 5th ed. (New York: McGraw-Hill, 1997).

8. Jean-Louis Comolli and Jean Narboni, "Cinema / Ideology / Criticism," in *Movies and Methods II*, ed. Bill Nichols (Berkeley: University of California Press, 1976), 25.

9. Williams, "After the Classic," 287, while acknowledging that the importance of the concept of ideology has been its alignment with the social, would still not support the continued use of the concept: "The concept of ideology should thus be replaced by whichever more concrete term is appropriate to the field under discussion."

10. Homi K. Bhabha, "The Other Question: The Stereotype and Colonial Discourse," *Screen* 24, no. 4 (November–December 1983): 23.

11. Michele Wallace, *Invisibility Blues: From Pop to Theory* (New York: Methuen, 1990), especially "Introduction: Negative / Positive Images," 1–10; Sander Gilman, *Difference and Pathology: Stereotypes of Sexuality, Race, and Madness* (Ithaca: Cornell University Press, 1990).

12. Ann duCille, "The Shirley Temple of My Familiar," *Transition* 73 (1998): 25.

13. Ibid., 27.

14. Steve Neale, "The Same Old Story: Stereotypes and Difference," *Screen Education*, no. 32–33 (autumn / winter 1979–1980): 34.

15. Tessa Perkins, in "Rethinking Stereotypes," in *Representation and Cultural Practice*, ed. Michèle Barrett, Philip Corrigan, Annette Kuhn, and Janet Wolf (London: Croom Helm, 1979), has been influential in arguing that, like the concept of ideology, stereotypes always contain a fragment of truth; thus stereotypes of women and blacks can be seen as telling us something about the real historical conditions that determine the circumstances of lives. More recently, Laura Kipnis, in "Female Transgression," in *Resolutions: Essays in Contemporary Video Practices*, ed. Michael Renov and Erika Sunderburg (Minneapolis: University of Minnesota Press, 1996), 343–344, refers to the "kernel of truth" in stereotyping with reference to images of aging. These arguments have had some influence over the past decades, but I am also persuaded that such arguments can be dangerous to make. David Freeman, in conversation, makes the point that although the image of an urban black stealing a television set may tell us something about real conditions, about systematic and structural racism, we need to answer such an image not with a "positive" one but with the statistics on the

disproportionate number of black as opposed to white men serving time in prison.

16. Neale, "The Same Old Story," 35.

17. Gayatri Spivak, interview in *Discourses: Conversations in Postmodern Art and Culture*, ed. Russell Ferguson et al. (New York: New Museum of Contemporary Art/MIT Press, 1990), 106.

18. Neale, "The Same Old Story," 35.

19. As quoted in Cornel West, "The New Cultural Politics of Difference," in *Marginalization and Contemporary Cultures*, ed. Martha Gever, Russell Ferguson, Trinh T. Minh-ha, Cornel West (New York: MIT Press, 1990).

20. Anthony Appiah, " 'No Bad Nigger': Blacks as the Ethical Principle in the Movies," in *Media Spectacles*, ed. Marjorie Garber, Jann Matlock, and Rebecca L. Walkowitz (New York: Routledge, 1993), 84. Later, Appiah cogently critiques the popular tendency to attack representations for the real that they are only standing for and the companion tendency to believe that nonstereotypical images will counteract stereotyping (p. 88):

> We need, in other words, to be careful in this political project not to conflate the representation of sin with sin; not to assume that the representations that are neither stereotyped nor prejudicial ipso facto diminish stereotyping and prejudice. I know that representations are also real, but we still need to keep a clear grip on the distinction between representations and the reality they represent.

21. See my "Introduction: The Real Returns," in *Collecting Visible Evidence*, ed. Jane M. Gaines and Michael Renov (Minneapolis: University of Minnesota Press, 1999), 2.

22. C. L. R. James, *Notes on Dialectics: Hegel and Marxism* (Detroit: Friends of Facing Reality Publications, 1966), 84.

23. W. E. B. Du Bois, *The Souls of Black Folk* (1903; reprint, New York: Penguin Books, 1982), 45.

24. J. Ronald Green, " 'Twoness' in the Style of Oscar Micheaux," in *Black American Cinema*, ed. Manthia Diawara (New York: Routledge, 1993).

25. Roland Barthes, *A Lover's Discourse*, trans. Richard Howard (New York: Hill and Wang, 1978), 129.

26. Ibid., 130.

27. Julia Kristeva, *Nations without Nationalism*, trans. Leon S. Roudiez. (New York: Columbia University Press, 1993), 50. Kristeva's diagnosis is that, in addition to knowing the other, we need to become familiar with *"strangeness within ourselves"* (p. 51). This could, of course, easily become another narcissistic exercise. Kaja Silverman, in *The Threshold of the Visible World* (New York: Routledge, 1996), 88, refers to a kind of identification with the self as spectator as "selfsameness," against which she posits a spectator who in the cinema is positioned in relation to unimaginable others.

28. See Scott M. Cutlip, *The Unseen Power: Public Relations, a History*

(Hillsdale, N.J.: Lawrence Erlbaum Association, 1994), 375–377, 398, for a fascinating account of the way the Klan used *The Birth of a Nation* as a recruitment tool in the year of the film's release, in the 1915–1920 period when the film was shown more or less continuously across the country, and again at the time of its rerelease in 1924.

29. Terry Ramsaye, *A Million and One Nights: A History of the Motion Picture through 1925* (1926; reprint, New York: Simon and Schuster, 1964).

30. Silverman, *The Threshold of the Visible World,* 102. Earlier she says, speaking of this new political cinema, "This cinema would project the male subject into the bodily parameters of femininity, the white subject into those of blackness, the middle class subject into those of homelessness, and the heterosexual subject into those of homosexuality" (p. 93).

31. bell hooks, in *Black Looks: Race and Representation* (Boston: South End Press, 1992), 12, quotes black theologian James Cone, who suggests that the "logic of white supremacy would be radically undermined if everyone would learn to identify with and love blackness."

32. Stuart Hall, in "Subjects in History: Making Diasporic Identities," in *The House That Race Built,* ed. Wahneema Lubiano (New York: Vintage Books, 1998), 292, appropriately says, "Remember: identifications, not identities. Once you've got identification, you can decide which identities are working *this* week."

33. See, for instance, Michael Renov, *The Subject of Documentary* (Minneapolis: University of Minnesota Press, 2001), particularly his discussion of Abraham Ravett's *Everything's for You* (1989) and the ethnographic other, based on an application of Levinas to film theory.

34. Emmanuel Levinas, *Totality and Infinity,* trans. Alphonso Lingis (Pittsburgh: Duquesne University Press, 1969), 80.

35. Emmanuel Levinas, in "Substitution," trans. Alphonso Lingis, in *The Levinas Reader,* ed. Seán Hand (Oxford: Blackwell, 1989), 93, says, "For Sartre as for Hegel, the oneself is posited on the basis of the for-itself."

36. Hand, ed., ibid., "Introduction," 7.

37. Vivian Sobchack, *The Address of the Eye: Phenomenology of Film Experience* (Princeton: Princeton University Press, 1992), 162. She continues, "Thus, even as human bodies engage the film's body in an always correlated activity (whether of filmmaking or spectating), the film's material body also always engages us in its possibilities as a nonhuman lived-body."

38. Sigmund Freud, "Interpretation of Dreams," in *The Standard Edition of the Complete Psychological Works of Sigmund Freud,* vol. 4, ed. James Strachey (London: The Hogarth Press, 1953), 150; J. Laplanche and J. B. Pontalis, in *The Language of Psycho-Analysis,* trans. Donald Nicholson-Smith (New York: W. W. Norton, 1973), 205, define identification as the "[p]sychological process whereby the subject assimilates an aspect, property or attribute of the other and is transformed, wholly or partially, after the model the other provides."

39. J. Ron Green, in " 'Twoness' in the Style of Oscar Micheaux," 45, has

remarked that "Micheaux has represented both the hope for and dangers of assimilation."

40. John Sibley Butler and Kenneth Wilson, in "Entrepreneurial Enclaves: An Exposition into the Afro-American Experience," *National Journal of Sociology* 2, no. 2 (fall 1988): 141, refer to an increase from 420 to 1,020 in the number of hotelkeepers between 1890 and 1920, and, in the same period, the number of merchants tripling from 7,181 to 23,578.

41. Tania Modleski, *Feminism without Women: Culture and Criticism in a "Postfeminist" Age* (New York: Routledge, 1991), 116, considers a similar point in a commentary on Thomas Cripps's description of this world. "Race movies," she says, "often had to do without white people," but this "lack of verisimilitude" had its positive as well as its down side in that lack of adherence to reality meant that these films were in an even better position to mock the white world. The relevant passsage in Cripps is: "Without whites, the requirements of dramatic construction created a world in which black characters acceded to the white ideal of segregation, and unreal black cops, crooks, judges, and juries interacted in such a way as to blame black victims for their social plight." See Thomas Cripps, *Slow Fade to Black: The Negro in American Film 1900–1942*, 2d ed. (New York: Oxford University Press, 1993), 322–323.

42. I am indebted to Susan Willis for this insight about "overlooking."

43. Stuart Hall, "Subjects in History," 299.

Index

Index

Godard, Jean-Luc, 179

God's Stepchildren: boycott of, 126, 183; passing in, 134–35, 143, 148

Gold Is Not All, 61

Goodjoe, Beatrice, 126

Green, J. Ronald: on Cripps, 125; *Straight Lick,* 277n. 22; on work of Micheaux, 148, 182, 264

Griffin, Farah, 12

Griffith, D. W.: as auteur, 123; censorship and, 6; crosscutting technique of, 176, 256; Eisenstein on, 178; Gish and, 202; *Gold Is Not All,* 61; *Intolerance,* 99; Micheaux compared to, 7, 123. See also *Birth of a Nation, The*

Grupenhoff, Richard, 148

Guardian (newspaper), 220

Guattari, Félix. *See* Deleuze, Gilles, and Félix Guattari

Gunning, Tom, 172, 258

Hale's Tours, 55, 289n. 10

Hall, Iris, *114, 212, 214, 215*

Hall, Jacqueline Dowd, 167, 168

Hall, Stuart: on construction of blackness, 43; on difference, 85; on double movement of popular, 35; on hegemony, 184; on identity, 28, 73; on impurity, 272; on popular culture, 145, 147; on race and class, 40; on self, 48

Hallelujah, 1–2, 96

Hand, Seán, 267

Harlem Renaissance, 5–6, 114, 127–30, 275n. 17

Hartman, Saidiya, 12

Haywood Gallery tour, 275n. 17

Hearts in Dixie, 1–2

Hegel, G. W. F.: on Desire, 200–201; Desire in, 62–63; gaze theory and, 71; interpretations of, 86; master–slave encounter and, 63–65, 79–81, 90, 263; *The Phenomenology of Spirit,* 62

hegemony: danger and, 35–36, 82; Gramscian notion of, 144, 183–84

Hemmings, Sally, 206–7

Heroic Negro Soldiers of the World War, 97–98

Hiller, John, 208, 330n. 80

history as narrative, 91–92, 94

Hitchcock, Alfred, 4, 55

Hoberman, James, 125, 180

Hodes, Martha, 192, 199

Hofstadter, Richard, 248–49

Hollywood: disappearance of race movie and, 96–97; race movie as parallel to, 1–2, 6, 270

Homesteader, The (film): booking route of, 121–22, 311n. 103; novel as basis of, 113, 117, 118; opening of, 121; publicity for, 124; scenes from, *114, 115;* success of, 119, 122

Homesteader, The (Micheaux, book), 154

homogenization, 134

homosexuality, 33–34, 37, 196–97

hooks, bell: on identification, 82; on imitation, 90; on interracial sex, 88–89; on "looks," 211; on race movies, 135

House behind the Cedars, The, xv, 156, 157

Howe, Frederic, 223

Hurston, Zora Neal, 12, 132

identification: assimilation compared to, 268; becoming other to become self, 135–36; cross-identification, 35, 37, 285n. 42; difference and, 20, 86–87; film's body and, 267–68; film theory and, 265; imitation and, 86–87; othering machines and, 81–87, 268–69; overidentification and, 251–52; overview of, 19–20; political drama of, 264–65; psychoanalytic theory and, 27, 60, 73–79; queer theory and, 34–37; stereotype and, 262. *See also* self–other dichotomy

identity politics and race movie, 9

ideology, concept of, 259–60

image: effect of, 250–52; lookalikeness of, 258–60; "positive" type, 261–62; terror of, 220–22; wanting something back from, 266

"Imaginary Signifier, The" (Metz): desiring machine and, 67–69; identification and, 83; Lacan and, 71; other in, 59; othering machine and, 81; politics of mirroring and, 24–26; worldview and, 87

"imaging black," 254–55

imitation: black spectator and, 251–52; class and, 257; Harlem Renaissance writers and, 128–29; inhabitation compared to, 135; popular culture and, 133–34; race movies and, 129–30

immigrants and assimilation machine, 134

incest, 185, 188–89

Incidents in the Life of a Slave Girl (Jacobs), 173

incorporation, 86–87